Christopher Marlowe
Poet & Spy

Park Honan

OXFORD
UNIVERSITY PRESS

OXFORD
UNIVERSITY PRESS

Great Clarendon Street, Oxford OX2 6DP

Oxford University Press is a department of the University of Oxford.
It furthers the University's objective of excellence in research, scholarship,
and education by publishing worldwide in

Oxford New York

Auckland Cape Town Dar es Salaam Hong Kong Karachi
Kuala Lumpur Madrid Melbourne Mexico City Nairobi
New Delhi Shanghai Taipei Toronto

With offices in

Argentina Austria Brazil Chile Czech Republic France Greece
Guatemala Hungary Italy Japan Poland Portugal Singapore
South Korea Switzerland Thailand Turkey Ukraine Vietnam

Oxford is a registered trade mark of Oxford University Press
in the UK and in certain other countries

Published in the United States
by Oxford University Press Inc., New York

© Park Honan 2005

First published 2005
First published as an Oxford University Press Paperback 2007

British Library Cataloguing in Publication Data
Data available

Library of Congress Cataloging in Publication Data
Honan, Park.
Christopher Marlowe : poet & spy / Park Honan.
p. cm.
Includes bibliographical references and index.
ISBN 0–19–818695–9 (acid-free paper)
1. Marlowe, Christopher, 1564–1593.   2. Dramatists, English—Early modern,
1500–1700—Biography.   3. Espionage, British—History—16th century.   4. Spies—Great
Britain—Biography.   I. Title.
PR2673.H57 2005   822'.3—dc22   2005019761

Typeset by RefineCatch Limited, Bungay, Suffolk
Printed in Great Britain
on acid-free paper by
Clays Ltd, St Ives plc

ISBN 978–0–19–923269–7

Christopher Marlowe

The putative portrait of Christopher Marlowe at Corpus Christi College, Cambridge. When it was found in a broken state in 1952, a quest to identify its sitter began. The legend at the upper left reads: 'ANNO DOMINI AETATIS SUAE 21 | 1585 | QUOD ME NUTRIT | ME DESTRUIT' ('Aged 21 in the year of our Lord 1585: That which nourishes me, also destroys me')

To my family and Ernst Honigmann

Acknowledgements

I especially wish to thank staff at the Canterbury Cathedral Archives and at the Canterbury Library, as well as at Cambridge University. At Corpus Christi College, the Master and Fellows let me stay over at Marlowe's former college time and again while work on this biography was in progress. I am very grateful to Ms G. C. Cannell, for constant help at the Parker Library.

I gladly thank the Huntington Library in California, as well as the Folger Shakespeare Library in Washington, DC, for fellowships while I was writing the book. In the Netherlands, I was aided at Naarden's museum, and very considerably at the Gemeentearchief Vlissingen, to whose staff, and especially Ad Tramper, I am obliged. In France, I was aided at Rheims and particularly at the Musée Carnavalet in Paris; also, for their interest and encouragement, I thank Pierre-Louis Basse, François Mouret, Marianne Sinclair and Sylvette Gleize, in Paris, and, in Brittany, Annick and Per Blomquist.

Closer to home, I am much obliged to the Bodleian Library at Oxford; the British Library in London; the Brotherton Library at Leeds University; the Centre for Kentish Studies at Maidstone; Deptford Public Library; the National Archives (formerly the Public Record Office), and the Yorkshire Archaeological Society. Members of the Marlowe Society, including Peter Farey, Michael Frohnsdorff, Alan Hart, and John Hunt, generously shared with me their research and often their time. At the Royal Armouries, Philip Lankester and Robert Woosnam-Savage tirelessly replied to my queries. For help with Renaissance Latin translations, and often debatable meanings, I warmly thank J. W. Binns of York University. I also turned to Moira and Gerald Habberjam in matters of genealogy and palaeography, and to Paul Turner for enlightenment on Greek, and other unique blessings.

Ian McDiarmid replied wisely to my questions about his acting Barabas's role in *The Jew of Malta*. As often before, Andrew Gurr answered queries on playing companies, and sent notes on sources. On English law and homicide, Nicholas Inge set me straight, or straighter than I was. For medical and physiological details, I thank Dr J. Thompson Rowling and

Andrew Lowsosky, and for much pertinent discussion, Dr James Birley and Julia Birley.

Ernst Honigmann, Michael Shaw, and Stanley Wells improved this book by reading some or all of it in draft. I am also grateful to Alistair Stead for his textual comments, and to Andrew McNeillie and Janet Moth for their editorial care.

No one mentioned in these acknowledgements is, in any way, responsible for the book's shortcomings. For help with matters bearing on Marlowe's life or the theatre, I am grateful to the following persons: Gerard Barker, David Bevington, Michael Brennan, H. Neville Davies, Ian Donaldson, Paul Hammond, Alan Haynes, G. K. Hunter, Arthur Maltby, Tom Matheson, Charles Nicholl, Veronica O'Mara, Anne Weir, Brian Wilks, and Laetitia Yeandle.

I thank former students and my colleagues at Leeds University, and particularly Raymond Hargreaves, John Scully, and Alistair Stead: all three will recall, as I do, the sensitive criticism of Douglas Jefferson. I benefited, too, from remarks by the late David Hopkinson and Richard Pennington. Also to be thanked are Ernst Honigmann for his intellectual generosity, and my family, though I mention only Roger and Natasha's keen interest, my son Matthew's aid in Europe, my brother W. H. Honan's comments, my elder daughter Corinna's editorial notes, some strange criticism (in odd French) by 'M. Harvey Slice-up', and my wife Jeannette's great help at all times.

I should like to acknowledge the following sources of facsimile illustrations:

John Bakeless, *Christopher Marlowe: The Man in his Time* (1937), facing page 196 (Plate 2), facing title page (Plate 4); The Bodleian Library, University of Oxford, shelfmark Arch A e. 125 (Plate 21); John Cavell and Brian Kennett, *A History of Sir Roger Manwood's School* (1963), facing title page (Plate 31); Centre for Kentish Studies, Maidstone (Plate 11); copyright Master and Fellows of Corpus Christi College Cambridge (frontispiece and Plates 7, 12, 13), and by courtesy (Plates 8, 9, and 10); Deptford Public Library (Plate 33); Dulwich Picture Gallery, by permission of the Trustees (Plate 23); *Essays and Studies by Members of the English Association*, x (1924), facing page 24 (Plate 18); Folger Shakespeare Library, by permission (Plates 20, 29); the Huntington Library, San Marino, California, by permission (Plates 1, 6, 27); J. H. Ingram, *Christopher Marlowe and his Associates*

(1904), facing page 21 (Plate 3); Richard Knolles, *The Generall Historie of the Turkes*, 1597 (Plate 17); the National Portrait Gallery, London (Plates 14, 30); Princeton University Library (Plate 22); Rijksmuseum, Amsterdam (Plate 25); J. Thompson Rowling, 'The Death of Christopher Marlowe', *Journal of the Royal Society of Medicine*, 92 (1999), pp. 44–6 (Plate 32); H. T. Stephenson, *Shakespeare's London* (1905), facing page 150 (Plate 24), facing page 170 (Plate 16), facing page 344 (Plate 19); University of Utrecht (Plate 15); Gemeentearchief Vlissingen, *Historisch Topografische Atlas*, cat nr. 1083 (Plate 28); C. E. Woodward and H. J. Cape, *Schola Regia Cantuariensis* (1908), facing page 86 (Plate 5).

Contents

I
A Canterbury Youth

II
Scholar and Spy

III
With Shakespeare, Kyd, and the Ralegh Circle

Illustrations

A Note on Conventions Used in the Text

In Marlowe's time the year began on 25 March (or Lady Day), but in this book it will be assumed that the year starts on 1 January.

My citations from Marlowe are normally to the texts and line numbers in the five volumes of *The Complete Works* (Oxford, 1987–2000), whose contents are as follows:

Volume i, ed. Roma Gill, *All Ovids Elegies, Lucans First Booke, Dido Queene of Carthage, Hero and Leander* (1987; we cite the corrected reprint of 1997); the volume also includes 'The Passionate Shepherd' and Marlowe's Latin works.

Volume ii, ed. Roma Gill, *Dr Faustus* (1990; repr. 2000). References give both the scene divisions from Gill's edition and, in square brackets, act and scene divisions from the Revels edition: *Doctor Faustus A- and B-Texts (1604, 1616)*, ed. David Bevington and Eric Rasmussen (Manchester, 1993; repr. 1995).

Volume iii, ed. Richard Rowland, *Edward II* (1994).

Volume iv, ed. Roma Gill, *The Jew of Malta* (1995; repr. 2000).

Volume v, *Tamburlaine the Great*, Parts 1 and 2, ed. David Fuller; *The Massacre at Paris with the Death of the Duke of Guise*, ed. Edward J. Esche (1998).

The spelling in poems and plays has been modernized. Roma Gill's edition of *Dr Faustus* uses scene divisions.

It has seemed helpful to respect the original spelling in brief quotations from documents when the sense is clear, but the older form of a letter ('v' for 'u', or 'i' for 'j') is changed in some instances. Italicized letters within a quoted phrase ('lectur*es to* be re*a*d') and [bracketed] words signify modern additions. For clarity, with longer extracts I have sometimes used modern spelling.

I have used M^r and M^{rs} for 'Master' and 'Mistress' as distinct from the modern 'Mr' and 'Mrs'. In Marlowe's day the rank (or title) of Master usually conveyed a certain well-regarded social distinction, or the gentlehood that came, for example, with a university degree.

Introduction

Christopher Marlowe's life is the most spectacular of any English dramatist. He has a quickness and glitter as if he were moving across the night like a gaudy comet, and yet the man is no more luminous than his art. His story continues to intrigue, not least because it includes an ongoing murder mystery. Just as thrilling for modern sensibilities is his reputation as a spy, an unceasing blasphemer, a tough street-fighter and a courageous homosexual. New material now adds to the picture of Marlowe's secret life; but it is important to recognize that he became a spy in another sense, as a highly critical and original enquirer into human nature and social behaviour.

When he died at Deptford, at the age of 29, he was thought of as the best and most scandalous of the Elizabethan playwrights. Admired by Shakespeare and other writers, he had become a figure of horror for the strait-laced. Even during his lifetime 'Kit Marlowe' was called a blasphemer and an atheist, and people knew of his odder scrapes. Who else would use a stick (*baculus* or dummy weapon) rather than a rapier to duel with a tailor in a Canterbury street?

In fact, he squeezed much into a remarkably short span. Born in Canterbury in 1564, only two months before his rival's birth in Stratford, Marlowe became one of the two most powerful dramatists of the Elizabethan period. In biography, however, much of the fine detail about his life has been neglected—his human relationships, the milieu of his family and friends, the tangible Canterbury in which he grew up, the shock of his schooling, and his strenuous experience later at Cambridge and in London.

Even the difficulty of assimilating the known biographical facts about Marlowe (and there are surprisingly many) can impede our understanding of him. A recent book, for example, offers a confused picture of his six and a half years at Corpus Christi College, Cambridge. This is not just a matter of giving him a roommate he never had, blandly neglecting facts about the college's master, Norgate, or failing to mention Francis Kett, a college Fellow with heretical ideas, who was later martyred; the book gives an inaccurate picture of Cambridge's Arts course, and of what is known of the people and various doings at Corpus in the poet's time. A close, unromantic alertness to politics and religion, as well as to explicit facts about individuals, has not always been found in works about Marlowe's life. His part-time vocation as an agent has inspired lively comment, but there has not been much exploration of his ability to make use of his adventures or of his carefully developed talent to write dramas that still tell us about ourselves. Some past biographers of Marlowe do help us, and their valid discoveries need to be understood and integrated as we try to add to them. We learn more about his life constantly. There are resources available now that help to illuminate his extraordinary loyalties, his need for the 'male gang', and his penchant for those who most stimulated his ideas and creativity.

He shared in London a tumultuous writing-room with Kyd, author of *The Spanish Tragedy*, and belonged to a coterie which included Sir Walter Ralegh and Henry Percy, the 'Wizard Earl' of Northumberland. Although some of his time was spent with booksellers, or with thugs or dangerous informers, he also befriended the finest scientist and mathematician of the day, Thomas Harriot, the first to see the moons of Jupiter. Also among his acquaintances were the foremost creative spirits of his age, Lyly, Peele, Nashe, Watson and Shakespeare among them.

Stratford's playwright, especially, is crucial in this group. We need to be able to see Marlowe and Shakespeare in relation to each other in order to understand either one as accurately as we can. Biographical light, in this case, is not easy to come by. Having read about both playwrights for thirty-five years, and spent a decade writing *Shakespeare: A Life*, I find nothing more helpful than a sense of my ignorance, and a delight in talk. Even at a trivial level (though I make no apology for this), my biographical 'camera' here will try to do its best, aided by a scratchy soundtrack. We have snippets of Shakespeare's own recorded remarks, as well as reported snippets of Marlowe's talk, for example, though I have not been able to catch the two playwrights in conversation. (I have tried to make the camera flexible in operation, though, to show evolving relationships in this account of playwrights.)

My aim, in this biography, has been to try to offer the facts of Marlowe's life reliably, and to bring our sense of him up to date. What we can discover becomes distorted if we dart back at an Elizabethan life in a narrow, retrospective way, so I have taken pains to set the subject in an ongoing historical context. I draw modest inferences about personal relationships, and believe that this is incumbent upon a biographer, but the details in this book are factual and true. I have tried to present a closer account of Marlowe's formal training than we have had before, and to say more about him in relation to the theatre and its actors. My account of the poet's early youth involves churches, colours, altar cloths, smells, 'prayers against the Turk', even rugs, furnishings, and other items in the Marlowes' household, but I think it important to show, with a minimum of speculation, the context of his beginnings and to set down what we can know of Katherine and John Marlowe. It has seemed right to examine a juvenile play attributed to Marlowe, and to discuss the development of his mind and flair. I hope the reader will be amused by a new, more accurate account of the putative picture of him at Corpus Christi, a reproduction of which appears as a frontispiece to this book. Sexuality and desire, I believe, represent central, fascinating themes in Marlowe's life, and I have drawn upon our modern debates about Renaissance sexuality in assessing pertinent evidence. Similarly, I have drawn on what can be known about his classical education. Some in his later circle were classicists, but none, not even Chapman, kept pace with Thomas Watson in fresh Latin composition. I have studied Watson's Latin writings closely to explore several aspects of his Canterbury friend's life.

We mistake Marlowe if we take him too literally. In his art, as in his talk, he can be quick, calm, savage, hyperbolic and 'Kind Kit Marlowe'. He drives far beyond satire, though Ben Jonson, understandably, admired *The Jew of Malta* for its satire and tragic farce. One of that play's modern critics, Tom Matheson, holds that its dramatic picture of entrenched 'religious prejudice and intolerance in the sixteenth century' is so satirically scathing that it makes Marlowe's own 'alleged' atheistic or violent tendencies look almost respectable by comparison. That is surely so, but Marlowe's violence, even in speech, is real enough. He could be outrageously insulting or perverse in his jokes or taunts, or in the theatre, when he deliberately exaggerated prejudice or xenophobia to expose folly.

Certainly, in his time Puritans moralized his death, and we can gather data from two of them. But after Marlowe died, there was a long, nearly unbroken silence until he was 'rediscovered' in the early nineteenth century, when his life and works looked more or less equally depraved. First, Germany came to his rescue, as it were. At Weimar in 1818, Goethe noticed that Marlowe's *Doctor Faustus* had a structure, perhaps not like that of any of Shakespeare's plays: 'How greatly is it all planned!' he told Crabb Robinson over the coffee cups. In general, when Marlowe has been thought to have no dramatic ideas of his own, or has been judged in the light of Shakespeare's dramaturgy, he has not been seen at all. So it mainly was in Victorian England, though the Victorians admired his superb poem *Hero and Leander*. His ranging works appealed abroad; some of the most alert criticism of them, later on, was to come from Turkey and Israel. In the nineteenth century he began to be read in Italy (to whose Renaissance writers he owed a good deal), and also in France and elsewhere in Europe: Victor Hugo's son translated *Doctor Faustus*. Then, in late Victorian England, there was a hint of change when A. C. Bradley, the Shakespearean, writing in 1880, found in Marlowe an 'intensity', 'a sweep of the imagination unknown before', and granted that he achieved effects which Shakespeare 'never reached'. With reservations, J. A. Symonds found in him one of the 'great craftsmen'. A poet such as Swinburne adored him. Even T. S. Eliot was to praise his 'torrential' mind in an influential essay, 'Christopher Marlowe' (1919), and find Marlowe immature and 'blasphemous' but (oddly enough) also '*thoughtful* and philosophic', in a key piece, 'Shakespeare and the Stoicism of Seneca' (1927).

In the twentieth century his plays were staged more often, and four major biographies were written. Tucker Brooke, in a fine work on Marlowe's reputation, immunized himself against reductive legends about Marlowe by looking into their origins and, in 1930, produced a brief, sensible *Life*. Of the major works on the life that followed, F. S. Boas's *Biographical and Critical Study* (1940) is not especially accurate; it misidentifies the poet's parents, overestimates the family's wealth, declares that Marlowe never returned to Canterbury once he had left home, and has other uncorrected errors. Yet Boas, a Victorian, brings from the past one observation that is so central, just, and finely stated that his work is invaluable. He understood that Marlowe's feeling for the classics—and not just a fondness for Ovid's images or Lucian's wit—influenced the whole shaping of his critical intellect and imagination. If we lose Boas's insight, we very nearly lose Marlowe the playwright.

G. C. Moore Smith, in 1909, had opened up details about Marlowe's life in Cambridge as a young man. In 1925 Leslie Hotson turned up the coroner's inquisition into his death; but John Bakeless, over a decade later in 1937, did something nearly as vital in identifying the 'Buttery Book' entries relating to his time at Corpus Christi College. These help us to trace Marlowe's whereabouts for six years, and illuminate his roommates, friends, and abscondings from the college. The nature of Cambridge's Arts course was another matter, which Lisa Jardine and Richard Hardin, especially, have brilliantly described. Bakeless's large, uneven *The Tragicall History of Christopher Marlowe*, printed in two volumes in 1942, remains a magnificently jumbled mine of useful data. William Urry's posthumous *Christopher Marlowe and Canterbury*, edited by Andrew Butcher in 1988, offers a lifetime of research into Marlowe's kinfolk and the King's School, and an initial guide to manuscript sources in the Canterbury Cathedral archive, though some relevant manuscript records lie outside the book's main interests, as do, by and large, the poet's experiences in the theatre, his life as an author, his London circle, and his work for the government. In our century, David Riggs's *The World of Christopher Marlowe* (2004) is intelligent on Marlowe's art. Constance B. Kuriyama's *Christopher Marlowe* (2002) is a thoughtful biography with debatable interpretations, and an ample appendix of transcribed documents. The critic Muriel Bradbrook long ago understood the 'smoke' of Marlowe's wit, his humour, his objectivity as an artist, and his capacity for indignation.

Many strands of data build up a picture of his government work. If Watson's Latin allusions are relevant, so are Ethel Seaton's and Eugénie de Kalb's researches into Robert Poley's Elizabethan ciphers and movements. The key piece has been Charles Nicholl's *The Reckoning* (revised in 2002), which, as its author emphasizes, is not a biography. Its factual material on secret agents and the intelligence system has helped me greatly. Extremely useful, too, with its new data has been John Bossy's *Under the Molehill* (2001), along with Roy Kendall's discoveries about the spy Baines, and Alan Haynes's books on the Elizabethan secret service (revised in 2000), and, in 2004, on Walsingham's life. I have drawn, too, on other sources dealing with Elizabethan espionage, including P. E. J. Hammer's work on the earl of Essex and Hammer's replies to Nicholl's speculations. We are now able, I think, to trace some details in Marlowe's relations with the government from his Cambridge years forward.

Fieldwork and archaeology at Scadbury help to tell us about his chief patron, Thomas Walsingham, and in this biography I include new material relating to the poet's death. Finally, I have not wished to take antecedents for granted. We need to go back to a time pervaded with religious concepts and practices, to politics, to martyrdom, to the embattled Turks and exiled English Jews, for the beginnings of a factual story about awareness and great creativity. Passionate in his aims, Marlowe followed a unique path and wrote plays which speak to us with as much intelligence and eloquence as any others we have. His life has something to tell us about living with endemic, provocative faults, as well as about gaiety, audacity, elated persistence.

P.H.

I
A Canterbury Youth

1
Birth

from every shires ende
Of Engelond to Caunterbury they wende,
The hooly blisful martir for to seke.

(Prologue to *The Canterbury Tales*)

Canterbury events

CHRISTOPHER Marlowe had the good luck to be born in Canterbury near a cathedral of high fretted stonework and sounding bells. This small, walled metropolis was the seed-bed of Christianity in England; in his day, it was a turbulent centre of politics and religion. His life began in February 1564—two months before Shakespeare's birth in the English Midlands—but Marlowe's mind and outlook had earlier origins in his historic city of eastern Kent, which at that point was bounded on three sides by the sea and was very accessible to Europe.

His attitudes were to be nourished by his city's tensions. Grandeur and beauty, along with squalor and civic corruption, were evident here. Marlowe's strong, enquiring interest in religion, his grasp of international trade, and his feeling for exotic influences, even his interest in a man's love for a man, are related to his days at school and university. In the year 2001 new data about Sir Francis Walsingham's secret service came to light which illuminated Marlowe's career as a part-time government agent, but even this aspect of his life has roots in his early experience. Threading through all that happened to him—the dubious or lethal friendships, the dazzling successes, the foreign episodes in his career—is the story of Marlowe's ambition, tenacity, and creativity.

He was peculiarly fortified by his city, and at first we shall look briefly into its history, since Canterbury's past was never quite past: myths, legends, and truths mingled here in a rich humus for a boy's development. In former times, the land had been a rich and attractive wilderness, beckoning to Europe and available to predators. Wolves had roamed in eastern Kent under a wide sea of greenery, and terrorized the early mining camps; but neither wolves, forests, nor marshes forestalled invaders such as the Belgae or the legions of Caesar and of Claudius. Engineers in the legions built excellent roads. Canterbury—or Durovernum Cantiacorum—became a half-swampy garden city in a Roman *civitas* or tribal province, but it had temples, elegant villas, and a theatre in which Latin comedies, later known to Elizabethan poets, could have been staged.

The Romans withdrew, and the *civitas* next fell under pagan Anglo-Saxon rule. King Æthelberht of Kent, luckily for the English Church, was wed to a Christian princess; hence the famous success of Bishop Augustine—who reached Canterbury with his forty Italian-speaking monks to convert the pagan English in 597—was no doubt less heroic than legend allows. Augustine's church was protected by Æthelberht until the king's death, when two suffragan bishops fled abroad. The fragile metropolis was later held to ransom, and sacked and burned by Vikings who kidnapped Archbishop Ælfheah before battering him to death. The city was rebuilt, but concessions to West Saxon kings depleted the church's moral authority, and in the early Norman period Canterbury was widely known for clerical bribery, simony (the selling of church offices), and petty warfare among its clergy.[1]

A legacy of corruption offset any ecclesiastical achievement. At that time, not even the building of a new cathedral or the appointment of a Londoner of mercantile background, Thomas Becket, as archbishop did much for local prestige. The burgesses viewed Becket's advent as a calamity. As a high-living royal Chancellor, he pleased King Henry II, but when he side-stepped to become archbishop of Canterbury, he infuriated his patron. Becket refused to reinstate insubordinate prelates, or to concede that a felon tried by a church court might be retried by a civil court. But his fatal mistake was to impugn the coronation of the king's son. Such prickliness, obstinacy, and 'dangerous audacity' might have seemed more typical of radical Kentish attitudes than of a bishop's politic urbanity.

King Henry at last had had enough of him, and it is only a myth that Becket was killed in an unplanned way. His murder was better arranged, so far as one can tell, than the eventual killing of Christopher Marlowe. Indirectly encouraged by Henry, four knights led a complex invasion of the archbishop's palace at Canterbury one afternoon. Finding Becket among his clerks, the knights left to call in aides. As the prelate progressed into the cathedral behind a cross, he managed to reach the north transept before the knights stormed in with swords and axes. As a baron stood on his neck, Becket's skull was sliced by a heavy blow, and with a sword's point his blood and brains were scattered on the floor. Among some of the burgesses there was a sense of relief at this death, which took place on 29 December 1170.

Becket had been declared a traitor, and royal troops then occupied the city, but his defiance and integrity could not be erased—and would be a part of Marlowe's mental inheritance. The archbishop's bloodstained garments were distributed to the poor. Six days after the murder, when Becket's torn corpse lay in a tomb, one of these rags touched the face of a woman named Britheva, who recovered her sight. Then the lame and sick began to be healed, as if Becket in death were invincible.

Silverlings

Canterbury, as a result, changed almost overnight. Miracle after miracle was recorded as happening in the cathedral. Until a generation before Marlowe's birth, the city was considered magical and sublime: a point of rare access to the deity, a magnet for pilgrims from Sweden to the Adriatic, and one of the most famous locales in Christendom. Becket, or St Thomas, was venerated in a Trinity Chapel shrine which filled up with trinkets such as a bright ruby given by Louis VII, silver-gilt candlesticks, and costly plate—all approached through a glazed ambulatory of inlaid stone roundels. Such wealth left a good precedent for Marlowe's ironic interest in rich jewels and 'paltry silverlings'.[2]

In his homosexual tragedy *Edward II*, Marlowe was to sketch the lovers, Gaveston and Edward, with an honesty well in advance of the practices of his time. In real life, King Edward II—the darling of Piers de Gaveston of France—had sponsored a useful cult for Canterbury in which kings were crowned at the cathedral; then, in need of money, he had gouged the monks with exorbitant taxes.³ In Marlowe's own day, monks would be accused of every vice, and his attitudes to religion, subtle as they were, undoubtedly had local roots.

Priory monks had sold *ampullae* of Thomas's supposedly diluted blood. Ten times a day, in an exhausting routine hardly broken for 470 years, the same order of monks that tended Becket's shrine celebrated the *Opus Dei* and prayed for the townsfolk. Local pride benefited, as did the merchants. The relations between money and piety were to intrigue Marlowe—and money and piety do not mix well. No worse off for crowds of well-heeled pilgrims, the Kentish church came to own about two-fifths of Kentish land. If the monks and nuns seldom knew luxury, they aroused envy, bawdy insults, fear, and rioting.

By the sixteenth century Kent was rife with heresy and anticlerical feeling. Canterbury's burgesses fought monks over the rights of pasture, rights of sanctuary, taxes, and boundary walls. There was a deep mental and spiritual change, in which routine observances and dogma came into question. Marlowe's mockery had precedents in the eastern and southern counties: typically, a blacksmith, with no love of dogma, claimed that he could 'make the sacrament as well as any priest between two of his irons',⁴ and preachers impugned not only pilgrimages but the idolatry of Becket's cult.

Then, at a swoop, Canterbury was pillaged by royal order, when King Henry VIII decided to erase all vestiges of papal power. St Thomas of Canterbury was declared a rebel and a traitor in 1538, and the heavy contents of his shrine were carried off in two trunks which eight men could barely lift. Bells from urban steeples and even the 'poor man's chest' at North Church were removed, and the local monastic orders for the most part were reduced to squalid pathos.

In the realm's next doctrinal change, local artisans were burned alive. Once crowned, Mary Tudor proved as fierce in restoring orthodox belief as her father Henry VIII had been in uprooting it. In seven separate martyr fires in 1556, forty-one Protestants were burned for sacramental heresy just outside Canterbury's walls. People thronged to these burnings and wept with compassion. Religion changed again when Mary's Protestant sister—the Lady Elizabeth—acceded to the throne in 1558.

By then, the city was hard pressed and in a miserable decline. Clothiers were moving out into the country, and high urban overheads with guild

The South West View of Canterbury.

J. Ryland del et fc.

1 'The South West View of Canterbury', from an engraving in 1751, made from an earlier sketch

restrictions discouraged other employers. West Kent gained from East Kent's losses. In this atmosphere, Canterbury's conservatives roused themselves and kept Catholics in civic office for ten years into Queen Elizabeth's reign. But there was no revival of a mainly unified ethos, no recovery of their saint's unusual allure, and the old walled city would be beset by economic hardship and intermittent social and religious turmoil for as long as Christopher Marlowe lived.

A shoemaker's son

In Canterbury's archives today one is surprised by the number of manuscript jottings relating to the poet's father John Marlowe—and these carry one back in time. So far as one can tell, it was in a year of martyrs during Queen Mary's reign, when the smoke and stench of burning human flesh drifted near the city, that John Marlowe first came to Canterbury. He was then about 20, good with his hands and alert to his chances. From the mainly legal evidence, John emerges as physically strong, optimistic, with a gift for winning friends and inspiring male loyalty. In rough moods, he used oaths or became violent, or insulted his helpers. When out of pocket he was tardy or unreliable in other ways, but he would not always be in trouble with employees or rivals. Although not very businesslike, he was a reasonably clever man who could write a few words and please those above his rank.

John Marlowe had been born in around 1536 in the coastal village of Ospringe, ten miles from Canterbury. Benefiting from gusty air and the commerce of the sea, Ospringe lay next to the port of Faversham, which is situated on a navigable arm of the River Swale. With its gulls and clamour, oyster fisheries and gunpowder-makers, Faversham was one of the 'Cinque Ports' which had privileges in return for defence commitments to the Crown. In its church was an altar to the shoemaker-patron saints Crispin and Crispianus[5]—and John had ambitions to be a cobbler.

Unfortunately, he had little money. The theory that he was a Canterbury-born man, helped by an ample estate as he learned the shoemaker's craft, was put forth by biographers in the twentieth century, but it is clearly incorrect. When he left Ospringe in 1556, John must have carried most of his assets on his back, or on a saddle; in the city, he had no choice but to work for anyone in the leather crafts who would take him. After two or three years, he was apprenticed to Gerard Richardson, a cobbler who scraped up 2s. 1d. to pay the legal enrolment fee after Michaelmas 1559. Richardson had the lowest possible tax rate in the Burgate ward; he paid reduced fines ('for that he is very poor'), so it is likely that he had delayed in paying the fee, and that his helper had been with him since coming to the city.[6]

The cobbler was in feeble health, but at least able to benefit from a hard-working apprentice. Encouraged by his skill in attracting custom, John Marlowe sought a wife, and probably did not find one on his door-step. He offered to marry Katherine Arthur. It has been assumed that he stood to benefit from her financial assets, and that her father was the Reverend Henry Arthur of Canterbury. In fact, she came from a family of limited means at Dover, and although her uncle visited Canterbury, she seems not to have been there when John's acquaintance with her began. Brought up beneath Dover Castle, she had known spectacular cliffs, vistas of green downs behind the port, and the colours and occasional stir of an open, rather shallow harbour, then unprotected by any sea-wall.[7]

Oddly, the marriage in 1561 did not take place at Dover, as might have been expected, and she rode to the groom's city to be wed. She was too far from home for frequent visits, and if the idea of the cobbler's city pleased her, she may not have foreseen its drawbacks. Canterbury, from a distance, resembled a grey fortress, with spires and towers above its walls; it lay in an oval shape about half a mile from east to west, a bit wider from north to south, with the western part enclosed by two branches of the River Stour. At the circumference were a few dingy settlements, militant walls, six twin-towered gates, and more than twenty watchtowers.

Entering the stronghold, one came into darkened streets, and saw cramped city gardens and queer old houses which jutted out at each storey. The wooden buildings also had overhanging roofs, often supported by goblins, leering monsters, elves with long tongues, or decorative runic knots or scrolls.[8] Having stayed perhaps with her uncle, Katherine came to live after her wedding on 22 May in a rented house near the city's eastern boundary in St George's parish. Here she found no vistas of greenery, but a high city wall, narrow and filthy lanes, and a stench from nearby slaughtered animals; in this locale, she bore a

2 Baptismal font of the church of St George the Martyr, Canterbury

daughter, christened Mary on 21 May 1562. The child was to die at the age of 6, but death often claimed the young. Many of the nearby churches were decayed or had ignorant ministers, if not empty pulpits; Matthew Parker, the archbishop, found canons in his diocese who were no better than 'drunkards, jesters, railers', as well as men in holy orders who seldom attended a service.[9]

Drunkards, railers, or idle pastors are unlikely to have cheered the cobbler's wife; nor did the deadly, terrible months when people fell ill and the skin might change its hue: the young shrieked, and the elderly often died in silence. Bubonic plague was in the city when Katherine went into labour again. A midwife lived near the Marlowes, but in the grave danger of childbirth a woman relied upon her female neighbours, and so Katherine faced her ordeal. In February 1564, she gave birth to a boy.

3 Extract from the church register of St George the Martyr: 'The 26th day of February was christened Christofer the sonne of John Marlow'

For the baptism, which was said to be a sign of regeneration, or new birth, in which he was 'grafted' into the new Reformed religion, the boy was taken to the flinty walls of St George the Martyr, with its tall, oblong windows. He was carried to an octagonal font, which was held up by eight shafts and a central pillar—as if it would have to endure for ever.[10] Then a promising entry was made in the register of St George, though it took no notice of the child's mother—

The 26th day of February was christened Christofer the sonne of John Marlow

2

Petty school and the parish

What is't, sweet wag, I should deny thy youth?

· · · · · · ·

Hold here, my little love, these linked gems
My Juno ware upon her marriage-day

(Jupiter, *Dido Queen of Carthage*)

Item, for two books of prayers against the Turks . . . 4*d.*

(Accounts of the churchwardens
of St Dunstan's, Canterbury, 1566)

The freeman's house

BORN on a winter's day and baptized in a cold church, John and Katherine's son proved to be healthy, and they had cause for joy since the plague epidemic had begun to relent in January. The father was an outsider—his birth at Ospringe did him little good at Canterbury—but his status improved after the boy's birth. Even a christening feast, with its easy jokes, harsh laughter, and sexual banter, could have helped John in his relations with a tight-knit parish.

Although the infant was baptized as a 'Marlow', the family's name had more than the usual number of variant spellings—

Marlowe, Marlow, Marloe, Marlo, Marle, Marlen, Marlin, Marlyne, Marlinge, Merlin, Marley, Marlye, Morley, Morle

With notable consistency—as if etching himself into the parish—John signed on seven occasions as 'Marley'. Indeed, his son's name appears in his one extant signature as 'Christofer Marley', though at the time—in 1585—he was signing a will and may have been following the spelling of his father's name, just above his own.[1] The name was fairly common in Kent and not unknown outside the county. Thomas Morle, a fuller, and Simon Morle, a vintner, had become freemen with the right to trade in Canterbury in 1414 and 1438. But there is no evidence that these or other city tradesmen were among the poet's direct ancestors.

For the Marlowes, his baptism was auspicious: only two months later, the father had good news. In April John Marlowe was made 'free' of the city, and this gave him the coveted right to trade independently as a shoemaker. Henceforth, he could 'holde craft and opyn windowes', or let down a wooden shelf before a ground-floor window at home to display and sell his goods. He paid to the Council 4s. 1d. (instead of a normal fee of between 6s. 8d. and 13s. 4d.) and swore to uphold 'franchises, customs, and usages', after which an entry was made in the city's accounts:

ye xxth day of aprill in ye yere a fforeseid [1564] John Marlyn of Canter*bury* shomaker was admitted & sworne to the lib*er*ties of ye citte ffor ye whitche he p*ai*d but iiij*s*j*d* becaws he was inrowlyd w*i*thyn ye Citte accordyng to ye customes off ye saeme[2]   iiij*s*j*d*

Thus he became a full-fledged Canterbury citizen who could be tried, judged, or imprisoned only by freemen of his own city, and he gained the protection of a local guild or trade company, and the Fellowshippe Companye Crafte and Mysterye of Shoemakers soon embraced many other workers in leather. John was to exploit his association with craft brethren, and his status helps to explain his perky self-confidence and resilience in hard times. As an 'outsider' who became a citizen, he took a certain pride in Canterbury, which still entertained foreign potentates in a lordly style (and, indeed, had an archbishop who continued to hold sway over the prelates of England).

For his family, he had rented a simple gabled and timber-framed house. Even if not all of it was leased, Christopher lived in an ample dwelling for his first ten years, near Canterbury's eastern gate and almost in the cathedral's shadow. According to a local tradition, the house lay at the corner of St George's Street and St George's Lane, the latter so narrow that a man could practically span it with his arms. On the opposite or northern side of St George's Street—a part of the High—stood the dark, flinty façade of St George's Church, with its clock tower. And so the church stood until the Marlowe house, most of the church, and nearly all of the parish burned down in an air raid on 1 June 1942, when the clock stopped for ever at 2.18 a.m.[3]

In Marlowe's time the High Street was narrower than today, and had a central 'kennel' or runnel, which sometimes clogged with rubbish. In front of the leaning façades, on either side, were tiny gardens with flowers and vegetables. St George's grey church had a bemused, ignorant pastor, the Reverend William Sweeting, who had been caught in a wild fling of the archbishop's recruiting net during a shortage of clergy. Sweeting, in fact, could not preach, nor could he get anyone to preach for him more than twice a year, though he asked parishioners to listen to the cathedral's sermons. Later, the poet was to be at school with the clergyman's son, Leonard Sweeting.

Flesh and spirit competed on the High Street, where even in a religious age the flesh often won out. No matter how poor conditions were, the alehouses were full. From his shop, John Marlowe only had to turn left and walk a few hundred yards to the Vernicle inn—then patronized by Germanic émigrés, such as Hermann or Harmon Verson the glazier, or Cornelius Gosson the craftsman-carpenter. The latter's son was Stephen Gosson (1554–1624), a scholar at the King's School who later took a BA degree at Corpus Christi College, Oxford, and left to write plays in London, but then, in revulsion, attacked the theatre in *The School of Abuse* (1579) and other pamphlets. No doubt, tensions in St George's small parish helped to produce in Marlowe and in Gosson the age's greatest theatrical innovator and its best theatre opponent, and religion was always a factor. Gosson—the semi-Puritan attacker of plays—turned up at the age of 30 in Rome to study for the priesthood, and then, in a final abrupt change, became Anglican rector at St Botolph's parish in London.

One day in the mid-1560s John Marlowe amiably took his wife to the Vernicle, where he and Katherine sat with the barber's wife Lora Atkinson, as well as Michael Shawe, the basketweaver, and Shawe's wife. Verson the glazier was on hand, as was Laurence Applegate, a tailor. Applegate was a close friend of John Marlowe, who had met him soon after moving to the parish, but he was nervy and light-minded enough to let filth from his privy flow directly into Iron Bar Lane, next to the alehouse. That day, the story that he told some of those assembled at the inn landed him in trouble.

Earlier he had told it to John Marlowe when, in February, the two men had walked out to Barham eight miles away. 'Good faith, cousin', Applegate had begun abruptly, 'I will open a thing unto you, if you will keep it secret.' Secrecy was agreed, and the tailor added, 'I have had my pleasure of Godelif—Chapman's daughter.' Applegate, as he put it, had 'occupied' the unwedded girl four times, but he explained that he was owed 6 shillings by Chapman's wife, who 'kept back' the debt and couldn't be made to pay. So, Applegate concluded, each time he bedded Godelif, he got part of his 6 shillings' worth.[4]

The randy tailor's boasting at the alehouse of his supposed feat, in the presence of more than one 'goodwife', led to a suit for defamation (after Godelif was wed); yet even the tailor's air of candour illustrates an easy, affable tone at the Vernicle where the Marlowes sat in their son's infancy. An alehouse, with its painted posts, walls daubed with slogans, and singing minstrels, was fuller on a Sunday morning than many a church.

Back at his shop, John had his own troubles; he was never affluent, or able to look forward to short hours or cash he didn't need. Only a month after becoming a freeman, he was sued by the two administrators of Gerard Richardson's estate; the old, distracted shoemaker had died intestate, and his former apprentice had taken some of his 'St Hugh's bones'—such as awls, shears, or hammers—or perhaps even his stock of hides.

At first, Christopher's father had no more than a cobbler's lad as a helper (there is no early sign of an apprentice). A boy cost 6*d.* a quarter if one paid for his meat, drink, and clothes, whereas a grown assistant received up to £3 a year. When trade picked up after Michaelmas 1567, Christopher may have been taken into the shop to see his father's first apprentice, Richard Umberfield. The son of a blacksmith who had wed a draper's daughter, he appears to have been thick-skinned, peaceful, and honest. Umberfield's father was a part-time gunsmith who repaired calivers, or light muskets, in the city's armoury, so the cobbler's son may have heard about weaponry at the age of 3 or 4. Evidently the apprentice whom Christopher knew the longest, Umberfield fled after getting a woman pregnant. Later helpers were more cautious, but less agreeable.

As he was engaging and forthright, John Marlowe was a popular figure in the parish, an easy man to forgive; like his son Christopher, he never lacked friends. One suspects that even his physique was reassuring, since

John carried no light caliver, but a bow—five or six feet long and needing good muscle to draw—when he exercised with the militia. He had to be civil and mild, or he could not have got along well in a guild; but in his workshop, demons came upon him, and at other times he was off colour. His irascible moods became more frequent, as when he struck his apprentice Lactantius Preston, and then got bloodied by William Hewes (a disgruntled employee) out near the buttermarket. Still, John rose to be warden of his shoemakers' guild—although, a few years later, as its warden-treasurer, he failed to produce a balance of 40s. 10d., was hauled off to court, and found guilty of misappropriating funds. The age was litigious, and as early as 1570 he was beset by law-suits. He was also capable of flaring up at good friends, as when he shouted at Shawe the basket-weaver: 'Michael Shawe thou art a thiefe or so I will prove thee to be!'[5]

These moods were the more likely to affect his children because he was not a habitual household ogre, but more usually mild or docile, and there is good evidence that he tried to please his wife and advance their son. Also, John Marlowe could use charm when needed, and discontent kept him alert. By 1570 he had taken up a loan of £2 from the Wilde Charity, and he may have turned to a rich benefactor such as Sir Roger Manwood (later Baron of the Exchequer—a corrupt self-server, but a man with a liberal hand).

It certainly seems likely that there was some connection. As we shall see, Manwood was in touch with men on the Queen's Council who employed couriers and espionage agents, and related to the family of John Lyly, whose brothers attended the King's School. Christopher Marlowe registered his admiration for Manwood somewhat belatedly in elegiac verses after the corrupt judge died, but the tribute is evidence that he felt obliged to this powerful figure. Moreover, during his son's childhood John Marlowe was attuned to sources of help, and well able to seek out those who could be useful. Well known in the city, Sir Roger Manwood had a house outside the Westgate and won even the archbishop's approval for founding a grammar school.

From time to time, the cobbler irritated the great by not paying debts, but at least he never badly offended Alderman John Rose, a linen-draper who lived close to the Vernicle. The linen-draper himself was affluent, and had numerous useful connections. A namesake of Rose was a master at the cathedral grammar school, and influence of one kind or another was surely attractive to John Marlowe, wherever it could be found. The elder Rose, at any rate, made use of a versatile cobbler who could sign his name. John Marlowe witnessed a deed for the wealthy linen-draper, borrowed sums from him, and still owed him 10s. at Rose's death. And so, at times by hook or by crook, he just managed to support his family. By the time Christopher was 6, the Marlowes had lost a little girl, but they had two more daughters, and the boy grew in an ambience somewhat removed from the dull, masculine routine of a marginally surviving cobbler's shop.

Katherine's child

Outside Katherine Marlowe's rooms, the sloping High Street had its mixed cries and an attractive changefulness, but it was hardly safe or clean. Bare posts and a few rails kept people from being run down by animals or wagons. The street was malodorous. Dripping blood or gobbets of bloody flesh stained the pavings, and the noises and smells of commerce were incessant even though the scene varied through the week. On market days, egg-sellers and other neat country folk were in the High Street and some of the lanes, through which horses or oxen came by with wagons loaded with offal, decapitated heads, or tubs of bloody entrails: on one side of the parish was a cattle market and on the other the butchers' shambles.

Marlowe grew up near the high, painted doors of the city's eastern gate, beyond which lay a wide, water-filled ditch and meadowland, but urban life filled his eyes, ears, and lungs. Darkness muffled that stir, though at 4 a.m. the bells of St George's, as effectively as the criers in the mosques of Damascus, would rouse the entire city. No boy could have been indifferent to the morning spectacle, and Christopher no doubt took it in with a taste for sensations.

Indoors, he was raised with little girls who were bound to think him superior for age and sex, if not for any high opinion he had of himself. In this kingdom, Christopher thrived. A Tudor boy was encouraged to rate himself more highly than his sisters, even if he cleaved to them or recognized his feelings in theirs, and this boy was a rarity. At first, boys were nearly indistinguishable from their sisters. Nearly all young children ran about in russet dresses, and for a few years Christopher would have

4 The Marlowe house, which survived into the early 1940s,
seen from narrow St George's Lane in Canterbury

had girls as his playmates. We have no direct evidence as to when he
became aware of his sexuality, or what he felt about it, though after
leaving home he took a self-conscious, oblique view of sex when he came
to translate Ovid's erotic *Amores*. In his version of that work he stresses a
self-obsessed hero's wry, dissatisfied regard for the male organ, as if it were
disobedient and unpredictable. The penis is viewed with detachment, as
it stands erect under the bed-sheets when the 'Student' hero is alone, and
viewed with dismay when it stays limp at a crucial time, to the scorn of a
lady friend, or when the hero talks to the offending organ. In the *Amores*,

Ovid sketches or implies all of this; but Marlowe interestingly makes the penis seem more aberrant and half-hostile to the hero's well-being. The almost vulgar explicitness of parts of his translation—a remarkable aspect of it, since Marlowe's *All Ovid's Elegies* is otherwise coolly sophisticated— has a possible bearing on his early days at St George's parish, when his sex set him apart from the female household. In coarse, more masculine garments, boys, at one point, were regarded as little men. The transition could be sudden. He may not have repined over that; but it does not follow that he thought little of his sisters, or happily fled from them. Inadvertently, they guaranteed his freedom by separating him from the unpleasant routine of a leather worker's shop.

Christopher was his mother's sole, surviving boy until far into his school years. Four of Katherine's nine offspring were male, but two died early. Baptized on 31 October 1568, her second son lived for only a few days (even his name is lost) and her first 'Thomas' survived barely longer in the summer of 1570. Twelve years after Christopher's birth a second Thomas Marlowe was baptized at St Andrew's Church, Canterbury, on 8 April 1576. Almost nothing is known about him apart from the fact that he became a choirboy, and one imagines him in a white surplice among the cathedral's singers, but he fades from view. Did he survive to work among his father's relatives back at Ospringe, as interesting research by Michael Frohnsdorff might suggest? We know that a Thomas Marloe, at Faversham parish, married an Elizabeth who gave birth to a John Marloe (in 1603) and a girl named Bennet (in 1614), but this Thomas is not mentioned in Katherine Marlowe's will. It is less likely that the missing brother was a footloose Thomas Marloe who turned up at Jamestown in Virginia in 1624, but it has become tantalizingly clear since 2003 that the poet had more interesting, helpful family connections in the Kentish coastal towns than had been previously thought.[6]

Katherine had better luck with girls, and gave birth to four healthy daughters, the first two of whom were well behaved though the second pair became known for quarrelsomeness or blasphemy. The more placid ones were Margaret and Jane, baptized at St George's Church on 18 or 28 December 1566 and 20 August 1569. With these two sisters to admire or torment him, Christopher had an early audience for his tears or wit. The second pair were Anne and Dorothy, and an astrologer might have held that cosmic storms or bad alignments had occurred at their births.

Both were to marry and bear children; but after the poet's time they were cited as harridans, sometimes even worse in bite than bark. Anne and Dorothy Marlowe were baptized at St George's Church on 14 July 1571, and on 18 October 1573.

Up to the age of 12 Christopher had no young male rival at home. His two infant brothers were dead: his rivals had disappeared, and their loss skewed things in his favour. It is not surprising, even in a family of moderate assets, that funds were found to abet his really superb education. He had ingenuity with an ability to take in much that fed his energy, and his relations with his mother, on good evidence, are of interest in this respect. At no time would he have seemed ordinary to her. Observant and alert, he was to prosper as a little scholar, and at an early age may well have struck one of her Dover relatives as having the potential to become a clergyman of note.

Clearly he was much admired, much was done for him, his parents had hopes for his advancement in a respectable career. They were not selfish, but apparently optimistic, keen, and resilient, at least when John was sober; they might have brought blue vistas and the fresh attitudes of Channel towns to the city. This was an optimistic age, in which failure mattered less than the promise to be seen in new prospects, and a certain optimism underlies Christopher Marlowe's self-confidence, as if he had been born to mock complacency and later transform the theatre.

The house he knew in boyhood was not bare of charms, and people indoors cared for sweet aromas and cleanliness. Working people bathed, soap was made in the home, children washed their hands before and after a meal, and boots and clothes might be lightly scented.

The cobbler's shop was on the ground floor at St George's Street. John Marlowe, by turns affable or truculent, made his presence felt at home, if one judges from his known outbursts or from reports of violence in his shop. Yet it appears that Katherine conceded to him, preserving order in the household and probably controlling a few of his worst traits.

She based her standards on daily routine, as a later inventory and her will both suggest. The former gives us a sense of her make-do prudence, which Christopher knew well enough, though he was to react against the constraints of semi-imposed poverty. The inventory was drawn up by Thomas Plessington the baker and two helpers in 1605, after the cobbler had died, but it reveals Katherine's preferences and suggests her habits.

At that later time, she had saved up 100*s*. in cash. It would appear, too, from this household inventory that Katherine, when in her kitchen, had worked chiefly at a raised dressing-board and had sat on a shabby cushion.[7] She had had a taste for elegance and style; in 1605 she owned two good, solid table-tops, with sturdy frames, and four chests, as well as a glass 'cage'—possibly a cabinet made by a skilled craftsman. There were, of course, fire-irons, including tongs, brand-irons and a fire-shovel in her rooms. Upstairs was her most costly item of furniture: a four-poster bed with a flock mattress and curtains hanging from rods—here, she had probably given birth to her children. There are signs of her frugality or cunning in saving up for choice items, as she had accumulated nearly a dozen silver spoons. Her cupboard was full of simpler but not insignificant treasures, such as eighteen pairs of sheets, four 'tableclothes' of good weave and four of coarser, a dozen very fine napkins, a dozen of rougher quality, four pairs of fine pillowslips and three pairs of coarser—and, elsewhere, she had blankets, rugs, pillows, and various chairs of wood or wicker.[8]

Similar items—if not in profusion—were likely to be in her house on St George's Street. Her will, dated from the same year as the inventory, takes one closer to the mother Marlowe knew. Here, she leaves items to three living daughters, all of them by then married: Margaret, then 38; Anne, 33, and Dorothy, 31. The last two had become bad-tempered. Even when approaching old age, Anne was cited for using a staff and a dagger to fight with a William Prowde of her parish, and she fought the same Prowde with a sword and knife. In 1603 the churchwardens of St Mary Breadman's parish had called her 'a scowlde, com*mo*n swearer, a blasphemer of the name of god', or 'a malicious contencious uncharitable person, seeking the unjust vexacion of her neighbours as the fame goeth in our saide parishe'.[9] What is especially interesting is Anne's predilection for stirring up smug fury in those who considered themselves fit to judge aberrant behaviour. And Dorothy was no angel either, even if she avoided knives. After she married, Dorothy was accused of stealing, and came up before the courts; she also failed to attend church and screamed at a blacksmith who was the object of one of her many law-suits.

All of this, anyway, is what fragmentary records say, though it is not clear why Anne fought with Prowde nor why the churchwardens were so appalled by outspoken women. There would have been some Doll Tearsheets in any parish, but Anne was 55, widowed and a mother of ten or twelve, when Prowde confronted her: it was he who brought the charges that she skirmished with a staff and dagger, and a sword and knife. Tudor widows cannot often have duelled gladly with able men, and only Prowde accused her of such warfare. Also there is something unconvincing in the wardens' reports that she upset sensibilities. Did Anne's blasphemy upset a parish, or chiefly its wardens? The implicit charge that she maliciously aimed to vex people may not be much sounder, I think, than the simplistic view that her brother can be pigeon-holed as an atheist (in our modern sense of the word).

With her more contentious daughters, Katherine was firm in her old age, and her care over precious belongings casts light back on her son's youth. To Anne, she leaves 'a golde ring' which Dorothy had taken—but 'which I would have her to surrender'. A 'silver ring' goes to one of her difficult offspring, a ring of posies to the other, but the 'greatest golde ringe' is left to her peaceable Margaret. That daughter is also favoured in graded allocations of 'one silver spoon', 'one great silver spoone', or 'one of ye greatest silver spoones of the sixe'. Katherine's stress on gold, silver, and even 'my red petticoate' suggests her love of rarity, value, and perhaps of colour.[10]

Her son's eye for colours and jewels may be traceable to his mother; equally, either she or another adult may have encouraged his interest in the night sky. Stars, comets, the Milky Way, and Northern Lights were to feed his lifelong interest in astronomy and cosmology, an interest clearly evident in his poetic imagery.

One clever sojourner at St George's Street was her younger brother Thomas Arthur, or Uncle Thomas, then in his early twenties. The city's records show him at St George's parish in the 1560s, but not as a settled resident. Born in Dover, he stayed with the Marlowes off and on before buying his freedom to work in the city in the mid-1570s. Though sane and dependable, he was restless, with a gift for mobility that led him to stay at Shepherdswell, then at Barham, then in four different parishes after he was wed to Ursula, a daughter of the blacksmith Richard Moore of St Mary Northgate's parish, who had come in from Ulcombe twenty miles to the west. Educated and literate, Thomas Arthur shared with his sister Katherine a capable mind, and one might conclude that Christopher's intellect derived genetically as much (or more) from the Dover Arthurs as from the Marlowes. In the 1580s, as joint-bailiff of Westgate, where Sir Roger Manwood had a house, this uncle in all probability knew of the judge for whom Marlowe wrote verses.

Well-painted inn-signs, the cosmos at night, or a stir of grandeur might equally have caught the boy's eye. The churches were not all derelict—many glittered—and one finds colours on view in Marlowe's youth, as in the new 'pulpit cloth of blue silk embroidered with gold', or in a 'pall of crimson velvet embroidered with angels, having a fine fringe of coloured silk a hand breadth round about it' at St Dunstan's Church. Streets were cleaned—for aristocrats—and pavings glistened outside one church before 'the French Ambassador came in'.[11] Canterbury had its exotic enclaves, as well as a quarter from which Jews had been expelled at high cost to themselves, and visitors from remote cities. The future poet of *The Jew of Malta* possibly heard the Mediterranean island discussed, well after its defence from Muslim armies had seemed crucial for England's safety. A terrible siege of Malta by the Turks—under Suleiman the Magnificent—had occurred in his infancy; but the event caused prayers to be said even after the island was saved, and Canterbury's wardens had paid out money for:

> one letelle [little] boke of prayer agaynste the Turke . . . ijd [2*d*.]
> another boke of prayer agaynste the Turke . . . ijd [2*d*.]
> Item for ij bokes of prayers agaynst ye Turkes . . . iiijd [4*d*.][12]

Far from being always solemn or austere, Canterbury's religion, on occasion, was carnivalesque, lavish, and spectacular. There was a blaze of pomp in the cathedral close, where Archbishop Parker—who had paid out £1,400 to restore his archiepiscopal palace—often showed himself in clerical dress. In processionals, forty yeomen in Parker's livery followed the heavy archbishop in his flowing robe, which had a collar of sables over a sparkling rochet or surplice. Such splendour was natural in a city in which dramatic acting had once been required by law. Sixty years earlier, it had been an offence for craftsmen not to act in one of the exquisite Corpus Christi mystery plays.

The city's council, or Burghmote, no longer gaoled anybody for not being on a pageant-wagon, or exacted of non-performers 'twenty shillings and their bodies to be punished', as the law had put it; in a Protestant era much had changed, but with no lessening of theatre. In Marlowe's youth there were well-sponsored itinerant acting troupes on view in the inns and churches. The city itself was like a gigantic theatre, always changing—if not prosperous, then full of opportunities and spectacles for a sharp-eyed viewer, and the outward stir of grandeur and colour might have suggested hidden rewards for the boy. A key experience of his life, or his schooling, had already begun. Though not undutiful, he learned enough to be uneasy about home truths, and intrigued by exotic Europe, and so in time acquired a perspective on an old city of martyrs, high walls, and wooden goblins.

After petty school

Not necessarily at first but in the long run, schooling for Katherine's son was a blessing beyond compare. His fascination with the night sky might have seemed romantic, but he hungered for actualities. Much would have appealed to his imaginative sensibility, and his education coincided with striking Dutch, French, and English events—all more or less palpably in the air at Canterbury—so that if his attention turned this way or that, he was saved from narrow obsessions, just as he was from any morass of idle contentment. He was to be hard-working and brilliantly effective in using his time, and although he later familiarized himself with international economics or some of the ways of espionage, he took a wider, freer interest in the human condition. Marlowe was at the borderline of things: he was neither an outsider nor an insider, and unlikely to be satisfied with the attitudes of any particular group.

Having grown up in a family whose lives were poised between genteel aspirations and the tawdry and shabby, he felt obliged to his parents, and went out of his way to gratify them on at least one occasion. But there are signs that he did not feel emotionally close to either of them, and that after his early years, Katherine's enthusiasms had to cross a wide gap to touch him at all. To an extent, he became a stranger in his own home—and we are to look into evidenced reasons for this. Even while a boy, he was a victim of conflicting impulses, and his temperament was not easy or settled. Though not callous with friends, he appears to have wrung some of them emotionally with his taunts; he was attracted to confrontation and the violent, provocative remark.

Yet schooling helped to discipline his artistic skills and intellect. Among the benefits were new views of power and of poetry, both ancient and modern; liberating discoveries about his society; and advances in his creative life. The dissatisfactions he knew at home no doubt added strength to his wings.

Where would a boy from St George's Street have started his schooling? At Canterbury down past the Vernicle and close to the Court Hall lay a half-empty shop called the Fyle. Since the 1530s, the Fyle had caught the municipal eye. Here a clerk did 'the duty of his office' and, with a concern for religious uniformity, the city ran a 'petty school' to teach young children.

Most petty schools were badly run, as Francis Clement shows in contemporary remarks in *The Petie Schole* (its preface is dated 21 July 1576).[13] Though the Fyle's registers are missing, Christopher would probably have known this school: here or elsewhere, under similar training, he would have begun with a 'hornbook' which had rows of numbers and an alphabet. Having learned to read the Lord's Prayer, he would have taken up an 'absey' or ABC book, such as *The ABC with the Catechism*, which, in theory, ensured that a pious child would defend the Anglican Church.

At 6 or 7, Christopher did not necessarily feel that he had much to defend. Had he been inspired by a vicar who couldn't preach, or moved to piety by Archbishop Parker's elaborate dress? Later he was to mock religion, and yet use it in his dramas to probe it, rebuke it, and indirectly honour it. For most small boys, religion centred on the simple advice given in homilies or official sermons read out by a pastor or literate clerk, but petty school at least taught Christopher to read, add sums, and probably to cast accounts. He was to be intrigued by money matters, and by spidery mercantile connections involving Russia, Turkey, Malta, or Africa, even before he studied Ortelius's great map of Africa. Arithmetic, at the moment, would have familiarized him with money, and, sooner or later, he learned about bills of credit and thus something of his father's problems.

His father lacked cash, always a grave trouble for the family. The chief cause of this lay not in John's imprudence, but in the fact that payments to shoemakers were often made by either bond or book, which meant that a cobbler often waited for cash while his tanning needs made matters worse. Still, if cash and credit's mysteries intrigued Christopher, his

father's shop did not. In a juvenile play—which may be his apprentice
work if it dates from about 1580—the script refers, somewhat condescend-
ingly, to Kent and cobblers. Certainly, throughout his writing career
Marlowe avoided his father's trade, and in this he was unlike the poet of
Stratford. Whereas Shakespeare, as the son of a Midlands glover and
processor of leather, readily alludes to a glover's implements or to animal
skins, Marlowe, in his known work, never uses words such as *shoe, shoemaker, sew,* or *sole* (as for a shoe), but distances himself from his father's
concerns. At various times, when he refers to *leather,* or *boots,* or even
when he uses the word *sell,* the allusions are oddly repulsive:

> Covetousness: begotten of an old Churl in a *leather* bag
> > (*Doctor Faustus* (1616)

> wormeaten *leathern* targets
> > (His version of Lucan's *Pharsalia*)

> As if he had meant to clean my *Boots* with his lips
> > (*The Jew of Malta*)

> our *boots* which lie foul upon our hands
> > (*Doctor Faustus* (1604)

> You will not *sell* it [a sacred crown], would you?
> > (*Tamburlaine, Part One*)[14]

Such lines may suggest hatred not of the cobbler but of his work, and we
can be sure that he never envied John Marlowe's slavery. Indeed, he may
well have pitied his father.

As a boy he was probably attracted to the drama of the unfamiliar.
Canterbury at this time was filled with émigrés, known as 'Flemings' or
'Dutch', who received news reports from across the Channel that would
have stirred his mind as much as anything he heard in class. Protestants,
just lately, had smashed churches and convents in the Lowlands, not
long before their Spanish occupiers sent in the duke of Alva. In 1572,
when Marlowe was 8, Alva's troops surrounded the town of Naarden,
and, except for a few who escaped in the snow, killed every man, woman,
and child. Brutality in the Dutch Revolt against Spain continued, and
there was also terror more widely afoot in France. In Marlowe's own
Massacre at Paris, he was to look into the less obvious causes of savage
inhumanity in modern Europe.[15]

Religious works, as boys noticed in grammar school, often depicted fierce modern struggles. In John Foxe's *Actes and Monuments* (1563) or 'Book of Martyrs', which Christopher came to know well, there was a good résumé of Turkish history, the best in English up to that date. Fascinated by the Muslim Turks, he was to read better histories of modern Turkey in Latin, such as J. M. Stella's *De Turcarum in regno Hungariae annis 1543 et 44 successibus*, or Philippus Lonicerus's *Chronicorum Turcicorum* (1578), which includes J. M. Stella's account. But even as a boy listening to recitals from the 'Martyrs', he may have enjoyed the 'black humour' of the siege of Alba Regalis in Hungary. As John Foxe tells it, in a 'church or Monastery', some defenders in 1543 had pretended to hold out, while filling the place with gunpowder, then starting a fire and leaving. As the enemy stormed in, the monastery blew up, causing 'great scatter and slaughter' among Foxe's 'barbarous Turks'. This was to be echoed in Marlowe's *The Jew of Malta*, in which his hero Barabas explains a trick with explosives, before the plan is carried out and 'barrels full of gun-powder' in a monastery destroy Selim's soldiers and 'batter all the stones about their ears'.[16] In Marlowe's play, the incident has a naive gusto, as if recalled from boyhood. His urge to get at the reality behind cover-ups, his sceptical view of authority, and his interest in the propagandistic uses of religion clearly had deep roots.

Moreover, there were troubles in the north of England that affected all schoolboys indirectly, with consequences that must have sharpened the views of a cobbler's son. Lately, Mary Queen of Scots had crossed the border to seek refuge from Scottish troubles, and her arrival stirred Catholic hopes for the English throne. A feeble rebellion of the Catholic northern earls was crushed, but the revolt of the earls of Westmorland and Northumberland had effects which became more apparent after Pope Pius V excommunicated Queen Elizabeth in 1570. In that alarmed climate, a governmental propaganda campaign began, even as a haphazard Elizabethan espionage system stretched its weak sinews.

Marlowe, like other boys, had been listening to homilies read out by a pastor or lay clerk. If Mr Sweeting did not recite these, somebody else did: lapses were felt grave enough to involve the archidiaconal courts. Printed in July 1547, one group of homilies that Christopher may have heard was honest and pithy, as when children were told a little about sex in 'Against Whoredom and Adultery'. Here, Christ was said to be mankind's friend, and the effects of adultery upon a household were evoked: the erring husband's 'wife is despised, her presence is abhorred, her company stinketh'.[17]

But that candour did not last, and the tracts grew darker. In a 'Homily against Disobedience and Wilful Rebellion' (1570), for instance, religion was used for political ends and there was no more talk of a friendly Saviour. Children heard that all protest was wicked, though some kinds were more wicked than others, as if the Bible were mainly concerned with the evils of unpatriotic Catholics. Marlowe would have learned that disobedience is 'the worst of all vices', 'the greatest of all mischiefs', and that 'a rebel is worse than the worst prince, and rebellion worse than the worst government of the worst prince'. Few citizens aimed to overthrow the queen, but boys must have listened in wonder.

They also heard about an exuberant rebel, and 'mother of all mischiefs', or Prince Lucifer. He was 'the brightest and most glorious angel', who had become 'the blackest and most foulest fiend and devil, and from the height of Heaven had fallen into the pit and bottom of Hell'.[18] That, surely, made a government obsessed with the Devil look intriguing to a listener who would one day imagine the fall of Faustus. Christopher had an early taste of the ease with which Scripture can be used to quell popular dissent, or 'rebellious' thought of any kind. He may not have been shocked to find articles of faith used for political ends, but he was to react with wit to what he heard.

The only book in the cobbler's house when he died was the Bible, and it is unlikely that he would have owned a library thirty years earlier. Books in the city were scarce. In Mary Tudor's day, the provincial press had been suppressed, and it was not until the mid-1570s that books were regularly shipped down the Thames to Faversham and thence to Canterbury. Thus, at first, Marlowe's reading was mainly limited to school texts, religious works, and a miscellany of pamphlets, stories, or poems picked up from itinerant sellers.

But it was easy enough to taste the culture of the streets. The Burghmote had decreed that beef could not be sold unless the animals were subjected to a public baiting, and the stake to which the bulls were tied was in the city's centre, south of St Alphage's Church, near the rush market. Here, there was carnage, with men shouting as the bull tried to gore snarling, foaming dogs. Public hangings organized by a sheriff were another diversion, and boys played in Shrovetide games (often mob combats with few rules) in which limbs could be broken.

Even boys of 6 or 7 knew rough-and-tumble battles, and Christopher was not squeamish. Attracted to elegance and fashion, he was to become adept with a rapier. But the evidence of his school progress also suggests that he knew quieter days and the benefits of Tudor family life.

After petty school, most boys would have been aware of their parents' arrangements of plans for their future, and to the extent that Christopher knew what they wished he was well placed to judge his elders. Briefly, what do his works suggest in their pictures of family relationships? In his choice of materials to dramatize, Marlowe later indirectly hints at his views—and it is interesting that he does not show us only cold, dominating parents. His tragedy *Edward II* displays Edward's keen, genuine affection for his son, the future Edward III. King Edward is warmly attached to his brother, and in the same drama the elderly Spenser adores his own son. In *Dido Queen of Carthage*, one finds that Marlowe's Venus is no more harsh, no more neglectful as a parent than is the same goddess in Virgil's *Aeneid*, upon which the play is based: a descent into callousness—from one generation to the next—is only lightly emphasized. In Marlowe's version, the god Jupiter's cavalier neglect of his daughter Venus is matched by Venus's crass behaviour with respect to her son Aeneas, who in turn neglects his own child, Ascanius. As one might expect, *Dido* elaborates on its classical source, but with no hint of any dire grievance of the author. Nor are there any signs that Marlowe had been brutalized as a boy when he writes of Tamburlaine's killing of his cowardly son, Calyphas (in the second part of *Tamburlaine*), or of Barabas's murder of his own daughter Abigail (in *The Jew of Malta*).

Interestingly, in his portraits of women, Marlowe is so forgiving of faults that it is hard to believe that he ever suffered at home. One might think that his sisters only abetted him or that Anne Marlowe, if she later took up swords or daggers, never struck him with a pin. He sketched women in ways that suited his art, but seldom demonized them. In *Tamburlaine* he implicitly approves of Zenocrate, who at first wisely doubts the hero's motives; in *The Massacre at Paris* he gives no inkling of the racy, scandalous Marguerite de Valois of history, whose lovers reputedly included the duc de Guise: instead, his Marguerite de Valois appears to be, as a modern critic justly puts it, the model daughter-in-law.[19]

Perhaps Christopher's parents gave him approximately what he wished for. Unwittingly, they instructed him in modes of survival: John Marlowe was like an acrobat with a trust in nets, able to recover from every plunge—as when he escaped trouble in the courts despite long-overdue debts to two landlords. Christopher discovered that nothing is lost in a law court if one keeps one's pluck, but that, in future, he might have to oblige powerful men.

Though habits varied in households, Elizabethan families often discussed aspects of personality, as if no other topic were more illuminating or profitable. Children in the home were subject to outspoken appraisal, and Katherine, as time went on, and the boy showed his promise, can hardly have failed to admire her dazzling son. To that extent Christopher was in sunlight, but there can be delicate problems in the quality, degree, and aims of parental attention. Well aware of an importuning, excessive love, or of too much domestic sunlight, he was to favour Ovid's remark, 'What flies I follow, what follows me I shun'. Having translated the line, Marlowe used another version in *The Massacre at Paris*: 'That like I best that flies beyond my reach'.[20] With amusement, he illustrates the excesses of female love in *Dido*, in which not only Aeneas but three spoiled boys— Ganymede, Ascanius, and Cupid—are petted and bribed by overly fond, slightly selfish women. And there are so many dominating mother-queens and dominated sons in Marlowe's plays, too, that one might imagine he had been spoiled and over-mothered in youth.[21]

Yet the truth of his situation in Canterbury, at any point, is unlikely to be pictured in exact detail in his writing for the stage. He had a fertile imagination, and invented what he chose. One picks up a few hints from his works, and in the end one must rely warily on documentary evidence about his parents and sisters to get at even a shadow of the truth about his formative life. Christopher Marlowe's energy, audacity, and enterprise as a young man, his interest in extreme emotional states, in the disordered consciousness, and in sharply tormented desire, hardly suggest that he had been lax, limp, or spoiled in boyhood, but, rather, that a phase of his struggle began early. He was tantalized by illusions of well-being as he came up against problems. One of them appears in the evidence that his parents, despite troubles, were unusually close or exclusive, and contented with themselves. We have seen them at the Vernicle, and Katherine and John Marlowe appear to have become companionable, as a rule, to the point of exclusion of other affections. Factual evidence points to the cobbler's solicitous attentions to his wife. Despite claims on his meagre and vexingly uncertain funds, he later allowed Katherine a maid-servant, one Mary May, and it is likely that she also had one while her children were young. As violent as he might have been, there is no sign that John physically abused his wife; in due course, he became an almost respectable churchwarden, and later clearly depended on her help when he became a licensed victualler (with the right to sell food in his own house). Finally, he made Katherine his sole legal executor, and she chose to be buried by his side. If John and Katherine were not undutiful parents, still, in relation to general norms of the time, the Marlowe children appear to have been kept well outside the periphery of the relationship between husband and wife. That may be one reason why Anne and Dorothy became unstable; in any case, these daughters profited little from such attentions as they had.

Christopher's position in the family was more central, and surely more complex, than that of his female siblings. He was fussed over no doubt, encouraged and coddled, but not with a selfless love; and, sooner or later, his status as the elder (and at last the only) son in the family meant less to him, if his needs were irrelevant to designs upon him. It would be to neglect other facts to say that he spent his early life in an effort to avoid his parents' settled ambitions. Though not in outright rebellion, he is unlikely to have wished to follow his elders' designs for his vocation, no matter how those were concocted or how befitting they were. On the other hand, he required his father's material support, and thus one of his problems would have been to escape any schemes imposed on him. He was not bound to rise or fall solely on the basis of obliging or dismaying his parents; but what seems true is that he felt an intolerable dependency, and that, as he withdrew from them, he became more fascinated by the external world and keen to take his chances in it. As his opportunities developed, he had good reason to look into the choices available to him, and in just this lay problems which are illuminated by our increasing knowledge of his career and even his secret life in espionage. Marlowe had a need to pierce the surfaces in life, and to try to see what lay in deep, alluringly mysterious shadows. His inquisitiveness hardly sprang up as a miracle in adult life; it was part of his temperament, and likely to have been encouraged at an early age by his parents' views about who he was and what he should do. Later he became a rapid explorer of society, and, as a writer, quickly developed an ability to relate complex material far outside his stage-settings to the intense, inward lives of characters. This suggests that in the years before he left home he was not incapable of finding out about his own historic city for example, or taking some note of its politics, its more popularly discussed contentions and ceremonies, or even its ghosts.

3
The King's School

Then haste thee to some solitary grove,
And bear wise Bacon's and Albanus' works,
The Hebrew Psalter, and New Testament;
And whatever else is requisite . . .

. . . .

First, I'll instruct thee in the rudiments.

(Valdes, *Doctor Faustus*)

The Jews of Canterbury

IN the cobbler's workshop, crises may not have tested domestic harmony, but they must have affected the family's income. As his son approached puberty, John Marlowe's troubles with the law, his apprentices, and his guild did not vanish, and he continued to struggle to earn enough to buy stocks of leather. Christopher, who lived at home during his schooling, no doubt developed some immunity to tense, meagre conditions later in his life. Any emotional gap between himself and his parents left him a little freer; and by the time he parted from their city he was ready to take high risks.

In about 1572 he was probably sent to grammar school. At 9, he would have been eligible to go to the cathedral's school (usually called the King's School) but, so far as we know, his entrance there was delayed. Meanwhile, he was absorbing more than Latin grammar, and gradually learning more about his metropolis, which had only about 4,000 souls though it was grand enough to entertain the queen. Thanks to a charter, Canterbury was virtually a county in its own right, independent of Kent, and so was entitled to a sheriff (an office once held by the cobbler's friend

39

Alderman Rose). Marlowe would have been aware that craftsmen of his father's rank had sat on the Burghmote, which had been made up of a court and a common council until the magistrates tore themselves away. The Council met every Tuesday during Marlowe's lifetime, and religion, money, and corruption usually figured in its annual elections. In the poet's boyhood, James Nethersole became mayor, only to be dismissed for forgery and then re-elected, and even the forger's son (Edward) later held office.[1]

Wealth made excuses for wealth, power bowed to power, corruption was tolerated to a degree, and religion had become a boisterous factor in politics. Although the Puritans triumphed, the Catholics did not give up without a fight: having tried to rig one mayoral election, they were foiled only by the intervention of the Queen's Council. To the delight of schoolboys, elections were accompanied by satires, slogans, and brief plays which usually mocked either Catholics or Archbishop Parker's clergy. Few could have avoided seeing anti-Catholic skits, which were often acted in local churches. Also, boys would have heard about the ghosts of a lost Jewish community, for although no Jews remained in the city they had become legendary. What could Marlowe, in time, have learned of these exiles?

He surely knew where they had lived, since the 'Jewish quarter', with its few, stone-built houses lay just off the High Street along Stour Street and in Jewry Lane. In this area, 'Luke the Moneyer' had once dwelt near 'Jacob the Jew' and 'Benedict the Jew'. Close by Benedict's home lay the old synagogue where, by law, announcements of loans had had to be made. There had been a Monetaria or Mint in Jewry Lane, opposite a Cambium Regis, or Royal Exchange, which dealt in gold or silver. In the England of the Angevin kings, perhaps as few as one in a hundred Jews had lived by money-lending, though in the myths of Tudor times that calling was supposed to have occupied most of the Jewish population.

Legends were repeated, but sooner or later Marlowe could probably have garnered a few shreds of fact. Before 1290, when all Jews were expelled from the country in the reign of Edward I, there had been at least some degree of fairness and tolerance at Canterbury.[2] Most details are lost to us, but Christian entrepreneurs had relied on Jewish traders, and amicable relations prevailed. When a man as beneficent as Rabbi Aaron lived in the city, his people had voluntarily aided the Christian religious houses, as in a well-recorded instance when the Jewish quarter sent food and drink to a convent in difficulties, and prayed for the nuns' recovery.[3] Yet the medieval relationship worsened, even as fantastic claims were used as a pretext for seizing money, land, or goods from a minority which had no recourse to law. After three Canterbury Jews were hanged on a trumped-up and standard charge of 'coin clipping' (robbing the king by cutting silver from coins), others in the quarter were imprisoned before the exodus of 1290, which brought a windfall of profits from confiscated Jewish belongings.

William Somner, an antiquarian writing about Canterbury only a few years after Marlowe's time, held that Jews had been banished for 'immoderate' profits, and a 'barbarous practice of crucifying, at places where they abode, any Christian's Child they could get at Easter time'.[4] Marlowe—who mocked lunacy in general—may have heard aspects of the truth, or that these myths had enabled the authorities to extort funds whenever they chose from their victims; accordingly, in *The Jew of Malta*, he was to show Maltese Jews at the mercy of extortionist knights and a perfectly urbane governor.

Almost no outward traces of the exiles' lives remained in eastern Kent. The nation had barely more than two small groups of supposedly con-verted Jews in London, some practising, but tolerated for services to the state. Even in the capital, Marlowe had no more than a small chance of meeting any of them. Yet preachers brooded over Christianity's Hebraic origins, and people applied the words 'Jew' or 'Turk' to anyone guilty of infidelity or greed, a practice which carried into stage-plays. The exiles were traduced, but not put out of mind, any more than they could be erased from the Bible. In the popular view they were linked with money, and, as if to display the link, the house of 'Jacob the Jew' or the lesser one of 'Luke the Moneyer' stood near Canterbury's Mint, which for years had literally made money and produced between a third and a half of England's coinage.[5] People heard Jews had thrived, even if their goods were tricked from them. And scurrilous legends were hardly dismissed by schoolboys: the image of the rich, amoral, twisted, and brilliant 'moneyer' of legend, with heaps of jewels and coins, was more likely to impress Marlowe than that of the murdered Jew of reality. One cannot assume that he quickly rid himself of legends, or saw through the gullibility of some of his teachers. Nevertheless, he thought about popular obsessions, and later reacted to the myths he had heard.

Anything exotic would have intrigued him, but if the city's German, Italian, or Dutch enclaves caught his eye, he was unlikely to forget the ghosts. The Jews figured in sermons at Cambridge, and in the talk of vicars who interpreted Scripture literally. In no simple way, he was to play on the assumptions of the public when, in the protagonist of *The Jew of Malta*, he created one of the most complex figures seen on an English stage. He did not forget Catholics or Jews when he took up a critique of the present, and he was to depict his Jewish hero, Barabas, with a mordantly hilarious but no less clear empathy. He reflected on paradoxes at hand, and, so far as we can tell, did not confuse reality with his imaginings. Taking in social facts which he later exploited for the stage, he managed to make his audiences question what he had learned to scrutinize. To be sure, as a boy he may have taken greater interest in the queen's visit to Canterbury than he did in jokes about the Jewish quarter.

Formerly, a king had expelled a helpless minority, and Jews had been treated as viciously throughout Europe. Well after Marlowe's and Shakespeare's day, England was to be relatively advanced in a politic, cautious fairness. In their own time, the queen was no friend to Moors or Jews, not that she was vindictive about converted Iberian Jews, or Marranos, who supplied her Council with intelligence, and for everyone, she was semi-divine and incapable of error. In the summer of 1573 her progress through Kent had been delayed, and this only enhanced an atmosphere of tense, awed expectancy in Canterbury. With fear for the sovereign, Archbishop Parker had heard of advancing epidemics of measles and of the 'pox' locally, and of plague at nearby Sandwich; but hopes were not disappointed, and trumpeters and a large entourage passed by on St George's Street near the cobbler's windows on 3 September. Then about to turn 40 and well disposed to pageantry, Queen Elizabeth played her role with aloof dignity and rode a little apart from others on her horse.

Archbishop Parker, who distrusted Archbishop Grindal of York, did not tell that colleague what he felt about the sovereign, but admitted he had met the queen at the cathedral's west door. 'After the grammarian had made his oration to her upon her horseback', Parker noted of her welcome by a Latin scholar, 'she alighted.' A hush came over the precincts when the assembled clergymen knelt in prayer, and then Elizabeth entered the cathedral, as Grindal was told:

The quire, with the dean and prebendaries, &c. stood on either side ... and brought her majesty up with a square song, she going under a canopy, borne by four of her temporal knights, to her traverse placed by the communion board: where she heard even-song, and after departed to her lodging at St Augustine's, whither I waited upon her.[6]

The 'grammarian' who orated before Elizabeth—his nerves in a riot, no doubt—was a boy from King's School, which Marlowe was to attend. The mayor and aldermen in their scarlet robes, sergeants-at-arms, footmen, Black Guards, 'Captains and Knights marshalmen', and even 'Walter the Jester' had swollen the royal party. Two French ambassadors with a hundred gentry appeared in or near the thronged precincts. The queen celebrated her fortieth birthday at the archbishop's palace, but for a fortnight she lodged at St Augustine's Abbey not far from the Marlowe windows, and it is supposed that the cobbler's son later recalled her arrival in *Tamburlaine*:

> Is it not passing brave to be a King,
> And ride in triumph through Persepolis?[7]

Boys such as Marlowe saluted the queen—but to assume, as biographers have done, that he merely waved his hat, and leave it at that, is to underestimate him or to neglect good, sound evidence of his intellectual growth and seeking curiosity. The city itself was alive to religious issues, and pamphlets gave schoolboys a notion of church politics and of a battle within the Anglican Church. Needing the queen's help against Catholic and Puritan enemies, Archbishop Parker himself was a moderate and not altogether naive figure, yearning wistfully for uniformity in church practices and a better-trained clergy. In earlier days as Anne Boleyn's chaplain, he had guided the spiritual welfare of the Princess Elizabeth, and yet, as queen, she had rebuffed his wish for fresh or more critical sermons and barely quelled his fears about Rome. By 1572 Parker was a weary, fading old administrator baffled by what he called Westminster's 'Machiavel' policies and by puritanical assaults on his hierarchy of bishops.[8] With his jowls and fondness for pomp, he might have aroused schoolboy laughter, but his charity was to help Marlowe. Having given away some £2,000 of his funds (well over £1,000,000 in modern terms), Matthew Parker had aided the King's School and set up scholarships for the most deserving.

When this benefactor died in 1575, he was replaced by Edmund Grindal as the new archbishop of Canterbury, and, far from opposing Puritans within the Anglican Church, he appeared to give in to them. It is significant that, in Marlowe's boyhood, the temper of life in the cathedral city was keyed to doctrinal changes. With Catholics in the dust, the magistracy pressed for a strict Sabbatarian regime, and public dancing came under attack even before a mayor took down the city's maypole.

Boys tasted the effects of a heady nonconformist enthusiasm. As Marlowe took in the air of the pagan classics, the Puritans—in the real world—made 'a show of strength'.[9] The boundary between politics and religion, though never distinct, had melted away by the time the so-called 'prophesyings' or biblical conferences came into vogue in Kent, and these seem to leave traces in Marlowe's writing. Ostensibly mild exercises, in which a group of clergymen would discuss a biblical text with laymen and then withdraw to censure their own group's deviant views, the meetings typified Puritan defiance. Since they were not initiated by the church, they struck at its episcopal structure and at Queen Elizabeth as its head. Furious at Grindal for not condemning them, the queen sequestered him, virtually depriving him of office.

Elizabeth had not punched him on the nose—and nothing else might have satisfied schoolboys. Marlowe, perhaps, knew little of church politics, but he noticed that Puritan zealots had damaged an archbishop and challenged Elizabeth with conviction, energy, and the attitudes of being among the deity's 'elect'. He seems to recall these attitudes when writing of an elect warrior in *Tamburlaine* who calls himself a 'scourge of God'. The city had martyrdom in its stones and arches, and the fall of a modern archbishop was notable (though local people hardly knew Grindal's face). As Marlowe's outlook matured, so did his capacity for taking an impartial view of the socio-religious fractures of the day. It was not a political view. He is not known to have sympathized with Puritans, but what he apparently found useful was an inner, intense force and self-confidence in their challenges.[10]

In his routine days, he faced Latin grammar. From time to time, epidemics gave boys an excuse for staying at home and flouting masters, but the death-toll at St George's rose alarmingly in the summer of 1575. In the autumn Katherine Marlowe was pregnant, and the family moved nearer the city's centre to St Andrew's parish, where the poet's only healthy brother, Thomas, was baptized the following April. John Marlowe became a sidesman in a new church, and earned a few extra pence as a bondsman for couples about to marry.

Katherine had a new infant to care for, and at the church there was a new, loud 'grete bell'.[11] With the cries of an infant and a brassy tolling in his ears, Marlowe was dipping into old English romances. This reading became his habit before he left for Cambridge, and his early writing shows a familiarity with the literature. Old meandering works about obscure, sandy battles and parching locales can be tedious, but the medieval translators of Jean Froissart, the French chronicler, had set a note for the best pieces. Looking for a motif to catch his fancy, Marlowe began to admire vignettes about armies: 'It was a great beauty to behold the banners and standards wavyng in the wind.' Dozens of poems expanded on such effects, as the anonymous *Generydes* does with a Saracen horde:

> Anon with all their Banners were displayed
> A royal sight it was to behold . . .
> Their cote Armers of silver and of gold . . .
> The trompettys blewe; it was A Joye to heare.

With John Lydgate's fifteenth-century verse, anyone with an eye for gorgeous effects might be especially thrilled. Though occasionally tepid in style, Lydgate could be at once colourful, vigorous and concise:

> Banners unrollid, & longe freshe penouns
> Of rede and whyte, greene, blew & blake.[12]

Even the most languid romances, such as Lord Berners' *Huon of Bordeaux* (*c*.1515) or the earlier, anonymous *Richard Cœur de Lion*, had militant, stirring allusions to trembling ground, falling snow, or glittering sun or stars. Marlowe was to develop such effects with subtlety by giving them a new psychological dimension in *Tamburlaine*, in which bright natural images match the calm, inward resolve of a Scythian genius, whose power is guaranteed by his words:

> And with our sun-bright armour as we march
> We'll chase the Stars from Heaven, and dim their eyes
> That stand and muse at our admired arms.[13]

His fondness for old tales had limits, and there are signs of a qualified regard in his *Dido Queen of Carthage* in which he mocks romantic ornateness, though the mockery does not lessen a tragic aspect of the play. His Dido, for example, describes a leaky ship—a perfectly useless gift—in which her lover Aeneas might not sail far off, and her nervy lines begin to suggest an abysmal fear of the hero's loss. 'I'll give thee tackling made of rivell'd gold', she tells Aeneas,

> Wound on the barks of odoriferous trees,
> Oars of massy ivory full of holes,
> Through which the water shall delight to play:
> Thy anchors shall be hew'd from crystal rocks,
> Which if thou lose shall shine above the waves:
> The masts whereon thy swelling sails shall hang,
> Hollow pyramids of silver plate:
> The sails of folded lawn, where shall be wrought
> The wars of Troy, but not Troy's overthrow.[14]

Apparently, as a schoolboy, he indulged in his fondness for heroics, setting enthusiasms off against each other, and they were unspectacular and normal enough. He gave in to his fancies by reading, in begged or borrowed texts, what he liked almost whenever he liked, and he was not unlike other boys in admiring warriors. Nor could he have cared much about a need for self-discipline, as he dreamed of far-off settings. He did not grow into a bookworm, but he did become an agile reader, not caught by any alluring text, but eager to find something else as alluring. His later translations show that he cared for Latin, but he hardly studied Ovid with a scholar's exactitude, and if he did well at lessons, a kind of truancy helped him imaginatively as he escaped into romances without being too enthralled.

At 14 he knew grammar pretty well, and he was not unreckoning in his habits—later, at university, he was to do private work while not offending anyone very badly until he had the BA degree. At Canterbury, his qualities to an extent spoke for themselves, and before he turned 15 he was elected a 'scholar' at the King's School.

A short walk from home, this institution had a relation to one of England's oldest schools, which in the seventh century under Archbishop Theodore had taught the monks about poetry, astronomy, the law, and the workings of the calendar. In late medieval times, both an Almonry School, and, for boys of the city, an Archbishop's School existed near the cathedral. Then, in 1541, Henry VIII granted the cathedral a new charter and re-founded its boys' institution. The King's School was told to hire two teachers of 'grammar', and to admit needy pupils—'fifty boys', as the statutes said,

poor and destitute of the help of their friends, to be maintained out of the possessions of the church, and of native genius as far as they may be and apt to learn: whom however we direct shall not be admitted as poor boys of our church before they have learned to read and write and are moderately learned in the rudiments of grammar, in the judgment of the Dean, or in his absence the Sub-dean and the Headmaster.[15]

The 'poor boys' were to be outnumbered by the well-to-do; but, rich or poor, they came into the school as vacancies occurred. Upon entering, a pupil had to be at least 9 years old, and not past his fifteenth birthday. In practice, not all were 'scholars', since the headmaster accepted fee-paying commoners and hired extra staff to cope with the numbers.

Marlowe may have begun as a King's School commoner, and as he appears in the school's registers at Lady Day in 1579, he must have become a 'scholar' by Christmas 1578. The lateness of the award suggests that he had already satisfied the masters—they might not have accepted an unknown boy, with only a few terms to go. John Marlowe, most likely, had met the early fees, and his friend Alderman Rose had a helpful purse. At any rate, Christopher Marlowe was encouraged. For his gowns and 'commons', or meals, he had £4 a year (payable at £1 per term), which was more than many a craftsman earned. Other benefits of the election were less amazing and less welcome to him, especially if he already knew the routine in the lower forms. Prayers among the canons were endless, and long hours on an often frigid bench might not suit an admirer of exotic armies, but he knew a master who opened up some doors of power and art.

Mr Gresshop's rooms

In a corner of the cathedral close, a few hundred yards from St Andrew's Church, lay the grey buildings of the King's School, which in deference to the monarch was then called the Queen's School. (The poet was a Queen's Scholar.) Here, in theory, no boy spoke any language at any time other than Latin or Greek. In replacing a boy named John Emtley, Marlowe had got his award two months before turning 15, so his stay was bound to be short. Still, he had been credited with knowing Latin well enough for conversation and exercises, presumably in the fifth form. The school occupied the site of an old *elymosynaria*, or almonry, where monks had dispensed charity to the townsfolk, and included a large hall, teaching rooms, offices, sleeping quarters, and a chapel. Class hours were long, but optimism was in the air and a vision of learning was fulfilling itself: the ideas of humanists such as Linacre, Grocyn, Erasmus, and William Lily were being put into practice. Reacting against an ignorant aristocracy and a dogmatic clergy, such men early in the century had believed in the power of language to form the mind for wise action. Christian worship was the bedrock of the programme, but Latin and Greek filled the curriculum, since it was felt the classics had lifted the mind to its highest levels.

The dark buildings and gowns of the masters, though dismal, could be offset in a class by nervous laughter. There were bizarre, silly figures at a Mint Yard gate—a carved figure who spits out his tongue and plays a harp, a juggler with spearheads, and a swinger of hand-bells with arms as long as his legs. If bored by routine, Marlowe had these wooden, somewhat well-worn but salutary reminders of medieval humour when, late in 1578 or early in the new year, he entered the room of John Gresshop, MA, the headmaster.

Gresshop lived alone, and judging from his dress, nobody ever accused him of worldliness. He had had appreciable successes. Having been a 'Student', or don, at Christ Church, Oxford, he had come to the school in 1566, and probably already had taught future dramatists such as Stephen Gosson and John Lyly. Marlowe sat under Gresshop for at least three terms in 1579, and may have heard him earlier. Pupils wore fresh purple gowns, or left to change into surplices to file into the cathedral; but Gresshop had an aspect of drab mould. Mercifully, he was not visible at 6 a.m., in the main hall, when the boys prayed for the queen and recited a psalm. By then, the usher had arrived, and verses and responses followed for the lower forms, until the master's entry at 7 a.m.

Gresshop materialized in 'olde carsey hose' with an 'olde mockadew cassock' of coarse wool, or his 'olde spanishe leather Jerkin'. He owned

5 The old King's School in the Almonry buildings at Canterbury, viewed from the south

nothing to dazzle the eye except the silver clasps of a round cloak. In bedrooms called 'Bul's chamber' and 'Darrell's chamber', he met with junior staff or played at chess, but, for all that, he was essentially a bachelor excited by books.

Of these, he owned more than 350 volumes, so he had a library greater than one might find anywhere outside the circles of noblemen, bishops, and a few eccentrics, and larger than the holdings of university dons. Marlowe was not bound to be awed by a bibliophile, but he was bound, in some respects, to find a kindred spirit in his master. Or, at least, he found no prude, but a man alert to drama, ribald humour, and the complexities of the moral life. It is no surprise to find Calvin's letters, his Geneva catechism, *Institutes*, or 'Calvinus de Praedestinatione' among the teacher's books: many an Anglican clergyman had fallen under Calvin's spell and wondered over the doctrine of predestination which saved or damned people before they were born, no matter how they behaved. Yet Gresshop had cast a wider net, and owned lurid prints, and a copy of the erotic poems which Théodore de Bèze, the French poet and theologian, had written as a society playboy in Paris before he married his mistress.

De Bèze, very often, is credited as author of the first French tragedy, *Abraham sacrificiant*, performed in 1550 and available in English in 1577, though well-structured medieval French drama surely antedates Bèze. In any case, the master had a copy of Palingenius's 'Zodiacus' with a defence of comedy, a copy of Aristophanes' plays in Greek, volumes of Sophocles' tragedies in Latin and in Greek, copies of the comedies of Terence and Plautus, a poetic dictionary and a Chaucer, the *Songs and Sonnets* of Surrey, and, very interestingly, 'Tragical discourses by the *Lord* Buckhurst'. The latter included Buckhurst's or Thomas Sackville's co-authored English play *Gorboduc*—and Marlowe's *Tamburlaine* has a relation to this play. It is reasonable to think that Gresshop had a feeling for verse and could impart his reactions; certainly he had guides to the art of teaching, such as Roger Ascham's *Scholemaster*, with its advanced theories. By coincidence, he had a source which affected Marlowe's fate: the religious polemic *Fall of the Late Arian*, extracts from which were involved in the arrest of the playwright Thomas Kyd. He also had texts which Marlowe was to consult for his dramas including modern historical works and Sebastian Münster's *Cosmographia*.[16]

Still, pupils may have lacked access to this library as a rule, though
some of it was produced in class; and what the teacher read for pleasure
was very far from those bleak mornings when Gresshop—in mouldy
cassock—promised Latin drill. What sent lightning through the room?
What excitements could he have stirred up, so that future writers at his
feet were galvanized?

With 'parchment note-books' open, pupils had plenty of hours of
Latin, and Marlowe heard much of Erasmus. Though influencing most
British grammar schools, that Dutch humanist—who taught at Queens'
College, Cambridge early in the century—had compiled texts which
especially affected the King's School. Typically, boys had snippets to turn
'exactly into Latin', such as this from Erasmus's *Praise of Folly*. 'The mind
of man is so constructed that it is taken far more with disguises than with
realities', or this, from the *Adages*: 'There would be less harm in being
frankly a Jew or Turk than a Christian hypocrite'.[17] Either might do as an
epithet for a Marlowe play, or gateway to his own ideas. Gresshop had
about twelve such texts, including Erasmus's *Copia* as prescribed by the
school's statutes, the great *Praise of Folly*, and *Enchiridion*—along with the
Dutchman's translations, annotations, and a book of *opera* or collected
works.

Erasmus, on the one hand, had viewed life as a field of combat. 'In the
first place', he declares in the *Enchiridion*, 'you should continually bear in
mind that mortal life is nothing but a kind of perpetual warfare—as Job
testifies, a soldier both widely experienced and consistently invincible';
and Marlowe's Barabas in *The Jew of Malta*, it seems accordingly, was to
liken his fellow Jews to 'soldiers slain' and a remembrance of lost Jewish
wealth to 'a soldier's scar'.[18] Erasmus's warfare, however, is not bitter or
narrowly entrammelled, but good-humoured and subtle as he turns to the
ancients. He recommends a ranging intellectual quest, with the pagan
classics in view, so that he seems to liberate the mind from the more
instinctive, unquestioned moralities of Christian societies.

Whether or not Erasmus alone lifted him by the ears, thrilled his
senses, or hurled him into another world, Marlowe came under the spell
of the classics. And that changed him. It is hard to grasp the depth, shock,
or the initial, naive thrill and sensuousness of *this* change, though to a
degree similar effects were felt by other Elizabethan schoolboys. Marlowe
was dazzled by the classics. Nothing in his imaginative life was to be the

same again, and it may be that no discovery he made, and no love he ever felt, affected his mind and feelings so terribly, so unsettlingly, as the writers of ancient Rome. Sitting under a good teacher, he probably was too moved to speak of what he felt; he found a stunning beauty in them, or more charm than he might have been able to explain. The ancients lifted one out of time, out of a mean, fussy, moral present, up to the clouds and the gods, over seas and continents, or in their stories defied every law of mankind. Sooner or later, he also found a sanity in the pagan viewpoints of Horace, Ovid, and Virgil, as they appealed to his rational sense; nobody ever raised in England, perhaps, has been more affected by the classics of Rome. They gave Marlowe leave to compare ideas freshly, to question the Canterbury society he knew, to find great allies in old and modern Italy, and to interrogate the value of any truth he heard.

Grammar-school masters were seldom worried by indelicacies in the ancient classics, and from time to time treasures from Gresshop's rooms appeared in the shape of a quotation, or an allusion, to jolt pupils. Despite Ovid's sexual explicitness, Erasmus, unshocked by erotica, in *De pueris statim educandis* had called Ovid's elegies (so far untranslated into English and taboo in schools) a fine achievement for a young poet, and had followed that up with a plea for the 'omniscient' Latin of Lucan.[19] Whether or not he heard that praise, Marlowe began his career as a poet at university by translating first Ovid's erotic *Amores* and then a part of Lucan's *Pharsalia.*

Most probably, he found useful surprises in a Greek author, since Gresshop's inventory in 1580 lists the following texts, with their current value:

> Luciani dialogi aliquot — viij d.
> Luciani dialogi Latini factj — 8 d.[20]

Both works contained Lucian's dramatic dialogues as translated from the Greek into Latin chiefly by Erasmus, and it is likely that the teacher recited from them in class.

Marlowe, in due course, identified in Lucian a tone, an ironic attitude, which took him closer to working up a style of his own. He found in him a gamesman, a brilliant showman, a detached wit and light mocker with sting but not rudeness, who, for example, had put the *femme fatale* of the ancients or Helen of Troy's sexuality into wry perspective in the briefest of dialogues. Lucian's 'Menippus and Hermes' unfolds in Hades, and Marlowe knew a version of it. 'I have no time, Menippus', says Hermes to his visitor in the Underworld. 'But just look over there to your right, where you'll see', adds the guide casually, 'all the beauties of old.'

MENIPPUS. I can see only bones and bare skulls, most of them looking the same.

HERMES. Yet those are what all the poets admire, those bones which you seem to despise.

MENIPPPUS. But show me Helen. I can't pick her out myself.

HERMES. This skull is Helen.

MENIPPUS. Was it then for this that the thousand ships were manned from all Greece, for this so many Greeks and barbarians fell, and so many cities were devastated?[21]

That is to translate directly from the Greek—it may be that school-children knew Lucian only in the wordier, faithful Latin version. The dialogue foreshadows lines in *Doctor Faustus*, when the hero says of Helen's image, 'Was this the face that launched a thousand ships, | And burnt the topless towers of Ilium?'[22] Still, Marlowe could have found Helen and the ships elsewhere, and it is more important that Lucian's cool irony generally caught his fancy.

I think that he reacted to Lucian in unique, unprecedented ways, took him over, even fiercely held him close as a private treasure. In contrast, nearly every boy who coped with Latin in school favoured Ovid. Relief and amazement were the usual reactions to Ovid's *Metamorphoses*, and that long poem, with its quick episodes about gods, goddesses, beautiful mortals, mishaps and follies, sexual exploits, and poignant transformations, appealed to Marlowe in different ways at different times. Ovid's poem had a prime value for him as a spacious, tightly ordered and seamed mine of data about mythology. At school, most boys knew of Arthur Golding's English version of the *Metamorphoses*, which opened up compact riches and showed off a glittering, hard-edged world to compare with the real one.

Otherwise, Marlowe heard more about verbal techniques than alluring topics. He would have memorized quantities of verse, but there is no sign that this dismayed him, or that the Muses did not crash through the roof for him now and then. The school's statutes of 1541 are not a detailed guide to the curriculum he knew, but they outline a basic programme, and though mentioning few authors they indicate poetry and original composition for the fifth form. Pupils, among other tasks, had to memorize 'rules for making poetry'. They had to be skilled in 'making verses' in good Latin, and in translating 'Poets and Historians'. All of this precedes the sixth form work of learning to 'make varyings of speech in every mood', and of composing original speeches or 'declamations'.

What is especially interesting is that, at university and just afterwards, Marlowe repeats this scheme as he develops as a writer. He is more patient than one might imagine. After close, but less imaginative, work at Cambridge as a deviser of phrases modelled on Ovid or Virgil, he was to practise making larger, bolder 'varyings' from a classic model in his writing—as in *Dido Queen of Carthage*—and only later on rise to full power and originality in composing the speeches or 'declamations' of *Tamburlaine*. Yet all of that is ahead. At school, he was, of course, eligible for awards, but his ingenuity, however exceptional, would have pleased his teachers less than his receptivity.

In 'making verses', flights of fancy counted for little. Rosemond Tuve, in a work that first appeared in the mid-twentieth century but withstands the test of time, has shown how much pleasure was taken by Tudor people in the craft of verse, and how difficult it was felt to be.[23] Pupils were not asked to depict what they saw, or to picture the beauties of nature or to imitate the visual world, but rather to find what was useful and intelligible in the visual. Form and significant good sense, above all, were wanted in a poem which would show a 'fit relation' in its parts, and boys were praised less for cleverness than restraint. The cosmos was felt to be so full of elusive, barely capturable significances that any 'helps' in catching them, including metaphor and the rhetorical devices, were to be prized.

Thus a master would stress the many benefits of classical rhetoric, and the usefulness of tropes and schemes. The trope is a 'turn' in a word's meaning from a literal to an imaginative level, as in metaphor or simile, so that the word may reflect awarenesses or feelings otherwise lost. The schemes, as Marlowe knew them, chiefly involved repetition or symmetry, as in having clauses of equal length, or corresponding sounds in matching structures, and other devices which can affect tone, clarity, or rhythm in phrases or sentences.

The Latin comedies owned by the master are a sign (though, at best, an uncertain one) that Marlowe knew both Terence and Plautus in class.

Admired for fine Latin, Terence would have given him lessons in syntax and exemplified a need to organize a sentence before adorning it with images or anything else. Marlowe's verse, from *Tamburlaine* to *Hero and Leander*, relies on a structural lucidity, which is the real basis of its flexible power and the strength of what Ben Jonson calls this poet's 'mighty line'.

Warned against excess, pupils tried to achieve a simple, luminous significance in writing. We lack his school poetry, but Marlowe displays that quality, a few years later, in his translations of Ovid:

> Thou ring that shall my fair girl's finger bind,
> Wherein is seen the giver's loving mind:
> Be welcome to her, gladly let her take thee,
> And her small joint's encircling round hoop make thee.
> Fit her so well, as she is fit for me:
> And of just compass for her knuckles be.[24]

Here the speaker's feeling is shown not so much in his gift as in his delight in small, luminous details, as when he notes the fair girl's 'finger', her 'small joint', her 'knuckles'. How else would we know that he cares?

In the sixth form Marlowe would have had sophisticated exercises to show how polished and skilled he was at Latin. But in effect he collected verbal bullets, and learned to shoot. He had to write *controversiae*, arguing now one view of a topic, now another, and these helped him later with quick dialogue. He had to master *imitatio*, in which he borrowed phrases from many texts in order to craft a new, compelling speech, and thus, as a writer, learned to assimilate new material from many diverse sources.

It is not hard to believe that he rose well to such challenges. In other ways, he was in an odd position as a cobbler's son, inferior in rank to most classmates. He might have seemed a vulgar interloper out on the green, a boy who could win plaudits, yet not accept the lead of well-mannered betters no matter how often they elbowed his guts, gave him a bloody nose, or smashed his ribs. Regrettable events occurred—a bone was broken, or a neck snapped—and nobody could explain how such accidents occurred in unregulated football. Not every boy got out of school with his life, or undamaged. Marlowe was not a fish out of water, but neither was he at home among the sons of old Kentish families, or brawny scholars of fashion, wealth, and social rank. Luckily, we know who some of his classmates were.

Questions

In Marlowe's fifth term at the King's School there was an abrupt, sad event, in that Gresshop the headmaster died. The death of the school's head affected the quality of lessons in the sixth form. Tudor funerals were revealing: at least in this case, black obsequies would have underlined the fact that Gresshop had worked with less scandal than a former master, whose dabbling in politics had offended the cathedral authorities. Yet the loss of a well-read teacher was grievous, and if his own future loyalties are a sign, Marlowe felt deprived.

In 1580 he turned 16. Before his baptismal day, or on 23 February, there was a stir at school when Canon John Hill arrived, with Minor Canons, to appraise the late master's belongings, and this created a problem. Gresshop had no living relative, it appears, and the faded red and green curtains, chessboard, dagger, old clothes, and books in his rooms had no visible inheritor. The estate's administrators, or the Parvishes of Guildford, lived too far away for the purpose, hence Hill and his assistants catalogued Gresshop's books and may have let his pupils have access to them. This, anyway, might account for Marlowe's having seen two or three texts owned by his teacher but unlikely to have figured in class.

The King's School was on amicable terms with the canons. To foster a communal spirit, the lower and junior members of the foundation—or all but senior clerics—had shared the school's dining hall. Later, when the Minor Canons were allowed to marry, they dined at home, though some still associated with the pupils. The school's hall became noisier and greasier, no doubt, with fewer staff and more boys, but Marlowe dined with about seventy vergers, choristers, fellow scholars and fee-paying boys. His meals, which he had to pay for out of his allowance, would have included salt fish, red herring and white herring during Lent, fish on every Friday, and peas, prunes, and mutton. The cook was one James Felle or Felles, a Lancashire man deficient in piety, and perhaps the butt of jokes, if not of clandestine satires in Latin. In this year, Felles was charged with stealing a ring from the purse of Esther Kemp, a prostitute.

Marlowe must have seen such women, but once inside the Mint Yard gate he knew routine and ritual. When evening prayer came at 5 p.m., boys stood up to recite a psalm, and more versicles and responses ensued.

Before 6 o'clock, there was a meal, and between 6 and 7, younger boys recited lessons to seniors 'ripe in learning' (*in litteris maturi*). Marlowe was possibly 'ripe' enough to listen to pupils himself, before the boarders were bedded down and he, as a dayboy, was allowed to go home.[25]

One of the small boys had a great name which lately had become more famous. He was William Lyly, already, at 12, a scholar for two years, and both a grandson of an author of grammar texts and brother of John Lyly, the future dramatist. Their father Peter Lyly had been a notary or recorder at Canterbury, but died early, leaving five sons. Of these, both Peter and William entered the school at the age of 10. It is likely that the eldest son, John, had been there, too, but the school's earlier registers are defective.

What is important is that the Lylys were of Canterbury, and the eldest son was already a star. Ten years older than Marlowe, John Lyly had gone on to Magdalen College, Oxford, and had then taken rooms at the Savoy Hospital at the Strand in London, where the custodian was one Absalon, a former King's School master. In 1578 Lyly's *Euphues* took the capital by storm. The smartness of this romance lifted it to a success so far unmatched in the age, and its style ushered in a new word—*euphuism*—though what the cognoscenti liked were its heaped-up similes, chiefly borrowed from Erasmus's *Similia*. (That might be a sign that Lyly had sat under the master at King's—but many a school used the *Similia*.)

Marlowe was to value John Lyly's comedies, though not to the extent of being over-impressed, but the fame of *Euphues* narrowed his prospects a little. If the school had a hero in Lyly, anything he himself might do in the sixth form would hardly shine by comparison. There is no sign that Christopher Marlowe was envious, and at this point he still had 'declamations' to write. But the school's mood was bound to be less exciting after Gresshop's reign, despite the talents of its assistant master John Rose, a Cambridge graduate with a clear interest in the school: Rose later established four exhibitions or scholarships at the universities for the boys. However, in Marlowe's time, the new headmaster was Nicholas Goldsborough, a mere time-server and lately chaplain at Corpus Christi College, Oxford. With no ardour for classrooms, he left the school in 1585 for the lucrative post of vicar at East Linsted, Kent, to be replaced by Christopher Pashley, to whose Cambridge scholarship Marlowe succeeded.

William Lyly, with no obvious sign of poetic gifts, was likely to be fond of an elder boy who had patience for him. Some others in the upper forms were from families as poor as Marlowe's, and Leonard Sweeting's was more wretched. Leonard's father, as the rector of St George's, had died a pauper, and his widow and her children lived in the dark, sheltering casemates (or enclosures) at St George's gate. Still, Leonard had endurance: he was to work for a church registrar and rise to be a notary, and since he enjoyed poetry and later owned a copy of Marlowe's *Hero and Leander*, he may have been an affectionate ally. Marlowe had known other boys since childhood, and one of them must have been William Potter, the son of a butcher who kept a stall in Iron Bar Lane near the Marlowe shop. The late headmaster had run up school debts, and when Canon Hill met fifteen of Gresshop's creditors in the cathedral's nave on 6 July 1580, Potter Senior, the butcher, got back 24s. 8d. Two shoemakers had also put in claims for goods rendered, and John Marlowe, at that time, recovered 16s. 4d. The claims, to the extent that they were known, advertised the fact that both Potter and Marlowe were sons of tradesmen, and John Marlowe's claim was for furnishing goods to boys who were not even scholars, but commoners.[26]

Two large echelons of the elite were at the school. On the one hand, they included well-groomed sons of the cathedral staff such as Thomas Walsall and Bartholomew Beseley, whose fathers were among the foundation's 'Six Preachers', and Bartholomew Godwyn, a son of Thomas Godwyn who was dean of Canterbury (1567–84), as well as two of the numerous Pownalls—Philemon and Barnabas—whose father had been a wedded priest at Calais before becoming a canon; or again, young Stephen Nevinson, whose imposing namesake, Stephen Nevinson, DCL, was prebendary of Canterbury by 1570.

Other classmates, of the gentry or rich yeomanry, might have carried the flags, plumes, and armour of medieval Kentish forces to the school. The Nevinsons owned vast tracts in East Kent, and Sidrac Kemesley's family had amassed land near Maidstone. Two boys came from families well placed enough to know the queen's great courtier and adventurer Sir Walter Ralegh, or his people. Marlowe's classmate Thomas Coldwell, a model of smiling piety no doubt, later went to a clerical office at Salisbury in the pattern of his father the bishop, who 'alienated Sherborne manor' to Ralegh himself. Edward Partridge, another son of the gentry, lived outside Canterbury either at Green Court or at Bridge, and had a namesake who married Ralegh's niece Katherine Throckmorton.

Of the other pupils, both Henry Drury and John Wilford were scions of old distinguished armorial families, and Christopher Digges, of Kent, was a careless, open-handedly spendthrift kinsman of Thomas Digges the mathematician, and of Leonard Digges, who later wrote two memorial poems about Shakespeare. Finally, boys such as Thomas Wyn, presumably of the local Wyns, had money to make up for anything they lacked in ancestry.[27]

Whatever their social rank might be, all pupils when under a teacher's eye were subject to strict rules of deportment; but outside the class, well-to-do boys could have a withering, brutal effect on the few tradesmen's sons. Quite apart from what happened in rough games, jaws were smashed or eyeballs gouged, and a prefect or 'praeposter' who tattled to the master about a calamity might later suffer a broken arm and never spy again. A bully can be met with a fist in the face, and wealthy boys in purple gowns can begin to look like other boys in such gowns, and yet the ease and style of the privileged clearly affected Marlowe. Poor and of low rank himself, he was tainted whatever he did, but he did not wilt for long at the King's School. His rank became a spur as well as a handicap, and later in *Tamburlaine* he was to draw intuitively on an upstart's feelings, without falling into simple autobiography. If school finally made him a better observer, he found some value in a cool, inquisitive sympathy, and at least the topic of religion kept him in a close, provocative alliance with the young men he knew.

Ritual, singing, and devotions were at the heart of his formal training. About eighty times a year, lessons were suspended as boys trooped into the cathedral for a service, and what they knew of Virgil or Ovid affected their reactions to the preacher. Pagan and Christian themes might conflict, and, even if Marlowe was bored now and then, not all the canons were soporific or lacklustre, nor did he daydream through all he heard. Erasmus had held that laughter purifies seriousness, and St Paul's many references to the 'foolishness' or 'madness' of Christianity (in 1 and 2 Corinthians) could not have troubled the cathedral's more skilful or effective preachers. Nor were the grinning figures at the Mint Yard gate unbefitting. To laugh at religion—especially when it is fragmented, besieged, or compromised—is not to deny or neglect it, and may be to affirm it; to reduce it to folly is to perceive a measure of its essence; and Christ, like Socrates, might be viewed as a holy fool, his adherents as vulnerable to ridicule as to martyrdom. The mocking, intense spirit of Erasmus, playing over Scripture as well as the classics, set a keynote for much that Marlowe would have heard or thought in the sixth form.

Later, by report, he was not to spare his friends in ridiculing Christ or Moses, whether or not he mocked God at school. This is not to say that Marlowe was secretly pious, orthodox, or fixed in his religious views, but there is no sign that he was indifferent to the Prayer Book or Bible. In his works he refers to biblical passages over a thousand times, and in most instances not ironically. He was to favour the low-priced Genevan Bible (1560), which was of a handy size. Matthew Parker had organized translators of the Bishops' Bible (1568), which must have been used by some members of the foundation, and Marlowe on occasion remembers it, as when he has Doctor Faustus say, 'View here the blood that trickles from mine arm, | And let it be propitious for my wish'. St Paul, in the Bishops' Bible, speaks of a *propitiation* through faith in Christ's blood (Romans 3: 25); whereas the earlier Geneva Bible had used the word *reconciliation* instead.[28] Crucial to Marlowe's training, too, were questions of Calvinism, which he could not have escaped if he had wished.

If only because he was impressed by the elusive in the cosmos, he absorbed, at about this time (or well before he wrote *Tamburlaine*), John Calvin's difficult concept of an unseen, mysterious, transcendental deity. That gave him one purchase on the obscurities of theology, helped him to judge other doctrines, and probably focused his mind on facile, casual evasions or hypocrisies he heard in pulpits. One rigorous canon attached to Canterbury Cathedral was no time-server or hypocrite, even if he was seldom present after going on to St Paul's Deanery: this was Alexander Nowell, a former Brasenose man inclined to Calvinism, and author of the official catechism which boys had to memorize either in Latin or in a translation. 'Why', asks Nowell as he offers a famous definition of the deity, 'is it not lawfull to express God with a bodily and visible forme?' 'Because', answers the catechism vividly,

there can be no likenesse or agreeing betweene God which is a spirit eternall, unmeasurable, infinite, incomprehensible, severed from all mortal composition, and a fraile, bodily, silly, spiritlesse, and vaine shape.[29]

Such a view hardly narrowed Marlowe's thinking, but it appealed to his imagination, sense of irony, and delight in paradoxes. He became intrigued by the catechistic question. What can one say of a being which is infinite, incomprehensible? In *Doctor Faustus*, his hero never summons Mephistophilis without drilling him with catechistic problems: 'What is Lucifer thy Lord?'; 'Where are you damned?'; 'What is Hell?'. This author can be irreverent, mocking, obscene, blasphemous; yet as there is far more than jejune cynicism in *The Jew of Malta* or in his portraits of *Tamburlaine* or Faustus, so it cannot be assumed that Marlowe at any time took an ignorant, obtuse, dismissive view of belief.

What plainly fascinated him as an artist was a calamity, in an age in which doctrines were so contentious that belief split the psyche, or led to doubt, hypocrisy, or inanition. At school, he was likely to find curious subject-matter in the feelings and hopes of his own mates. The new Protestant faith taxed the conscientious mind, and a boy might be caught up in a terrifying drama with himself as protagonist, his everlasting future at stake, as he struggled in a Satanic world without much guidance.[30] Stephen Gosson of St George's parish, only a few years older than Marlowe, had left the King's School to begin his career as a playwright, forceful anti-theatrical pamphleteer, then Catholic convert in exile, and finally Reformed priest. Gosson's mission in being abroad, perhaps, is open to question; we lack evidence to settle the matter in his case; it is not impossible that he worked briefly in espionage for Walsingham. But no mere listing of what happened to Marlowe's clerically inclined school-mates might suggest the plight of some of the sensitive young in the 1580s, or of pale, overwrought 16-year-olds with doubts, of timidly defiant graduates fated to go to poor vicarages, or of those to be punished as heretics, or of nervous if not suicidal college Fellows, or of limp, guilt-ridden souls who planned to serve the church but, for some reason, never did. Mostly, we know of King's School pupils who survived in clerical careers. Henry Jacob—a boy of Marlowe's age—after conforming at Oxford University went abroad as a worried, fastidious 'Brownist' or anti-ritualist follower of Robert Browne, later helped to found England's first Congregational church, befriended a Pilgrim Father and set up a Virginia community, only to return for unknown reasons and die in London. Benjamin Carrier followed the poet to Cambridge, conformed satisfactorily as a Fellow of Corpus Christi College, then became an unexceptional vicar in Kent, a rector in Sussex, and chaplain to King James I, before pretending to visit a spa for his health, defecting to Rome, and dying as a papist in France. Marlowe's classmate Samuel Kennett (whom we are to meet again) was another who conformed thoroughly, but then, in bizarre circumstances, fled after a quick conversion to the Catholic seminary at Rheims and came back to England secretly under an alias.

Others, of course, saved their sanity. The Canterbury school was not full of nervous wrecks, and the queen's religion still had its priests, rites, and veneration of the Church Fathers. Day after day, schoolboys as they sang took on a collective identity, and Marlowe was to make dramas partly out of traditional rites and rituals. The plainest version of a psalm obliged pupils to assume the voice of David, Christ, or the church, as in Matthew Parker's very simple rendering of the first psalm with its strong, undeniable ritual efficacy, as boys cracked their voices to sing it:

> Not so, not so: the wicked do,
>   lyke dust or chaff they bee:
> Uphoyst by winde: as light by kinde,
>   From face of earth to see.
>
> Therefore these men: so wicked then,
>   in judgement shall not stand.
> Nor sinners bee: in companie,
>   of righteous men at hand.[31]

Marlowe's showy enthusiasm for singing, his musical skill and obviously good voice, were to be factors in his crucial academic advancement, as we are to see; music not only drew boys together, but offered careers to a few pupils. Roper Blundell, who drops out of the list of scholars when Marlowe does, became a *substitutus* or supplementary member in Canterbury's choir and later choirmaster at Rochester Cathedral.

What also drew boys together were their play productions, and drama had had a lively history at the school. An entry in the cathedral's accounts, for 1562–3, shows that the sum of £3. 6s. 8d. had been paid to the headmaster Anthony Rushe for this purpose: 'To Mʳ Ruesshe for rewards geven him at settynge out of his plays in Christmas *per capitulum* iijli vjs viijd'. Such a grant may indicate a capital expenditure, as for fitting out a stage, but a note in the cathedral's Act Book shows that it applied to the school for purposes that were common late in the reign: 'agreed that the Scolemaister and [scholars] shall have lxvjs. viijd. towards . . . settyng furthe of Tragedies, Comedyes, and interludes this next Christmas'.[32]

School plays would have helped Marlowe to find his *métier*. Pupils only needed a master's approval of a drama to stage it, and that gave them more freedom than many of the fifty or so acting troupes flourishing in the nation between 1530 and 1580. A 'lewde play' was pounced on in the city, but city authorities left the school alone.

Just which plays were staged in his tenure is uncertain, but the works of John Bale, a Canterbury canon when he died in 1563, would have been felt appropriate. Once a Carmelite friar, 'Bilious Bale'—to give him a later sobriquet—had turned into a fierce mocker of Rome with a knack for mixing doctrine with farce. In his *King Johan*, when corrupt friends bear on stage their bulky master, Sedition, the latter is pleased. 'Yea, thus it should be', cries Sedition from a lofty perch,

> Marry, now I am aloft
> I will beshit you all if ye set me not down soft.[33]

Bilious Bale's spirit of iconoclasm would have kept boys awake. For holiday stagings, there was much else available—and a torrent of invention in converging, darting streams of fashion in medieval and modern drama was on offer. Marlowe found almost too many styles amid the welter—even if he had a hand in a satire. Brief theatrical 'interludes' had begun to show diversity and psychological tact. Even the deity, at this time, was being challenged on the London stage. A strong Calvinistic emphasis on divine justice (rather than on divine mercy) had led to a tragic interest in persistent, resolute impenitence, for example in scripts such as W. Wager's *Enough is as Good as a Feast* or Nathaniel Woodes's *The Conflict of Conscience*.

Schoolmasters preferred moral plays which taught pupils 'good behaviour and audacitye'. Yet classical dramas were also acted, and the introspection later favoured by Marlowe suggests that he knew Seneca's tragedies. There were good examples of Senecan form in recent English plays, such as *Apius and Virginia* by 'R.B.', Thomas Preston's *Cambyses* and John Pickering's *Horestes*, or even Norton and Sackville's *Gorboduc*. The latter, about the evil brought upon a country by a king's folly, rises to genuine tragic feeling.

Whether or not he acted on a raised platform, Marlowe had a chance to judge a few plays. What he came to dislike were works which denied an audience the right to think, and there is a link between his mockery of the

Protestant clergy, on the one hand, and on the other his distaste for mere 'morals' on show. That which lulls the mind, soothes feelings, or supports a popularly held view is fatuous, irrelevant, or belittling in any drama, in Marlowe's view, and his opinions of the theatre formed early, if we judge from *Dido Queen of Carthage*, which he wrote at Cambridge. He favoured what was jagged, ironic, or unsettled in a script, as well as mixtures of the comic and epic, or of divine authority and the human will as shown on a stage. He was to set himself against any plain, educative, moral purpose, with Lucian or Ovid among his exemplars. Yet, in avoiding simplicities in theme and feeling, he was to respect, even so, a community of spectators. He was to privilege an audience above all of his characters, and write so as to get people to adjust their responses, to take in the unexpected, in form as in content, throughout the whole spectacle of a drama. Even at school, he was likely to try his hand in writing a sharp, ridiculing piece. Whether or not Lucian gave him a model, in his last days at the King's School he might have envied that cool, witty Greek.

All of this time, his school allowance had been handed to him in arrears at £1 a quarter. The sum which he had received from the King's School on Lady Day, 25 March 1579, had applied to his time since the previous Christmas, and he was to get his final payment at the end of September 1580. This summer, he was at the top of his form, and not among those misfits who, as the statutes put it, were 'strangers to the Muses'.

He cannot have spent all of his days within the trampled cathedral precincts, and a fifteen-minute walk would have taken him to what he calls 'the meads, orchards, and primrose lanes'. Marlowe uses local details in his works—and many interestingly occur in his *Jew of Malta*, in which the friars inhabit a 'monastery | Which standeth as an out-house to the Town', as St Augustine's Abbey stands. The nuns' cloister has a 'dark entry' matching the cathedral's so-called Dark Entry opposite the school itself. Or again, 'Jerusalem, where the pilgrims kneel'd', might reflect stony floors where pilgrims had knelt ever since St Thomas Becket's days. In his walks, he clearly knew 'running streams | And common channels of the City',[34] since the River Stour divides into streams which flow both in and around Canterbury. What often appealed to Christopher Marlowe's fancy, too, were wide panoramic views and the notion of uncannily large, sudden astronomical or geographical events. Earthquakes, quite obligingly, had rattled through Kent in April, and then in September came a report that Francis Drake, who had family roots in Kent, had come back from circumnavigating the globe.

Souvenir-hunters, in fact, were then greeting Drake's ship at Deptford, and his plunder of Spanish ships *en route* only led the queen to delay his knighthood for the moment. Rejoicings at King's School may have been keener because a relative of Drake (Francis's younger brother Thomas, it seems) had been a scholar there. At this point, vivid travel books existed, but, so far, Marlowe cannot have read a purely jokey, modern account of a world trip.

Yet, after Marlowe's last school payment, an unknown poet mocked Drake's great world voyage in a play called *Timon*. This work—a school play—offers a Kentish–Grecian landscape. The author cites 'Cinqueports' and cobblers, but he has not heard of Plutarch's account of the Greek Timon, and he knows very little about punctuation and less about apostrophes (he writes *ti's, tha'ts, pla'cd, h'ees, accur'sd*). With Lucian's dialogues, however, he is very familiar; at times, one wonders if he approves of anything else. He lifts Timon's story from Lucian's *Misanthropos*, and borrows other details from two or three Lucianic dialogues. The playwright's vocabulary includes expressions soon to appear in Marlowe's own works—fairly unusual words, such as *brabbling, insinuate, ruinate, stratagem, adamantine*, or *invocate*, which are unlikely to have been used by other young playwrights, as well as phrases such as 'cruel Scythians', and other proper names which Marlowe uses and favours, such as these, to mention a dozen: Lybia, Boreas, Hecuba, Antarctic, Caucasus, Zodiac, Pylades, Tantalus, Amazons, Proserpina, Ganges, or Antipodes. What especially indicates that Marlowe may have written a part of this play, at 16 or 17, is that its use of place-names suggests his style:

> This man is rare, and hath noe pararell
> Hath travaild *Africa, Arabia*
> and the remotest Iles; yea ther'es noe nooke
> or crooke in land or sea, but he hath seene.[35]

Exactly when *Timon* was completed is unclear, but its humour depended on people's having Drake's voyage freshly in mind. As for the play, its dialogue is trivial but funny. Satire gives way to the aim of showing off an unparalleled wit, a knowledge of geography, and some urbanity. A 'lying traveller' named Pseudocheus, who favours cheap travel by air, claims to have ridden a wooden Pegasus on a round-the-world journey lasting 'three years six months & four days'. (Having left Deptford in March 1577, Francis Drake had returned to port after some three years and six months at sea.) The play's references to air-mileage, or to 'duckes and drakes'—to make certain no one misses Drake's name—or to an inn high up in the air at Zodiac, a city with a view, all belittle Drake's feat of circling the globe by water. The traveller has supposedly seen the Antipodes, Africa, Arabia, and the Ganges (four places from which Drake had just returned).

The author—again, like Marlowe, who includes aerial viewpoints of Europe's cities in *Faustus*—is bemused by the high-flying traveller and by Pegasus, who needs no hay. Less emphasized is a foolish Timon, who might be a figure in a farce. Then, abruptly, farce shifts to tragedy. When Timon's friends leave him, he rises to crude power in speeches which a gifted adolescent might have penned, as when he lashes out at absent roisterers who have eaten his food, drunk his wine—

> Fire water sworde confounde yee, let the crowes
> Feede on your peckt out entrailes, and your bones
> Wante a sepulchre: worthy, o worthy yee
> That thus have, falsifi'd your faith to mee.
> To dwell in Phlegeton. rushe on me heav'n
> Soe that on them it rushe, mount Caucasus
> Fall on my shoulders, soe on them it fall
> Paine I respecte not: O holy Justice
> If thou inheritte heav'n descende at once
> Ev'n all at once unto a wretches hands
> Make mee an Arbiter of Ghosts in Hell
> That when they shall with an unhappy pace
> Descende the silent house of Erebus
> They may feele paines that never tongue can tell[36]

This is not beyond the ability of a schoolboy, and flashes of poetry and, above all else, a dramatic surge in the writing suggest that Marlowe, or a good imitator, had a hand in the script. Elements of the work, including a besotted 80-year-old female, look like comic drafts for his *Dido*. The style, vocabulary, and allusions here suggest his authorship, and in our time John C. Baker argues that the play is, indeed, Marlowe's own.

If his own writing *is* here, what we have is a young Marlowe trapped in amber. The script has not been attributed to anyone *but* Marlowe, and it would be foolish to deny his authorship on the frail, easy assumption that he never wrote anything less than a whole, well-integrated work. But I am sceptical. The trouble is that *Timon*'s manuscript, now at the Victoria and Albert Museum in London, is not that of the original play; what we have is a transcript, by two different hands, which includes later additions which cannot be his own, since they imitate works written after his time. An able editor of the manuscript, James C. Bulman Jr., believes that Shakespeare borrowed from this work to write *Timon of Athens*.[37] As a borrower, Shakespeare could be a magpie, of course; but how and when he would have been able to see the *Timon* manuscript is not clear to me, at least. Nor do we know that this satire of Drake's voyage was performed at Canterbury or elsewhere, and Marlowe may have thought little of the work if he did scribble it around October or November 1580. Nobody has extracted the original script from its later additions—but the piece is a symbol for what we lack, or for any of his early scripts lost to us. Such a *jeu d'esprit* may suggest that he had had to write unevenly, to find out how to write well.

It is not impossible that he spent time, this autumn, in writing the odd satire. Nonetheless, his prospects changed. By November, he knew he had a chance to go to university, and so would be less dependent on his parents. Thanks to Parker, there were funds to send boys on to Corpus Christi College, Cambridge. Six scholarships, providing 8*d.* a week initially, had been arranged. The allowances were raised, and the archbishop subsequently had set up 'Norwich' scholarships, and then, in 1569, 'Canterbury' ones. Deriving income from Westminster rents, the latter were open to boys nominated by the cathedral's dean and chapter. When the archbishop died in 1575, his will provided for three more scholarships under the control of his son John Parker.

Marlowe was nominated for one of the latter, and the award was a high honour. The field of selection had included not only Canterbury, but the Aylesham and Wymondham schools in Norfolk. Recipients had to be 'forward in learning, and also well minded in the service of God', but did not have to prepare for the church at first. Instead, Marlowe would have leisure to write and study as he wished, and the honour made him more attractive to men of influence. With hope of patronage, he was surely buoyant in the late autumn.

He had worked hard enough to excel, and in time might afford to be less cautious. He would need boldness, or a show of talent, to attract more help, but in his enthusiasm he would now lack parental guides. He had a certain fund of kindness, with charm to attract sensitive friends, and a strong incentive to write, though poets had not always fared well. The Roman poet Lucan, at a very early age, had lost his life for the crime of offending the politically powerful, and Marlowe, who could give offence, needed the stability which he had found in his schooldays. Though restlessly ambitious, he may have cautioned himself after all, since he knew that he couldn't afford to jeopardize his award. Having said good-bye at last to his sisters, a brother, and his parents, he set out through a high, mossy, medieval gate early in December—or, at any rate, after the leaves had fallen—to conquer as he could beside the river Cam.

II
Scholar and Spy

4
Corpus Christi College, Cambridge

❧

A Royston horse, and a Cambridge Master of Arts,
are two creatures who will give way to nobody.

(proverb)

The inland sea

LATE in the year, the roads in Cambridgeshire gave small comfort to
a traveller: the sun shone fitfully, and white drenching mists and
a chill might pierce one's clothing whether one sat in a carrier's
wagon or rode on horseback. On his journey, Marlowe must have
followed the Thames estuary, and had a sight of the capital or its environs
before he came to lonelier roads. He would have passed Hauxton, beyond
which the land rose before the Gog Magog Hills, and then, around
December 1580, come into Cambridge in between the King's Ditch and
the River Cam. Except for weeks of absence, he was to be at Corpus
Christi College for nearly six and a half years.

In this period he knew a dance in which the steps he took were as
bizarre as any modern choreographer could devise. The steps involved his
nerve, friendships and commitments, and a rapid emotional, intellectual,
and artistic development. He met regularly with a tutor, but fashioned a
verse style of flexible power; he heard lectures in Greek and Latin but
befriended a cousin of the spymaster Sir Francis Walsingham; and he took
part in genteel and often polite 'disputations' to earn a Bachelor's degree,
but became an agent in a calling which employed fraudsters and thugs.

His opportunities were good, and yet he was in danger of being tactless or over-confident at his college. The university imparted a deceptive

71

feeling of safety, and at first the place was odd enough to suggest that any behaviour—with the exception of a crude mockery of sermons—might be tolerated or even go unnoticed. On a wintry day gowned figures scuttled here and there, and no one would have conceived that they were ghosts, but the setting was bizarre in the fading days of Michaelmas term. To the north, one gazed at a smear of horizon and a large, improbable sea of water which stretched up past low, grassy, outcropping islands to the Isle of Ely. From Castle Hill beyond Magdalen College, the minster of Ely was visible when mists cleared over the strange, dank, undrained Fens.

Though built on dry earth, Cambridge's colleges had arisen like independent islands, and students had had to huddle in poor hostelries or in freezing convents among monks and friars. As late as 1310 there had been only one college, Peterhouse, which in itself housed no undergraduates and barely provided for fifteen senior scholars and three choristers. As new foundations arose, the townspeople had begun a warfare against rowdy students and there had been clashes between 'town' and 'gown': deeds and charters of the university had been burned and students were killed, but one college had seemed to bring peace. Sponsored by the united guilds of Corpus Christi and the Blessed Virgin Mary, Corpus Christi College was the peaceful agent, founded in 1352. It, too, was raided, yet it helped to appease the townsfolk; it was officially 'the College of Corpus Christi and of the Blessed Virgin Mary', but came to be called Bene't College, since the late Saxon church of St Benedict was joined by a gallery with Corpus.[1] That umbilical cord might have promised much, and a truce with the town existed in Marlowe's time, when glass-breaking boys could be sent to the Tolbooth or local prison.

Marlowe was unlikely to damage Corpus, which lay to the east of the High—or Trumpington Street—in a half-mile area in which most of the foundations clustered. The university's fourteen colleges and halls differed in size, but in no way more radically than in attitudes to the theatre. Further to the east lay Christ's College, so puritanical that its students were forbidden to act in plays, and Emmanuel College, which opened in 1584, was to be as hostile to theatre. To the west, the royally founded colleges of King's, Queens', and Trinity welcomed stage productions. The most populous college, St John's, had made play-acting mandatory, and Trinity and Queens' had done the same. The master of Gonville and Caius, Thomas Legge, had written a play about Richard III

CORPUS CHRISTI COLLEGE, & ST BOTOLPH'S CHURCH.

6 Corpus Christi College, Cambridge, and St Botolph's Church,
engraved in 1827 from a view looking north from a corner of
Silver Street and Trumpington Street

and yet, typically, *Richardus Tertius* was not acted by his own scholars at
Caius, but in 1579 by those at St John's.[2]

Marlowe knew other confusions, but had time to settle in before a new
term began. Corpus had an old, four-sided court—the first closed court
built at Cambridge—and here he would have found neatly plastered
rooms, with glazed windows, on the north, east, and west sides. To the
south were a kitchen with the Fellows' library over it, the Buttery, Great
Hall, common parlour, and Master's Lodge above. Cambridge had been
expanding so that about 5,000 townsfolk were rivalled by a university
population of 1,862 in 1581, and some Corpus men lived in an annexe
outside the court.

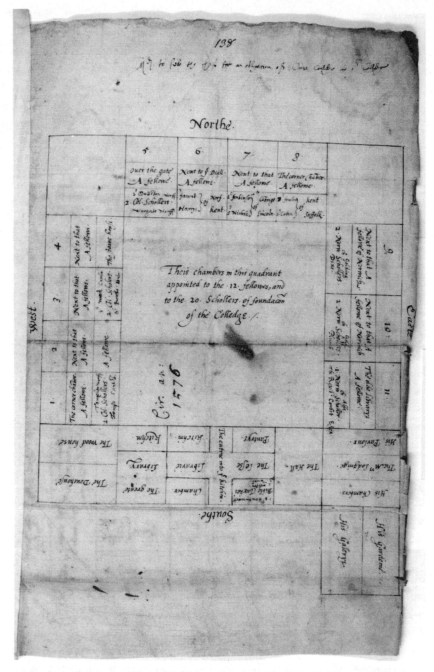

7 A plan of Corpus Christi College, showing the 'Store house' room where
Marlowe lived, as No. 4, near the north-west corner of the Old Quad

Marlowe slept in a converted 'Storehouse', as the late archbishop had referred to it, a bedroom which had a garret over it, and, what was welcome and unusual, a chimney with two flues, which had been added in 1542 when the chamber served for storage; this was a ground-floor room next to a staircase at the north-west angle of the court. I very much doubt that he had any other accommodation at the college. He could have slept in another chamber, as is sometimes supposed, but this would have contradicted the wishes in Parker's will, under its provision for three scholars drawn from the Canterbury, Aylesham, and Wymondham schools; so, if tradition is valid, he had the storehouse with its angled view of the hall's large oriel. Six Parker scholars, on Norwich grants, lived on the court's east side, where the archbishop had left a few books chained 'within the Under-Chamber of the Tenth Chamber on the East', according to the stipulation. Here Marlowe found a few Latin and Greek bibles, Erasmus's New Testament, a concordance, lexicons, thesauri, and even a history of Cambridge called *Historia Antiquitat. Cantabrigiae*, printed in 1574.[3] Bachelors and Fellows had access to more texts than the undergraduates, and there was an international flavour in what some Fellows perused. 'You cannot step into a scholar's study', Gabriel Harvey wrote to his friend Edmund Spenser in 1579, 'but (ten to one) you shall likely find open . . . Leroy's *Exposition* upon Aristotle's *Politics* or some other like French or Italian politique discourses. And I warrant you some good fellows amongst us begin now to be pretty well aquainted with a certain parlous book called, as I remember me, *Il Principe* di Nicolo Machiavelli.'[4] Not everyone read anything so truthful about statecraft as Machiavelli's *The Prince*, which Marlowe, later on, seems to have encountered in French. At present, he made do with standard texts, usually issued from chests under care of a Fellow, who ensured a book's safe return. Bookshop prices in the town were low, mainly under the university's control. Once he had his BA, he would have access to two of the best collections in the British Isles: Corpus's rarer books and those in the university library in the public schools quadrangle.

The archbishop, too, had bequeathed a priceless collection of volumes—but this nearly ruined the college. Corpus's Master, Robert Norgate, had planned to build a new chapel with an attic library for these treasures, and as a result a good deal of slate, lime, and sand, with 700 tons of stone, 500,000 bricks, and much timber, had piled up south of the court, but when Marlowe arrived the new chapel was a mere shell. Even when he had his Master's degree, he may have lacked access to Parker's books, and, at the moment, the price of Norgate's attic had exceeded £200 on hand for the project, the donor of that sum was dead, and Norgate stupidly had forgotten to allow for the cost of nails, scaffolding, ramming of foundations, or even the labourers' wages. This must have been a topic when Marlowe arrived—since the Master's folly ran the college into debt, and their financial troubles were to worsen.[5]

Norgate was a bemused martinet, a man of unreckoning fervour, and so fearful of Romanists that he imagined a papist takeover of the quad. He was a Calvinist without common sense, and with no sane notion of money he left the college and, in fact, his own household bankrupt, but he was not indifferent to Latin or Greek. Just when Marlowe began to annoy him is unknown, but Norgate either took steps to thwart the cobbler's son, or thoroughly approved the steps taken. Before his main offence, Marlowe was perhaps likely to be impertinent with men whom he did not respect, but there is no sign that he offended anyone at first. Whatever he did at the college, he had to get along in close quarters, and this winter he slept near two other Parker scholars: these were Thomas Lewgar, who later took several holidays when Marlowe did and graduated with him (BA and MA), and Robert Thexton, a vicar's son and already a Bachelor of two years' standing. Thexton, in 1582, gave place to Thomas Munday, a former King's School boy, and Munday, after taking his degree in 1584, was replaced by William Cockman. The Parker men were often dutiful souls, eager to please and bent on careers in teaching or the pulpit; the eldest in the storehouse slept on a bedstead, and the others, such as the poet at first, had pull-out beds. All had desks or small carrels for study, and since there was a chimney, a fire may have been permitted; elsewhere in the quad, boys ran up and down steps to warm their feet before retiring.

After chapel at 5 a.m., Marlowe would have appeared in hall dressed like a monk in a black, demure gown reaching to his heels, a round skullcap on his head. He kept his hair uncut, if he wore it knotted, but students were deluged with orders about dress. These came from the authority of the queen's minister, Lord Burghley, who was also the university's Chancellor, and one might have thought that he cared for nothing but show. In one year, a particularly gigantic edict was produced as a result

of Burghley's anxiety—and doubtless its terrible contents were made
known:

Orders of Apparell for Schollers of the Universitie of Cambridge, made by
the Right honorable the Lord Burleigh Lord High Treasurer of England and
Chauncelor of the Universitie of Cambridge, with the assent of the Vice-
Chancellor, Master of Colleges, and the Doctors of all
Degrees within the saied Universitie.
Anno 1585
First, that no Graduate remayninge within any Colledge, Hostell, or Hall, or
clayminge to enjoye the priviledge of a Scholler, doe weare any stuffe in the
outwards part of his gowne, but woollen cloth of blacke, puke, London Browne,
or other sad color . . . .

Such advice went on for pages. In their emergency repair of gowns,
boys were told to use nothing but a plain hem, 'without cutt, purle,
stringe, jagge, carving, lace, twist, pynke, or any such like'.[6] The repeating
of these laws suggests that they were disobeyed, but even an army of
invaders could not keep Whitehall from thinking of the colour of a boy's
hose, and in the Spanish Armada year Burghley was still hard at his
dress rules—a boy must avoid anything but 'sad' colours—until he found
the sumptuary laws almost unenforceable. One effect was to feminize
students in ankle-length gowns, if not to conduce to homoerotic fantasies.
The male form was covered as if it were too alluring for the eye, but this
charade was given the lie every night when boys undressed. Marlowe
made a good deal of the 'bed' in his first known work, and his interest in a
man's love for a man was undoubtedly encouraged by the lascivious
authorities.

As Christmas approached, he dined in hall with about 130 boys and
men. Some of the undergraduates were as young as 12 or 13, others as old
as 21; as he was not yet 17, Marlowe was not over-age for one awaiting
matriculation. The highest-ranking students were fellow-commoners,
often sons of the wealthy. The bulk of the others were pensioners as
Marlowe was, and so he appears as the last but one among 'Pensionari'
in Corpus's *Registrum Parvum*, or Admission Book, for the year ending
25 March 1580/1. A third group were sizars, who had menial duties such
as bed-making or chamber-sweeping to pay their way. Cambridge's
sizars often included gifted men, such as Spenser, lately over at Pembroke

Hall, or Marlowe's future enemy Robert Greene, then at Clare Hall after taking his BA at St John's in 1578. Or a thin, boyish satirist with a tooth or two that poked out at angles, Marlowe's great friend Thomas Nashe, who began at St John's in 1582. At the lowest rank were half-sizars or *quadrantarii*, mainly college servants who were allowed to study.

All boys were supposed to attend college lectures given in the three trimesters, from 10 October to 16 December (Michaelmas term), then from mid-January to the second Friday before Easter, and from the eleventh day after Easter until the Friday after Commencement Day (always the first Tuesday in July). There was also a Midsummer quarter, in which less work was usually done. Rules for the Parker scholars were rather strict in theory, and they were allowed only a month's absence per year if they had leave. Many students, evading lectures, were anything but exemplars of hard-working future clergymen: 'At Cambridge', wrote Robert Greene, 'I light*ed* amongst wags as lewd as my selfe, with whom I consumed the flower of my youth.'[7] Some scholars hunted from dawn to dusk, as Simon Forman recalled of his Oxford days, and John Lyly implied that he himself had indulged in dice, drink, and women. At both universities, there were protests over dry lectures and silly disputations, or the 'Philosophy of Aristotle'.

On his first day at Corpus, Marlowe had spent 1*d.* at the college Buttery, and this was recorded by the bursar as occurring in the tenth week after Michaelmas or probably on 9 or 10 December:

> septimana 10ᵃ post ~~Nativita~~ Michael . . . ño co Marlen——id

He had to pay for what he consumed—and his grant allowed a shilling a week for food and drink. Just one week later, he had spent 3*s.* 2½*d.*, or three times his weekly allowance,[8] but he was then near the Christmas season when laws were relaxed. Gabriel Harvey had been pilloried for studying when others were 'hardest at their cards'. At Corpus Christi, a large fire burned far into the night, and torch-links (of flax and pitch) usually lit up college theatricals. These were staged in hall, where lately a guard had been attacked in a riot, and at Christmastime students from rival colleges arrived to see any play on offer. As a precaution, glass might be removed from windows—unless they were netted—and 'stagekeepers' kept order in metal visors and used torches as weapons. Before his formal study began in January, Marlowe knew of a demand for plays, well evidenced by shouting, marauding students from every college.[9]

At Corpus he found an unusual emphasis on singing: he had won his award partly for his musical ability and skill in making verses. The archbishop had laid down requirements for Canterbury scholars, but his son John Parker, as recently as April 1580, had made these more specific by asking that scholarship-holders

at the time of their election be so entered into the skill of song as that they shall at first sight solf [or accomplish the scale] and sing plain song . . . and if it may be[,] such as can make a verse.[10]

Those demands were unlikely to be unappetizing, and so, presumably, Marlowe joined in plainsong; it is interesting that, although he became an espionage agent, he was deliberately to present himself, for the rest of his life, as a scholar, one with a Master's degree and a programme of his own. To survive in the Arts course, he had to avoid stepping on the toes of the lecturing professors, but so long as he was not a vile nuisance he had some freedom to do as he pleased. One difference between the King's School and Cambridge was that here, in all fields, there was a higher proportion of the gifted, though anyone with original ideas might fear that his tongue could get him in trouble. Religion was full of traps for the unwary: since nearly all dons were clergymen, 'atheistical' talk would not be tolerated. And at this time, Marlowe was dining in hall with Francis Kett, who suffered martyrdom.

Not that this shy, introverted man was likely to be talkative, but Marlowe knew him. Born in Norfolk, Kett had taken his Master's degree at Corpus in 1573, when he became a Fellow. His crime was to follow in the steps of a third-century priest, Arius, who had denied the Saviour's divinity. As an 'Arian heretic', Kett believed Christ was 'not God, but a good man' who suffered for his sins and was to 'suffer againe for the sinnes of the world', and be made God after a 'second resurrection'. Whether or not he advanced these views at Corpus, Kett remained until the eleventh week of Easter term in 1581, so Marlowe saw him in the three or four months before he left for a Norfolk vicarage. Later, the bishop of Norwich charged him with heresy and condemned him to be burned in a ditch. In January 1589 Kett was watched at the last by a Puritan divine, who apparently found that the former Fellow was lightly tied, and went

8 Marlowe and Francis Kett, who was later burned for heresy: in Corpus Christi's Buttery Book for Easter term 1581. 'Marlen', at the bottom of the list, has spent 5*s.* 4*d.*; 'Mr Kett,' second from the top, has spent 13*d.*

'leaping and daucing: being in the fire, above twenty times' and 'clapping his hands, he cried nothing but *blessed bee God*', and so he continued 'untill the fire had consumed all his nether partes, and untill he was stifled with the smoke'.[11]

Kett was burned by a bishop—not by Cambridge—and that such a man had been a Fellow is one index of an atmosphere in which deep feeling, along with eccentricity, folly, and intelligence, had thrived at Corpus Christi. The dates of Marlowe's compositions are open to question, but it is likely, as scholars believe, that he wrote versions of *All Ovid's Elegies* and *Lucan's First Book*, as well as of *Dido* and the first part of *Tamburlaine*, at Cambridge. If that is so, Marlowe produced creative work of a higher quality than anyone else in residence at a Tudor university ever did, and his college's tolerance of eccentrics probably helped. As for other heretics, the university tried to protect people from outside interference. Ecclesiastical commissioners had lately ordered one Corpus Fellow, named Stannard, to appear before them at Lambeth. Stannard was obviously a Catholic, but the Vice-Chancellor forbade him to go to inquisitors, foiled them, and encouraged the college to keep him on.

Not every Vice-Chancellor had the pluck of the one who saved Stannard. Marlowe could hardly have avoided seeing the princely estate of Dr John Hatcher, whose tenure as Vice-Chancellor had ended in 1580, since this domain covered a large area at the back of Corpus. As regius professor of physic, Hatcher had kept up a medical practice while writing a little poetry and encouraging poets, but he gouged his well-to-do patients expertly enough to make a palace behind the college out of an old Austin friary, where he had twenty-seven rooms. The former Vice-Chancellor's parlour, with a ceiling seventy yards long and nine feet high, was decorated with tapestry carpets and lit by a window twelve feet broad, and there was an immense hall above it. Hatcher kept 'a large chest filled with copes and other spoils' of Catholic churches, as well as an array of gold and silver plate.[12] As Vice-Chancellor, he had not put a foot wrong to judge from his few, bland edicts, and in his façade anyone who looked behind the college might have seen evidence of greed's rewards.

Yet when spring came and the sky cleared over the Fens, the palace of greed must have shrunk a little in significance. People noted a green, tranquil Cambridge, which foreigners envied, equipment for sport came out in the colleges, and a student might have found his room a palace and a workshop, too.

Beds, Buttery Books, and elegies

Early in 1581, Marlowe fell into some trouble which was not of his making, though as it involved money it had an ominous aspect. He became a semi-legal resident at Cambridge with no scholarship, and in all probability with little in his purse. If he was advised by a bursar, he was no better off by the early spring.

His plight was odd. Lacking cash, he might have been recruitable as a government agent at any time: indeed, fate divided him from other young men, as if to underline the fragility of any source of ordinary, official help. His King's School award had come so late that he was nearly over-age for it, and then, owing to a mix-up, his Parker stipend had vanished. Had he been invited to Corpus too early? The fault was not that of Christopher Pashley, the Parker scholar whom he was supposed to replace. In Corpus's bursary records, Pashley's name appears until the first quarter of 1580–1, when it is dropped and the poet's name occurs; but Marlowe's name is crossed out, and 'Pashlye' is inked in above it. Pashley, it appears, had an indisputable right to the Parker money until mid-1581: certainly he is described as *ex fundacione Matthei Archiepiscopi Cant[uarensis]* and, having entered on 15 June 1575, he was allowed to hold the stipend for six years as an ordinand.[13] The bureaucracy at Cambridge may always have worked in mysterious ways, and in former times a tenth of the students had died each year owing to the fetid King's Ditch or the plague, but few died of hunger. Marlowe did not starve, and the bursary may have let him draw on credit at the Buttery, but even so he was not allowed to matriculate at the university, despite a ruling which required him to do so within a month. Others may have known the same dilemma since there appear to have been conflicting rules for matriculation. Weeks after the deadline for this formality had passed, his name was listed in the University Registry's *Book of Matriculation* on 17 March 1581:

Coll. corp. x͟r. Chrōf. Marlen

Finally, an entry in Corpus's *Registrum Parvum* headed '*Nomina Scholasti-corum*' shows that he has his award in place of Pashley:

9 Marlowe loses his scholarship: in Corpus Christi's Audit Book for 1580/1, 'Marlen', second line from the bottom, is crossed out, and the name 'Pashlye' is substituted

1581. Maii 7 Marlin electus et admissus in locum domini Pashley[14]

If these delays struck him as absurd, they can hardly have reinforced his respect for authority, nor did they bring him closer to solving another problem. The Parker scholarship was tenable for three years, or barely time to qualify for a BA degree under a special provision, but if he opted to read for holy orders, the award might be held for six. He may not have wished to die in a Kentish vicarage, but unless he found outside help, he might be forced to take holy orders. Meanwhile, if he broke rules, he could lose his stipend and be sent home, so he tended to be cautious at the outset. Thanks to Corpus's Buttery Books and audits, we can follow his university career almost week by week, and the evidence is interesting.

The Buttery Books were kept in succession by the bursars Richard Chever and Sophynam Smith, who as college Fellows spelled his name in nine different ways, beginning as 'Marlen', 'Marlinge', or 'Marlin', and evolving to 'Marlie', but they noted the cost of what he ate or drank. The initials 'R.C.' or 'S.S.' were jotted under his entries at the end of a term, when he paid his bill, though, as some totals are uninitialled, he still seems to have owed for lamb chops and beer.[15]

If he took a brief holiday he might let a friend use his grant, and so the bursar notes, 'he left *P*eters in commons being absent', or 'Ds Grenewood in commons'.[16] John Greenwood, the second beneficiary of Kit Marlowe's largesse, was a fervent Christian who qualified for a degree in 1581. Later, for holding radical Puritan meetings, he was sent to prison at the Clink, and Greenwood was finally hanged at Tyburn in April 1593 for writing subversive tracts.[17] Marlowe's college friends cared about beliefs, ideas, or literature; what mattered was whether they took a fresh line on anything.

On the whole, the Buttery Books suggest that he was prudent until the BA, when he became an absentee with an excess of money. The audits, which record scholarship payments, show that he was more often at Corpus as an undergraduate than any of his roommates. A boy was paid a shilling a week for being *actually* resident, but lost a shilling if away, so we can tell when Marlowe was in the college.

In his first year, the audits show the following for 'Marlin' and his chambermates, in trimesters from January to September:

10 Marlowe's name in the Buttery Book again, 1581. When away from
Cambridge, he left his food allowance to William Peeters or to the ardent
Puritan John Greenwood, later executed for heresy. Opposite 'Marlen',
near the bottom, is the entry 'he left peters in c̄omons being absent'

1581	in 2a Trim. [Lent]	3a Trim. [Easter]	4a Trim. [Summer]
	Ds Thexton xiijˢ	Ds Thexton xiijˢ	Ds Thexton xˢ
	Leugar xiijˢ	Leugar xiijˢ	Leugar iijˢ
	Marlin xiiˢ	Marlin xiijˢ	Marlin xijˢ

He took a week's holiday in Lent term—when he was paid a shilling less than Thexton or Lewgar—but, overall, the regularity of his attendance at the college was exemplary.

In 1581–2 he was about equally correct; he took a longish holiday in the summer quarter, when he was paid 7 shillings for so many weeks in residence during a fourteen-week term—but that absence at a lazy, warm time was hardly excessive:

1581–82	in 1a Trim. [Michaelmas]	2a Trim. [Lent]
	Ds Thexton xijˢ	Ds Thexton ⎱ xijˢ Mondey ⎰
	Lewger xiijˢ	Lewger xiijˢ
	Marlin xiijˢ	Marlin xiijˢ
	3a Trim. [Easter]	4a Trim. [Summer]
	Munday ijˢ	Munday xiiijˢ
	Lewgar viijˢ	Lewgar ijˢ
	Marlin xiijˢ	Marlin vijˢ

In the next year, he took his seven weeks' holiday in May and June of Easter term. Again, he was more often at Cambridge than either of his chambermates:

1582–83	in 1a Trim. [Michaelmas]	2a Trim. [Lent]
	Munday xijˢ	Munday xjˢ
	Lewgar iiijˢ	Lewgar xiijˢ
	Malyn xijˢ	Marlin xiijˢ
	3a Trim. [Easter]	4a Trim. [Summer]
	Munday iijˢ	Munday xiˢ vjᵈ
	Lewgar ixˢ	Lewgar xiˢ
	Marlin vjˢ	Marlin xiiijˢ

In the following session, his name is preceded by 'D.' or 'Ds.' for 'Dominus', as he became a Bachelor of Arts. The bursar erred in thinking he had the baccalaureate in the first term, though Marlowe became a BA in the Easter session, 1584:

1583–84   in 1a Trim. [Michaelmas]   2a Trim. [Lent]
D Munday xij^s D Monday x^s vj^d
D. Lewgar xii^s D Lewgar viij^s
D. Marlyn xij^s D Marlin xiij^s

3a Trim. [Easter]   4a Trim. [Summer]
D. Monday iii^s Cokman iiij^s
D Lewgar viij^s D Lewgar xiij^s
D Marlyn xiij^s D Marlin xj^s vj^d

That summer his habits began to change—and the next year, when he turned 21, he began to abscond for long periods. He was away for three weeks before Michaelmas, but his absence continued (whether or not he had leave) during almost all of Michaelmas term of 1584–5, and other long absences followed.

These changes are reflected in the next audit:

1584–85   in 1a Trim. [Michaelmas]   2a Trim. [Lent]
Ds Lewgar   Ds Lewgar
Ds Marlin iij^s Ds Marlin vij^s vj^d
Cockman xij^s Cockman xiij^s

3a Trim. [Easter]   4a Trim. [Summer]
Ds Lewgar   Ds Lewgar
Ds Marlin iiij^s Ds Marlin v^s
Cockman iij^s Cockman xiiij^s

Marlowe came back to Corpus at the end of January 1585; he stayed until the middle of April, when he vanished again until the term's end. The audits are missing for 1585–6, and it may be that plague (or another crisis) emptied the college from about 22 April to 17 June 1586. Anyway, Marlowe was constantly present from mid-June until that October, when the Buttery Books close. The following volumes are lost and the Buttery series does not begin again until 1721, so we lack details of his expenses during his last year at Cambridge.

We have a few, final glimpses of him in these records, since the audits of 1586–7 show him present for nine weeks after Michaelmas, and for five and a half weeks around Lent, after which he left for good:

1586–87   in 1a Trim. [Michaelmas]   2a Trim. [Lent]
Ds Lewgar   Ds Lewgar ij^s

Ds Marly ix^s Ds Marlye v^s vj^d
Ds Cockman xiij^s Ds Cockman xj^{s18}

Still, he was ready to gain what he could when he began the Arts course in January 1581. Formerly, the course had been designed as a survey of human knowledge, and medieval students in cold rooms had taken up grammar, rhetoric, and dialectic (the famous *trivium*), and gone on to arithmetic, astronomy, geometry, and music (the *quadrivium*), before rising to the wonders of philosophy and divinity. In Marlowe's time, the core programme had been simplified, and the new course aimed to provide a basic training for the mind. There would have been less memory-work than Marlowe had known at the King's School, and students were encouraged to improve their grasp of logic and their ability to think on their feet and to develop imaginative resourcefulness. In fact, the university's statutes had ordered the colleges to teach 'rhetoric the first year, dialectic the second and third', and in the fourth year philosophy, as well as a few ancillary subjects.

Also—as if to fill in idle hours—Norgate had set up a college programme which required men to be in hall six days a week for a battery of topics and exercises. A copy of his plan (dated a little earlier) survives, and, with minor changes of detail from year to year, this was the Corpus week:

> The exercises of Learning in Corpus Christi Colledg*e*
>   in Cambridg*e* every daye in the weke from
> the beginning of the terme untill the ending thereof.
>
> On Mondaye after morning prayers, be re*a*d in the hall at vi of
>   the clock, these thre*e* Lectur*es* 1. Aristotle's *Naturall*
>   *Philosophy*. 2. Aristotell's *Organon* 3. [John] Seaton'*s*
>   [*Dialectica*] w*h*ich continewe for the space of one whole
>   houre.
>
> At xii of the clock *to* be re*a*d two Gre*e*ke lectures, one of
>   construction, as Homere or Demosthenes, or
>   Hesiod, or Isocrates. etc. The other of the gra*m*mer
>
> At iii of the clock *to be* re*a*d a rhetorick lecture, of some
>   p*a*rt of Tully [Cicero], for the space of an houre.
>
> At iiii of the clock beginneth the schollers sophisme, w*h*ich
>   continueth untill 5

On Tuesdaye be the same lectures & exercise at the same
　　houres.

On Wednisdaye, after morning prayers in the chappell one of
　　the fellowes in his order handeleth some place of the
　　scripture, wherupon he taketh occasion to entreat of
　　some common place of Doctrine, the which he proveth
　　by the scripture, & doctors.

After the common place be the same lectures & exercise at the
　　same houres as upon the former dayes.

On Thursdaye after morning prayers, at vi. xii. & iii of the
　　clock the same lectures to be read which be on the
　　dayes before. At iii of the clock, a probleme for the
　　Bachelours of Arts & generall Sophisters.

On Frydaye after morning prayer A common place, as upon
　　Wednesdaye. At vi. xii. & iii of the clock, the same
　　lectures to be read as before. At iiii of the clock the
　　Deane keepeth corrections; At 5 of the clock doth beginn
　　the fellowes probleme in Divinitye which continueth
　　ii hours.

On Satterdaye after morning prayers at vi. xii & iii of the clock,
　　the same lectures to be read as on the former dayes. At
　　vi of the clock after supper doe ii bachelours or ii
　　schollers declame.[19]

How did Marlowe react to this deluge? Clearly he responded well to
'Rhetoric', as we can tell from his later skill with it; but so far as the
official programme was concerned, he was a poet-in-residence waiting to
be amused. It was normal to skip many events (or doze through them),
but one secret of his success as a poet is that, even if he sat dreamily
through lecturers, he remembered what was intriguing or unusual. Like
Doctor Faustus, he read Aristotle, not in Greek but in the philosopher's
Latin dress, and later as a writer he referred to the *Analytics*, the *Organon*
generally, and the *Nicomachean Ethics*, and adapted quotations from
Aristotle. Glosses and commentaries on Plato, Aristotle, and Pliny
supplied the 'philosophy' part of Norgate's programme, and there were
doses of Greek, although Marlowe avoided them, or anyway did not
swallow many of them. He never read through the Homeric epics in the
original, nor did he delve far in the Attic tragedies, though Ovid appears

to have led him to Sophocles and, sooner or later, to Thomas Watson's elegant Latin translation of the Greek *Antigone*.

In his second year as 'Merlinge', he figured in a list of those due to hear about Cicero's *Topics* from Mr Johnes, professor of dialectic.[20] Even if he chose not to attend the talks, he would have known related exercises involved in what Norgate called 'the scholars sophisme'.

Much depended on Marlowe's skill with logic, the syllogism, and dialectical argument. A college's 'disputations', at this time, were usually friendly affairs, in which students twisted their tongues around Latin syllogisms before taking part in formal debates in the university's public schools building. To qualify for the BA degree, Marlowe had to offer two 'Acts' or 'Responsions' and two 'Opponencies' in the schools: his future hinged on whether he came off well. As a 'Respondent', he had to announce three philosophical ideas which he was willing to defend, and young men from other colleges acted as his opponents. At best, a dispute had the agility of a Spanish bullfight, and success could lead to local fame, or a Fellowship.

In a surviving transcript of a dispute, for example, the Respondent holds that 'The threat of punishment is sufficient to deter the crime' (*Sufficit in rebus humanis scire locum esse in carcere*). Then there is a verbal scuffle, in which an Opponent counters with an obliquely related syllogism:

> Natural liberty as the philosophers say is to live as one pleases.
> But this liberty is bridled by the threat of punishment.
> Therefore the threat of punishment is a bridle of natural liberty.[21]

Such exchanges often had the unpredictability of good theatre, and Marlowe respected them. His Faustus was to hold that disputing well is 'logic's chiefest end', but mistakenly to regard the syllogism as trivial argument instead of a means of piercing to truth and saving his soul. Probably the fashionable ideas of a modern professor in France, Petrus Ramus, whose *Dialecticae* was in use at Cambridge by 1576, helped to reconcile Marlowe himself to dialectic. Defying the rigidity of Aristotle and humanizing the study of logic, Ramus not only helped students to get through their formal exercises but stressed that dialectic could be of use in poetic composition. In *The Massacre at Paris* Marlowe sympathetically brings Ramus in person on stage, only to kill him off rather quickly.

While studying dialectic, he had chances to hear preachers who displayed logic, or its lack. Vigorously expressed Calvinist and anti-Calvinist views rang in the pulpits even before William Perkins, a Fellow of Christ's, began to win over the undergraduates with persuasive, step-by-step Genevan discourses over at Great St Andrews Church. Marlowe preferred the imagistic, vivid Calvin to his apologists, and must have recalled Calvin's graphic imagery from school. That theologian's sketches of the 'abyss' of unbelief, for example, can be felt in the last act of *Doctor Faustus*, and his doctrine of aspiration, his stress on the need 'to climb up to eternal felicity', or his belief that it is 'the chief action of the soul to aspire', mingle in *Tamburlaine*'s remarkable theme of striving. In a persuasive study in 2000, Christopher Haigh showed that Calvin's followers were already on the defensive at Cambridge and Oxford by the 1580s[22]—and yet Marlowe found Calvinist theology no less provocative because it was under siege.

Above all else, he had to please a tutor, whether or not the tutor was alert to poetry or the intellectual flux of the times. His Corpus tutor's name, as 'praelector', appears at last in a *supplicat*, which enabled Marlowe to appeal for a Bachelor's degree after getting past his college's hurdles, and then three days of oral and written university examinations. The conventional *supplicat* avows in Latin that one Christopherus Marlin prayeth

that twelve completed terms in which he hath heard the usual lectures (even though not wholly according to the form of the statute), together with all opponencies, responsions, and other exercises required by the royal statute may suffice for him to be admitted to the question.[23]

As many others did, he qualified for the BA in fewer than twelve terms, and, just at this time, faced a final 'question' on Aristotle's *Prior Analytics*. Thus he was close to success when the *supplicat* was signed by Thomas Harris, his tutor. Not much older than Marlowe, Harris had begun as a Corpus pensioner and taken his Master's degree in 1580, after which, as a Fellow, he was listed directly under Norgate's name.

Even if that is not a sign of prestige, he was a well-thought-of young scholar, who may have known of Marlowe's effort to translate Ovid's *Amores*—which, for all its emphasis on seduction, focuses on the stylish remarks of a Roman 'Student', a persona usually distinct from that of his poetic creator. Marlowe had meant to render into English, with the accent of a contemporary voice, the first erotic work of Ovid. The *Amores* had struck the dons as salacious, no doubt, but it had the endorsement of Erasmus. In the poem, Ovid begins (and later intrudes) in his own voice, but Marlowe is fully alert to the delicacy and subtlety of the author's essentially dramatic method. The 'story' that unfolds is not particularly complex in itself. Ovid's vain, mean-minded hero seduces the wedded Corinna, then displays his jealousy of her husband and strategies of deceit, enjoys the lady rarely, sometimes fails in his sexual performance, and bitterly loses her to a rival as if he were a cuckolded bachelor, before he emerges with a dim sense of his folly. All along, the Student focuses on himself, and Corinna is, for the most part, his prey. We find him tossing on a lonely bed, and Marlowe makes more of the bed than the Latin original does:

> What makes my bed seem hard seeing it is soft?
> Or why slips down the coverlet so oft?
>
> .   .   .   .   .   .
>
> 'Tis cruel Love turmoils my captive heart.[24]

The last line with its fine verb 'turmoils' suggests what Marlowe chiefly gained from translating. He put his poetic talent into a furnace to get rid of its fat, its excesses. He even made a difficult task harder for himself since English is not an inflected language. Ovid's elegiac lines, in their hexameter and pentameter pattern, are unusually concise, and Marlowe attempts to translate them into the even tighter form of the English heroic couplet: it might be easier to squeeze a genie back into a bottle.

What is notable, though, is that he often catches his Student's voice, while reflecting the cool, citified tones and epigrammatic smartness of the Latin text. He associates love with topics seldom discussed openly in the halls of Tudor Cambridge, such as the abortion of the foetus, bitter sexual jealousy, the characteristics of a self-deluding liar, or even the unpredictability of the penis.

The Student talks naturally to that organ, berates it, or recalls with shame a limpness when 'like one dead it lay', though the organ rises in bed with unruliness when he is alone. 'Now', he tells himself,

> when he should not jet, he bolts upright,
> And craves his task, and seeks to be at fight.

Lie down with shame, and see thou stir no more,
Seeing thou wouldst deceive me as before.

Even as the Student recalls a sexual disaster, the vagaries of the affair
lead the poet to appraise male prowess from unheroic, wry, and psychologically detached viewpoints. 'Nay more', laments the hero, in light of a
recent encounter,

the wench did not disdain a whit
To take it in her hand and play with it,
But when she saw it would by no means stand,
But still drooped down, regarding not her hand,
'Why mock'st thou me,' she cried, 'or being ill,
Who bade thee lie down here against thy will?'[25]

Corinna, just then, had flung herself away from the lover in her 'long
loose gown'. On an earlier occasion, he had been sexually capable, though
his memory of the incident is oddly idealized, as if his success were a
daydream. Again, the lady is little more than a luscious target. Unlike
Ovid's hero, Marlowe's Student—in his imagination, at least—was
violent at a crucial moment when he 'clinged her naked body', or pushed
Corinna back until she fell:

How apt her breasts were to be pressed by me.
How smooth a belly under her waist saw I?
How large a leg, and what a lusty thigh?
To leave the rest, all liked me passing well,
I clinged her naked body, down she fell.
Judge you the rest: being tired she bade me kiss;
Jove send me more such afternoons as this.[26]

For the most part, nevertheless, Marlowe's hero is sullen or driven to fits
of jealousy or petty recrimination, as when at a banquet he threatens to
expose Corinna's adultery, if she so much as dares to kiss her husband, or
again, when he urges her to throw meat in the man's face if he tastes it
before handing it to her:

If he gives thee what first himself did taste,
Even in his face his offered gobbets cast.[27]

This is a good deal cruder, or more evocative of Canterbury market brawls
perhaps, than anything suggested in the Latin text, but Marlowe is usually

faithful to Roman details. Even so, what he adds to Ovid is a pathos of self-recognition in the Student's hunger for love: Marlowe's hero lacks the twisted ferocity or vitriol of Ovid's monster, even when he remarks—cruelly enough—that Corinna has probed her entrails and aborted a foetus to avoid stretch marks. Marlowe is enough of an Elizabethan to seek out cruelty and to use it to fine—sometimes even to grotesque and hilarious—effect, but not without good reason.

Again, he is often more tender-hearted than Ovid. On a day at the races, the hero observes his lady with an innocence more suggestive of guileless need than of the Ovidian hero's self-concern. The Student adores the races not for 'the noble' horses. Rather, 'To sit and talk with thee I hither came', he tells Corinna, while picturing himself as a charioteer as he sits at the edge of a curving race-course:

> Such chance let me have: I would bravely run,
> On swift steeds mounted till the race were done.
> Nor would I slack the reins, now lash their hide,
> With wheels bent inward now the ring-turn ride;
> In running if I see thee, I shall stay,
> And from my hands the reins will slip away.[28]

Marlowe's grasp of Latin can appear feebler than it is, since Renaissance texts of the *Amores* differ from our modern texts. But he can be simply wrong, and classicists wonder if he would get a degree in Latin today. Anyway, there are famously damaging howlers in his uneven, but usually amusing and often exquisite lines, as when he assumes that Ovid's *Carmine dissiliunt abruptis faucibus angues*, which literally means, 'Song bursts the serpents' jaws apart and robs them of their fangs', can even make sense in English as: 'Snakes leap by verse from caves of broken mountains'. He may have seen adders in Kent, and recalled Virgil's serpents in the *Aeneid*—all boys like snakes—but 'snakes' is the only word he gets right in the line. Pondering the verse, *Plena venit canis de grege praeda lupis*, which means 'From the flock a full prey comes to the hoary wolves', Marlowe simply twists and mangles it as: 'From dog-kept flocks come preys to wolves most grateful'.[29] He did find a commentary—possibly with his tutor's help—or Dominicus Niger's *Ennaratio*, which saved him from a few blunders, but now and then he translates Niger to escape a difficulty in Ovid. His tutor Harris, surely, did not correct this translation, if he ever saw it, and one doubts it was meant for print. Its publication history is unusually complex. After Marlowe died, the work appeared in three early editions, one of which was ordered to be publicly burned by the bishop of London and the archbishop of Canterbury, no doubt because it was bound with John Davies's even more objectionable *Epigrammes*. That volume, which includes only ten of Marlowe's translations, under the title, *Certaine of Ovids Elegies*, was published by 1599; there was another early edition under the same title, with textual changes in the ten translations; and Marlowe's almost complete rendering of Ovid's three books appeared in an undated quarto as *All Ovids Elegies*. All three of these editions (according to their title pages) were supposedly printed beyond the arm of English censorship at Middleburgh, near Flushing or Vlissingen in the Lowlands.

Since manuscripts circulated among poets, it is just possible that Marlowe's sexually explicit work was in Shakespeare's mind when he wrote the so-called 'Dark Lady' sonnets. What is more certain is that Marlowe made Ovid's *Amores* more accessible to dramatists generally. Slightly adapting from Marlowe's work, Ben Jonson incorporated a version of the fifteenth elegy in Book I in his satirical comedy *Poetaster*; he may have done so, in about 1601, partly as a signal of his deeper indebtedness to Canterbury's poet, and the unknown playwright who wrote *The Insatiate Countess* (1613), perhaps John Marston, freely extracts from Marlowe's lines. Nashe quotes from one of these couplets in the novel *The Unfortunate Traveller* (1594). On the other hand, a line in *The Merchant of Venice*, 'Peace ho! the moon sleeps with Endymion', has been said to imitate a line in Marlowe's Book I, 'The Moon sleeps with Endymion every day', but Shakespeare could have been translating directly from Ovid for himself. Marlowe, at any rate, was the first to treat any classic as an equal, a friend, or a genial, entertaining crony, a part of the reader's daily experience of life, and he was one of the first to achieve in English in many of his lines a verbal beauty commensurate with, if different from, the startling beauty of Ovidian verse. In his interpretation of a twisted, self-incriminating hero, he opened up a new sensibility, and, one suspects, he really found the Student's defeats, jealousies, and self-betrayals more amusing than any victory in the 'schools'.[30]

The Queen of desire

After finishing with the self-obsessed 'Student' Marlowe next undertook a graver exercise. He admired the dark visionary poem *De Bello Civili* or *Pharsalia*, on the wars between Caesar and Pompey, which the Roman poet Lucan had left unfinished when he died at an early age in AD 65. Lucan had followed his brilliant uncle, Seneca the Elder, to Rome, where as a teenager he worked on the *Pharsalia* before taking part in a conspiracy against his jealous friend, the young emperor Nero. The conspiracy was betrayed, and Lucan quite simply was ordered to die; his veins were opened, and he bled to death in a bath. He left behind nine books of the *Pharsalia*, along with some 500 lines of a tenth book; and Marlowe produced a line-by-line translation of the first book into English blank verse. His version of Lucan was eventually published in 1600, by Thomas Thorpe in London, as *Lucans First Booke Translated Line for Line, by Chr. Marlow*, though its dates of composition are uncertain. In this matter, as in several others, we can follow only tentatively a likely hypothesis about dates or events in the poet's career. There are clear signs that Marlowe thought well of his verses—or well enough to save them—and that after finishing a version of the 694 lines at Corpus Christi, he revised the text later when thinking about history plays and when his fellows and rivals included Shakespeare and Kyd.

Ironically, he may have put Lucan aside to investigate the theatre. Anybody with an interest in plays at Cambridge is likely to have enjoyed St John's College—especially in its winter dress. Not even the rich mercantile city of Antwerp, in the view of Roger Ascham of *The Scholemaster*, had seemed a match for St John's Hall when 'decorated theatrically after Christmas'. Red hangings of a serge-like cloth known as 'say' were exhumed and hung up, and properties and costumes—such as multi-coloured, bushy beards or more than one 'Woman's kertle' for boy actors—were removed from wainscotted chests in the Master's room.[31]

Yet for Marlowe there would have been a drastic difference between lavish stagings and the quality of new plays staged. In the normal run of things, the best plays at Cambridge were weak imitations of Italian neoclassical comedies. One trouble was that the thunder of Calvinistic Geneva was loud enough to make the dons nervous, and sexuality on stage gave them headaches. Boys with painted lips! 'What comes of it?', as Calvin had remarked (with Deuteronomy 22: 5 in mind), when he thought of men dressing up as females—

Whosoever doth it, is an abomination. Ought not this saying to make the haire of our heades stand up, rather than wee would provoke God's wrath upon us wilfully?[32]

Calvin's fears, of course, confirmed the theatre's emotional power, but it was not often on display. When, in June 1580, the fearful Burghley hoped that the earl of Oxford's troupe might entertain the university with a few harmless plays which the queen had seen, the request was turned down by the then Vice-Chancellor, Dr Hatcher, on the grounds that Leicester's men were refused a similar permission. Burghley had to be reminded that assemblies, in open spaces suitable for acting, were forbidden within five miles' range of the town by a Privy Council order of 1575. Very distant was the fate of Serjeant Roo, flung in the Tower fifty years earlier after a play was taken as a lampoon on Cardinal Wolsey!

A few good scripts were acted in the halls, such as Legge's three-part *Richardus Tertius*, which brought English history more objectively to the stage than did the *King Johan* of 'Bilious' Bale. Or there was Edward Forsett's *Pedantius*, which aimed at collegiate pedantry and took as its object Edmund Spenser's quirky, ego-ridden friend Gabriel Harvey, then over at Trinity Hall as a Fellow. Staged at Trinity College in Marlowe's first year, *Pedantius* borrowed from Harvey's works to sketch him as a pedant even in lust. 'I beg you to regard with compassion the eviscerated, lifeless corpse of Pedantius', the hero laments.

His poor liver is being gnawed at and chewed upon by the eagle of Prometheus, which is to say, by love. His intestines are being burned by desires, as if by blazing torches. His stomach (whether you inspect its upper portions or its lower) burns like a raging fire pent-up in a furnace. Thus in all quarters I am afire with the love of you.[33]

Prometheus's eagle possibly amused a cobbler's son with a bent for mythology. Out of boredom, Marlowe might have penned a Latin satire, but he had embarked on a series of careful English exercises, and it is likely that he did not write a play at Cambridge until he had news of John Lyly.

Lately, the author of *Euphues* had excelled again, and had begun to appeal to the royal court as a dramatist. Lyly's plays *Campaspe* and *Sapho and Phao* were both printed in quarto editions in 1584, near the end of Marlowe's time as an undergraduate. Lyly, in fact, was about to conquer a slightly wider audience of play-goers. Historically, the powers of Westminster and London had imposed upon Canterbury; but in this decade, two Canterbury writers were to impose on the capital and change its theatre decisively, and these men were Lyly and Marlowe.

John Lyly, just then, was an odd source of aid for an unknown poet at Cambridge. He was a tidy, rather elegant, short-statured man who, since his wedding in 1583, had been living next to a theatre at the Blackfriars in London. He had a cool, clear, analytical mind, much talent as a writer, along with a heaven-sent gift for play structure, and a desire to impress the queen. Though ambitious, he was not smug. At some point he recognized Marlowe as a fellow Canterburian, and the two were to be in the same friendly set in London.

So far, Lyly had played his cards well. At university he had failed to enlist the help of his distant relative, Lord Burghley, in getting a fellowship, yet in London he hardly forgot the Lord Treasurer. He praised Burghley by name in *Euphues'* sequel—*Euphues and his England,* in 1580—and three years later the young playwright captured a first-rate prize in the marriage market: he was wed to Beatrice Browne, an heiress from Mexborough in Yorkshire and a relative of Joan Cecil, Lord Burghley's aunt.[34]

With his bride, Lyly put up with large, old, queer rooms at a former Blackfriars monastery, and found them convenient after he became a 'servant' to Edward de Vere, seventeenth earl of Oxford, who was interested in the theatre. This earl was Lord Burghley's son-in-law and formerly his ward, and Lyly, no doubt, had grander concerns than Marlowe's welfare. Of course, there had been Canterbury—Lyly's brothers went to the King's School where Marlowe had known two of them. And not only through his own wife, but also through his employer, the earl of Oxford, Lyly had immediate connections with Burghley, who was Chancellor of the university in which Marlowe was taking his degree.

In turn, Lyly's career at the Blackfriars had a magnetic effect on those who cared for theatrical success. The earl had an acting troupe which, as an element in a group known as 'Oxford's boys', performed Lyly's *Campaspe* and *Sapho and Phao* before the queen at court on 1 January and on Shrove Tuesday, 3 March 1584; Lyly was the payee for these showings. Marlowe knew Lyly's plays after they were printed, and he may have seen them on stage at the Blackfriars that year and met John Lyly then.

At any rate, Marlowe, interestingly, knew a good deal about boy troupes and the requirements of child actors when he began to write *Dido Queen of Carthage* in about 1584 or 1585; he could not have hoped for a performance by boy choristers in London much later than that. The title page of *Dido* claims that it was 'Played by the Children of her Majesties Chappell', a troupe which seems to have been a component of 'Oxford's boys' when they were at court. Even so, there are problems here. The Chapel Children, so far as we know, were not in the capital between 27 December 1584 and 1600, but 'flitted in a shadowy way across the provinces', so it may be that *Dido* was first acted on tour. Also *Dido*'s title page, in its quarto of 1594, shows Christopher Marlowe and Thomas Nashe as its joint authors, although Nashe's name is in smaller print. It may have been felt that Marlowe's scandalous name had more selling power at that time; but though Nashe had lyric talent, most of the verse in his only drama, *Summer's Last Will and Testament*, stays at jog-trot level, and it still seems likely that he only copied out Marlowe's play and changed a few lines, as an act of homage soon after the latter's death. *Dido*'s title page, anyway, testifies more nearly to friendship than to a collaboration.

Marlowe did not imitate John Lyly's works, but understood their precedents in form. Lyly's *Campaspe* pictures Alexander the Great after his conquest of Thebes, when he falls in love with a captive, the beautiful Campaspe, but magnanimously gives her up to Apelles, an artist who has been ordered to paint her picture. Interest is sustained by clever debates on kingship and love, as well as by the finesse of Lyly's language. There is an appeal here similar to that of opera or ballet, in which technical virtuosity is more important than characterization or acted-out feelings. The boy choristers who staged *Campaspe* may not have been strong actors, but they depended on cool ensemble delivery, neatness, and precision. Marlowe probably found even more to admire in Lyly's *Sapho and Phao*, a mythological play in which Venus confers male beauty upon Phao, a common ferryman. Cupid strikes the queenly Sapho in love with Phao, but queens do not marry ferrymen, so Sapho displays her power and limited pity by resisting love. Very pretty lines in the work flatter Queen Elizabeth, who is also criticized implicitly for being icily aloof.

Marlowe's *Dido Queen of Carthage* also gives boy actors pretty lines to say, and calls for more attention to techniques of speech than to the feelings behind speech. The play interprets Virgil, but many of its lines are translated directly from Books I, II, and IV of the *Aeneid,* and some of Virgil's own Latin is included.

At the two universities, few stories had enchanted the dons more than that of Aeneas's visit with Queen Dido in the *Aeneid.* Having fallen in love, Dido commits suicide when the hero leaves her—and Virgil's exquisite episode had inspired many a drama. Queen Elizabeth at Cambridge in 1564, for instance, had sat through a slow *Dido* play in Latin by Edward Haliwell, and just kept herself from falling asleep. In writing his work in English, Marlowe ignored most of the *Dido* plays, but took something from Ovid's Dido in the *Heroides,* Ludovico Dolce's Italian *Didone* (1547), and John Lydgate's medieval *Troy Book.* Yet, in many ways, he put his own stamp on Virgil's story. For one thing, he made his Aeneas extremely unheroic. In Lydgate's *Troy Book,* as he must have found, the heroic Aeneas is portrayed as a traitor, and again Virgil's hero is diminished in Dolce's *Didone.* Marlowe respects Aeneas as a charismatic soldier, but portrays him as a likeable, unstable man who succumbs to desire and has a terrible, embarrassing time in trying to leave his lover. The limitations of boy actors (in the mid-1580s) encouraged Marlowe to depict love, anger, and despair with restraint, but he develops the relationship of his lovers more fully and less gravely than the *Aeneid* had done. Whereas Virgil had not shown the increasing intimacy of Dido and Aeneas in detail, Marlowe invents scenes in which love's processes unfold. In Virgil's poem, there is a conflict between Aeneas's passion and the political destiny which calls him from Carthage on to Italy to found a city-state. At any cost Dido would keep Aeneas, and when he leaves her, she must die—her desire has become a condition of her being.

Yet Marlowe thinks of the tragic episode in relation to what he himself feels and what he observes of friendship and love. The materials have a comic aspect. Any mutual feeling between lovers, and the individual's wishes and needs, are not necessarily rigged together to last in time, but may coexist in a chancy game. Not much in Virgil had suggested a homoerotic context for the game, but Marlowe's play begins with a comic sexual scene.

Jupiter, ruler of the gods, has a craving for the lovely, willing boy Ganymede. As scene i opens, Jupiter is seen wantonly playing with him. 'Sit on my knee, and call for thy content', he coaxes the boy,

> Control proud Fate, and cut the thread of Time.
> Why, are not all the gods at thy command,
> And heaven and earth the bounds of thy delight?
> Vulcan shall dance to make thee laughing sport,
> And my nine daughters sing when thou art sad;
> From Juno's bird I'll pluck her spotted pride,
> To make thee fans, wherewith to cool thy face.[35]

This is lyrically tender, subdued in rhythm and tone—as if a father were consoling his child. Yet Marlowe makes a rich, half-concealed joke out of the frightening, overwhelming power the ruler of the gods offers to his minion. After kidnapping Ganymede away from Troy, Jupiter had given the comely, amusing boy eternal life to gain sexual favours. Now, besotted, he ridiculously offers him power over life and death: 'Control proud Fate, and cut the thread of time.' Ganymede is offered the job of Atropos—one of the Fates—whose work is to determine the deaths of men and women by cutting the threads of life. As a further bribe, the boy will be sung to by the nine Muses, and so anything ever conceived of in the Cambridge Arts course will be at his fingertips, since the Muses preside over all thought, as well as controlling poetry, mime, dance, music, tragedy, and comedy.

The joke is that these offerings are airy nonsense: Jupiter's relatives, Juno and Venus, intervene to show that the hen-pecked ruler of the gods is full of bluff, though he stirs up jealousy. Already, his homosexual dalliance has caused the Trojan war and the deaths of thousands. As much as they hate each other, Jupiter's sister Juno and daughter Venus nonetheless manage to ensure that poor, wandering Aeneas, after the defeat of Troy, will survive to enjoy a fine love affair.

As zany as the plot sounds, Marlowe had found a homoerotic theme in the *Aeneid*—though Virgil holds that Juno's jealousy of Ganymede was only a minor factor in causing the Graeco-Trojan war. Marlowe endows the immortals with pettiness, boasts, pride, and bickering that seem typical of half-uninteresting social climbers, but he does not imply that their hegemony means much. Humans still have free will, and interest soon focuses on the plight of Aeneas.

What is really distinguished in *Dido Queen of Carthage* is the exquisite beauty of its verse as well as the varying registers of its styles. The drama has the aspect of a poem, even of a courtly *jeu d'esprit,* but it is free from heaviness, as in Venus's complaints about Aeneas's pains since the fall of Troy. Juno, her deadly rival, as she says

> Made Hebe to direct her airy wheels
> Into the windy country of the clouds,
> Where finding Aeolus entrench'd with storms,
> And guarded with a thousand grisly ghosts,
> She humbly did beseech him for our bane,
> And charg'd him drown my son with all his train.[36]

Aeneas himself, when we see him, is in tears over his plight as a survivor of horrors perpetrated by the Greeks when they broke into Troy, though he is more concerned for his soldiers. Almost nothing he says lacks pathos—in this, the author differs from Lyly—and yet feeling, in *Dido,* is keyed to psychological realism and to the plain, lucid tones of boy actors. The hero has hallucinations; he is pitted with grief for the slaughtered at Troy. Altogether he is 'comfortless', but comrades yearn for the light of his face, for 'lovely Aeneas' or 'sweet Aeneas'.

When he reaches Dido's palace, the queen tears off his 'fisher' rags to clothe him in finery. Painfully, Aeneas tells her about Troy's downfall and offers an insider's view of events. He has witnessed Hecuba's cruel fate,

> At last the soldiers pulled her by the heels
> And swung her howling in the empty air,

or he has seen

> Virgins half-dead, dragg'd by their golden hair,
> And with main force flung on a ring of pikes.[37]

These fine, vivid details are too icily pictorial to shock, and one feels they belong to a nightmare of the classic past—Troy is Troy and it is over—but they serve as a backdrop for an ironic view of love and fate. What Marlowe emphasizes is a kind of farcical tragedy of the present, or the sweetly bitter results of Cupid's rakish, mischievous act of assuming the shape of the hero's son, the better to strike Queen Dido in love with Aeneas. Jupiter's homosexual dalliance, as it turns out, has set a tone for nearly all that follows; he is no more fatuous than mortals who pursue love despite a lack of reciprocal feeling. Not without sympathy for their dilemmas, Marlowe invents lovers who have no chance of success. As Dido is hopelessly loved by Iarbus, so the heroine's sister Anna loves the same, unresponsive Iarbus. A comic, 80-year-old female lover in the anonymous play *Timon*—the spoof which could have been written in some version by Marlowe at Canterbury—now has a parallel in a gummy, 80-year-old Nurse, who is in love with love. 'Say Dido what she will, I am not old', the Nurse tells Marlowe's Cupid. 'I'll have a husband, I, or else a lover.' Cupid is unimpressed: 'A husband, and no teeth!' The Nurse doubts her qualifications, but hopes to enjoy passion just as others do. 'O sacred love!' she says, before wondering if at 80, she has a right to begin at love's shrine:

> Blush, blush, for shame! why shouldst thou think of love?
> A grave, and not a lover, fits thy age—
> A grave? why, I may live a hundred years,
> Fourscore is but a girl's age, love is sweet:
> My veins are wither'd, and my sinews dry,
> Why do I think of love?[38]

Marlowe, though, offsets all of this with two deeper motifs. Aeneas is too weak-minded to give Dido up on his own volition, so at first he plans to build a city-state at Carthage, rather than in Italy as is ordained by heaven. Abruptly, he is jarred to a sense of destiny by Hermes, winged messenger of the gods. What is at stake is the hero's understanding of his creative mission, which would take him to Italy to found the metropolis of Rome.

'Why, cousin, stand you building cities here', Hermes sharply asks him,

> And beautifying the empire of this queen,
> When Italy is clean out of thy mind?[39]

That question is direct enough to suggest that Marlowe is critical of his own prettinesses. Hermes implies that Dido's Carthage is a distraction, that its story is not Aeneas's story, and that major work lies ahead for the hero—and author. An English poet who takes line after line from the

Aeneid, or strains his effects through an Ovidian sieve, may feel that he needs Hermes' rebuke.

Yet the poet's view of Queen Dido, in effect, rebukes other elements in the playscript. Dido's lines are more compelling than cool pictures of Troy. She has more intensity than any of the gods, and though the play treats sex as a game, its heroine exposes the triviality of gamesters. She can be far-fetched in her conceits, but her images accurately convey her desire. 'Ten thousand Cupids', she tells the hero,

> hover in the air
> And fan it in Aeneas' lovely face!
> O that the clouds were here wherein thou flee'st,
> That thou and I unseen might sport ourselves!

Dido's lines even have a spatial, graphic range which extends the language of Petrarchan love which Marlowe inherits. And, perhaps, any poet raised at Canterbury might recall that its saints had altered the ways in which inanimate things are understood, or in which tempests overhead or the earth underfoot can be allied with the martyr:

> O blessed tempests that did drive him in!
> O happy sand that made him run aground![40]

The Queen's love is limitless, and what interests Marlowe is that passion frees the mind from literalness, with a dialectic of its own—in this, in some respects, he anticipates both Shakespeare's Juliet and his Cleopatra.[41] In effect, Dido turns to the wind and the seas not fancifully, but to express herself with a valid new logic—

> O that I had a charm to keep the winds
> Within the closure of a golden ball;
> Or that the Tyrrhene sea were in mine arms,
> That he might suffer shipwrack on my breast.[42]

The boy choristers who said these lines did not need to 'act' them, but to articulate them as pieces in an aesthetic ritual. Little here, other than the queen or the comic Nurse, is as pulsating as life. The only emphasis given to the Queen's tragic suicide, at last, is that two other unrequited lovers, Iarbus and Anna, kill themselves in the flames that consume her.

Dido is a lovely, amusing, and shrewd technical exercise, and it might well have suited the royal court. What we do not know is how far afield its poet went to find a sponsor for it, or whether he cared to have the play staged at all. One infers that he showed it to Nashe, who, as an undergraduate at St John's, thought that Lyly's *Euphues* was *ipse ille* (or the very thing itself) and may have been keen on Lyly's plays, too. But there is no certain proof that Marlowe's friendship with Nashe began at Cambridge.

Dido—at any rate—is the last of Marlowe's works which he may have begun as an undergraduate. Having leapt the hurdles for his baccalaureate, he scraped through to a degree. His time spent on creative work probably kept him from a close knowledge of set texts, even if he was 'ravished' by a few authors. He had lost nothing by testing his art, and in that way he was ahead of any student who sneered at him, although his academic rank was not high. In the Cambridge *Ordo Senioritatis* of bachelors, Marlowe ranks 199th among 231.

But he had succeeded, whereas a few had dropped out of the course. Turning 21, Marlowe at last had a chance to become as arrogant as any Fellow, if he did not offend the master, and if he stayed alive.

5
Into espionage

The first law for every creature is that of self-preservation.
You sow hemlock, and expect to see ripening ears of corn!
(Machiavelli)

Well, do it bravely, and be secret.
(Lightborn, *Edward II*)

'Aetatis suae 21'

IN the middle of 1585, on leave from Corpus Christi College, Marlowe took a long ride south, and then he must have pressed eastward below the Thames estuary, which had low meadows on either side, as he made his way to Canterbury. At 21, he was a cobbler's son with a BA degree and might have seemed remarkable anywhere. After due consideration, he had taken a new step in his dance. Although enrolled in an Arts programme for his final degee, his *magistratus* or the goal of 'Master of Arts', he was obliged to take up some theology, and this enabled him to draw renewed aid from Archbishop Parker's funds.

Also, there is reason to think that he had made contact with a petty functionary or minor secretary in the government, and had begun secret work: this began well before he took the *magistratus*. He had extra money in his pocket, and Corpus's records show that he was spending in excess of his grant. To judge from his finances and the vigour of *Tamburlaine*, written in the next twenty-four months, he was full of nervous energy and confidence. He would have had good opportunities in view, or a consciousness of new possibilities for himself as a part-time employee of the Queen's Privy Council and also as an independent playwright. Outside his college's gates, he had no need to dress with restraint. His BA made him a gentleman, whether or not there was an Apollonian glitter in his clothes.

His family knew troubles, which inevitably this summer would have drawn him in. He cannot have gone home without hearing about matters that had nothing to do with Cambridge or the government. His second-eldest sister, Jane, when less than 13 years old, had married John Moore, at St Andrew's Church on 22 April 1582. Almost at once, she had become pregnant, and then had apparently died in January 1583 with her newborn infant son. Christopher was not so callous as to be unaffected by his living sisters, or by losses which flattened hopes and led to new difficulties. In the cobbler's milieu, the attempts of family and kin to profit from goods of the deceased were constant; rows ensued, and the firmest, most affectionate and enduring kinship ties came under strain. The Canterbury blacksmith Richard Moore, as it happened, had lately died. His daughter Ursula—a sister of John Moore the young widower—had lately been accused of improperly handling goods and chattels belonging to her father's estate. This trouble, unfortunately, dragged on. Both Ursula and her mother Thomasina Moore were taken to court by the grocer George Aunsell, vowing to protect the heritable rights of his sister Mary, who had wed one of the blacksmith's sons. Since Ursula was married to the poet's uncle Thomas Arthur, these contentions would have had brisk, possibly even heated, argumentative echoes in the Marlowe household. The poet's father the cobbler was to be accused of meddling with a deed of gift connected with a residue of the Moore estate.

Too many bees buzzed over a small pot of honey, but Marlowe took one chance to rise above legal frays and talk of the Aunsells. He agreed, no doubt readily enough, or with a sense of relief, to witness the will of a family friend. This year, the friend's son, John Benchkin, had entered Corpus Christi on 30 June, as a fellow-commoner able to pay his way at Cambridge. Marlowe had not ridden down with the boy, but he knew him.

Benchkin's mother lived in St Mildred's parish at the southern end of Stour Street, adjacent to a blocked alleyway known as Ballock Lane. The neighbourhood was not salubrious; but Widow Benchkin's wool-loft and seven large rooms may have been proof that her late husband James, a beadle of the cathedral, had profited from illegal trading in grain as well as

11 The signatories on Katherine Benchkin's will of August 1585: John Marley, Thomas Arthur, Christofer Marley, and John Moore. As the third witness, Marlowe signs beneath the names of his father and uncle, and above the name of John Moore, a shoemaker who had wed young Jane Marlowe

from dealing in wool. James Benchkin's collection of lutes and virginals, swords, javelins, and tapestries, as well as a fine table with the queen's arms, ornamented the widow's house. It was in her parlour one Sunday that Christopher, with his father, his uncle Arthur, and his brother-in-law John Moore, appeared after church services. Katherine Benchkin received them all, and then fetched two legal wills, burned one in the fire, and asked Christopher to read her new will aloud. Its handwriting gave him no trouble: he began with, 'In the name of God, Amen', and went through item after item in the presence of John Moore, whose sister Ursula had been at issue with the Aunsells. 'Item I give to Aunsells widowe of St Mildreds aforesaid twenty shillings', Marlowe intoned. 'Item I give to

Agnes Aunsell the daughter of the foresayd widowe Aunsell twenty shillings.' But Moore—a shoemaker himself—may not have blenched. Later, with the poet's father, on 30 September 1586, he gave evidence relating to the widow's will and remembered that Christopher had read it 'plainly and distinctly'.[1]

The Benchkin text gives us some words Marlowe spoke in his city, presumably on 19 August 1585—the date of the will—and his witnessing as 'Christofer Marley' gives us his only known signature. Riding back to Cambridge a few days later, he put miles between himself and the shabby semi-poverty of his father's house, or between the petty, scrimping narrowness he found in his father's parish, and the creative amplitude of his own views. Yet, for all his distaste for a cobbler's shop—or at least its tools, leather, and smells—he did, contrary to what biographers have implied, revisit his home on more than one occasion. We know of several of his Canterbury stop-overs, and, of course, it is not necessarily true that every visit he made left its record in the archives of a law court.

At this point, well before he took his second degree, he had begun to live a complex, tense, inspiriting double life. He involved himself in some duplicity, if not in faithlessness and treachery, with regard to fellow scholars at Cambridge; as he did so, the more or less forthright pursuits of his family may have steadied him. If he came to the edge of a worrying bleak abyss, in so far as his relations with himself were concerned, he was not, so far as we can tell, unguarded or reckless at his college. He avoided any appearance, at first, of being a delinquent absentee. Indeed, it is clear now that he had a good chance to cover himself, since from the time of the University Statutes of 1570, candidates for the Master's degree had been allowed 'discontinuance'. Not strictly tied to residence at Cambridge, they could apply for leave from a college's head, or a deputy, to study privately elsewhere as 'discontinuers' and support themselves, as they might, by parish work or as schoolteachers.

There was a catch, for anyone doing extraordinary, secret work. To qualify for the *magistratus*, one had to supply the Vice-Chancellor with testimonials from landlords and three clergymen, to certify that one had 'lived soberly and studiously the course of a scholar's life'.[2] So far as we know, Marlowe left that to the future, though we shall have to return to the matter. Other obstacles, he could not avoid. The university prided itself on its courses, and the *magistratus* called for public disputations, exercises, and declamations—all subject to exacting appraisal. Students listened to sermons, and often copied them down word for word; there was much ferment in theology, and waves of doctrinal fashion replaced one another as lecturers took up what have been called 'other positions' on ecclesiology, soteriology, Mariology, sacramentology, moral theology, or liturgy. At a sophisticated level, there was hair-splitting debate, and one might have to argue whether Adam and Eve's fatal Fall in the Garden might be best explained by distinctions, virtually lost to us today, such as those between supra- and infralapsarianism.

Christopher Marlowe seldom tired of learning. Theology, as an element of his course, appears to have bothered him less than the mincing airs, abstractions, or evasions of fellow divinity students. Partly in reaction, he was to seek out low, cruder company, and also plunge into ironic skirmishes and gratuitous blasphemy with his friends, though, on occasion, he went to somewhat worse lengths than that. Yet off and on, through nine terms, Cambridge's divinity lectures aided his speculative thinking and refined his mind, and he did not fail to react to what he heard. One proof that theology did not chill his brains is in the freshness and variety of thought about divinity and the human will in *Tamburlaine*. The first part of that two-part drama—it is, really, two semi-independent plays—was planned, if not chiefly written, before he took his degree.

Another aspect of *Tamburlaine*, especially in its opening scenes, may suggest features of his secret life. Nothing is more bizarre in a drama about the victories of a Scythian warrior than its focus upon personal appearances—that is, upon looks, textures, plumes, crests, colours, and above all, on vestments or clothes.

Was anything more vital for battle, on Asia's steppes, in the Near East and in Africa one wonders, than the equivalent of a catwalk? Did an army's dress-designers achieve more than swords or horses? Or is it that the hero and his opponents never tired of mirrors?

'And with thy looks thou conquerest all thy foes', says the hero's enemy Mycetes to Theridamas, in scene i, in which militant frowns supplement the effects of costume. 'Lie here, ye weeds that I disdain to wear!' vows Tamburlaine in scene ii, when satisfied that the 'fair face and heavenly hue' of Zenocrate—a captured princess—befits a man of his aims who takes a chaste designer's view of her potential: he will drape her in garments 'made of Median silk | Enchas'd with precious jewels of mine own', and pull her with 'milk-white harts upon an ivory sled'.[3] Lovely, if a bit chilly in winter. . . Soldiers, as scouts, do not report on an enemy's locale or tactics, but on their 'plumed helms' or 'massy chains' glittering over the neck and dangling about the waist. Sometimes, opposing ranks are about as deadly as rival groups of couturiers:

> Lay out our golden wedges to the view
> That their reflections may amaze the Persians.

An enemy marvels that the hero is 'so embellished'. The hero, in turn, puts trust in Theridamas's 'outward habit' to 'judge the inward man', and one is hardly surprised that Act II opens, in the hostile camp, with a twenty-four-line description of Tamburlaine's limbs, fingers, jewellery, complexion, and curls.[4]

All of this, it seems to me, is very effective; a great deal depends on our sense of the hero's palpable presence, and on his own view of his attributes and destiny. But one cannot deny that for all the poet's concern for divinity—or the Calvinist and Lutheran thesis that we are irremediably flawed—Marlowe takes a lively interest in how people actually look.

His own dress cannot have seemed to him a trifling matter. He was more likely now, than as an undergraduate, to resent the university's mercilessly reiterated and slightly maddening sumptuary rules. There was no leeway to dress as he wished as a student of theology. The most immense, detailed edicts about apparel, for all ranks at Cambridge, had been issued by Lord Burghley and the Vice-Chancellor in 1585, the very year in which Marlowe for the first time had funds to buy what he liked. He had no option but to appear in a drab, ankle-length gown at lectures, at disputations, and in chapel. But out on the road he could dress as he pleased. In about 1585 it is certain that he had money to commission a portrait, if he wished. Did he, by any chance, return to Cambridge one day with a painted picture of himself in his finery?

Anyway, it is important to know what he looked like. Today, the famous alleged or 'putative' portrait of Marlowe reproduced in the frontispiece to this book, and now at Corpus Christi College, is all we have. It lacks the name of its sitter and painter alike. Though the circumstances of its discovery—exactly where it was found, when it was found, or by whom—

have been misreported, the portrait turned up at the college in the last century when Marlowe's reputation was on the rise.[5]

Does the picture show the playwright? Its mystery is worth looking into briefly, I think, as a kind of a gateway to other mysteries before we follow him into espionage.

Superficially, this panel painting on stout oak boards, measuring 24 × 18 inches, looks about right. It is inscribed near the upper left-hand corner:

ANNO D[OMI]NI AETATIS SUAE 21

1585

So the fashionable young sitter who gazes at us was born when Marlowe was, in 1564, and had himself painted in 1585, when the poet was flush with funds, as we know from the college's Buttery returns. Beneath the date is a motto, 'QUOD ME NUTRIT ME DESTRUIT' ('That which nourishes me, also destroys me'): this is often taken as a sign that the sitter is in love—maybe the beauty which charms will also bury him.

He has been called 'a bit flashy', but he is not melancholy, or a conventional type of the Elizabethan sad lover, though his dress might suggest that he puts a high value on himself. The padded black velvet doublet, with decorative slashes to show golden-red material underneath, bulges slightly below the chest. If new, the garment will improve with wear. Bossed golden buttons run down its front and along the sleeves, fourteen on each arm.

With one arm folded over the other, and hands concealed, the sitter does not beg for approval. His left hand has been said to hold a dagger, but might conceal nothing. The brown or hazel eyes, oval cheeks, and high, pale brow have been thought to give him a 'feminine tone'; but he has also been called stark, intellectual, even unfashionable, 'a bit unhealthy'. One hardly feels that he is about to dance or to enter a boudoir: his simple collar is of 'cobweb lawn', though lace collars were far more frequent in this period: he might be ready for action or travel.

In a poor state by 1953, the picture was later said to have 'come from the Spencer Room in the Master's Lodge', where it was noticed 'lying face downwards on the floor' below the club fender.[6] This might be a good sign that the portrait has nothing to do with Marlowe: the Master's Lodge is a part of Corpus's New Court, built by William Wilkins in the 1820s.

For many years after he died, Marlowe was a scapegrace too disreputable, it seems, to be honoured by a painting kept first in the old Master's Lodge and later transferred to the one in Wilkins's New Court. The picture could show some long-forgotten college worthy, known, perhaps, to the poet who shared his birthdate.

This may be so, but facts which relate to Marlowe are precious enough for us to be accurate about them. The portrait was not found in 1953—despite what is often said—nor did it come from the Master's Lodge in the New Court, nor is there any evidence that it was especially valued.

In 1952 Mr Peter Hall (not the famous theatre director, but an undergraduate who was to become 'Captain of Boats') was living in the Old Court. By coincidence, his room was just over the old, converted 'storehouse' assigned to Marlowe. Another coincidence is odder; by the autumn, Hall had moved to the main locale of the Parker scholars, on the east side of the Old Court; here, he had a room at the south-east corner, on the first floor, but a staircase as he recalls went up to his bedroom 'in the roof space above'. The 600th anniversary of the founding of the college was at hand, and while stripping old fixtures from rooms workmen had left a large metal skip, or dumpster, outside: this filled with builders' rubbish, and passers-by glanced at what was being thrown away.

In Peter Hall's bedroom, there was an antiquated gas fire on metal supports. 'Workmen', as he wrote on 26 May 2000 to Ms G. C. Cannell, sub-librarian at the Parker Library,

took the gas fire out of the fireplace in what was now [in 1952] my bedroom above my room in the Old Court, in order to install a more modern fire. In doing so, they found two planks of oak underneath the old fire, and these were put into the skip. When I saw this happening, I asked if I could have the oak planks as I was building a case for a hi fi system and thought that they might be suitable.[7]

It is bizarre to think that a student who could afford a hi-fi would dispense with it, or delay in setting it up; yet the hi-fi's needs were forgotten: there was an oddity about the oak supports for the wooden case. 'When', Hall remembers, 'I looked at the planks closely, I saw that there was a painting on them, you could vaguely see a head, so rather than build my hi fi unit, I took them to Pat Bury, the Librarian, to ask if he thought they were of any value.'[8]

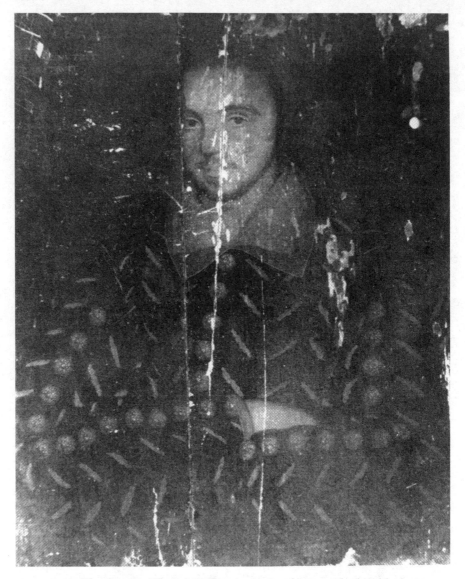

12 The Corpus Christi College portrait, photographed in black
and white before its restoration. Painted in 1585, its old
flaking boards had split apart by November 1952

John Patrick Tuer Bury (1908–87), or 'Pat' Bury, formerly dean of the
college and its librarian since 1937, felt that he 'could just see a date' on
the picture, and consulted with the holder of the Anglo-Saxon chair,

Bruce Dickins (1889–1978), who was less impressed. Dickins later claimed that another Peter, Peter Wimbush, had found the boards in the skip, and that they 'proved to have come from the Spencer Room', whereas it is certain that they lay there, for inspection, only after Hall and Bury first saw them. Dickins had the planks arranged together and photographed, not in colour, but in black and white.

They looked execrable. 'The boards were thick in grime, nails had been driven through them, and the paint was flaking badly particularly on either side of the fracture.'[9] The right-hand board itself had a deep split. At some time in the past the painting had obviously disintegrated into two pieces, and the nail holes suggested that the oak planks had served some other purpose even before they supported Hall's gas fire.

Dickins was implicitly right about one matter: a portrait left in such a state of delapidation had mattered little to the college, so perhaps it may never have had much significance. Of course there was a date on the work, though the sitter's identity appeared to be utterly (or mercifully) lost in time. Pat Bury, less sure, noted that the date coincided with Marlowe's twenty-first year: he 'found out that there were no other portraits of Christopher Marlowe and thought that it was worth getting the painting restored'.[10]

But if restored, the painting would be changed, so Bury at first sent copies of the photo to experts and enquired as to the motto, in a quest which began on 15 November 1952. G. K. Adams, of the National Portrait Gallery, could say nothing of the motto, but advised that 'inscriptions on Elizabethan portraits very rarely help in identification'.[11] Before the year's end, two Marlowe biographers, F. S. Boas and John Bakeless, said that they had never seen the motto. More helpfully, Rosemary Freeman of Birkbeck College, University of London, wrote on 9 December to say that, in emblem books, she had seen versions of the inscription, such as 'QUI' or 'QUOD ME ALIT ME EXTINGUIT', often accompanying an engraving of an inverted torch with wax dropping into the flame. There was one such phrase in Samuel Daniel's translation of Paolo Giovio's *Imprese* (1585), and this was echoed in Shakespeare's *Pericles* (II. ii. 33–4); but she had never seen the odd phrase '*Nutrit* & *Destruit*' as in the Corpus portrait.[12]

By March 1953, by which time the fragile painting was being kept face downwards to protect it, Bury had accepted G. K. Adams's advice that

Messrs Holder & Sons of London would be good restorers (though, as Adams warned about sending the painting, 'you are not likely to see it back for two years'). In August, Holder submitted an assessment: the Tudor picture, in 'a very bad state', would need extensive reparation as 'in many places the original paint has flaked away & in other parts the pigment is very insecure'.[13] However, less than a year later, the repaired painting was hanging in Corpus' Hall, where it stayed until 1998, when it went to a safer locale. Meanwhile, it was X-rayed, with the college's wary permission, by those hoping to find some hint that Marlowe was the author of Shakespeare's plays, or that Shakespeare penned most of Marlowe, or that the sitter was the seventeenth earl of Oxford.

The portrait attracted 'lunatic attention', wrote Noel Purdon in *The Cambridge Review* in 1967, though its inscription looked odd:

This is a most unusual motto; it belongs to no crest of arms, has no heraldic significance. It is rather a *personal* emblem, one chosen by the sitter himself as an indication less of his public symbolism than of his private drama.[14]

There was, as the college seemed to agree, only suppositional proof that the sitter was Marlowe. The art of oil-painting in Tudor times was a long process, 'much of which was done away from the sitter', according to Roy Strong,[15] so if Marlowe wished for a portrait, he may have had to accept one finished by studio assistants; but why would he have needed to show off some 'private drama'? There is no sense of one-to-one, romantic intimacy in the picture, which does not look like a gift for a lover. On the other hand, young Tudor artists had themselves painted—as did, for example, Thomas Whythorne the musician, at first when he was 20 or 21, and again a year later.[16]

If the sitter was not Marlowe, who else could he be? Rivalry among the Cambridge colleges was strong and pride was fierce; it is not likely that the portrait of a youth, of university age, was sent to Corpus, or hung on its walls, unless the person had been of that college. Twelve men from Corpus were admitted to the BA degree in Marlowe's year, when there were fewer than sixty pensioners, fellow-commoners, and sizars in residence. In theory, of course, the sitter might be a devil-may-care nobleman who violated university dress regulations, which were never more stringent than in 1585.

The difficulty is that it is unimaginable that such a person, so attired, would have been honoured in a portrait kept at Norgate's college. A youth in a sumptuous doublet, capless with loose hair, was not exemplary, and noblemen at the university were few. The name of no other candidate for the portrait—save Marlowe's—has turned up in over fifty years. Peter Hall's new account in 2000 is important at least in showing that the work was found in the Old Court, just across from Marlowe's former bedroom. The picture was not well cared for, nor cherished by the authorities; there is no record of it in Corpus's archives, so it cannot have been included in their collection. Its nail-holed, broken, flaking condition, when, in two pieces, it lay under Hall's gas fire, shows that it had been at the college for years.

No one had authority to confiscate a work owned by the Parker scholars, and virtually nothing but the painting's being kept in the archbishop's sanctuaries, or in a room delegated for his candidates, would account for the work's survival until it fell apart. The boards were found at the south-east corner of Old Court, a few paces from chambers which he had set aside for entrants from his native city, Norwich, and here in fact he had placed nine chained books for the cream of his elected men; a Bible clerk served those students. Either Marlowe left the painting behind or gave it to a fellow scholar, after which it was never discarded, if only because the two oak panels were stout enough to have nails driven in them and serve for practical uses. This is now the most likely explanation of the work's survival. The new data in Hall's letter, the unique motto, and what we know about the poet's life and finances give us a firm biographical context, so it is reasonable to relate the work to Christopher Marlowe.

Other Parker men were headed for the church; he was one of the few likely to wish for a worldly portrait. He had funds to dress fashionably, and an artist's motive for having himself painted in 1585. He was adjuring himself, cozening, or egging himself on to write about a showy hero when the work was painted. His Tamburlaine would be one who 'can never have enough of being looked at', as L. C. Knights has noted.[17] With some irony and complication, the poet expresses a theory of appearances even in *Tamburlaine*. Through what a soldier chooses to wear, and manifestations such as his physique, manner, or confidence, rather than his actions, we may have the best chance to judge inner qualities; even the disguise, exposing motives, will portray the disguiser. In dress, we make of ourselves what we intend to be.

13 Matthew Parker, archbishop of Canterbury,
from a painting made in about 1573

Marlowe had not only money to commission a picture, but a good
reason for wanting one, and a developing theory of appearances and
perception: he also had a certain sanction. The designations of founded
scholarships today may mean little, but nothing comparable was true of

Corpus's Parker awards. The name of Matthew Parker (the queen's first archbishop, a former master of Corpus, and its greatest benefactor) had prestige after his death, and this was not dependent on his gift of books and manuscripts to the Fellows. As a Parker scholar, Marlowe belonged to an almost sacrosanct elite; as *Dominus*, he was enrolled in the greatest of Corpus's programmes. His memorializing of himself was, in one sense, a tribute to the status of other Parker scholars and divinity candidates; and there is no reason to think that his friends would have discarded his picture after he left. It lasted through the years in the Parker rooms, or close by in their side of the quadrangle, partly because of the archbishop's immense distinction.

It is worth noting, too, that this likeness has passed the most subtle of tests in that it 'matches' our sense of the playwright. Actors, directors, critics, scholars, and others have felt, on the basis of their familiarity with his works, that this was Marlowe. I do not say that intuitions can be definitive; what I believe is that a sense of an intelligent, ready, alert, creative writer is apparent here: the picture looks right. Many agree that this is so, and now there is a good probability that what many have felt to be true, is true in fact.

Even if we were to put aside Hall's letter and other contingent facts, the portrait might still suggest the poet's aims. As Marlowe's horizons expanded, he needed a new, sharp and enabling awareness of himself, a sense of his own audacity, gaiety, and capability as a writer: he was conceiving of a hero who makes actual what is imagined, and dares to imagine on the grandest possible scale.

Amusingly, the Corpus picture has an odd aspect in the sitter's swirl of hair. (Tamburlaine's 'amber locks' also seem remarkable, since they are admired by his enemies.) The effect of the stiffly padded doublet, in the portrait, is offset by mousy-coloured but flowing locks, which suggest a liberated mood. There is a similar, polarized effect in Marlowe's elegy on the grim justice Sir Roger Manwood, who is shown to be crime's 'harshest scourge', but is wept over by a lovely mourner, 'with hair spread o'er her neck'.[18]

At any rate, Marlowe did not have to scissor his own locks, under dress regulations which applied to Cambridge men. Nobody required that his head actually be *shorn*, but it is reasonable to think that he looked well groomed when he became an employee of her majesty's government.

The Walsinghams

The recruitment of secret agents at Cambridge was urgent for the Queen's Council by the mid-1580s, and students had not been difficult to recruit. They were picked up as couriers—who were often in short supply—or as informers on those intending to defect to Catholic colleges abroad, and they occasionally had duties involving the foreign legations. A few were trapped in France, Spain, or the Low Countries and all were thought expendable, but good work was expected; there was a close selection, and an officer such as Walsingham's Nicholas Faunt was aware of the advantages of keeping the secret service lean and taking on temporary help. In fact, the queen's chief adviser Lord Burghley, her military expert the earl of Leicester, and the Secretary of State, Sir Francis Walsingham, all had separate intelligence services, but Walsingham's was the largest, most efficient, and most subtle in existence. Faunt happened to be the only one of Walsingham's officers to have attended Cambridge. A Canterbury man himself, he had gone up from the King's School to Corpus Christi with a Parker grant in 1569, and seven years later had begun as Walsingham's 'confidential clerk'. It is extremely probable that Faunt had a role in the recruitment of Marlowe. Though Faunt will not much concern us, he appears from his letters to have had a conscientious view of the French service. He regretted the moral laxity of Westminster's court, its 'dissolute manners and corruption generally', though he befriended Anthony Bacon, who was imprisoned at Montauban in France for pederasty with his page.[19]

Respectable men, anyway, were needed in the French service into which Faunt himself had gone. Recommendations counted, and the Lyly brothers, in this case, were in a position to help Marlowe. Their father Peter Lyly had married Jane Burgh, of a well-to-do family from Burgh Hall in the East Riding. In about 1558, Jane Burgh's sister Catherine was wed to John Manwood of Sandwich, a brother of Sir Roger Manwood the judge, about whom the poet later wrote his elegy.

A word in favour of Marlowe from Sir Roger, a former friend of the archbishop and protégé of Walsingham, may have sufficed. The judge was to sit at the trial of Mary Queen of Scots, and his reputation was never to be higher than in about 1586. Disbursing sums for education, he could have aided a Canterbury man applying himself to theology. The trouble is that we do not know that the poet benefited from this source, and such aid may not explain his initial good luck, or just why the Council intervened to get Marlowe his MA degree, or why, when others were dropped, he later continued to serve the government.

The facts of the matter are not wholly obscure, since we shall see that Marlowe, in due course, impressed an officer truly close to the spymaster—Walsingham's own cousin. One reason for Marlowe's success in his new flight, too, was that he proved to be a good catch for his employers. His qualifications may have been evident at once if he had the keyed-up, winning alertness and pluck which high ambition gives a young man. With a taste for foreign locales, he almost certainly knew some French. Claude Hollyband's language guides, or the *Dictionarie French and English* of 1571 (the first French–English dictionary, possibly by Hollyband) could have enabled him to work up a veneer of skill. He looked intelligent, if the Corpus portrait can be trusted; his tutor could have added that he was industrious. His talent for friendship was obvious. He was a divinity scholar, not a ruffian, and a voice which was suited for choral ensembles might have suggested his refinement. It is important, too, (as the earl of Leicester noticed) that Walsingham had taken an interest in the popular theatre, and that he sponsored a few energetic, gifted editors and writers.

At any rate, Marlowe was hired, though agents lacked contracts, or any promise of being retained. He was on trial, and most likely to be dropped with a nod unless he did unusually well. If his beginnings were normal, he did not plunge at once into hazardous work; the intelligence services were not known for throwing Latinists to the wolves, or giving rough, unseemly tasks just at first. In Burghley's (or Cecil's) early days, Cambridge recruits, such as Thomas Chaloner and William Pickering, both keen translators, were sent abroad to improve their language skills; both may have used cipher on occasion. Chaloner survived in Spain; Pickering sent back books from Paris, including a strange 'Euclid with the figures in a small volume'.[20] In recent times, overseas work had become more urgent and problematic; a misstep, by a naive agent, could upset vital, costly plans and drain away time and funds. And yet, while awaiting an assignment, a new man did not necessarily learn much from any officer's chit-chat or evasions. There was no network of intercommunicating agents for him to be aware of, no training programmes, no sessions on espionage or formal means of indoctrination, and the chances are that Marlowe bided his time.

His feelings about his employment, when he was 21, were unlikely to be particularly complex, if we judge from his university and creative life so far. One suspects that the deeper he tiptoed into this acid, murky sea, the more aware he became that he could not escape its taint and smell, or refresh himself if he climbed out of it. But at the moment he no doubt thought well of secrecy, travel, and risk; also he needed a choice, an alternative to entering the church or trying for a fellowship: he probably hoped for a bridge between the archbishop's grant and his good luck in finding a patron, and trusted that the bridge would be short. John Marlowe's son knew of official power, which at times offered a licence to the poet, radical thinker, or dreamer, along with a chance of protection. Another poet, Sir Philip Sidney, had lately countered suspicions of his loyalty to the queen by marrying Sir Francis Walsingham's only child, Frances, in 1583. Sidney's sympathies were hardly with his father-in-law's avid Puritanism, but the Walsingham alliance helped to whiten a blot on his reputation, left by friendships with Catholics such as the Jesuit martyr Edmund Campion. Striving to suit his employers, Marlowe was to prove dependable and of special use partly because of his theatrical success, and the Council, having drawn him in, kept hold of him.

He was to benefit in several ways. He confronted himself, his identity and culture, freshly even at Cambridge, but his attitudes became more complex partly as a result of his secret work; he looked anew at the state's power, at rivalries and threats from abroad, and benefited from travel. His international perspectives, his interest in politics and 'policy', in loyalties, duplicity, secrecy and the nature of the self, relate in part to his new career. Yet no matter how unobjectionable his duties, he was at least prone to a sense of guilt or degradation, whether or not he betrayed scholars; and his new part-time association with agents shortened his life and led to his death.

The consequences of his employment alone suggest our need to look into the Elizabethan intelligence system itself. Thanks to recent research, we have new light on Marlowe's role as an agent, and it will be worth considering the Walsinghams and departmental arrangements before we look into evidence of his part-time duties. Marlowe's route of travel, to and from home, led through London or its outskirts, and it is likely that he visited the capital before he lived there. Agents knew that the Privy Council had an eye on London's French embassy. Faunt was familiar with the building in question, Walsingham visited it, and Marlowe sooner or later would have heard it described; the importance of the secret, official work of the legations whetted interest in this particular hornet's nest, even if one did not meet the hornets.

The French embassy lay near Fleet Street in Salisbury Court—where on a summer's day the area was fairly empty. The hornets might then have seemed asleep. An agent who hoped to be of diverse use to the Council had to know how operations might be co-ordinated, and it is sufficiently clear that Marlowe heard something from the spymaster's own cousin (virtually a specialist in this matter) about the French presence in the capital.

There was not much stir at Salisbury Court, even with the monthly arrival of a diplomatic bag. The embassy's staff was dense with family relationships, and not all were diplomats. One or two were moles reporting back to Walsingham's staff, and in that sense the place was full of holes through which much trivial data passed, but the sieve was zealously watched. An earlier French ambassador, La Mothe-Fénelon, had lived there while musing about *rapprochement* between Catholic Europe and England's Protestant queen, but had given up any such hope. 'It is impossible to make any serious arrangement [*de pouvoir rien establir de bien asseuré*] between those whose religion is different', he had felt.[21] His more active successor Michel de Castelnau, seigneur de Mauvissière, trusted that the queen could be killed, and made the embassy into a clearing-house for messages to and from the Continent in support of plans to set up Mary Queen of Scots once Elizabeth was dead.

Genial and slightly dissipated, Castelnau had high hopes even as he entertained his friend Walsingham, who for his part had managed to turn the ambassador's secretary Claude de Courcelles. By 1583, Courcelles had run a secret correspondence between Castelnau and Mary for more than a year while ensuring that each message, or a copy, reached the spymaster's desk. Gilbert Gifford, an English agent, became a postmaster for Mary's further correspondence. Laurent Feron, a French resident and clerk, worked as a mole to check on Courcelles, with the aid of 'Henri Fagot', a mole whose identity is still elusive, though he had recruited Feron.

The upshot was that a regicidal plot was crushed: a Spanish ambassador was expelled, and Castelnau was blackmailed and watched in London to avoid upsetting Henri III and volatile France. Walsingham took a wide view of the politico-religious schism, and his concern with Salisbury Court is proof enough that he was more than a priest-hunter. Marlowe began as an agent when his employers were seeing Europe as a delicate interlocking maze, best viewed, unfortunately, from the mole-ridden embassy at Paris, which gave Walsingham nightmares; Burghley's correspondence shows that he himself knew the English ambassador was selling data to Madrid, but the Lord Treasurer tolerated abnormalities. A Cambridge man such as Faunt, though he worked for Walsingham, ascribed the troubles there and elsewhere to too many 'intelligencers' at work.

Piecing together what he could, Marlowe would have found the spy-master's house at Seething Lane a well-run den, in which murder, now and then, was arranged without the use of torture rooms. One of its supervisors was Walter Williams, a veteran of seven years' courier work on the Continent, an ex-papist who had spent months in a Rye prison trying to extract treasonous data from a Catholic. Williams went to extremes if need arose: he knew what 'There is but one way with him' meant, but little was gained by killing useful double agents, and the service depended on men in the field to whom loyalty was fatuous. Patient work was the order of the day. Coded letters came in to be processed by Thomas Phelippes, an expert decipherer. And traditions which historians of British espionage often neglect affected the office and inevitably Marlowe's view of his part-time calling. From about 1514, when Henry VIII's diplomatic service became efficient, there had been monthly payments to couriers in France—militarily and in other ways a country of prime interest—and an operational espionage system with agents in Scotland. What were called 'exploratori' or spies had been used much earlier: captured agents were tortured, and Edward IV and Henry VII had interrogated their prisoners personally. The modern system, which Marlowe knew, was still based on collecting data from the Continent, with Paris always a key post, except that there were contacts or place-men in about fifty-three different locales outside England, some as far off as Turkey, and information accrued from diplomats, soldiers, merchants, sailors, even itinerant clergymen. In London and at the ports, moles and watchers, turncoat papists and agents provocateurs were used: Jesuit missionaries were trapped, tortured, killed, or simply deported, and three plots against the queen were exposed in two years.[22]

Marlowe's stage demons, such as the Duke of Guise or Mephistophilis, are creations fed by his fascination with secret power, and in this vein the Secretary of State as a black spider had much to offer. Walsingham aroused horror in his lifetime, though for his swarthy face he was called by the queen her 'Moor', just as she called the pale, gouty Lord Burghley her 'Spirit'. In his bust portraits, Walsingham appears as a scholar in a black skullcap, an ageing undergraduate, but his image at the National Portrait Gallery in London shows him with dark hair, doleful eyes, well-sculpted beard and eyebrows, and a lean head—from which a single ear juts over his ruff; in his mid-fifties, he looked the part of Lucifer.

Not that he was a villain to colleagues, who mostly were fond of him. One reason for the Council's collegial solidarity, which has a bearing on Marlowe's fate, is that the government was largely being run by Cambridge men. Several in power were old 'Athenians', classical enthusiasts and acolytes of John Cheke, formerly Regius Professor of Greek. Burghley (or Cecil) had gone up to St John's College and married Cheke's sister. Walsingham had been at King's College when Cheke was Provost, and Walter Mildmay, of Christ's, who excelled in financial administration, had married one of Walsingham's siblings.

Other factors, too, fed the *esprit de corps*, and, despite what has been claimed, factional warfare was rather slight when Marlowe was hired as a petty cog. The Council's driving powers—Burghley, Walsingham, and Leicester—frequently opposed Elizabeth's parsimony, delays, or favoured policies while working for her, and in the summer of 1585 a decision to send an army to the Lowlands drew ministers closer, until Leicester began to bungle overseas. If there was some fierce, grudging rivalry among spies, there is little sign of this among their employers, at least until the Secretary of State died in 1590.

Walsingham, with the largest number of place-men abroad, had the most crucial interests in France, and Marlowe probably worked for him rather than for Lord Burghley. This cannot be proved, but, I think, more than a few factors make it likely: the main evidence is that the Council linked Marlowe's name with Rheims, a known object of Walsingham's anti-Catholic operations, and that the poet had a close association with

14 Sir Francis Walsingham, from an oil painting of about 1585, now at the National Portrait Gallery, and attributed to John de Critz the elder

the spymaster's cousin and aide Thomas Walsingham, and incidentally with the latter's friend Thomas Watson. Marlowe came to know Richard Baines, who had been at Rheims as a Walsingham informer. Whether or not the poet learned of operations chiefly from the Secretary's cousin, he would have heard of the Secretary's chief problems.

The most urgent was mundane—spies had to be paid. Sir Frances believed 'Knowledge is never too dear', but knew its costs. After using his own money for secret work, he benefited from the queen's subventions. To fund the office, he was paid £750 a year in quarterly instalments in 1582, and that grant was dwarfed as tensions with Europe increased. The Signet Book, which records payments, shows that Walsingham received £5,000 in June 1585, £6,000 ten months later, and then another payment of £4,000. Yet nearly all agents were paid on a low *pro rata* basis for specific tasks or information. Phelippes, who had a role in fatally tricking Mary Stuart in connection with the Babington plot, was given a pension of 100 marks a year, and Gilbert Gifford had an annual salary of £100. Otherwise, as a rule, a spy was rewarded with a signed warrant for anything between a few shillings and £30. Agents were desperate for money and shrieked for it. Marlowe could expect £5 or £10 for a few weeks' courier duty abroad, but nothing else unless he worked again.

The typical agent was susceptible to bribery, or 'greedy of honour and profit', as Thomas Morgan, an agent of Mary Stuart, once described Phelippes. Marlowe came to know turncoat Catholics such as Richard Baines and Robert Poley, who at first risked themselves for small, intermittent payments and uncertain prestige as agents provocateurs. Very often, turncoat spies profited from victims, as Walsingham's man Nicholas Berden did: the spymaster himself knew of the practice and must have condoned it. In 1586, Berden told Phelippes about two incarcerated priests: 'If you can procure me the liberty of Ralph Bickley at his honour's [Walsingham's] hands, it will be worth £20 to me, and the liberty of Sherwood, alias Carlisle, will be worth £30.' He added that he was in 'extreme need', and this kind of bribery was a useful part of Berden's operations: he could pose as a Catholic sympathizer with friends at court, who could ensure the release of priests, and then keep bribes paid to him by victims, or by their supporters, for himself. Marlowe's later associate, Richard Cholmeley, played similar tricks. Employed by the Council 'for the apprehension of papists and other dangerous men', as he put it, he took bribes from Catholic prisoners and 'let them pass in spite of the Council'.[23]

There was not only tawdriness but deep insecurity in the system, and Marlowe must have noted that it was built on sand. Seething Lane had to hire in the short term, withhold trust, and use agents to check on agents. Less apparent may have been the Secretary of State's belief in the system and his deviousness. Having left Cambridge without a degree, Walsingham had absorbed lessons in five years abroad, especially at Padua, which in the middle of Italy's Cinquecento was then struggling with other small cities against Habsburg and Valois control. Italian politicians, who knew the maxims of Machiavelli by heart, had spoken to him about the uses of cunning and deceit against oppression while viewing moral considerations as irrelevant. It was best to catch a foe unawares, to 'trick him by false promises, and betray him by false hopes'.[24] Walsingham, as I judge, found this inverted idealism much too simple when he became ambassador at Paris, where he had to put up with Queen Elizabeth's vacillations over marrying the duke of Anjou, or her 'Monsieur'; but, in time, he brought a hard, ruthless practicality to Seething Lane, and his office introduced Marlowe to a Machiavellian system which somehow worked: at least it trapped hostile interlopers (priests included) and scotched conspiracies.

What especially favoured Marlowe's prospects were Walsingham's flexible opportunism and his odd, unlikely interest in the popular theatre. The Secretary (it is said) took little pleasure in watching actors, who might have been amazed late in the 1580s to see him on a cushion at the Rose on Bankside, but he was ahead of his time in appreciating mass communications. For example, he had been prepared to create an acting company in the queen's name and to abet actors and therefore their suppliers. Marlowe stood to gain from this interest, which has been neglected in studies of the Privy Council and illuminated chiefly by Scott McMillin and Sally-Beth MacLean's research in 1998. Their work suggests that there is more to learn about Walsingham's sponsorship of original talent. How may the Secretary, at first, have responded to Marlowe, and what could he have heard of him? Up to the end of the poet's stay at Cambridge, his translations and some version of his *Dido*, all in manuscript, would have been known to a few friends, if not to his tutor or one or two other Corpus Fellows. There were informers in the colleges, and it is likely that a notion of Marlowe's skills reached Seething Lane, and that he made an impression before anything he wrote was printed or staged. Walsingham kept track of part-time agents: he almost certainly heard from his cousin about Marlowe, and he saved one of

Marlowe's fellow writers from the law. One suspects, too, that successful plays such as *Tamburlaine* and *Faustus* did not lessen his interest in their poet.

It is clear, in any case, that for years Walsingham had kept an eye on the popular theatre. As a student of maps, he had taken an interest in how far the playing companies travelled, also in the sort of works they staged, and whom the actors influenced. His colleague Robert Dudley, earl of Leicester, had sponsored an acting troupe which toured from Cornwall to Newcastle and further north, and a few other groups even took their chances abroad.

Backed by Leicester, the Secretary had at last ordered, in 1583, that Edmund Tilney, Master of the Revels, should select the best actors from existing troupes to form a new playing company, the Queen's Servants. This had entailed some arm-twisting, as well as shrewd hand-picking. Leicester had released to the new company the actor-playwright Robert Wilson, and skilful performers such as John Laneham and William Johnson; Oxford's group had probably given up John Dutton, and the earl of Sussex's troupe had yielded the best prizes of all in its famous comedians John Adams and Richard Tarlton. Monopolizing professional shows at court, the Queen's Servants soon shouldered out other troupes competing for royal favour. Though created by a Privy Councillor's fiat and bearing the queen's name, they did not quite break down defences against professional players at Marlowe's Cambridge, but by and large they succeeded elsewhere.

In several ways, they aided and relieved the Secretary. The Queen's players were not, so far as we know, paid spies, but offered a good 'cover' for a spy system, while giving the impression of extensive court influence within the country. It was plain to the Council that vocal, outraged Puritan attacks on the theatre were becoming more dangerous as they became more strident. A troupe with royal approval drew lightning from the extremists, who threatened to cause such a rift in popular culture and feeling as to make the nation almost ungovernable. The Queen's Servants chose Protestant dramas, or anyway those not inconsistent with an Anglican outlook, whether or not they incidentally carried letters for agents.[25] Thus Walsingham, who in other circumstances might have looked askance at the players, took an interest in the state's role as a provider of entertainment.

The troupe which he called into being did not disappoint him, and playwrights benefited from the officially sanctioned and (at first) thriving company. A new, clear, medley style of composition was soon encouraged, and the Queen's men's history dramas—such as *King Leir, The Troublesome Reign of King John, The True Tragedy of Richard III*, and *The Famous Victories of Henry V*—were to help release the talents of Marlowe and Shakespeare.

It would also seem that Walsingham's regard for poets improved, and that a report of Marlowe's potential concerned him; he may well have delegated his cousin to look after the Canterbury poet. Walsingham knew that a vigorous writer, drawn into espionage, could not easily be dangled as a puppet on strings, but could be watched and might be made to feel obliged to the government. He did not handicap talent, but nurtured it and lightly censored a work when he saw much to gain by doing so. Partly to augment trade with Russia for example, he was aiding in these years his protégé Richard Hakluyt, who had trained as a priest at Oxford, and had wound up as an agent and chaplain in the unsafe molehill of the Paris embassy. For five years after 1583, Hakluyt snooped at the exiled court of Don Antonio of Portugal (where he met the 'best pilots and captains'), and fretted over 'sluggish security' and how far England was lagging behind in opening up the New World. To the fury of the Merchant Adventurers, the richest of the Europe-oriented trading companies, which he belittled, he was to publish accounts of Cabot's, Drake's, Harriot's, and other voyages in *Principal Navigations, Voyages and Discoveries of the English Nation* (1589), one of the most graphic and valuable works of the age.

Hakluyt dedicated this to Walsingham, who had supplied access to government documents and personally licensed the book for publication.[26] Marlowe knew the *Voyages* (though not its expanded edition), and could have met Hakluyt in Paris in 1585 or 1586. However that may be, he could see who the dedicatee was. Having slightly doctored Hakluyt's text, Walsingham was keen to help writers, especially if they were dutiful; but as a busy, obsessive man he left a few arrangements to his second cousin Thomas.

Marlowe, in due course, met Thomas Walsingham, who was then a young officer in the French service. About three years older than the poet, Thomas was a good Latinist; he was also cosmopolitan, pleasant, and ready to oblige. His duties as a courier may not yet have hardened him, or made him crass or cynical, and we know that he awaited an inheritance. If he had an obvious fault, it was only, perhaps, that he was overly anxious for his reputation; unlike his famous, powerful cousin, he did not mean to devote his life to the Elizabethan intelligence service. Loftier, more ornamental roles awaited him as a gentleman and friend of the court, so he was boyish, cheerful, and somewhat inscrutable. He impresses one as a man who practises facial expressions in a mirror and finds disapproval the hardest; he might have touched pitch without being defiled. Thomas employed thugs, but seemed no more affected by this than if they had been cherubim and seraphim.

Lately, he had been promoted at Seething Lane, where he served as Marlowe's case-officer, or at least as one of his contacts. Some such arrangement, at any rate, led to a warm friendship, if not to an early invitation to visit the finely appointed, handsome Scadbury, the Walsingham family estate out at Chislehurst in Kent. Thomas's eldest brother, Guldeford, had been employed in military intelligence, but had predeceased their father, and the estate devolved to a second brother, an apparently frail Edmund. When Thomas did inherit Scadbury in 1589, his career as an officer had ended; by then, despite a few initial contretemps, as will emerge, he was one of Marlowe's patrons.

When barely out of school, Thomas, as a protégé of his cousin, the Secretary of State, had been popular with an English community in Paris. In halls among diplomats or at soirées, he appears to have been grave or amused, as occasion required, if a little noncommittal; but on the highways, as a bland, well-bred gentleman, he had proved ideal in courier work. In fact, we first hear of Thomas at the age of 19 or 20, when he was already well trusted.

On 13 October 1580 he brings 'letters in post for her majesty's affairs' over to England from the ambassador at Paris, and on 11 November carries others back. He repeats the same task on several occasions the following year; he is at Blois with the ambassador, Sir Henry Cobham, in February, and in August with Sir Francis at Paris. His duties in connection with the duke of Anjou or 'Monsieur' once saved him when a troop of French soldiers caught him on the road in Picardy. Cobham, the ambassador, described that very awkward moment in a letter to Sir Francis dated 12 November 1581:

They stopped Walsingham and Paulo, my Italian, whom they resolved to rob, but that he showed them Monsieur's packet. They spoiled another Englishman in his company, called Skeggs as I remember.[27]

The Italian in the group was Paolo Citolino, who was often employed by the English ambassador. The name 'Skeggs', in Cobham's letter, might be a reference to 'Skeres'—and Ethel Seaton, in recent times, was the first to show that Skeres was an agent in the Babington affair. It is quite certain, then, that Nicholas Skeres, a witness to Marlowe's murder, was an early associate of Thomas Walsingham.[28]

Thomas had connections with two other men present at Marlowe's death, Robert Poley and Ingram Frizer, but it hardly follows that he himself deliberately conspired with a killer or secretly planned to eliminate the author of *Doctor Faustus*. We know that Thomas befriended a variety of ambitious politicians without badly injuring his own prospects. Moreover, it is clear that he had pleased his cousin upon returning to a room at Seething Lane, and within a year or two he was thought proficient for duties involving the Babington plotters against the queen. As a young agent in Paris he had met the poet Thomas Watson, and later appears to have introduced him to Marlowe. That meeting—it occurred some time in the late 1580s—was important, since the habits and views of 'witty Tom Watson' were consequential for the poet who studied at Corpus Christi. Sir Francis's cousin had close contacts with both Watson and Marlowe, and went out of his way to please the talented.

Tom Watson after France

At Cambridge one day, Marlowe had apparently found, with pleasure, a translation of Sophocles' tragedy *Antigone*. This was among the best of recent translations from Greek into Latin, and one suspects that he read it closely. Thomas Watson, the translator, had begun with an amusing verse-letter to the earl of Arundel, who declared himself a Catholic in 1581 and whom the translator had not yet met.

'Let Momus himself', Watson tells the earl,

murmur empty words beneath his breath, and envious Zoilus mark it with his pitchy claw, the verdict of your judgment will prevail over both, and place on my brow the wreath of laurel.

The writer adds that he hopes to be 'like Ganymede, the attendant of Jove'.[29]

If Marlowe read that, he was amused. Nearly 30 by 1583, Watson did not much resemble the erotic boy Ganymede—if he was ever like him—but he was a famous, innovative writer. His hundred or so lyrics in *Hecatompathia* have been neglected in our time, but Watson's works appeared in their first adequate edition in 1998, and were fully listed, with data about his lost pieces, in 2001, so we can begin to see why Marlowe admired him.

That poet had set a high mark in productivity. Marlowe himself, in these years, was seeking out works by Spenser or Sidney even in manuscript; he would have made notes about verses he liked, or even memorized stanzas.[30] There was a vogue for the 'art of memory' inspired by books on mnemonics by Giordano Bruno or by Thomas Watson; if the 'memory' fashion was zany, at least it helped actors and poets. And Marlowe's work as a spy has to be seen in the light of his devotion to his art. To reduce him to the status of a mere hero (or victim) in a spy story would be to forget that his attention to verse, language, and the stage kept him hard at work at Corpus. In contrast, his dabbling in espionage might have seemed at times a stop-gap, a wretched insurance against future poverty; no doubt, he could be in many moods about selling his soul. The intellectual integrity of *Tamburlaine* and *Faustus* is, in one sense, a response to the compromises of his work as an agent; and one link between his writing and his subservience to the Council was his friendship with Thomas Watson.

To be sure, Marlowe may have read this poet's works before meeting him, but a friendship developed. Watson was a bohemian, a disciple of French and Italian poets, a prankster and joker fit to have drunk wine in ancient Greece with Lucian; he was among the earliest of the so-called 'University Wits'. One suspects he was tall or gangly with a long reach of arm, an English Don Quixote bronzed by the Italian sun. Though not given to street fighting, he was to intervene and virtually save Marlowe's life in a duel. With an ear for music, he knew William Byrd and helped to introduce Italian madrigals into England. In recent years, he had befriended the Walsinghams, and, with some encouragement, had published the first loosely connected cycle of sonnets in the English language.

What else would Marlowe have found out about him, and why was their friendship important? Born in London and raised at St Helen's, Bishopsgate, where his father began as an attorney, 'Tom Watson' was a law-scholar, but one without a degree. He signed himself *i*[*uris*] *u*[*triusque*] *studiosus*—a student of both canon and civil law. He was always *studiosus*, the eternal student, never a Bachelor or a Licentiate, and he was always 'young'. It is no surprise that he is called a young man (*juvenis*) in the *Antigone* of 1581, but he was still applying that word to himself at 29 and 30. In his escapades in Paris and London, he was watched by spies, an odd fact in light of his affection for the Walsinghams; but there was something hidden in this poet's relations with Seething Lane and the Paris embassy.

A mystery about him no doubt added to his allure. From the first, Marlowe may have assumed he was a double agent. Raised as a Catholic, Watson was cited by an informer even in April 1580, for being a 'great practiser' among 'sundry Englishmen, Papists, presently abiding in Paris'.[31] Yet there was nothing especially religious in his poetry.

Marlowe nonetheless clearly knew that the man had associations overseas. As a boy, Watson had been to Winchester and then briefly to Oxford, where, writes Anthony à Wood some decades later, he excelled in the 'smooth and pleasant studies of poetry and romance'. Not having impressed the dons, the young man withdrew, and for the next seven and a half years travelled abroad. Watson briefly studied Roman law at the University of Padua, and avoided scenes of war; he implies in his lines to Arundel that hostile 'camps' never appealed to him, but poetry did:

> *castra tamen fugi, nisi quae Phoebeia castra*
> *cum Musis Charites continuere pias.*

> [Yet I shunned the camps, save for the camps of Phoebus,
> which contained the pious Graces together with the Muses.][32]

At first, in Europe, he wrote about the sexual exploits of Greek gods, or 'the love abuses of Jupiter', and translated a few of the Psalms. Then he woke up to find a new refinement in the poetry of Ronsard, Petrarch, Serafino, and others, and so began to imitate or translate their lyrics. In his *Hecatompathia*, Watson scrupulously advertises the names of twenty-six modern European poets. As Marlowe surely noticed, Watson does not just 'absorb' the influence of Italy (as the poet Surrey had done), but rather he brings the tones of Italian lyrics straight into his work, though his manner is deceptively simple—

> I'll praise no star but *Hesperus* alone,
> Nor any hill but *Erycinus* mount,
> Nor any wood but *Idaly* alone,
> Nor any spring but *Acidalian* fount,
>   Nor any land but only *Cyprus* shore,
>   Nor Gods but Love, and what would *Venus* more?[33]

Marlowe was to be as delicate and subtle in 'The Passionate Shepherd', but Watson's passionate Europeanism above all stimulated a Corpus Christi poet fond of exotic locales. Marlowe was surely thinking of the career of a heroic Eastern warrior, 'Tamerlane', by 1585 or 1586. If Watson's foreign perspectives had power, might one not bring exotic viewpoints to bear upon war, religion, and the human will in a new, unmoralistic parable for the stage? In writing *Tamburlaine*, Marlowe drew on wide reading, and that work's strands of Muslim thought, as well as its Jewish, Arabic, and Moorish elements, show him to be quite as coolly objective with foreign motifs as Watson himself.

That friend's experiences abroad, at last, had led him to a Catholic college famous in Europe. Keen to study the law, Watson had recalled his fondness for 'Bartolus' and 'Baldus'. Bartolus of Sassoferrato—in commenting on the Code of Justinian—had won renoun as a lawyer, and his pupil Baldus de Ubaldis, at the ripe age of 17, had begun to reform Italian jurisprudence. Much impressed by such authorities, Watson had enrolled for further law study among Roman Catholic exiles at the English College of Douay, in Flanders.

His episode there no doubt intrigued Marlowe, whose employers had been obsessed by Douay. When the English College later moved to Rheims in northern France it became a training ground for Jesuits, who aimed to invade Elizabeth's realm, convert her subjects, and prepare for armed rebellion. The college had been founded in 1568, with the help of Dr Robert Parsons, though largely by Dr William Allen (later Cardinal Allen), an open-minded, genial scholar, who has been wrongly linked with the spy Charles Sledd's supposed sketch of a fanatic, with fingernails like talons—

his beard cut short & somewhat red of colour; his face full of wrinkles; under his right eye a mole—not very big; long-handed; the nails of his fingers long & growing up.

In Flanders, Dr Allen had been willing to admit men of different faiths to read 'humanities, philosophy or jurisprudence'. His students were kept 'at their own and not the common charge', or having to pay their way. He hoped that all might see the light as Catholics, but not a few who came there in the 1570s, as he put it, 'were heretics, or even heretical ministers and preachers'.[34]

Listed with other law students (*juris studiosi*), Watson stayed at Douay for months, so he was presumably later able to give Marlowe a view of the college different from the reports of Walsingham's spies. Disliking the food, Watson had withdrawn from 'commons' or taking meals with his fellows, who typically dined on 'a little broth, thickened with the commonest roots'. Despite the ascetic fare, some meant to risk their lives as missionaries in England. For Dr Parsons, at least, the word 'conversion' had meant the forcible restoration of Protestants to the old faith; and that priest had applauded 'about two hundred youths' who went to Belgium in 1577, 'to take up arms against the heretics'. Just as laudable, in Parsons's view, was their willingness to fight for a 'Catholic King'—Philip II of Spain—and to be 'ready to shed their blood for the Catholic religion in England, if occasion should offer'.[35]

Since Watson knew of that militancy, Marlowe probably heard a mixed report about Douay. The college offered instruction in the liberal arts and admitted some Protestants—while also beginning to train Jesuit enemies of the Elizabethan state. But if Watson, at any time between 1586 and 1589, spoke of the wider humanist features of the programme, that may have added to Marlowe's reluctance at Cambridge or later to betray anyone planning to go overseas to Rheims.

Watson himself had left Flanders for a tour of Paris, where a lawyer as famous as Jacques Cujas was holding forth (German students doffed their hats at the mention of Cujas's name), but when he returned, he found the college in dangerous straits, with an enrolment down to forty-two. The Spanish army had withdrawn from Flanders, and popular feeling turned against English scholars at Douay. On 6 August 1577, one townsman asked at the gates, 'Were not all the Englishmen's throats cut [*jugulati*] last night?' Inevitably, the college's diary records that 'Mr Watsonus' and others left the next day for England.[36]

Back in the English capital, Watson had settled in St Margaret's parish, Westminster, where he shared a room in a boarding house with a clergyman, a Mr Beale whom he had known at Oxford. Unluckily, he met a boarder named Mrs Anne Burnell, a butcher's daughter from East Cheap, who believed she was a child of the king of Spain: a witch of Norwell had told her so. Confronting the bemused lady one day, Watson gave rein to his delight in pranks. 'The best Spaniard that ever came in England was your father', he told her (meaning King Philip II) and added:

You have marks about you that shall appear greater hereafter. You shall have a lock of hair like gold wire in your head, and a mark in the nape of your neck like the letter M, and three moles standing triangle upon your right shoulder, and upon the reins of your back you shall have a mark of the breadth of twopence, which in time shall grow to a greater compass.

Soon after that, nervous glances in a mirror told Mrs Burnell that a red spot on her kidneys had grown to form a crown, lion, and dragon, and so reveal her as Spanish royalty. Her husband examined her and laughed: 'You are branded on the back like one of the Queen's great horses is on the buttock.'

There, as it must have seemed to Watson, the joke ended. But a year before the attack of the Spanish Armada, Mrs Burnell was taken to court for babbling in public about the forthcoming, welcome arrival of the king of Spain. At the time, this was treasonous talk. Summoned to court himself, Watson claimed he had 'said nothing' to Anne Burnell, and had never heard her explain that she was a king's daughter. The case was dismissed, but at last in 1592, as Stow records, the lady was 'whipped through the City of London for affirming herself to be the daughter of Philip, K. of Spain'.[37]

That outcome puts Watson's joke in a crass and cruel light, and he was to blunder again and cool off in prison. If Marlowe breathed a freer air with his fellow poets, his friend's quixotic pranks led to calamity or fatality. But in 1580 Watson had returned with happiness and relief to his beloved Paris, where he had met the two Walsinghams. Sir Francis possibly displayed some urbanity, especially when in need of unpaid couriers, and anyway young Thomas Walsingham and Watson melted into each other's ways. Later, in two versions of a eulogy, *Meliboeus* and *An Eclogue* (1590), written upon the death of Sir Francis Walsingham, Watson pictures himself as the poet 'Tityrus', young Thomas as 'Corydon', and the much-lamented spymaster as 'Meliboeus'. At one point, the mourners discuss their happy days in Paris together, and Watson reminds 'Corydon', or the former courier Thomas:

> Thy tunes have often pleas'd mine ear of yore,
>   When milk-white swans did flock to hear thee sing,
> When *Seine* in *Paris* makes a double shore,
>   *Paris* thrice blest if she obey her King.[38]

In his Latin version of the same poem, Watson more interestingly expands upon the same passage, to give a fuller picture of escapades in France. Here, he expansively tells Thomas, or 'Corydon':

Once your strident reed used to please my ears, when it would sing to the swans of Paris, that divided city washed by the waters of the Seine, a happy city, if it would obey a lawful king. I recall how our youthful plucking was dear to men of good sense, you seemed like a swallow to us hoopoes. But now, o Corydon, how you have changed from those days! Your erstwhile Muse has been overwhelmed by these new complaints, and while you mourn Meliboeus' death with your pious song, to all of Arcady you seem a swan.[39]

The 'milk-white swans' in the English version change sex in the Latin poem; instead of seeming to be young ladies, they appear as young male poets. Yet why should the English and Latin versions of the poem be different? Not exactly in what they say, but in their degrees of reticence, the two versions are puzzling. A few days before he died, Marlowe was to stay over at Thomas's house at Scadbury, where his own killer was present; so it is helpful to have any light we can on the manners, tones, or conversation he may have known before his death. In *Meliboeus* and *An Eclogue*, Watson's two versions of Thomas Walsingham's activities in Paris are about equally innocent, but whereas the English poem, for the public, really shields Thomas's activities, the Latin poem for friends and scholars is more explicit. It would appear that Thomas's associates took pains not to embarrass him with revelations; he is fairly brush-stroked out of the English poem, but less obscure in the Latin. Different levels of candour and comment are natural in view of Thomas's career as a Seething Lane spy, but will be worth considering when we come to Marlowe's visit at Scadbury and subsequent death.

Back in 1581, Watson had entered into a grovelling relationship with the senior Walsingham. At the time he had little in common with the great Protestant spymaster, except that they had both studied law at Padua University. In *The Jew of Malta*, the author has a courtesan refer to such law students or 'gentlemen': a canny, affecting Bellamira had lured to her bed scholars of the University of Padua, just before her trade declined. 'I know my beauty doth not fail', she says petulantly,

> and from Padua
> Were wont to come rare-witted gentlemen,
> Scholars I mean, learned and liberal;
> And now, save Pilia-Borza, comes there none.[40]

If Watson laughed over that, Sir Francis Walsingham hardly lived long enough to know the courtesan joke in Marlowe's play.

The spymaster, obviously, had lacked couriers in Paris, and Watson obliged him. Walsingham had landed at Boulogne on 27 July, and had then had audiences with Henri III and Catherine de Médicis in August. In that month, three men with despatches from Sir Francis reached England in the space of a week: one courier was called 'young Walsingham', surely Thomas himself. A second was John Furriar, who later had a role in trapping the Babington conspirators. A third man, named 'Watson', reached court on 13 August, with 'letters from Mr Sec. dated 10 August'. Watson is a common name, but Marlowe's friend had been at Paris with Sir Francis, so Tom Watson is very likely to have been the third courier.[41]

Even so, there is no proof that Watson was involved in espionage for Sir Francis or anyone else. Though spied upon, he was not, after all, a double agent, nor was he a con man who had tried to fleece Mrs Burnell (though this has been supposed). But after befriending the Secretary of State, Watson began to release a flood of poetry back in London, with the result that his fame began in 1581.

As Marlowe knew, and as any reader could see, the literary assault was well prepared. Watson's *Antigone* blossomed that year with laudatory poems by William Camden the antiquarian, John Cooke the headmaster of London's St Paul's School, and other luminaries. To Sophocles' tragedy Watson had added choric figures such as Death, Violent Impulse, and Hatred, who step out to discuss the Greek *personae*; Marlowe, if well disposed, can hardly have looked back approvingly on that moralistic aim to explain the play to an audience.

But his friend's star had kept rising—for a while. After *Hecatompathia* appeared in 1582 with its eighteen-line 'sonnets', it became a textbook for later poets. Marlowe found in Watson's lyrics in the book not only a display of foreign sensibilities, but a tonal felicity rare in earlier English verse. Spenser exchanged compliments with Watson; and Lyly wrote a euphuistic puff. Shakespeare admired the work, and for his own felicity was later to be called 'Watson's heir'. Even Robert Greene paid compliments after the London poet's pastoral *Amyntas* appeared in 1585. Watson had flattered other writers in advance of *Amyntas*, but he won praise from both Nashe and Harvey, who seldom agreed on anything else.

Marlowe found in Watson's later works few original ideas, but could not have denied his industry, his alertness to modern thought, or his internationalism. Watson's tract on memory, *Compendium memoriae localis*, printed in 1585, for example, modestly called attention to works on the same topic by the much more original Italian philosopher Giordano Bruno.

At that time, Bruno was electrifying Europe, and, to judge from *Faustus*, Marlowe himself was intrigued by the Italian philosopher of magic. If Tom Watson was a realist, Bruno was a vain theoretician who had amazed Henri III in Paris, before coming over to lecture to Oxford's dons and cause tumult. Born at Nola in the foothills of Vesuvius in 1548, Bruno was, in several ways, true to his volcanic origins. As an ex-Dominican monk who fell into heresy, he was to be burned alive; but well before that he developed a chaotic, interesting view of magic based on Hermetic Egyptianism.

Having crossed over to London in 1583, Bruno had stayed two years with the French ambassador, Castelnau, who sheltered him from most of the uproar caused by his ideas. Oxford's dons, listening to 'little' Bruno at formal disputes and lectures, believed he was a plagiarist, and in a sense he was, since he was heavily indebted to two authors Marlowe possibly heard about at school. At Canterbury, Gresshop's inventory had listed works by both:

Zodiacus vita Anglice
Marsilij ficinj opuscula[42]

The first text—or Palingenius's *Zodiacus Vitae* (1534), which Shakespeare also knew—goes systematically through the signs of the zodiac to attach vices, virtues, and magical meanings to each one. The other book contained writings by Marsilio Ficino, who had translated and interpreted treatises by the supposed Egyptian seer 'Hermes Trismegistus'.

Hence Bruno, mad as he might seem, perhaps struck a familiar note for Marlowe. At the same time, the philosopher of magic scorned texts praised at Cambridge, since he felt that 'poor Aristotle' was to be pitied for literalism, and that Erasmus was a destroyer of philosophical traditions because he was so ignorant of the Middle East. As Frances Yates has shown, Bruno picked up the ideas of Averroës, or Ibn Ruoshd (1126–98), who in expounding the Koran had founded a Muslim philosophy of religion. Though Bruno oddly dismissed Moses and Hebrew thought, he also reflected or borrowed without acknowledgement from doctrines of the Jewish poet and philosopher Avicebrón, or ibn Gabirol (1020–c.1070).[43] He used these and other sources to expound an infinite universe with innumerable worlds, as well as the notion that living beings in outer space rule over human life, and that memory is to prepare itself by taking in arcane spatial truths. In his *Spaccio della bestia trionfante* (1584)—dedicated to Sir Philip Sidney—Bruno gives a particularly good example of his devotion to the Egyptian seer Trismegistus. Egyptians, he holds, had once contemplated divinity and found it in seas and rivers, metals, stones, or fruits. Even planets and constellations had been considered gods, and, says Bruno, a magical view will show their deific presence on earth. 'For Mars', he writes typically,

is more efficaciously seen in natural vestiges and modes of substance, in a viper or a scorpion, nay even in an onion or garlic, than in any inanimate picture or statue. Thus one should think of Sol as being in a crocus, a daffodil, a sunflower, in the cock, in the lion; and thus one should conceive of each of the gods through each of the species.[44]

In two treatises published in England, Bruno is especially concerned with invocations needed to call down power from the planets, and with memory as an instrument in the formation of a Magus.

Marlowe may have read or skimmed Bruno's *Explicatio triginta sigillorum* or his *Sigillus sigillorum* (both printed in England by 1583), and could hardly have avoided hearing of them. Nobody, just then, knew that the Egyptian Hermes Trismegistus never existed, or that his supposed works in the *Corpus Hermeticum* did not pre-date Moses or Christ, but were composed around AD 100–300 by unknown Greeks. Bruno was mistaken, outlandish, and unscrupulous, but he was not literal-minded; his descriptions of 'astral magic' called attention to a need for fresh insights into the divine, and he appealed to young poets. Marlowe took an interest in arcane forces, and what he knew of Bruno helped to prime him for the magic of *Faustus*.

Unlike Bruno's grandeurs, Watson's ideas were rational; he advertised the best European poets, and developed a new kind of pastoral lament himself. In Marlowe's view, nonetheless, there must have seemed a difference between the ferocious, genuine uproar caused by Bruno, and the tepid praise won by England's own *littérateurs*. Writers from the colleges were often ignored; genteel puffs were as lasting as the wind; even Lyly's vogue did not last. Scholars in gowns, of course, felt that Watson had given a fresh Continental tone to the lyric. His *Antigone* and French and Italian imitations in *Hecatompathia* were keenly admired in the universities, and yet by the time Marlowe met him in the latter half of the 1580s Watson's success must have begun to look threadbare. Watson found no security in the applause of the learned, and no practical employment gave him status. He wrote a number of plays, but none survive. He frequented London's Inns of Court and Chancery, where residents may have seen his works in the holiday revels, but acclaim tended to die out. If the Walsinghams helped in more than one emergency, as will appear, they found for him no regular or well-paid office.

This poet did not starve, and yet after getting back from France, Watson might have illustrated for Marlowe that the scope for artful talent even in London was limited. Already English poets were being reduced to popular entertainers if they meant to eat. The optimistic ideas of the century's earlier humanists were going down, as the sun plunges into the sea, and no fresh dawn seemed likely for Linacre, Grocyn, Lily of St Paul's, or their ilk. Whatever the good sense of Erasmus or Thomas More, the humanists' dream that *learning* might contribute to statecraft was nearly a joke. In view of Watson's apparent failure to get a good position, a steady income from work, a tangible recognition of his efforts, or anything really substantial from his poetic fame, Marlowe might have felt lucky to have in sight any employment at all.

A government man

High, nervous, or unsettled spirits at Cambridge usually prevailed as spring approached and men thought of clerical offices. Marlowe, who had ample time to consider the benefits of joining the clergy, had remained in a Master of Arts programme while studying theology and taking into account the modest expectations of future clergymen whom he knew. Yet it came to pass that Corpus's chapel—with a good, stout floor overhead for the archbishop's books—was finally built despite the Master's gross neglect of its costs. Scholars no longer edged into old, narrow pews at St Benedict's Church, which was left to the townsfolk. The religious life began to look more prosperous, central, and inescapably in evidence than in the past, and men who went through the green quad to the new chapel would have included a few of the poet's friends.

Also, his divinity studies had evidently gone well. His *supplicat* for the MA was signed, and a degree was conceded to 'Chr. Marley' (among six others at the college) on the last day of his final month in the course:

Conceditur . . . ultimo Martii, 1587. . . . Ex coll*egio* Corp*oris* Chr*isti* d*o*mino Thome Lewgar, Rob. Durden, Chr. Marley, Edw. Elwyn, Jo. Burma*n*, W° Browne, Abr. Tylman.[45]

Just then, he did not *have* the MA, and there can be slips 'twixt cup and lip, but he was eligible for clerical preferment. There is no sign that he was deeply committed to espionage, or that the Council guaranteed him future work.

As he awaited fate, what he had heard of other spies and knew from his own secret work no doubt influenced his choices or last-minute plans. How had he been used by the Privy Council? Spies such as Robert Poley and Richard Baines, both Cambridge men, illuminate his own secret experience by way of contrast, and it will be useful to look into their roles briefly before we attempt to trace Marlowe's secret path up to this point.

One odd circumstance had been that a relative of Tom Watson, his sister or a cousin, had apparently married Robert Poley in 1582. Poley never lacked nerve; but Sir Francis distrusted him, though the Secretary had befriended the more eccentric Watson. If Poley used his marriage to Mistress Watson to better his chances with the spymaster, he fared poorly at that game, and soon left his wife. In about 1583, he had called at Seething Lane to see Thomas Walsingham, and then for a short time had worked for the earl of Leicester before being taken on as an agent, belatedly, by Sir Francis.

Marlowe may not yet have glimpsed Poley, but must have heard of his role in the Babington affair. A Catholic, Poley had studied at Clare Hall after matriculating as a sizar at Michaelmas 1568; he was considerably older than Marlowe and an exact contemporary of Baines, who, in the same term, had matriculated at Christ's. Starting as a 'gentleman pensioner', Baines had moved on to Caius, taken a Master's degree, and at last, like Poley, gravitated to Walsingham's French service. Still, there were marked differences between the two agents. By turns shrewd and asinine, Baines gulled the gullible and pocketed bribes, but failed in more sensitive duties. Uneasy among the reticent, he made a show of bluff, good-spirited candour, and in that mood he had appeared at the Catholic English College after it moved from Douay to Rheims in 1578. As a Walsingham informer, Baines may have been seen by one of his own kind at Paris on his journey, but what we know is that he became a sub-deacon at Rheims on 25 March 1581, a deacon on 8 May, and a priest on 21 September.

Marlowe, who knew him, sooner or later had wind of this episode, if not of the sheer, futile idiocies of which Baines was capable if left to his devices. To kill everyone at the English College, he had planned to 'inject poison' into a well or communal bath, and so he anticipated Barabas, who is said 'to poison wells' and does kill off a whole nunnery in Act III of *Jew of Malta* with Ithamore's help: 'Here's a drench to poison a whole stable of Flanders mares: I'll carry't to the nuns with a powder.'[46]

When thwarted, Baines became contrite and tattled on his colleagues for profit; later, he was to denounce Marlowe to the authorities twice, and leave a famous 'note' about the poet's seditious atheism. Failing to poison a well at Rheims, he had tried to sow dissent among new recruits: 'I found means', he admitted later, 'to insinuate myself to the familiarity of some of the younger sort, that methought might be easily carried into discontentment.' However, Baines had fallen from grace. When he tried to bribe a seminarist with a promise that Sir Francis in London would pay a vast sum of 3,000 crowns (or £750) for information, his colleague reported this to Dr Allen, who did not act at once. But, as Allen recalled, 'while Baines was daily celebrating mass, believing himself unsuspected, his treachery and illicit dealings with the Privy Council had became known'.

Finally, on 29 May 1582, the college's diary shows that he was imprisoned: 'Richardus Baynes presbyter in carcerum conjectus est'.[47] In fact he was also physically tortured, kept on low rations or half-starved, and transferred after about a year in Rheims's gaol to a chamber in the seminary, where he wrote and signed a confession. When this was printed in six pages in 1583 by Jean Foguy, in a small quarto called *A True Report of the Late Apprehension of John Nicols* (it included certain recantations by other priests), the book blew Baines's cover, so that he was of little more use as an English spy in France.

Marlowe would have had a sharply contrasting view of Robert Poley. That agent was sent, presumably by Sir Francis, as a 'plant' to absorb data at the Marshalsea's dungeons. There, and later at the Tower, Poley had a chance to observe the state's chief interrogation officer, or 'rackmaster', Richard Topcliffe. Topcliffe once said he could add height to a priest's body with the rack. That device, in use at the Tower until 1588, consisted of a raised oak frame, under which a prisoner's ankles and wrists were attached by ropes to rollers. By means of levers, the victim was raised until hanging by his limbs; then, if he remained silent, levers were worked until his bones started from their sockets. At the Tower, close by Seething Lane, there were various manacles, as well as officers such as the London attorney and playwright Thomas Norton, co-author of *Gorboduc*, who until 1584 helped the vicious, psychotic Topcliffe.

If Marlowe did not know that *Gorboduc*'s poet aided in the reign's cruellest acts, he would have heard a little more of Poley. After his free run at the Marshalsea, Poley had emerged to meet a young, idealistic Anthony Babington, who, with others, aimed to kill the queen and set Mary Stuart immediately in her place. Then aged 24, Babington had asked for aid in getting passports, and Poley saw in this a chance to improve his own credit with M[r] Secretary Walsingham, or, as he wrote later,

I thought that someone fit, at his honour's appointment might be enforced into Babington's service, who following him in his travel might do the State some good service; which course Mr Secretary liking willed me to put Babington in hope.

Poley's later 'Confession', preserved in the *Calendar of State Papers*, suggests that he had played Babington like a fiddle. There is no way to check his story, but Poley had no need to lie grossly about his great success. At first, he had expressed horror over regicide; he advised Babington to confess frankly to 'Mr Secretary', and led the naive plotter to an interview with the surprised Sir Francis. When that came to nothing, Poley tuned his approach and hinted that he, as a Catholic, whatever the conspirators did, was a loving friend. Catching him red-handed one day, Babington discovered that Poley had been copying from a secret letter, lately sent by 'the Queen of Scots' or by someone close to her. 'But suddenly demanding the paper again', Poley recalled,

all unawares he saw the abstract I had taken, and lest he should suspect me that I should show it to Mr Secretary I rent it before his face saying I would not keep any such papers.[48]

Anyway, that is Poley's brief report of an incident which quickly might have undone him, had he not covered up his errors with a shrug and a few apt words. Finally as the authorities closed in on the plotters, Babington sent to him a last letter which suggests that 'Robyn' Poley, all along, had worked more or less on a psychological knife-edge to keep any shred of trust. Babington concluded warily,

Farewell, sweet Robyn, if as I take thee, true to me. If not, adieu, *omnium bipedum nequissimus* [of all two-footed creatures the vilest].

Return me thine answer for my satisfaction, and my diamond, and what else thou wilt. The furnace is prepared wherein our faith must be tried. Farewell till we meet, which God knows when.

Thine, how far thou knowest,
Anthony Babington[49]

In 1586 the conspirators were taken, and then executed with due horror on 20 and 21 September. Poley was sent to the Tower, not just as a 'plant' this time, but because his tactics were bizarre enough to put his loyalty in question. Babington had been naive, but Poley appears to have run the relationship with exquisite subtlety; he controlled a delicate situation expertly, judged his victim well, and let little or nothing get out of hand.

The poet is unlikely to have matched Baines in gross presumption, nor Poley in devilish skill; but he was ready for risk. It is apparent that Marlowe chiefly took on assignments which led him abroad, if not quite to Baines's Rheims, though he was later to be caught in the Lowlands. Absent from college briefly in 1583–4, he could not have been of much use on the road then; but in 1584–5, when the Corpus portrait was painted, he was away from Cambridge for 32½ weeks. It has been argued that his missions began in the latter academic year, and fresh evidence supports this. Again, the Council's own memo about him in 1587 suggests that Marlowe's work was not hazardous, but complex and fairly important: in all his actions, 'he had behaued him selfe orderlie and discreetlie', runs the wording, 'in matters touching the benefitt of his Countrie'. The fact that his payments were not recorded, or not in a usual manner, indicates that what he did was secretive, and there are signs that he was in France and the Lowlands. In *Massacre at Paris*, he relies not only on printed texts, but, in its second part, on 'hearsay' evidently picked up in France. At this time, there was a dire lack of couriers in Paris, where the ambassador Sir Edward Stafford had to use his own chaplain in that capacity. It was during this shortage—when British troops were engaged in the Lowlands—that the Council and Paris embassy had the most crucial need for extra help.[50]

Post horses were fiendishly expensive; one might pay 33 shillings for post horses from London to Dover, but Walsingham kept over sixty mounts. For his own agents, he favoured the five principal routes in England, and three on the Continent to Paris, the Low Countries, and Italy; letter-carriers not in the government's service normally favoured these routes. The poet would have received his orders in London. If we knew nothing of the Privy Council's words about him, Marlowe's writing would still suggest that being overseas gave him keen sensations of power and self-possession. He was less braced by 'spying', than by a spy's locales, it seems, and by associations made along the way. From Calais, he was likely to go to Paris, and from there to the Lowlands, where he either met Paul Ive (or Ivey) or someone else who had access to Ive's unpublished works. A military engineer, Ive was a secret agent for Walsingham in the Netherlands in 1585. The poet borrowed a long passage from that agent's *The Practise of Fortification* for *Tamburlaine* two years before Ive's book was printed and seems also to have talked with him. A few years later, Marlowe returned for work at Flushing (Vlissingen), situated on an island

near the mouth of the River Scheldt. In *Faustus*, he alludes closely to events
in the Netherlands which date from 1585, such as the Dutch attempt to
use a fireship on the Scheldt to destroy a bridge during the Spanish siege
of Antwerp. At one point, Faustus ceases to be German, sounding like a
Netherlander in defying forces of occupation led by the Prince of Parma:
'I'll levy soldiers with the coin they bring', he vows in scene i,

> And chase the Prince of Parma from our land,
> And reign sole king of all our provinces:
> Yea, stranger engines for the brunt of war
> Than was the fiery keel at Antwerp's bridge
> I'll make my servile spirits to invent.[51]

The sending of an English army over the Channel that year had been
tantamount to a declaration of war against Spain—a war which lasted for
the rest of the playwright's life. Walsingham and Burghley struggled
to stay in touch with the Paris embassy and officers in the field, and
Marlowe's role seems to have involved excursions over a period of several
months, during which he may have accumulated as much information as
Thomas Walsingham and others in the French service gathered in their
tours. Most couriers for the Council, for example, would have learned
something of a delicate situation in Paris involving the Catholic and weak
Henri III, who was in a half-secret alliance with England's Protestant
queen. In youth, Henri had thought of little beyond the *chasse de palais*,
or seducing of court ladies, and had been the despair of his mother
Catherine de Médicis. Lately, he had begun to rouse himself; he was
threatened within France by Henri de Lorraine, due de Guise and a
militant Catholic League which aimed to overthrow him, and by the
Protestant Henri de Navarre, who hoped to succeed him. France was
enfeebled by internal warfare, open or implicit, between Guise, Navarre,
and the king—'the three Henrys'. If Guise brought France into full
accord with Spain, Elizabeth might have a small chance of resisting the
united forces of Europe.

For the Council, the situation was fragile, but far from hopeless; and to
judge from his *Massacre at Paris* and *The Jew of Malta*, Marlowe became
aware of shadowy factors which influenced politics inside and outside
Paris and London. One of the findings in John Bossy's research in
2001 into spying in Tudor London involves a 'Chérelles', who wrote

occasionally as 'Arnault'. In this, there is no mystery: a Frenchman could be known by his family name or by that of his *seigneurie* or lordship, and Jean Arnault became Seigneur de Chérelles in 1585. Early in the decade, Arnault had left Castelnau's London embassy on a mission in Rome for a certain Horatio Pallavicino, a Genoese financier then in the English capital. Ostensibly, Arnault's aim had been to free from the prisons of the Inquisition in Rome Pallavicino's brother, Fabrizio, then in custody on a charge relating to immense profits of the financial syndicates which controlled the export of alum from the papal territories. This was a business on which most of Europe's clothiers depended. Arnault, after several years abroad, had returned to London to be secretary to the legation at Salisbury Court. In view of his status, English agents were obviously interested in his Roman activities.

It would have been clear to those in Walsingham's French service—and presumably to Marlowe, if he talked with Thomas Walsingham—that Henri III's officer Arnault had negotiated advantageously with the alum syndicates. Typically, religion and politics in this case were tied up with matters involving vast entrepreneurial profits in Europe, a theme which fascinated Marlowe. Behind Protestant–Catholic controversies of the day, or the showier, more generally understood issues between modern states, were down-to-earth considerations about where large profits were to be had, which governmental policies were best to aid and then to milk the international syndicates, or how a regime might feed upon monopolies, while also fattening the companies involved. There was another side of the picture, too. Loyal to Henri III, Arnault knew that the French king was in imminent danger of being toppled by a massive revolt of French Catholics flocking to the Guise's party. Hence, there had been something else for him to do in Italy. He had stayed in Rome with his king's ambassador, Paul de Foix, who, with concern for stability, aimed to prevent a Catholic attack on either Henri III in Paris or on Elizabeth's realm. In their dealings with the Curia, both men had cultivated Cardinal Montalto, who as Sixtus V, in 1585, emerged as a new pragmatic, reformist pope, who was sceptical of the success of any enterprise against England.[52] The pope did not discourage Spain's Philip II, who was preparing an armada of invasion against Elizabeth. Marlowe himself may not have approved Sixtus V, who had no fondness for England; but the pope's disbelief in the success of French armed attacks on Elizabeth's Protestant kingdom weakened the duc de Guise. In Rome, a second English College had already been working in concert with the duc de Guise's party, which by the mid-1580s was having better luck in Paris.

In Paris itself, an English agent would have found trouble. Henri III's lax grip there had been giving the Privy Council headaches. Yet a courier such as Marlowe might have wondered if the entire embassy's staff had not been 'turned'. Needing cash to pay his gambling debts, Stafford the ambassador had agreed to take sums from the Spanish throne. His lengthy, detailed letters were read by Walsingham with fury, though Burghley withheld any judgement against the embassy. If Marlowe did not see the impugned ambassador, he may have met his secretary William Lyly, who (despite what is said in a modern work on espionage) was not one of John Lyly's brothers of that name who was born in the 1560s. Stafford, at about this point, referred to William Lyly as one of his two 'oldest servants'.[53] A shadow then hung over that figure: Lyly was at that time in the pay of the agents of the Scottish Mary Stuart, although, like Stafford, he used his position chiefly to aid the Privy Council. Less respectable at the embassy was a half-mad Irishman named Michael Moody, who was genuinely corrupt.

It is not certain whether or when Marlowe, in a bright doublet, sailed through the Paris embassy, but there are signs that he delivered and picked up letters there. For one thing, he became familiar with the French capital; he depicts Paris with easy confidence. The Catholic city was then a fortified metropolis surrounded by thick, thirty-foot high walls and a large earth dike beyond them. One did not see the pleasant brasseries, restaurants, monuments or wide boulevards of modern Paris, though one heard the ragged, itinerant street criers, the *cris de Paris*, which sounded odd in dank, stony lanes of an ecclesiastical centre: they are represented today in documents at the Musée Carnavalet—*A bon lait! Qui veut de Leau!, Fromage de Hollande!, Voila du bon vinaigre!*

If one walked along the Seine near the Pont Neuf, one saw an unending collection of religious houses, colleges, or medieval churches, all in grey stone. In his *Massacre at Paris*, Marlowe gives a similar if exaggerated impression of the city in the Guise's boast—

> *Paris* hath full five hundred colleges,
> As monasteries, priories, abbeys and halls,
> Wherein are thirty thousand able men,

Besides a thousand sturdy student Catholics,
And more . . . in one cloister keeps
Five hundred fat Franciscan friars and priests.[54]

In Paris, too, Marlowe seems to have absorbed a French view of the
Tartar warrior, Timur or Tamerlane, or at least he offers a more nearly
French than English idea of the hero in both parts of *Tamburlaine*.
Cambridge, of course, had foreign books, but it is not certain that he
found there, or would have been prompted to read in England, a text such
as *La Vicissitude ou Variété des Choses en l'Univers* (1575), in which the
author, Loys LeRoy, argues that the representative man of the modern
age is the 'grand & invincible Tamberlan'. Such a view may have been
current enough in France to be picked up by the poet even from his talk
with young men he met.[55]

Among a fair crush of new couriers in Paris in 1585 was the young
English poet Samuel Daniel—who had left Magdalen Hall at Oxford the
year before—and there is evidence that Marlowe, at this time or later,
made his acquaintance. He was to write a dedication to Daniel's employer
the countess of Pembroke, with a bold assurance which suggests Daniel
had encouraged him to do so. At any rate, young Englishmen abroad in
the mid-1580s, such as Daniel and Marlowe, would have been well aware
of Leicester's hopeful campaign in the Spanish Netherlands, where the
earl arrived with fanfare and even a troupe of players in that December.
Leicester's vanity and failure in leadership soon ensured his ruin, even as
his troops in the new year largely came to grief. Soldiers involved in the
unprofitable skirmishes included George Chapman, the future playwright
and translator of Homer, who was hospitalized, and Sir Philip Sidney,
who was wounded at Zutphen and died on 17 October 1586. Yet
Marlowe—as others did—probably heard of one useful English general.
John Norreys, with a force of only 500 men, pushed back 1,000 of the
enemy on a slippery dyke near Grave early that year. The ranks were
reinforced, but even after a chest wound made him 'all bloodie about the
mouth', Norreys led troops in driving rain until the enemy withdrew,
'leaving behind nearly 700 casualties'.[56] For that, he was knighted, but
promptly excluded thereafter from the jealous earl of Leicester's Councils
of War. The poet may not have used Leicester as a model for the hero's
vain enemies in *Tamburlaine*, but, when he returned to Cambridge, he
had probably had some experience of England at war.

Did Marlowe, at some point as a spy, visit the English Catholic seminary at Rheims? Lying eighty-one miles north-east of Paris, the Université de Rheims had offered that organization a secure, well-protected home on the rue de Venise. After Baines's debacle there, the number of Cambridge students defecting to the college had steadily increased. About 200 Englishmen were at Rheims as early as 1583, and between then and the year in which Marlowe went off to London, the college prospered. Dr Allen himself set off for Rome for a cardinal's hat, even as English seminarians at Rheims in their black gowns and tricorns met with hostility among the French townsfolk. Meanwhile, the seminary was well alert to the chance of receiving spies.

Marlowe could hardly have risked entering the college in disguise, or under a name other than his own. At Rheims, there were too many Cambridge men to expose him if he sauntered in under a false name. There is no record of him in the college's diary, nor other evidence that he infiltrated the place, nor does the Council's memo say that he was there. In his *Massacre*, he alludes to the well-known fact that Guise had supported the seminary's removal from Douay to Rheims—

> Did he not draw a sort of English priests
> From Douay to the Seminary at Rheims
> To hatch forth treason 'gainst their natural Queen?[57]

But that distanced reference is not enough to suggest that he spied at the college. The removal from Douay to Rheims was known not merely to Walsingham's and Burghley's agents, but to freshmen in the halls of England.

In Marlowe's country, scholars at times would have talked of little else. Defections to the Catholic colleges overseas affected both of the English universities, now and then inhibiting free speech or doctrinal debate, adding to undisclosed anxieties, tempting rivals into slander or silence, or making gossip dangerous and putting a whip into the hands of spies. Back at Cambridge, Marlowe would have heard of young scholars who did cross over to become priests. Especially from Caius, Peterhouse, King's, and Trinity, there was a steady leakage to Rheims, Louvain, or Rome, and the exodus increased after 1580 and peaked around 1587. In a single year, more than a dozen had gone abroad for Jesuit training from Peterhouse alone. From Caius, there were students such as John Ballard (Rheims,

1581, martyred 1587) and John Fingley (Rheims, 1581, Jesuit martyr 1586) or Robert Sayer (Rheims, 1581, later a monk at Monte Cassino), not to mention others who followed such as William Deane, Francis Bloundeville, Richard Holtby, Charles Yelverton, or Christopher Walpole.

Marlowe's schoolmate Samuel Kennett had rather better luck than some. On leaving the King's School at Canterbury, Kennett had become a yeoman warder at the Tower, where he was converted by a prisoner; he reached Rheims in June 1582 and was then ordained priest at the Lateran in Rome. Still later, he crossed to England under the alias of William Carter. Eluding the queen's authorities, he went back to Rome, became a Benedictine monk, and found himself, as late as 1611, dangerously in England again as part of a 'mission to the north'.[58]

For his part, Marlowe may have been asked to report on scholars likely to bolt to the papists. In one way, he blundered as a secret agent: he gave rise to a rumour that he meant to go to Rheims himself. He paid a high price in anguish for selling his soul to Seething Lane, if he turned in anyone's name. Yet we cannot be certain that he betrayed Corpus men, or lured them as a *provocateur,* even though a certain disenchantment informs his mature plays. In *Faustus* or even in *Tamburlaine,* a sense of grandeur is sometimes coupled with a deflating triviality: Faustus cannot define his desires and only receives trifling, sham rewards for bartering his soul. Yet Marlowe displays a control which does not suggest, at any time, that he is merely venting his despair over being tied to the labours of petty or major treachery. He could not afford to cut his ties with the government, I suspect; but if there is an edge of cynicism in his outlook, his devotion to his art saved him from any self-indulgent posturing, at least in his work, and deepened a rigorous objectivity.

The rumour of his wish to go overseas reached his college's master, Robert Norgate. An odd train of events began after Marlowe's *supplicat* for the MA was signed by Norgate and by Henry Ruse, praelector, on 31 March 1587. There had been trouble between the college's head and the Chancellor Lord Burghley. Having been Corpus's head since 1573, Norgate was slow in taking a required DD degree, but rather quicker to profit by holding a number of clerical livings *in absentia,* such as Lackingdon in Sussex, Forncet in Norfolk, and Little Gransden in Cambridgeshire. Lord Burghley surely was used to profit-hungry, inefficient masters or vice-chancellors; he might even have forgiven Norgate for improperly selling some college property, and for gross financial mismanagement. Less forgivable, it seems, was his high-handed favouritism, neglect of undergraduates, and indifference to rebellion. In the teeth of a mutinous staff, Norgate had kept one Antony Hickman as a Fellow and elevated him over claims of others, despite Hickman's lack of qualifications: the man was not even in orders. When Norgate died in November 1587, his successor Dr John Copcot—a Burghley man— ordered Hickman to be ejected from his Corpus room 'by violence'.[59]

By May or June, Norgate's tenure was under threat. Word that Marlowe meant to go overseas surely irked the master, and if the poet had failed to supply credentials to explain his previous, long absences, that made matters worse. News that he was denied the MA degree reached Marlowe, whose only recourse was to seek the help of an officer in touch with the government.

In due course his case was taken up. Meeting in St James's Palace on 29 June 1587, the Privy Council grandly drafted a letter to the Cambridge authorities to scotch the idea that he was headed for Rheims. That letter has vanished, but a clerk's memo about it is fascinating: 'Whereas it was reported that Christopher Morley was determined to have gone beyond the seas to Reames [Rheims] and there to remaine[,] Their Lordships thought good to certefie that he had no such intent.'

The Privy Councillors, with evidence of his behaviour, could tolerate no false tale about him:

in all his accons [actions] he had behauved him selfe orderlie and discreetelie wherebie he had done her majestie good service, and deserued to be rewarded for his faithfull dealinge[.] Their Lordships' request was that the rumor thereof should be allaied by all possible meanes, and that he should be furthered in the degree he was to take this next Commencement: Because it was not her majestie's pleasure that anie one emploied as he had been in matters touching the benefitt of his Countrie should be defamed by those that are ignorant in th'affaires he went about.[60]

At the meeting that day were Burghley himself, Archbishop Whitgift, Lord Hunsdon, Sir James Croft and the queen's new lord Chancellor, Sir Christopher Hatton. Sir Francis—often ill—was not on hand, but his cousin Thomas presumably had spoken about the poet's 'faithfull dealing' to Burghley, who was exasperated with Norgate and ready (the very next day) to complain, as he did, of the high pay of Cambridge dons and their neglect of students.

In consequence of the meeting, the poet was awarded his MA degree in July. Marlowe was sixty-fifth among the masters in Cambridge's *Ordo Senioritatis*, but only two of the seven MAs from Corpus ranked ahead of him. He was well versed in history as well as theology, and the power of his first great play owes much to his college. Still, he had depended on conscientiousness and his lasting energy to get through an apprenticeship as an artist. He had trained himself through translation exercises from Latin into English and by writing *Dido*, if not also by beginning a play, with which he was about to enchant London and make a new kind of drama possible. He had mixed feelings, no doubt, in leaving Greenwood or Lewgar, and there is good, sound evidence to show that he had not been isolated, or too wrapped up in himself to sympathize with others, for all his extraordinary talk or antics. He lived in no vacuum of irrational, static, puerile or self-indulgent dreaming; his poetry was the centre of his life, but by no means all he cared about. At 23 and on the verge of success, he was to profit from his art and his rivals, and even from the intelligence services, while finding himself either willingly or compulsively drawn into the ranks of men such as those who were eventually to take his life.

III
With Shakespeare, Kyd, and the Ralegh Circle

6

The Tamburlaine phenomenon

Tamerlane oft a lusty Herdsman, a most valiant
& invincible Prince.

(Gabriel Harvey's notes at Cambridge, 1576)

If you are putting something untried on the stage and
venturing to shape a new character, let it be maintained to the
end and be true to itself.

(Horace, *Ars Poetica*)

Tamburlaine the Great

THE road south from Cambridge was better in the green spring than in the winter, and many poets had taken the route, but the capital was not always kind to them. There was a glut of talent in London, a surfeit of those hoping to justify their fine rhetorical training, and Marlowe in the spring and early summer had no obvious means of support: there is no sign that the Privy Council as yet had further use for him. His MA, of course, enhanced his status, but in intervening to get him his degree, the Council had blown his cover: he had no guarantee of being used again; and, having failed to take holy orders, he could expect no further help from Cambridge.

It was normal for recent graduates to live together, as Thomas Watson had done with Mr Beale at Westminster. Marlowe was later to share rooms with the poet Kyd, who was not a graduate though he knew Latin well enough. Some theatre men were at St Helen's, Bishopsgate, within the city, and many others were in the suburbs, north of the urban walls, at Norton Folgate or Shoreditch. The latter was a bohemian, sleazy, 'red

15 The only known illustration of James Burbage's famously popular flag-topped 'Theater' or 'Theatre', north of London's walls at muddy Shoreditch, where plays by Marlowe and by Shakespeare were staged. Its two flanking staircases may be evident in this invaluable sketch, made in the 1590s. Marlowe lodged not far away, in Norton Folgate

light' area, cheap and convenient for actors and poets. Before living at
St Helen's, Shakespeare came to stay briefly in Shoreditch, according
to John Aubrey. There had been an earlier theatre, the Red Lion, in
Whitechapel; but it was at Shoreditch that James Burbage, formerly a
member of Leicester's troupe, had built a galleried playhouse called the
Theater or Theatre (the two spellings were used interchangeably), and a
year later, Henry Lanman or Laneham's Curtain playhouse rose close by
at Moorfields.[1]

These two tall structures, with interior staircases and colourful flags,
stood out in the landscape as boldly as church spires, and people of all
ranks came to their doors. On six days a week, one heard the actor's
trumpets and saw placards announcing the title of a play and its per-
forming troupe. Living near taverns and brothels, Cambridge men had
begun to write for northern troupes playing at the Theatre, although the
edifice, in fact, was continually under threat from the authorities. It could
be dismantled in a crisis, and to brace its scaffolding the building was
shored up by a tiled timber barn which might have reassured audiences
fighting for space in the galleries. One found a seat in church more easily
than at a packed theatre, as a clergyman had told Walsingham in January,
and even the royal court encouraged actors inasmuch as the Master of
Revels needed plays for the queen's 'solace'. Her Council contravened
rules given out by the elected mayors at Guildhall, who sometimes—in
vain—prohibited acting within the city. In fact—as Marlowe surely
noticed—there were regular afternoon city performances at inns such as
the Bel Savage on Ludgate Hill below St Paul's, or the Bull, in Grace-
church Street, which ran north from London Bridge. At these venues,
inn-yards were used, whereas the Bell and the Cross Keys in the city had
upper rooms for playing.[2]

The Queen's players—whom Walsingham favoured—dominated the
stage when Marlowe arrived, and so far had acted in every urban locale
available to them. Richard Tarlton, their plebeian clown, drummed on a
tabor, fingered a pipe, and shuffled in a jig obscenely while giving his
court, city, and country *Jests*; audiences shouted remarks, which he topped
in reply. There was a timid variety in many shows, which could be
followed by fireworks, or even by bear-baiting or bull-baiting. The serious
fare included dramas about famous people such as Preston's *Cambyses
King of Persia*, comedies such as Robert Wilson's *Three Ladies of London*,

moral allegories such as Ulpian Fulwell's *Like Will to Like*, or lurid romantic pieces such as the anonymous *Sir Clyomon and Clamydes* about two
royal knights.

Actors followed public tastes, but a new kind of clientele was emerging.
The repertory system meant that a troupe frequently staged several different plays in a week, so there was a keen demand for fresh shows—
including dramas which mocked traditional offerings. On the other hand,
jigs, jokes, and acrobatics often jostled together, and the poetry or ideas
of a Sidney or a Spenser seldom came to a theatre (though Spenser, just
possibly, penned a few comedies). On foggy or rainy afternoons when the
suburbs contracted into their narrow lanes, Marlowe might have longed
for Cambridge; there is no sign that he adjusted easily to the loss of a
college ambience. But on luminous days the city seemed to expand on its
low hills, and then the throngs at Cheapside, the busy waterscape of the
Thames, or the splendour of London Bridge might have suggested a
certain promise in this metropolis of about 170,000 souls.

In the west and around Holborn, Marlowe would have found the Inns
of Court and Chancery, where idle, gentlemanly residents took time off
from dancing, fencing, or law-books to go to the Curtain or Theatre.
Apprentices, too, escaped work to see a show, and flat-capped young
people, in blue, could be seen everywhere. They had to be unmarried and
in their early twenties when completing an apprenticeship. Normally,
they resented long, indoor hours, demeaning rules, and their vague social
status, and a quarrel between a gentleman and an apprentice could bring
out wild, frustrated mobs. Lately, three brawls outside the Curtain theatre
had involved some 1,000 of these workers, who rescued imprisoned
fellows and attacked an Inn of Court.

Marlowe sympathized well enough with the flat-caps; and they were to
respond to his shepherd Tamburlaine, who conquers kingdoms as 'the
amazement of the world', never loses a battle, and emerges as Emperor
of Asia, Africa, and the Near East. The theatrical revolution just ahead
was to move beyond Lyly's courtly, passionless works and involve Kyd,
Marlowe, Shakespeare, and the temper of the capital itself. And Marlowe
appealed not only to cutlers and tailors, male and female, but to ranks of
accountants, land-agents, investors, and attorneys down from Cambridge
or Oxford. The investors often met at the colossal quadrangle of the Royal
Exchange facing Cornhill, an ornate palace which owed its origin in 1566

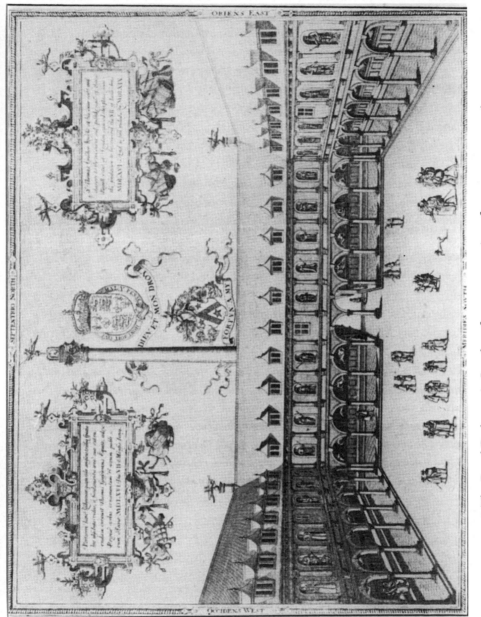

16 The Royal Exchange in London, from an engraving of a contemporary print

to Sir Thomas Gresham, the queen's finance minister, and had a giant interior court with arched entrances north and south. Like a parody of Corpus's quad, it had sprung up like a mushroom. When a bell rang at noon and again at 6 p.m., entrepreneurs gathered here to haggle or arrange for far-reaching transactions.

This was a base for overseas trading companies such as the Merchant Adventurers—which interested Walsingham's spies—or recent import-export consortia such as the Muscovy, Spanish, Levant, or Venice companies. The Crown had given exclusive privileges to these concerns, which were opening up the Mediterranean and Near East.[3] In odd contrast, religion in the capital was visibly slack. St Paul's Cathedral was larger than the Exchange but crumbling and half-desecrated by prostitutes, hucksters, masterless men, and the homeless within its precincts. Despite preachers, tolling bells, and a forest of spires, attendance at services in London was low.

Some of the capital's paradoxes had been guiding Marlowe's pen. He finished his new play by the summer or tidied up what he had written at university, and offered *Tamburlaine the Great* to a troupe. Its hero has a representative quality in reflecting the zeal of overseas traders, as well as the dreams of young people in the shops; and, as if to appeal to the thoughtful, the poet includes a strong theological interest, although his sketch of a 'scourge of God' is neither Christian nor limitedly doctrinaire. He meant to win the public with a new kind of heroic tragedy, and his Tartar's victories were just as impressive as the play's flexible, brilliant verse, so there was reason, here, for authorial confidence. In major crises of his life, he relied on his friends, and Watson, Lyly, or even young Walsingham could have said a word about him to actors in the Lord Admiral's men. Even if his drama had a brief, early debut on a stage under different auspices, it soon became one of the Admiral's chief offerings.

Marlowe's work had a glowing, challenging part for an actor with good lungs. The nation still lacked a 'Roscius' (or any such serious ancient Roman performer of large fame), but the Admiral's men had as their best hope young Edward Alleyn, a tall, athletic, and golden-voiced idol with a handsome nose, splendid eyes, and dazzling skill. Born in London in 1566, he had been raised for the stage. At 16 he had been a star in Worcester's troupe; at 21 he picked up *Tamburlaine's* tones as his own, and understood well enough that this work was unmatched in its

17 A picture which may show the actor Edward Alleyn in the dress of
Tamburlaine, from Richard Knolles, *The Generall Historie of the Turkes*, 1597

spectacle and verbal music. Marlowe's drama rises to sublimity in its tonal
effects and grandeur, and Alleyn's oratorical manner, even in its slight
excesses, suited the part: no doubt he felt so himself. The ring he wore on
his little finger as Tamburlaine still survives, as does his personal seal and

chalice. He went on to play Marlowe's Faustus and the hero of *The Jew of Malta* and to become, with Richard Burbage, one of the age's two most famous actors and by far its richest, though his stalking gait, blazing eyes, and frightening voice were mocked. Ben Jonson later huffed over the age's Tamburlaines with their 'scenicall strutting and furious vociferation'. (He was no kinder with *Titus Andronicus*). But there were two equally good, equally honoured acting traditions, and just as Alleyn's rhetorical style flourished at theatres such as the Rose, Fortune, Red Bull, or Cockpit, so Burbage's quieter realism served in his own roles as Shakespeare's Richard III (most likely at the Theatre), or Hamlet and Othello, at the Globe or Blackfriars.[4]

Alleyn's presumed portrait—now at Dulwich College in south London—suggests that he was 5′9″ or 5′10″ in height, or 6′ tall in his boots, about the same height as the historic conqueror of Asia, Africa, and the Near East. Born in 1336 in Samarkand (or modern Uzbekistan), the real Tartar was exhumed as recently as 1941. 'Within the coffin', reports the anthropologist Mikhail Gerasimov,

lay a skeleton on its back with folded hands and outstretched legs. The skull lay on its left side, the face turned towards Mecca. [His] contemporaries described him as a red-bearded man of tall stature and extraordinary bodily strength.[5]

A Muslim, this hero had large thighs, and a fused, immobile right elbow and knee. Marlowe himself found that the Tartar ruler Timur (1336–1405), also known as Timur-i-Lenk (Timur the Lame), was in Western versions Tamerlane or Tamburlaine. Having conquered Samarkand in 1366, he led brutal military campaigns in India, Persia, and Syria. He wantonly destroyed Delhi, sacked Damascus with terrible savagery, and, after defeating and humiliating the Turkish sultan, Bayazid or Bajazet, in 1402, he died three years later while still campaigning.

About a hundred versions of his story were available to Elizabethans. Ignoring the hero's bad right leg or crippled elbow, Marlowe selects his details from a variety of sources. There is no need here to cite any but the chief ones, and it would be hard to say where his reading in Latin or French stopped. He clearly knew of Pedro Mexía's account of Tamburlaine in *Silva de Varia Lección*, published at Seville in 1540, though he seems to have used its English version in Thomas Fortescue's *The Forest* (1571). He had read the succinct biography in Petrus Perondinus's

Magni Tamerlanis Scytharum Imperatoris Vita (1553), and had found an elaboration of Mexía in George Whetstone's *The English Mirror* (1586), and some of Perondinus in a book called *Beautiful Blossoms, gathered by John Byshop.*[6]

Evidently, though, his project had evolved slowly. Is it likely that any of Marlowe's dramas pursue a topic which he had not contemplated for years? He was often in no hurry to write. Foxe's 'Book of Martyrs' was known to Canterbury's canons and masters at the King's School, and there are good indications that Marlowe at an early point had seen the book and read its brief account of Tamburlaine and of the Christian Sigismund. For Foxe, Tamburlaine was a deific agent raised by a wrathful God to defeat the Turkish Bajazet, and this Protestant view entered into Marlowe's dramaturgical design. The play itself opens with a Prologue, which is, at once, a sales pitch and an art manifesto, the most important so far heard in a London theatre. Indeed, these eight lines do more than bash at commercial skits, and, at least in what they imply, they amount to the most influential lines ever written, in this age, about the theatre's purposes. 'From jigging veins of rhyming mother wits', Marlowe writes sharply,

> And such conceits as clownage keeps in pay,
> We'll lead you to the stately tent of War:
> Where you shall hear the Scythian Tamburlaine,
> Threatening the world with high astounding terms
> And scourging kingdoms with his conquering sword.
> View but his picture in this tragic glass,
> And then applaud his fortunes as you please.

Dozens of plays had moralized on 'War'. But in asking spectators to hear, view, and judge as they please, Marlowe does not treat the stage as a place of moral example, proof, or beneficial demonstration, but as a place for story and experience. He implies that drama is artful, free, unfettered, or it is nothing. Moral verdicts are secondary to truth. An audience must freely interpret what they behold. The theatre cannot offer object lessons, only paradoxical interpretations of life.[7]

Having rebuked 'clownage', he introduces a silly and nearly clownish Mycetes, King of Persia, the most inept of monarchs. This king has homosexual crushes. His brother Cosroe, who means to overthrow him, insults him to his face. 'I might command you to be slain for this', cries Mycetes, with a glance at his minion. 'Meander, might I not?' But crass mockery of the anointed one follows:

MYCESTES. Well, here I swear by this my royal seat—
COSROE. You may well do to kiss it then.[8]

Entrenched power is often a sham. Yet the silly king interestingly becomes a chorus of truth, as when he later tries to hide his crown before a battle. Like Shakespeare's Falstaff, he would save his skin rather than his honour, and he is the only one of the hero's enemies to visualize death before it arrives. 'Accursed be he', Mycetes moodily tells himself,

> that first invented war,
> They knew not, ah, they knew not, simple men,
> How those were hit by pelting cannon shot,
> Stand staggering like a quivering aspen leaf,
> Fearing the force of Boreas' boisterous blasts.[9]

This allusion to Boreas is one of many signs of the poet's immersion in the classics and mythology of Rome. Even the Prologue uses a device of Ovid (in *Fasti* and *the Amores*), by which an older artistic practice is denied in favour of a new one, and as in Seneca a 'choric' element is diffused and distributed to the speeches of key characters.

The poet, in effect, stands back from the action, and yet, at 23, Marlowe brings his full concentrated intelligence and driving power to this remarkable tragedy. He offers a comprehensive view of life, and involves the audience in the Tartar's urgency and purpose. The play unlocks sources of strong feeling such as wonder, horror, repulsion, terror, or prolonged awe, as one of its more alert critics, Brian Gibbons, has noticed, and no doubt it appeals also to wish-fulfilment in its vast, exotic, territorial scope, impassioned speeches, and depiction of unusual exploits in love and war. Only the most shallow reading of his dramas will support the charge that Marlowe was a careless artist, and here he is sustained by what Muriel Bradbrook has called his 'capacity for objectivity and self-criticism'.[10]

That view, I think, is right. But there is something personal in his work if only because in each mature play, in some way, he appears to come to terms with aspects of his experience. In this case, experience has supplied him with a fund of strong feelings and memories. He draws on a central motif of his days at school and Cambridge, since *Tamburlaine* is a critique of eloquence, and of the ideals of Grocyn, More, Erasmus, or Lily. Schoolmasters had credited the humanists' view that eloquence—or persuasive language—is a sign of the well-ordered mind.

In several ways, Marlowe represents such a mind in a hero who is charming, easy, genial with comrades, and respectful of a captive Zenocrate, whom he loves; he speaks of the princess with chaste restraint, whether or not he yearns to bed her. Compared with the cruel or effete leaders whom he overthrows, he is refreshingly humane. In Acts I and II, he persuades an enemy to join him, and defeats a vicious Cosroe, while affirming his own role as 'God's scourge'; he inspires others, and avoids bloodshed when he can. His banners are nearly those of coercion and reform: he would parley rather than fight; when he fights, he scorns the odds and leads with courage. One sign of his purpose is in the very tone of his blank verse, the finest so far heard on an English stage. Marlowe, of course, in *Dido* and *Tamburlaine* did not invent blank verse, which had appeared in more than a dozen works, such as Surrey's version of Books II and IV of Virgil's *Aeneid*, or Norton and Sackville's *Goboduc*, at the Inner Temple Hall in 1561.

Yet here in his Tartar drama his verse conveys inwardness, personality, and thrilling force as well as delicate nuances of feeling. It is not inconceivable that Shakespeare started as a dramatist as early as Marlowe, but, so far as we can tell, this is the first play to mix blank verse effectively with speech rhythms, to break it up with dactylic feet and to give it lightness, flexibility, and a haunting power. When Tamburlaine enlists his embattled Persian enemy, for example, he is mildly boastful in a patently homoerotic scene. 'Art thou but captain of a thousand horse', he tells the handsome Theridamas,

> That by characters graven in thy brows,
> And by thy martial face and stout aspect,
> Deserv'st to have the leading of an host?
> Forsake thy king and do but join with me
> And we will triumph over all the world.

The last line is not emphatic, but has an aspect of quiet litany which concludes each picture of himself—

> I hold the Fates bound fast in iron chains,
> And with my hand turn Fortune's wheel about,
> And sooner shall the sun fall from his sphere,
> Than Tamburlaine be slain or overcome.[11]

Nobody else in the drama has just these tones, and yet in his claims and preenings he begins to undo himself. He is neither really creative and reforming nor bent on fulfilling a sacred mission, though he affirms a new view of human possibilities. The play, in general, celebrates the power of the unfettered human will, along with some of the crass, solipsistic results of pure or unchecked self-reliance. Moreover, it gains a kind of impetus from a random opposition to existing norms and notions. In *Gorboduc*, a chorus had warned against 'growing pride' and the 'climbing mind' or 'climbing pride', but here, sheer aspiration is at first glorified. In the play's most famous speech, the hero apologizes for stealing the Persian crown from Cosroe, who had turned against his brother Mycetes to claim it. By this time, one is perhaps well attuned to what Seamus Heaney calls a Marlovian 'poetic equivalent of a dynamo hum, a kind of potent undermusic', and Tamburlaine can be thrilling—

> Nature that framed us of four elements,
> Warring within our breasts for regiment,
> Doth teach us all to have aspiring minds:
> Our souls whose faculties can comprehend
> The wondrous architecture of the world:
> And measure every wandering planet's course,
> Still climbing after knowledge infinite,
> And always moving as the restless spheres,
> Wills us to wear ourselves and never rest,
> Until we reach the ripest fruit of all,
> That perfect bliss and sole felicity,
> The sweet fruition of an earthly crown.[12]

But, I think, it is well said that Marlowe's most ringing pronouncements are ironic, and I would add that they have much more intellectual complication than those in Shakespeare's early set speeches and soliloquies, at least up to those in *Richard II*. Tamburlaine describes a hunger for power which, after all, cannot be sated, if one is 'always moving', never at rest. His lines suggest a psychological weakness in human personality: the inner self begs, from time to time, for Narcissus-like mirrorings of itself, which neither pictures nor words are likely to show.

In the grandest speeches of the play—and they are operatic, and more than a few—Marlowe suggests how entwined a psyche can be in speech and dress, which are the psyche's crucial parade; if the parade slows or falters, a sense of the self may dwindle or die. The doublet or coat of mail, in *Tamburlaine*, has the same status as a soliloquy. But then the Tartar moves into action to validate his talk, or destroys cities to justify his militant looks. He projects formal images of himself as if in dire need of endorsements of them. It is, of course, possible that Marlowe sets himself up as a revealing case, or studies his own impulsiveness, love of show, or attraction to the theatre in order to understand his hero. But if this is the case, he is, as Muriel Bradbrook says, self-critical enough to view his contribution as fairly slight. He assimilates what he needs to compose an astute portrait, with its various foils, starting with a homosexual king. Any simple, boyish ardour he once had felt for Foxe's God-touched pagan has been overcome.

Tamburlaine is more complex than he seems, and repeated readings of the play will, I think, always reward. He is seldom merely in the skies: he has his feet on the ground, and his eye on Eastern and African maps. At Cambridge, Marlowe may have found a copy of *Theatrum Orbis Terrarum* compiled by the German geographer Abraham Ortels or Ortelius. This was the first great atlas of the world. A copy of Ortelius had been given in 1581 to Cambridge's library, where it was available to any Master's candidate, and another was included in the Parker bequest to Corpus. First printed in 1570, the atlas had been revised, reissued, and translated, with coloured maps in some copies. Ortelius had aimed for accuracy, and Marlowe understandably respected the work. As Ethel Seaton claims, one can nearly follow his finger down a page as he plans a campaign for his hero or an ally.

The trouble is, of course, that atlases date quickly. No one kept Ortelius up to date. In his map of Africa, Zanzibar is marked on the east coast, but a more imposing ZANZIBAR appears in large type as a part of western 'Africe', and the sea between Africa and South America becomes the *Oceanus Aethiopicus*. Thus, in Part Two, Tamburlaine's confederate Techelles reports absurdly on a march

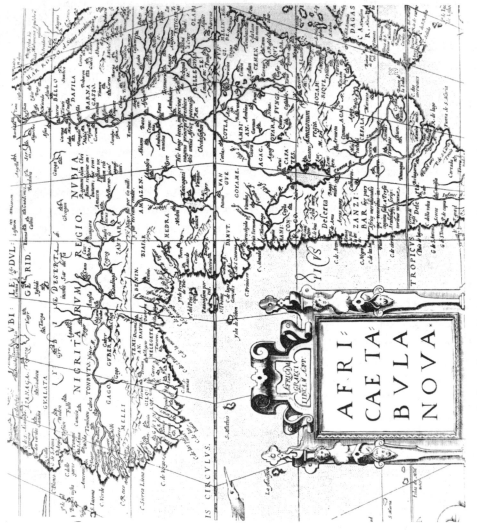

18   Map of Africa, from Abraham Ortelius's *Theatrum Orbis Terrarum*, 1574

to Zanzibar,
The western part of Afric, where I viewed
The Ethiopian sea, rivers and lakes,
But neither man nor child in all the land.[13]

That muddle is not the fault of the playwright, who one feels, has selected place-names not just for their sonority. Place-names chart spaces on the globe which tantalize the ego, and become as collectable as rare coins or orchids: Tamburlaine need not worry over populations associated with them. His virtues at least qualify his monomania up to Act III, which involves Turkey and Ottoman power.

Marlowe's connections with Seething Lane, his stints as a courier, and his fascination with overseas trade primed him to study the East. In 1578 Walsingham had penned a 'Memorandum on the Turkey Trade' about exchanges with the Ottoman Turks. A year later, Anglo-Ottoman relations had formally opened, and Queen Elizabeth's letters to the new sultan, Murad III, began to ensure a boom in trade. English cloth went to the Levant market, and tin, steel, and lead were shipped directly to the Ottoman Turks. Perhaps, then, it was no longer necessary to pray 'against the Turk'. Something more, too, was involved in this *rapprochement* between Christianity and Islam. English Protestantism encouraged the Turks to view the queen as an enemy of 'idolatry', and thus of Catholic Spain and Italy. After the Ottoman–Venetian war—which figures incidentally in the background in *Othello*—support for Protestantism became a tenet of Ottoman policy, according to Halil Inalcik's *From Empire to Republic*, published at Istanbul in 1995. Walsingham's own memo is free of qualms about an increased contact with Islamic culture, and one might think that the 'Turkey trade' was no mystery at Cambridge, where there was keen interest in Ottoman power and the medieval sophistication of Islam. At any rate, Marlowe knew enough to find 'the Turk' intriguing when he considered Timur's prime enemy, Sultan Bajazet.[14]

In Act III he introduces a Turkish motif with a surprise typical of his methods. The dignified Sultan of history at first appears as a joke, a misfit, a buffoon unaware of his absurdity, as when he responds to royal flattery. The King of Argier tells Bajazeth obsequiously, 'All flesh quakes at your magnificence.'

BAJAZETH. True, Argier, and tremble at my looks.

KING OF MOROCCO. The spring is hindered by your smothering host,
  For neither rain can fall upon the earth,
  Nor sun reflex his virtuous beams thereon,
  The ground is mantled with such multitudes.
BAJAZETH. All this is true as holy Mahomet,
  And all the trees are blasted with our breaths.[15]

Humour, exaggeration, and hyperbole are carefully used on Marlowe's stage. At first, one is led to feel that Bajazeth must be another hollow monarch to be crushed: he is boastfully cruel when he aims to make a eunuch of Tamburlaine, or to have the latter's captains draw the chariot of his own Zabina. And he is indifferent to sacrificing easily replaceable volunteers and enslaved recruits—'I have of Turks, Arabians, Moors and Jews | Enough to cover all Bithynia'. Also, he sensibly desires a truce, or he can comment on the hero's 'valiant mind', and his traits become half-comic contrasts to illuminate his opponent. The chief difference between the two is religious. Bajazeth's attitude to the Muslim faith is not shallow, but fatuously lazy. In contrast Tamburlaine's nearly egalitarian view of 'Jove' and his belief in an unknown transcendent god well above Jove become lively, varying sources of his empowerment, and for the moment his pragmatic, flexible attitude to deity insures his sanity. Bajazeth and his wife Zabina are not martyrs to a faith, but to their marriage, and nothing is more deftly suggested in Act IV than Zabina's ardour for her husband, whose defeat in battle leads to his humiliation in Tamburlaine's iron cage, then to Bajazeth's and Zabina's suicides.

'Ah Tamburlaine, my love, sweet Tamburlaine', Zenocrate warns,

> That fights for sceptres and for slippery crowns,
> Behold the Turk and his great emperess.

The heroine's maid, Anippe, speaks of Tamburlaine's 'ruthless cruelty', but Zenocrate's own views are useful guides for an audience. She is barely more than a choric voice in Part One, but the voice warns, intuits, and chastises as much as it praises—although, rather like the poet's mother, Zenocrate does not keep a cherished upstart from behaving exactly as he wishes. Marlowe's play, of course, is too artfully controlled to include self-apology, and he takes pains in tracing a subtle diminishment.

In Act V, we see the Tartar at the siege of Damascus. Its governor has not yielded despite clear, terrible warnings. On his siege's first day, Tamburlaine's white tents signal his mercy or lenience; on the second day, red tents signal his intention to kill the city's soldiers. Since the governor does not respond, black tents, on the third day, are a sign that Tamburlaine will massacre the populace. Dressed in black when the city falls, and 'very melancholy', as the directions say, he confronts the virgins of Damascus. 'Behold my sword', he tells the hapless virgins at a tense moment, 'what see you at the point?'

VIRGINS. Nothing but fear and fatal steel, my lord.

TAMBURLAINE. Your fearful minds are thick and misty, then,
    For there sits Death, there sits imperious Death,
    Keeping his circuit by the slicing edge.
    But I am pleased you shall not see him there:
    He now is seated on my horsemen's spears,
    And on their points his fleshless body feeds.
    Techelles, straight go charge a few of them
    To charge these dames, and show my servant Death,
    Sitting in scarlet on their armed spears.[16]

In this utterly savage taunt, he traps himself. In his view of himself, he obeys a divine edict that he purge the world; but here the notion that 'imperious' Death is meted out by Justice quickly shifts to an admission that Death is only the conqueror's 'servant'. Even so, the Tartar's pragmatism and pride, as he degenerates into sterility, do not leave him insensitive to poetry or aesthetic charm. To be sure, there are some 'poetic' Corpus Christi additions to the Tamburlaine legends in Act V which have little to do with the Samarkand tyrant, or, for that matter, with the astute psychology of the play, though allowance might be made, I suppose, for an often college-bound dramatist of 22 or 23. Having debated his aims in the light of Zenocrate's beauty, the hero spares the life of her father, the Soldan of Egypt who controls Damascus. Critics argue that Tamburlaine's elaborate soliloquy on beauty—which leads him to contradict his purposes and save the Soldan—is his greatest 'battle', but this critical view is faulty. In his monologue on poetic and female beauty he is far too much at ease, not merely self-indulgent but aware of a conclusion before reaching it. He loses nothing by not murdering the father of his beloved, and indeed this leaves Tamburlaine at last in the position of Jove after ousting Saturn: in full control of an enormous polity. He is to wed the princess whose chastity he respects; the dead will be honoured, and Zenocrate's father, the Soldan, will have a richer kingdom than ever before.

So ends Part One of *Tamburlaine*, and only in a special sense has Marlowe used the 'Tragic glass' of the Prologue. The drama is hardly a tragedy, but for the hero's growing savagery and self-deception. Playgoers, at any rate, enjoyed a gorgeous spectacle and a plausible sketch of a grand, historic conqueror. More responses to this play exist than for any other of the period, as Richard Levin has shown; and in its reception, mockery and parody were not absent.[17]

And that, one feels, was appropriate. In sketching King Mycetes or Bajazeth, the poet had brought laughter to tragedy, as he would do very differently in his future plays.

Of what use is laughter in tragedy? Let us take up the question with *Faustus*. Just here, he seems to play with laughter's relation to the sacred. In Jewish culture, Yishak means 'he who laughs', and, as Vladimir Propp notes, 'Yishak was connected with Ishakel (God laughs)'.[18] Does Jove laugh down at Tamburlaine? Marlowe surely knew of the boy-god in Virgil's Fourth Eclogue, who laughs when he is born. The Greeks had honoured Gelos, the god of laughter, and for the Romans the laughing deity Risus was felt to be *deus sanctissimus* and *gratissimus* (the most sacred and beautiful god).

In making Bajazeth especially absurd or laughable before he is caged, mocked, and driven to death, Marlowe achieved a rich, if brief, tragic pathos. He had changed the nature of the theatre by getting idiosyncratic character into his style, and had related Tamburlaine's paradoxes to modern ideas about freedom and the will, while giving a feast for the senses. His drama may not be as perfect, technically, as *The Spanish Tragedy* or *Richard III*, but his work is as powerful as Kyd's, and rivals Shakespeare's early works. Marlowe expands one's sense of what tragedy can be, while crediting an audience's ability to interpret lifelike paradoxes, and to decide on moral issues themselves. He had offered a well-sustained, unified portrait in Tamburlaine, with minor dramatic foils in Bajazeth, Cosroe, or Mycetes. Also he had supplied high emotion with a riveting story, and in no other way had he shown himself more in command of the theatre.

Part Two of *Tamburlaine*, and rumours and charges

Marlowe's success gave him new credentials in the eyes of Cambridge and Oxford men. A few were envious, and attacks on him as a heretic or 'atheist' soon began. One interesting aspect of his career is what it tells us about a writer who changes the nature of an art form, and how envy, rivalry, and popular fears affect how he is seen.

His name was mainly unknown to the public; only a few cared who had written a drama. Yet by the winter of 1588, in well-lit, steamy taverns outside Bishopsgate and north of Petty France, St Botolph's Church, and the White Hart inn, actors and university men alike must have been discussing *Tamburlaine*. The writer of such a script was clearly in demand. The Admiral's men, with no extraordinary supply of playbooks, it appears, felt that the further exploits of a murderer of Eastern virgins would be welcome, and probably asked Marlowe for a sequel.

At any rate, he began to write for actors known to him. The life of a troupe, as he must have found, was chancy—with hasty rehearsals, six afternoon shows a week, and often tiny margins of profit. A new play's debut was treated as a final rehearsal, in which gross mix-ups could occur. Patrons usually held aloof from their troupes, although Charles Howard, the second Lord Effingham, yearned to have his men play at court. He had become Lord Admiral at 41 in 1585, but still cared for his prestige. The queen's wishes or whims made him nervous, even if his influence at court was as sound as his finances; she took pleasure, as he knew, even in bear-baiting. Luckily, the queen was fond of watching his star, Edward Alleyn, who later retired from the stage only to return to it at her request.

Alleyn's fame, however, was only beginning in 1587; the Tartar material had given him a good start. No doubt, Marlowe felt encouraged. He had used up only his chief sources for the Tartar hero, such as those by Mexía or Perondinus. He had invented a love story, and brought the conqueror to a pause in marriage, while no doubt thinking of a Part Two even before he finished Part One.

To seize his chances quickly, he drew on what he already had begun to work up imaginatively. The figures of Tamburlaine and of one Faustus of Germany had been talking points at Cambridge. To an extent, Marlowe had already been drawn back to his six years of student life. He knew of the fussy, vain, academically embattled Gabriel Harvey—the famous hero of *Pedantius*—who habitually annotated texts. As early as 1576, Harvey had acquired a remarkable synoptic history of the world, A. P. Gasser's *Historiarum et chronicorum totius mundi epitome* (1538), and had begun to jot marginalia on 'Faustius', and also next to its account of Tamburlaine, who, in the chilly perspective of a Fellow's study-room, had looked like a 'lusty herdsman' and a 'most valiant & invincible Prince'. Harvey's approval is interesting, and so are his spelling changes, as when he writes 'Calapinus' for Gasser's 'Celapinus'. Since Marlowe follows several of these spellings, he had presumably seen Harvey's notes while looking for sources.[19]

If Gasser and Harvey supplied keys for his project, Alleyn as a versatile, brilliantly intuitive actor offered a certain way ahead. He varied his personality easily from role to role—and Marlowe meant to capitalize on variety. As a playwright, he was not to repeat himself in a choice of dramatic kinds; none of his plays is much like anything he had done before. Whereas Shakespeare's artistic development is fairly progressive up to his mature history plays, Marlowe had reached his stride in *Tamburlaine*, a well-structured advance over the comic *Dido*. The pattern of his enterprise might resemble the spokes of a wheel: he moves out in a wholly fresh direction with each new attempt. His talent is mature, in full flower in the two Tartar dramas, just as it is in *Faustus, The Jew of Malta*, or *Edward II*, and, so far as one can tell from its cropped text, *The Massacre at Paris*. In about 1587, he aimed to test the genres by shattering them, recombining them as needed, and giving the Admiral's men a different kind of playscript in each one he wrote.

Though it is another heroic drama, his Part Two of *Tamburlaine* is more sombre, ritualistic, even more nearly liturgical than Part One; its hero is grave, formal, and in retreat from bonhomie. On fifteen occasions, for example, the characters enter in solemn processions. At the outset, the poet admits that his first script prompts him to take up a quill again, if only to show the death of Zenocrate, and the downfall of God's Scourge. The 'general welcomes Tamburlaine' had had 'when he arrived last upon our stage', states Marlowe in a Prologue,

> Have made our poet pen his Second Part,
> Where death cuts off the progress of his pomp,
> And murderous Fate throw all his triumphs down.[20]

Here, a touch of sour grapes suggests that his first Tartar had been rejected by one or two troupes before the Admiral's men bought it. Understandably, of course, he wishes to consolidate his success, or to appear as more than a flash in the pan. He is mildly boastful in implying that his first play was greeted with such wild rapture that he had to write another to keep the peace. Possibly, he had noticed less than rapture at the Inns of Court and Chancery, among men who had barely left off their campus gowns. Marlowe hopes to show off his intelligence, his command of ideas, and to appear as a 'scholar' who uses thrilling situations to convey nuances of thought, or a dialectic of opposed themes.

But he needed to appeal to an often unlettered public. The main action of the sequel is keyed to military strategy, with opposing desperate armies moving over large tracts of desert, mountain, and forest. Hoping to crush the Tartar's men, Turkish forces are seen at their outposts on the Danube. Since Tartar legions press at their eastern frontiers, the Turks make a binding, tactical peace with Hungary's Christians, and then withdraw along divided routes into Asia Minor, only to suffer the Christian King Sigismund's vicious attack on their exposed forces.

Either fate or the deity—Marlowe leaves this ambiguous—causes Sigismund, the Christian perjuror, to die in battle. Though Tamburlaine had been 'at peace with all the world', after a lapse of years he is seen on the move again—at Alexandria, Larissa, Aleppo. He defeats the Turks and their allies near the boundary of Natolia and the Turkish frontier, and then, with captive kings in tow, turns to conquer Babylon. Having subdued the rallying Turks, his last victory, he disposes of that city's populace, before facing 'the wrath and tyranny of death'—his only defeat.

Counterpointing the military action is a fine, subtle, psychological study in which religion comes under scrutiny. For the Sigismund events, Marlowe has kept Foxe's 'Martyrs' in reserve—and he has unused material in Lonicerus's Turkish history and in Münster's *Cosmographia*. Imaginatively, he conjures up a domestic life for the Tartar, who—to the despair of Zenocrate—is training their three sons for war. Exploring the results of the hero's view of himself as a God-appointed scourge, the author is in pursuit of elusive truth, and he is obliged to account for the fact, implicit in his sources, that no evil or folly ever reverses the hero's fortunes. It has been argued that Tamburlaine's three worst acts of cruelty and impious pride occur in Act V, when he destroys Babylon, breaks his oath with its governor, whom he kills in cold blood, and mocks Islam while burning copies of the Koran. That is valid, if one focuses on the play's episodic structure as it echoes that of Part One, but Marlowe's dramaturgy is more complex. He includes a delicate structure of feeling, with a manic, estranged, but by no means crazed or ruined psyche in focus; and in this scheme, the Tartar's killing of his pacifist son Calyphas in Act IV is his most horrendous crime. Deprived of wife and son, he lives on with the sole, bizarre hope of turning his other boys into conquerors.

Even at the outset, the poet strips Tamburlaine of charm—or of what had been transcendent in his talk—and portrays his enemies as superior in their morality. The Tartar's first opponent is Orcanes, King of Natolia, a devout Muslim who attracts 'Sicilians, Jews, Arabians, Turks, Moors' and others to his side.[21] The supposed 'atheism' of Marlowe, in his time, arose partly from the fact that he exhibited the moral weakness of Christians—and none of his defiers or perjurors is worse than Sigismund. This European breaks a treaty pledged in Christ's name since he regards faith as purely dispensive or negotiable. 'Can there be', reflects the Muslim Orcanes in horror,

> such deceit in Christians
> Or treason in the fleshly heart of man
> Whose shape is figure of the highest God?[22]

This viewpoint might be Marlowe's own, and it is, I suppose, arguable that he favours the candour or lack of hypocrisy he finds in Muslims (in so far as he has met them in his sources). But the mortified feelings of a Natolian Muslim are not central, and the emphasis really shifts to the hero's unquenched aspirations, along with the relations between faith and desire. What deeply intrigued Marlowe (and was soon to intrigue Shakespeare) was the worth of our natural desires, the warrants we seek to sustain them, and what results from a wilful pursuit of them. To explore aspiration, or the will, is to investigate the psyche and, at Cambridge, he had been aware of a debate over human identity, in which Calvinists and anti-Calvinists had plumbed questions about desire, the will, and earthly rewards. Calvin's *Institutes* had figured ambivalently, and both parts of *Tamburlaine* have scenes which might be commentaries on that work. The seeking for God's rewards is endorsed by the Calvinist, who, nonetheless, sees humankind as depraved, lost, and helpless. Lutheran and other viewpoints had been heard at Cambridge, but little in the debate had run counter to a Puritanical emphasis on the limits of human self-sufficiency.

Tamburlaine, in Part Two, opposes just that. Though his aims are military, he sets no limits upon desire, or upon what he (or his warlike sons or allies) may achieve, so he speaks for freedom or gives lip-service to it. Marlowe does not mock or even quite undercut his hero's individualism, which seems an antidote to a passive acceptance of rules which can cripple a society. Curiously, the play, in this respect, anticipates the anti-Puritanical ideas of Richard Hooker, who, in *Of the Laws of Ecclesiastical Polity* (which began to appear in the 1590s), argues for a scheme of law evolved by our needs, and for a faith which leaves aspiration relatively free.

Yet Marlowe—like Shakespeare—does not appear as a critic of doctrines, and instead delves beneath them to represent the mind in its paradoxes. He remains aloof—hence the difficulty of calling him an 'atheist', 'a secret Catholic', an 'ironic humanist', or 'a Protestant in disguise'; he eludes each label, though all of them together might be befitting. It is impossible, on the evidence, to assert that he has a religious faith or that he eschews faith. One of Marlowe's assets as a playwright was that he profoundly and urgently concerned himself with religion, not as a theologian, but as an intellectual and artist in pursuit of truths about feelings, attitudes, motivation, and behaviour. It is clear that his views of history, of society, and particularly of social violence begin to evolve in the Tamburlaine plays. Vouching for the fearless mind, the hero is withered by his own brutality, in a story which pertains to violent Europe and England as well. We are never quite sure that the catastrophic past (in Marlowe's outlook) has settled into oblivion, or exists to shape events in the future. So Orcanes, when he alludes to filling the Danube with 'slaughtered bodies of these Christians', implicitly evokes corpses in the Seine after the St Barthomew massacres of 1572. 'Cleave his pericranion with thy sword', says the hero with an echo of Becket's heroic death at Canterbury. (Even Becket's murder is not 'past' for the poet, who was fascinated by the killing of priests, and also by churchmen who had directed French violence in the episodes to be taken up in *The Massacre at Paris*.) In Act V, Tamburlaine's order to kill every man, woman, and child at Babylon reflects the fate of the Dutch town of Naarden in the poet's own youth.[23]

Marlowe is sensitive to gender, though his females close their lips when religion is at issue. In Part One, he had used Zenocrate as a choric voice; but, in the sequel, she comes alive in her apt, worried protests over the Tartar's warlike talk to their three sons:

> My lord, such speeches to our princely sons
> Dismay their minds before they come to prove
> The wounding troubles angry war affords.[24]

By idealizing her, the hero has isolated her speech and mind. In Part Two, she inspires him a good deal less than his power-hungry allies and lieutenants who live without women, unlike his soldiers who rape in the conquered cities. Tamburlaine must still preserve the image of what he is trying to be, and so he discusses his role and keeps himself on show. His militancy may suggest that Tartar wives must toe the line, or have their heads chopped off, but he is skewed out of his wits by Zenocrate's death. Since she has not commented on his false view of himself as God's scourge, she may unwittingly have validated his religious conceit.

Marlowe evokes four or five different religions in this play. His Christian king is a perjurer; but Muslims and Jews appear to be valiant. At one point, the Jews send 60,000 fighting men to defend their Muslim neighbours. Also it is left to a Muslim to refer to a transcendent God who reflects the deity of the Koran and Calvin alike. 'Open thou shining vail of *Cynthia*', Orcanes prays when looking for divine justice against Sigismund,

> And make a passage from the imperial Heaven
> That he that sits on high and never sleeps,
> Nor in one place is circumscriptible,
> But everywhere fills every continent,
> With strange infusion of his sacred vigour
> May in his endless power and purity
> Behold and venge this traitor's perjury.[25]

This God is not circumscriptible, not subject to the limits of space. Saint Augustine's '*Deus* ... *solus incircumscriptus*' must have been in Marlowe's mind when he wrote the speech. He could have recalled the words as quoted in John Proctor's *Fall of the Late Arrian*, a copy of which had been on Gresshop's shelf.[26] Both Tamburlaine plays expose convenient, self-authorizing assumptions about God, without necessarily impugning any creed. The hero is portrayed at times as if he were Herculean, but when he harnesses the kings of Trebizon and Soria with bits in the mouth to pull his chariot in Act IV, he is farcical. There is nothing especially deific or heroic in his silly, triumphant cry, easily parodied in the aftermath of the play:

> Holla, ye pampered Jades of Asia!
> What, can ye draw but twenty miles a day . . .[27]

One might imagine the quick ruin of a soldier who indulges in trivial, time-wasting pursuits on the march, but Tamburlaine is victorious to the last breath. One of the play's shocking aspects, for generations living after the Holocaust, is that there is no final scene of a maniac in his bunker, no retribution, or sense that a leader of killers has anything to apologize for. Neither is there an apology *for* him, in a drama which attempts to depict the historic Tartar in depth, as he was in life. In the end, Tamburlaine calls for a map to savour his vast conquests, and dies after acknowledging 'necessity'.

Elizabethan audiences, weary of didactic plays, thrilled over him without racking their brains to decide if he were moral or not. Machiavelli had admired the real Tamburlaine, and Marlowe has fully credited the hero's practical ability, despite evidence of Timur's manic fury, as in Paolo Giovio's account (copies of Giovio's works were in Cambridge's library). The general reception of the second *Tamburlaine* appears to have been no less enthusiastic than that for the first. One wit noted that the Tartar 'ravishes the gazing Scaffolders', and yet Marlowe's friend Nashe later compared Tamburlaine with Christ. When the two plays toured in Shropshire, little boys were christened with the Muslim hero's name, which turned out luckily for some. Later on, Tamberlaine Davies (1620–85) rose to be High Bailiff of Ludlow, and his fellow mercer Tamberlane Bowdler, born in October 1620, also became prominent. The name alluringly lived on, and one Tamburlaine Davies—baptized in 1695, or more than a century after the poet died—left assets of £854. 14s. 4d., as if he had found the rank-scorning hero a good model to emulate.[28]

Years earlier, Philip Henslowe of the Rose had noted a 'Tamberlyne bridel', and some gorgeous costumes Alleyn must have worn for revivals of the Tamburlaine plays from October 1594 to April 1595, before audiences as large as 2,000. One staging of an Admiral's men's play had been criminally negligent. On 16 November 1587, Philip Gawdy reported in a letter to his father that an actor in an Admiral's production had been tied to a post, to be shot at. Unluckily, the caliver taken on stage was loaded. When the assailant's hand swerved, he missed the fellow he aimed at, and 'killed a child, and a woman great with child forthwith, and hurt another man in the head very sore'.[29]

This may have occurred in the last act of Part Two, in which Babylon's Governor is hung up on chains and then shot at by Theridamas, Tamburlaine, and others. The play involved is still unknown, but the Admiral's group barely escaped ruin and disappeared from record until well into 1588.

By then, Marlowe had come under fire of a different kind. If his success boosted the self-confidence of a few poets, one of them was not so pleased. This was Robert Greene, formerly down from Clare Hall with two degrees, several prose romances, and a fluent pen. His red beard, brisk talk, and servile cronies were known in the alehouses. He imitated *Tamburlaine* so ineptly in his first play *Alphonsus King of Aragon* that it failed, and with jealous irritability he blamed Marlowe and began to traduce him. Greene's attacks are allusive enough to trouble interpreters today, but they can be fun to examine. Lately, 'two Gentleman Poets' had mocked one of his dramas—it seems the woeful *Alphonsus*—as he admits in an epistle for *Perimedes the Blacksmith* (licensed 29 March 1588). This pair of critics

had it in derision, for that I could not make my verses jet upon the stage in tragicall buskins, everie worde filling the mouth like the faburden of Bo-Bell, daring God out of Heaven with that Atheist *Tamburlan*, or blaspheming with the mad *priest* of the sonne: but let me rather openly pocket up the Asse at *Diogenes* hand, [rather] th*a*n wantonlye set out such impious instances of intollerable poetrie, such mad and scoffing poets, that have propheticall spirits as bred of *Merlins* race, if there be anye in England that set the end of scollarisme in an English blanck verse, I thinke either it is the humor of a novice that tickles them with selfe-love, or so much frequenting the hot house . . .[30]

Greene uses tags culled from the classics, or from some of the 12,000 English proverbs then in daily use—a rich store for dramatists. Here, perhaps, Christopher Marlowe ('Marlen' back at Cambridge), whose name links him with the faithless, magical race of Merlin, uses blank verse to blaspheme with the demented, atheistical Bruno ('mad priest of the sun'). Since Tamburlaine's own atheism does not bring him to grief, his creator must be godless. The phrase 'daring God out of Heaven' may refer to the last act of 2 *Tamburlaine* (ll. 42–5), in which the hero insolently dares Mahomet to drop down and work a miracle.

Greene did not stop with a charge of atheism, though that was the most invidious and dangerous of his smears. Unable to reach a wide mass of playgoers, he tried to make Marlowe seem pretentious, absurd, and conceitedly ambitious chiefly to a group of educated fellow wits. Hence his recondite, teasing manner served well, and he probably kept up a refined fire each year until he died. In *Menaphon*, licensed 23 August 1589, he calls a shallow love passage a 'Canterbury tale' which, he adds, is told by 'a prophetical full mouth that as he were a Cobbler's eldest sonne'. That could be a slur against Marlowe, unless Greene, who hated actors, is thinking of some invective against the comedian Tarlton printed a few months later in *The Cobbler of Canterbury* (a linked series of tales by an unknown author, who does not target Marlowe). But, clearly, in *Francesco's Fortunes* of 1590, the tormentor turns on Alleyn as 'Roscius', and on the 'Cobbler' (Marlowe) who supplies a vain actor with star roles: 'Why *Roscius*, art thou proud with Esops Crow', inquires Greene, 'and if the Cobbler hath taught thee to say *Ave Caesar*, disdain not thy tutor because thou pratest in a King's Chamber'. The double insult applies to Alleyn speaking Tamburlaine's lines (*1 Tamb.* III. iii): 'My camp is like to Julius Caesar's host, | That never fought but had the victory.' Next, in *Farewell to Folly* of 1591, Greene implies that the first edition of *Tamburlaine*, printed the year before, has sold so badly that its 'unsavoury papers' are fit to wrap up a peddler's smelly powders. Finally, he deals with Shakespeare and Marlowe at a swoop in the most polished of his assaults, *Greenes Groats-worth of Witte*.[31]

The two parts of *Tamburlaine* were licensed as 'twooe commical discourses' on 14 August 1590, but were published together that same year in black-letter octavo as 'two Tragicall Discourses', that were 'sundry times shewed upon Stages in the Citie of London | By the right honorable the Lord Admyrall, his servantes'. Marlowe's name does not appear in the volume. Its ostensible printer, Richard Jones (who may have been Thomas Orwin), claims in an epistle for gentlemanly readers that he has excluded poor, feeble, comic passages from the two plays about the Tartar, some fond and frivolous *G*estures, digressing (and in my poore opinion) far unmeet for the matter, which I thought, might seeme more tedious unto the wise, than any way els*e* to be regarded, though (happ*i*ly) they have been of some vaine conceited fondlings greatly gaped at, what times they were shewed upon the stage . . .[32]

Jones protests a little too much here. We know that he had to print from a non-theatrical manuscript (the author's own or a good copy), so, in his apology, he may invent an excuse for not including popular material added in the theatre, which he could not use because he lacked it. That is Fredson Bowers's explanation of the 'epistle', but the matter is still unresolved. Jones could have tailored the two dramas to appeal to an upmarket clientele, of course, although few printers in London (in their right mind) would have deleted anything that had done well on a stage.

In any case, once Jones's volume was in print, other playwrights climbed aboard Marlowe's rolling bandwagon, or tried to overturn it. The anonymous *Troublesome Reign of King John*, a Queen's men's drama printed the next year in a two-part format by 'T. Orwin', told audiences that they would do better to applaud a Christian king than a foreign infidel such as Tamburlaine. Imitative works such as the anonymous *Selimus*, or George Peele's *Edward I* and his later *Alcazar*, or Charles Tilney's *Elstrild*—quickly rewritten heroically as *Locrine*—swelled the Tamburlaine phenomenon, and the imitations gave added strength to the charge that he had celebrated an atheist. Lyly's plays faded in a wave of patriotism after the defeat of the Spanish Armada, even though *The Woman in the Moon*, his only comedy in verse, and the only one he wrote for men, not boys, had a twilight success in the early 1590s. Times changed, but the public flocked to the theatres, and Marlowe began to be noticed by a new actor-poet, of some unusual energy, humour, and talent, down from Warwickshire in the Midlands.

Shakespeare of Stratford

At Shoreditch, the jutting, far-overhanging storeys of shops often broke off the sunlight so that, on a good day, the lanes were in shadow. This was a crowded area at all times. As night fell, the area's lurid life became evident in the light of tallow candles, or low hearth fires. The theatres drew clientele north to this locale—and young actors were glad to find cheap rooms about 500 yards from the Theatre or Curtain. In the streets beggars and men from Oxford, Cambridge, or the counties might rub shoulders. By 1589 or 1590 at the latest, Shakespeare reached Shoreditch and remained there during some of his apprentice days in the theatre. Marlowe, at this time, lived in the adjacent liberty of Norton Folgate, just north of the capital's walls.

Both suburbs were served by the major artery of Bishopsgate Street, which connected one prime locale of taverns with another. Often located above a shop, a tavern was a place 'where men are drunk with more credit and apology' than at an alehouse, as John Earle put it, but legal sessions were held in taverns, as in 1589 at the Castle in St John's Street.[33] Also troupes met *en masse* at taverns to decide whether to accept or reject a script. When Drayton, Dekker, and Chettle's play *The Famous Wars of Henry I* was recited at the Sun in New Fish Street, the impresario Henslowe lent money for the wine, as he did later for a play called *Jephthah*. An Act of 1553 had allowed London only forty taverns, but many had at least ten rooms. One entered to find drinking booths, and walked up one or two flights to panelled rooms with trestles, arrays of pots, and barrels of Rhenish or Bordeaux.

Food could be served, and a poet who wrote for a troupe might join its members. Ben Jonson later dined with actors once a fortnight, and Marlowe would have seen Shakespeare at a play-reading or a supper.[34] Few meetings between Elizabethan poets are on record, but the theatre's circles were tiny. Actors and poets nodded to each other in the lanes. Even in a tavern, however, there were invisible barriers—matters of rank, affiliation, status—which kept men apart. A good deal would have divided a common, Stratford-born player from a Cambridge trained, elite writer. Probably at first, Marlowe viewed Shakespeare with cool indifference.

Did they meet often? Or become intimate? Plainly, no record of their talk together survives. No obscure diary tells us of their meetings, though shreds of the truth can be discovered if we are willing to be patient, indirect, or somewhat roundabout in assessing Marlowe's friendship with his prime contemporary. In this very small theatrical community, Shakespeare and Marlowe saw each other dozens of times, in an evolving relationship between 1590 and 1593, though the fact that no camera, no pen, no talkative host of the 'Four Swans' records their exchanges, is daunting. Even so, I want to offer a kind of circular report, a tentative

19 The galleried 'Four Swans' inn, known to Elizabethan actors

approach to the most fascinating of all relationships in Marlowe's working life. This matter is extremely delicate, since it leaves us always at the edge of the unknown.

Sooner or later, Marlowe became curious about the man from Stratford. What was there to learn about him? We know that John Aubrey, talking with William Beeston not long before he died, heard that Shakespeare had been a 'schoolmaster in the country' and that he had been cautious while living at Shoreditch. As Mark Eccles points out, this testimony should be accurate, since Beeston's family had been at St Leonard's, Shoreditch late in the sixteenth century. His father had acted with Shakespeare after being a servant to Augustine Phillips, who left a bequest to the Stratford poet. Beeston the younger duly inherited his own parent's Shoreditch property, which included 'a lease of part of the Curtain estate and the freehold of the King's Head Yard, north of Hog Lane'.[35]

Thus Aubrey's informant belonged to one of the suburb's well-established acting families, one of whose members had close daily associations with Shakespeare. In Marlowe's time, another theatrical family nearby took a most particular interest in the actor-poet from Stratford. Here again, we can be quite factual. Between 1574 and 1576, the robust, sometimes feisty James Burbage had settled at Holywell Street in Shoreditch. He and his sons Cuthbert and Richard, baptized at St Stephen Coleman Street on 15 June 1565 and 7 July 1568, were at Holywell Street when Marlowe was at Norton Folgate.[36]

Though Shakespeare did not seek out company he was well liked by his fellows—agile and hectically busy. On stage, he may have taken up to a hundred brief roles in a season. Greene called him a 'Johannes factotum', or one who both wrote and acted, but Stratford's poet also found time to talk and listen (as he did with the difficult Jonson). To be sure, Marlowe's two Cambridge degrees set him apart as a gentleman, but he had a habit of seeking out fellow poets such as Watson or Daniel, and later shared a room with the playwright Kyd, who, like Shakespeare, had not been trained beyond grammar school. *Tamburlaine*'s fame had imparted a certain status, though the publication of two works, without his name, did not mark him out as awesome or unapproachable (normally, publication reduced a play's value). Like his rival, he wrote to supply a group, and met with other suppliers. However, whereas Marlowe was outspoken and eager, ironic or challenging, Shakespeare appears to have been prudently guarded. 'Mr Beeston . . . knows most of him from Mr Lacy', Aubrey later scribbled, when tracking the man of Avon: he was 'the more to be admired' since 'he was not a company

20 Shakespeare of Stratford, from Ozias Humphrey's drawing in 1783,
based on the Chandos portrait

keeper'. He 'wouldnt be debauched, & if invited to *be*, writ *that* he was
in paine'.[37]

This defensiveness was Shakespeare's light armour to protect himself
against time-wasting evenings, but if he pleaded the toothache to avoid
carousing, by day he was likely to be inquisitive about the author of *The*

Jew of Malta. He knew that play intimately—it was not in print—years before conjuring up Shylock, and his allusions to Marlowe seem to include an alehouse joke as early as *Venus and Adonis.* Mutual curiosity would have broken down walls, and Shakespeare was to recall the poet of *Hero and Leander,* in a warm, close tribute of a kind he paid to no other contemporary, by quoting a line of Marlowe's ('Whoever loved that loved not at first sight?') in *As You Like It.* Poetry was a common bond, and Shakespeare talked freely about his interests (as seems clear from Jonson's remark about his 'open' manner), even if his odd tones set him apart. His accent was, no doubt, that of Stratford in the Midlands, where the Henley Street of his birth was pronounced 'Heanley', as William Dugdale noted with despair. In the pamphlet in which Shakespeare is attacked as an Upstart Crow, Greene describes a country author whose 'voice is nothing gratious'. Interestingly, the rumoured roles of Shakespeare were those of old men—King Hamlet's Ghost, or the octogenarian Adam of *As You Like It.* In contrast, Marlowe had grown up with the clipped tones of Kent, which had already contracted 'Medweys Towne' to Maidstone, or lazily changed 'Eglesford' to Aylesford.[38]

Differences in tone or rank could melt at a play-vetting, and other threads had begun to knit theatre poets together, and even to set Marlowe and Shakespeare in a group apart. Writers cared about rivalry, parody, satire, company loyalty, and box-office receipts, but few were out to cut throats. There was a kind of cheerful, well-tolerated mutual robbery from 1587 into the 1590s. Not merely the hacks but good poets lifted one another's poetic images, conceits, lines, and stanzas as deftly as pick-pockets. Playwrights also imitated each other's main ideas, as Greene had tried to do in *Alphonsus.* Marlowe borrows a whole stanza from Book 1 of Spenser's *Fairie Queene* (starring 'Like to an Almond tree ymounted high') for *Tamburlaine,* and he would have found Shakespeare's strategies as a literary borrower amusing, perhaps, in light of that poet's tact in daily life.[39]

That tact was remarkable. Marlowe did not hear the following examples of Shakespeare's speech—but they tell us about a poet who surely chatted at Burbage's Theatre as often as Marlowe did. A little later, for example, it happened one day that Shakespeare was asked by Sir George Buc, who eventually became Master of the Revels, to name the author of *George a Greene.* This comedy—about a pinner or impounder of stray beasts—refers to 'martial Tamburlaine', but it has an odd love-plot which requires a grown man to wear female clothes. *George a Greene* was written by 'a minister', Shakespeare testified urbanely, 'who act*ed* the pinner's p*art* in it himself'.[40] If that saved a fellow author from trouble, on a later occasion when asked to testify in the court case of *Belott v. Mount-joy* Stratford's poet balanced his replies so well that neither the plantiff's nor the defendant's case was affected. Some of Shakespeare's talk may have been blandly factual, but he marshalled details rapidly in a crisis, as when he calmed the nerves of a worried official when asked in London about a party of aggressive or ruthless Stratford land-developers (whom he slightly favoured). 'They meant', he said, 'to enclose no further than to Gospel Bush, and so up straight, leaving out part of the Dingles to the Field, to the gate in Clopton Hedge and take in Salisbury's piece.'[41]

These are very approximate, banal survivals of his talk (though they show a restraint that contrasts with Marlowe's rashness), and the last example reminds one of the rapidity and fluency he was bringing to his work by 1590. It is not that Shakespeare's style is rapid, but that his mind works swiftly, and affects even his habits of theatrical borrowing. His early history works, including the *Henry VI* trilogy and *Richard III*, for example, appear to lift about two dozen verbal phrases from the Tamburlaine plays, and I expect more echoes are to be found. Marlowe could not have resented such thievery, nor would writers have felt that a drama, once in print, was not a larder for anybody's use. The Stratford poet's borrowings are minor, and the borrower changes what he takes. Thus Marlowe's phrase 'dreaming prophecies' (*1 Tamb.*, I. i. 41) becomes Shakespeare's 'prophecies and dreams' (*Richard III*, I. i. 54); or Marlowe's 'sweet fruition of an earthly crown' (*1 Tamb.*, II. vii. 29) is changed to 'How sweet a thing it is to wear a crown' (*3 Henry VI*, I. ii. 29); or again Marlowe's 'all the wealthy kingdoms I subdued' (*2 Tamb.*, I. iii. 19) is echoed in 'all the wealthy kingdoms of the west' (*2 Henry VI*, I. ii. 153). There is no need to multiply trivial examples, though Shakespeare also borrows more broadly, I think, as in *1 Henry VI*, in which a Marlovian treatment of the 'scourge' infects what is said of Talbot and Joan la Pucelle.

What was more important for Shakespeare is that Marlowe's *Tamburlaine* and *Faustus* faced backwards and forwards; they assimilated the powerful emblematic methods of morality plays, or the theatrical tradition which David Bevington examines in *From 'Mankind' to Marlowe*, but these tragedies also leapt ahead of their time. Marlowe, one suspects, took Shakespeare's minor borrowings as a compliment. No doubt, he noticed something else. His tragedies began to teach Shakespeare major new psychological techniques. Marlowe, after all, suggested how to isolate, analyse, and broadcast the feelings of a Faustus, Barabas, or Guise, how to let that hero 'speak past' interlocutors, how to dramatize an intriguing, aberrant psyche and get a mind to lend its tone to a drama. The teacher became a pupil, they switched roles back and forth, and up to the year in which both turned 29, neither really was the better artist, despite Marlowe's innovations in tragic form. Neither found out more about dramaturgy, theatrical spectacle, or the blank-verse medium; neither was more experimental, challenging, lyrical, or in some way more humane than the other. The idea that Marlowe was only a herald, a forerunner of a matchless Swan of Avon arose from our blinkered sense of the London stage. For at least two or three years, with equivalent artistry, the two poets were hard-working, originating contemporary rivals, in some ways alike, but far more importantly unalike and on different paths. Their dynamic relationship was a basis of the greatest flourishing of the English theatre. Lyly, Peele, Greene, and especially Kyd were involved, but the boldest innovations in dramaturgy were those of Shakespeare and Marlowe. There was no slackening in the quality of their discoveries about play structure, theme, story, or the possibilities of staging. Indeed, they kept pace with each other for as long as Marlowe lived. Shakespeare knew of that artful equivalence, and used Marlowe's precedents as late as *Antony and Cleopatra*. His verse style is never the same as Marlowe's, except in deliberate echo or parody, and the parody usually becomes a compliment, as in Pistol's lines in 2 *Henry IV*,

> Shall pack-horses
> And hollow pampered jades of Asia
> Which cannot go but thirty mile a day,
> Compare with Caesar and with cannibals
> And Trojan Greeks?[42]

The point is that this is inept parody—Pistol fudges every style he mimicks, and Marlowe's 'Jades of Asia' hardly suffers from the attention.

A nearly collusive relationship between the two dramatists, starting around 1590, really ensured that *Tamburlaine*'s revolution in form and significant ideas would not die out. Much depended on a fresh attitude to creativity itself, and it was Marlowe who most encouraged Shakespeare to bring stateliness and a high poetic habit to the drama. Both writers pressed material to extremes and risked absurdity in exploring new patterns of feeling, as Shakespeare does, not quite slavishly, when borrowing from the speeches of Ithamore in Marlowe's *Malta* for the Moorish Aaron of *Titus Andronicus*.

Both, too, were practical enough to see that stage innovations were necessary to attract the idle, moneyed gentry at the Inns of Court and Chantry, whose own enthusiasm could affect the mercantile ranks. Even in *Dido*, Marlowe had changed tack in mid-scene, mixed humour with pathos, and tried out flexible options. His aim, at least partly, was to plumb his sources well enough to try out flexible tactics for works ahead, while crediting likelihood and psychological reality. In *Tamburlaine*, he had boldly exploited the emotions of an audience without veering into the improbable. Similarly, in the tense confrontations of his *Henry VI* trilogy, Shakespeare has an eye on what is normal in human nature. Placing a weak King Henry at the centre of his sequence, he depicts the feuds of competing nobles who circle round his idle, ineffectual monarch. He looks below the level of ideology to evoke an audience's sympathy and repulsion, and without indulging in excessive detail concerns himself with loyalty and disloyalty, fidelity and subterfuge, ignorance and machination, patriotism and betrayal. That exploration of scenic and thematic strategies was encouraged by his chief rival, and their artistic relationship had open-ended possibilities for both. Marlowe had much to gain from a seemingly tireless actor down from Stratford who 'wouldnt be debauched'.

At the moment—in 1590—Shakespeare had less artistry to show than his rival. He may not have expected to learn from Marlowe's talk, or from the bright radiance and collateral light of his dress. But Marlowe, in a theatrical sense, had changed everything. He had transformed the mere 'jigging veins' of the national literature. Nashe, in his *Pierce Penilesse* of 1592, commented obliquely but justly on the result. Audiences had been lifted above the commercialism of banal comedies and shown a grander, finer, more intelligent 'Scene', one 'more stately furnished' and not consisting 'of a Pantaloon, a Whore, and a Zany, but of Emperors, Kings, and Princes, whose true tragedies (*Sophocleo cothurno*) they do vaunt'. He meant, by 'Sophocleo cothurno', that the elegant, symbolic Greek shoe or boot of Sophoclean tragedy had come to the Elizabethan stage.[43]

Marlowe had done more than anyone else to lift the theatre to that level. In *Tamburlaine* he had begun to free tragedy from its old inter-pretative frames, and create finely opposing views of character and event. Rather than display a hero as 'good' or 'bad', he explored aspects of motive and psychological metamorphosis which elude narrow judgement. Even Tamburlaine's portrayal opens a way much later for Hamlet or Lear, and it may be a conscious tribute that Shakespeare, at the outset of *King Lear*, has the vain, enraged king allude to an aspect of Marlowe's Tartar hero in likening Cordelia to 'the barbarous Scythian'.[44]

The extreme haste and endless, taxing round of duties in repertory theatre could be exhausting. Energies were stretched to the limit, and one's social circle had to consist mainly of co-workers. Burbage's hive-like Theatre drew in actors like bees, and no doubt Shakespeare took part in morning rehearsals. But how often did he detach himself from this buzz? The relationship between the two poets was anything but static (as I hope we shall see); but, until about 1592, Marlowe's intimacy with Shakespeare was impersonal, abstract, unreal, superficially theatrical, a matter of grudging rivalry or mild envy, but probably chiefly one of cool nods and banality. Shakespeare borrowed from *Tamburlaine* more than he gave back to Marlowe, and the case of early indebtedness is all too one-sided. The Stratford poet did little, at first, to advance the art of tragedy, and less to make comedy a vehicle for ideas. Nauseatingly self-protective, he had fingers in everyone else's porridge. Shakespeare's robbery looks harmless or pardonable, except that he deftly took what he could use in limitless thievery, while sequestering himself in blandness. He offended almost no one but Jonson and, more sharply, Greene, who in his bitter anecdote of the thrifty Ant and spendthrift Grasshopper in his *Groats-worth* implies that Shakespeare is an 'olde acquaintance' whose parsimony and indifference he has known for some time.[45]

Whatever else divided them, Shakespeare's busy, politic defensiveness and attachment to actors were real barriers, at least at first. There is no sign that Marlowe quickly developed a close friendship with this grammar-school rival. None of Shakespeare's early heroes has an intellect comparable even to that of the wayward Faustus. Further, there was a painful lack of self-analysis in this rival's early personae, and nearly a denial that feeling can have anything to do with intelligence. Still Marlowe may, at last, have sensed that Shakespeare was detached from the actors he served.

Both men supplied the theatre by defying official restraints upon it, and worked under threats of plague, rioting, Puritan indignation, or the animosity of Guildhall's mayors. A script-writer who took the chaotic theatre too seriously might have been defeated by it, and neither Kyd nor Greene was as disposed to irony, jokes, and self-satire as their two rivals. Shakespeare among his fellow actors blended stoically into the maelstrom. Marlowe kept himself slightly aloof from the mania of the entertainment industry. Both poets were bringing a wealth of metaphor and new structures to the popular stage, and yet, after all, they had to appeal in part to a dull-brained mass who shouted and stamped in theatre yards. Sidney and Spenser did not betray the vocation of poetry, whereas theatre poets often grovelled to please. Marlowe, at least, took immense pains with his work, and clearly had a sense of himself as a Cambridge poet and scholar who believed, as Ovid did, in the transforming power of intense emotion in art. There is no sign that he was indifferent to the quickly produced scripts of his Stratford rival. He was to learn from Shakespeare's new, supple techniques in exploiting the sources of English history, but he had other rich material at hand. He had perhaps no immediate need for a man of Stratford who occupied himself almost as a Jack-of-all-trades in a troupe, but made himself scantily available to others, while producing exceptional scripts. Marlowe, in any case, was singularly free of jealousy, and not unaware of his own resources. Lately, he had drawn on his days at university to create a great modern myth.

7

Doctor Faustus

Thou talk'st of Christ, contrary to thy promise.
Thou shouldst not think of God. Think of the devil,
And of his dame, too.

(Lucifer)

Heaven and Hell

O N hot summer days in crowded Shoreditch, the difference between sweaty actors and poets in the alleys was not great. Rehearsals and performances filled the day, and the entertainment industry was a hungry demon. An actor who wrote scripts—such as Shakespeare—was hard-worked, and Marlowe followed up his own chances by writing new tragedies. Good tragedies were rare—few poets ventured into that genre—and as we have seen, an acquaintance between himself and Shakespeare became a stimulus for both writers.

The Tamburlaine plays had helped to form taste, and the gentry who came up to the Curtain or Theatre expected intelligence—some unusual *frisson* or intrigue in exchange for what they paid for cushioned seats in a gallery. Shakespeare, by 1590, had begun to look into the scandals of English history in *Henry VI*, and Marlowe, more daringly, in *Doctor Faustus* had set a precedent in delving into religion.

A change for the theatre had been in the air since the death of the Queen's men's popular comic actor Richard Tarlton back in 1588. He had faded slowly. On his deathbed, he had written a beseeching letter to Marlowe's former employer, the spymaster Francis Walsingham, to complain that a crafty 'sly fellow' named Adams was trying to bilk him of his estate and so deprive his elderly mother and son, 'a sillie old widdow of fourscore years of age and a pore infant of the age of six yeares', as the dying comedian put it. Whether or not Walsingham tried to help, he no doubt noted the circumstances: he took an interest in the fate and foibles of theatre men, and the success of the Tamburlaine plays was hardly lost on him. At any rate, Tarlton had died in the house of 'one Em Ball in Shordiche'[1]—possibly the same Em Ball who became the poet Robert Greene's mistress—and the theatre world had grieved. But if it seemed that comic ingenuity suddenly died with Tarlton, Marlowe lifted the genre of comedy to a new level in *Doctor Faustus*, which combined slapstick farce and tragedy with new and terrifying effects.

A good deal about the early performances of this play is lost to us, and the popularity of *Faustus* has had the odd effect of diluting Marlowe's writing with revisions made, sometimes long after the piece was first staged, by other authors. It is fairly clear, however, that he finished a whole playscript without help, though his comic scenes are likely to have been altered by revisers.

He appears to have found the topic of Faustus at Cambridge. Few intellectual enthusiasms in the colleges had been better known than those of the outspoken, laughingly satirized, but well-read Gabriel Harvey, whose marginal notes in A. P. Gasser's world history, *Historiarum*, on a legendary German magician, suggest that the career of 'Joannes Faustius' was talked about in the halls. Half a century earlier in Germany, stories about magic had gathered around a Georgius of Helmstadt who studied at Heidelberg between 1483 and 1489, though it is equally possible that the real Faust was born at Knittlingen, a few miles north of Pforzheim in the county—later the Duchy—of Württemberg, and never had any formal university training. What is surprising, in view of our meagre facts about him, is Faust's notoriety in his lifetime. It seems reasonably certain that he became a schoolmaster at Kreuznach in 1507, but fled when accused of pederasty. In one German source, he appears as 'Georgius Faustus, Helmitheus Hedelbergensis' at Erfurt in 1513, a few years before he was paid to cast a horoscope for the bishop of Bamberg. Pederasty, almost as much as black magic, led to his infamy. At Nuremberg, he was called 'the great sodomite and nigromancer', and others described him as 'a stinking privy of the devil', or a lewd scamp, glutton, and drunkard who lived from quackery. According to the *Zimmerische Chronik*, he died mysteriously and perhaps explosively, amidst shattered glass during an

alchemical experiment, at Stauffen in around 1540. But his name
'Faustus'—meaning 'fortunate' or 'auspicious', and also 'fist'—was linked
with crude pranks and scrapes such as those associated with the comic
rogue Till Eulenspiegel, and about forty years after his death he became
known, above all, as a man whose lust for fame, riches, knowledge, and
pleasure had led him to make a pact with the devil.

Cambridge men may have read of Faustus in a Latin tract now lost,
but which, later at Frankfurt in 1587, possibly became a basis for the
famous *Faustbuch*—the *Historia von D. Johann Fausten, dem weitbesch-
reyten Zauberer und Schwartzkünstler* ('History of Dr Johann Faust, the
Notorious Magician and Necromancer').

This work's author, who strikes one as a fanatical Lutheran, turned
the legends into a kind of exemplary story about an anti-saint, relieved
by comic anecdotes or *Schwänke*. The book was later translated into
English—by a mysterious 'P.F.'—as *The History of the Damnable Life and
Deserved Death of Doctor John Faustus.*[2]

Just when Christopher Marlowe read this so-called 'English Faust
Book'—the main source for his play—is unknown. The earliest surviving
edition is of 1592, but the title page says it is 'newly printed' and
'amended'; he could well have seen a version of it in 1587 or 1588. By 1589
at the latest, his own *Doctor Faustus* appears to have been completed, since
the play had an early staging at the Bel Savage at around that time.
William Prynne later referred to

the visible apparition of the devil on the stage at the Belsavage playhouse, in
Queen Elizabeth's days, to the great amazement both of the actors and
spectators, whiles they were there playing the History of Faustus.[3]

So far as we know, the Bel Savage in the city was in use until 1588, and
possibly as late as 1589. A popular sheet called 'A ballad of the life and
deathe of Doctur Faustus the great Cunngerer', registered on 28 February
1589, seems to have responded to the play's vogue. Marlowe's *Faustus* is
also likely to have encouraged new dramas about magicians, and, thanks
to I. A. Shapiro, we can positively date one such play, Anthony Munday's
John a Kent and John a Cumber, the manuscript of which (now at the
Huntington Library) existed in 1590.[4]

All of this interestingly confirms other evidence to suggest that
Marlowe, then aged about 25, struck while his iron was hot. With *Doctor*

Faustus, he followed up *Tamburlaine*'s success when Cambridge divinity studies were fresh in his memory, but when he also had some perspective on them in London, and managed to write the first great English tragedy with strong mythic and universal qualities.

All the same, none of this takes us closer to the problem of deciding how much of *Faustus* he actually wrote and to the matter of recovering his original text. Parts of the drama, to meet special tastes, could have been changed by actors or their aides over a period of ten or twelve years after the playscript left his hands, or well before Philip Henslowe, the Rose's impresario, paid the good sum of £4 to William Birde and Samuel Rowley, on 22 November 1602, for supplying additions or 'adicyones in doctor fostes'. Moreover, it was only after these alterations that the play was printed in two different versions.

The first of these—the so-called 'A-text'—was published in quarto in 1604. A second and longer version of *Faustus*, or the so-called 'B-text', appeared in quarto in 1616. So which is the more likely to contain Marlowe's writing, if we consider that both appeared years after the play was first staged (around 1589) and after it had weathered much theatrical success and revision? 'The substantial differences between the A-text and the B-text', write two modern editors gravely, 'pose an immense problem.'[5]

Off and on, scholars have favoured one version of Marlowe's *Faustus* or the other. Fashions change, and this is all very well, but *both* the A-text and B-text include writing that cannot be Marlowe's. Both are corrupt, and both include passages that are clearly superior to those of the other text. The problem is not quite hopeless. The A-text, though short, is based for the most part on an authorial manuscript or a good copy of it, gives the better account of Marlowe's chief source, and seems in its language to influence other plays of the 1590s. Hence it is likely to contain more of his writing than the B-text.

To my mind, Leah Marcus is right to insist that 'different versions of the play carry different ideological freight'. Scholars quarrel with her conclusions, but her premise bears on Marlowe's aims. Henslowe, in calling for additions, wanted more anti-papal feeling in the play and indeed the B-text, in which the hand of Samuel Rowley, the actor and minor writer, is plainly discernible, makes Faustus an anti-Catholic hero. It adds a rival German pope called Bruno as a foil to the Italian pope,

21 Title page of the first edition of *Doctor Faustus*, 1604 (the 'A-text')

makes Faustus engage in additional pranks in disguise as a cardinal, and amounts to what Michael Keefer calls 'a general relapse from the tragic ironies of the A-version in the direction of the more grotesque features of the Faustbook'. Also, as the editors Bevington and Rasmussen say, 'the B-text trivializes the very nature of Faustus's tragic experience by its endless appetite for stage contrivance'—and in fact (with its 2,121 lines) it is longer than the A-text (of 1,517 lines) mainly because of its rather silly expansion of the hero's antics in Acts III and IV. On the whole, the A-text of 1604 does more justice to the poet's ambiguous attitude to religion, as well as to Faustus's subtle psychological portrait, and will be followed here unless otherwise indicated.[6]

It has been argued that Marlowe had a collaborator, to whom he 'farmed out' the writing of comic scenes. Those scenes are related in subtle ways to the drama's emotional pattern, but (so we are told) the collaborator 'worked with only an imprecise knowledge of what he was up to'. Nashe, Rowley, and others have been dismissed as this co-author because of their different styles, and an elaborate case for one Henry Porter of Christ's College, as Marlowe's helper, also falls flat for technical reasons. Nor, I think, is a collaborator evident from the supposed fact that *Faustus*—in the printing-house—was set from an authorial manuscript 'compiled of separate scenes'. (Marlowe's papers may have been rearranged, partly crossed out, or recopied more than once betwen 1589 and 1604. How can we tell how much of his original handwriting was left, on *any* sheet, by the latter date?) There is no reason to think he needed help in penning scenes of horseplay. To believe he did, as James Shapiro notes, is to turn him 'into a tragedian incapable or uninterested in writing comic material. Even the briefest glance at *The Jew of Malta* would show how shortsighted such a view is.'[7]

Even so, *Doctor Faustus* begins in high seriousness and offers troubling problems which can lead one to question its author's outlook and artistic control. The sheer intensity of Marlowe's writing owes much to his drawing on recent experience and finding ways to distance himself from his feelings and transmute them. He is impulsive and censorious, believing in himself but in the stage even more, and devoted to a concise, objective art. As with Tamburlaine, he advertises himself in a prologue— which becomes a 'Chorus'. Here, he evokes a little list of dramatic topics or plays before turning to the German Faustus.

Is the first play he alludes to in the first two lines below one of his own?

> Not marching now in fields of Trasimene
> Where Mars did mate the Carthaginians,
> Nor sporting in the dalliance of love
> In courts of kings where state is overturned,
> Nor in the pomp of proud audacious deeds,
> Intends our muse to vaunt his heavenly verse.[8]

All this is very grand. In fact, no drama about the 'fields of Trasimene', the Italian battlefield near Lake Trasimeno where Hannibal defeated a Roman army in 217 BC, now exists. The allusion could be to a lost work, or to one Marlowe *thinks* of writing; but the lines about a 'dalliance of love' suggest his *Dido*, and those about 'proud audacious deeds' point back to *Tamburlaine*.

A brief biography of Faustus next relates that this scholar excelled over all his fellows in academic disputes on 'theology'. He was no dunce, certainly. But unlike the impartial prologue of *Tamburlaine*, the Chorus is not neutral about behaviour. Swollen with self-conceit, the hero wickedly mounted above his reach, became glutted with learning, fell into a devilish exercise with magic, and forgot his 'chiefest bliss'. Far from crediting the theatre as a place of new experience that we are to evaluate for ourselves, as in *Tamburlaine*, Marlowe's speaker appears to pre-judge what is to unfold. Faustus was despicable in defying God and unwise in losing his chief bliss. But in offering that sane, orthodox verdict, the Chorus invites us to judge our normal ideas about God's order, and to question the premises of our lives.

Much depends on what we think of Faustus, as he sits alone with books in Act I. The Chorus warns us not to expect to hear of kings or conquerors, but of an individual who awaits his fate, whether 'good' or 'bad'.

The trouble is that in his opening monologue he seems to create his fate—with a good deal of headlong rashness and impudence if not forgetfulness. No Cambridge freshman could fail to bridle over such a theologian's mangling of Scripture. The Faust Book (or the *Damnable Life*) offered no clue as to how the hero intellectually came to the point of bargaining away his soul, and critics—with some reason—wonder over Faustus's blunders. His scholarship looks shoddy. He misrepresents learning—or at least the chief disciplines as they were at Cambridge, starting with logic or philosophy.

Like Marlowe, he enthuses over books—which give him an oddly sexual thrill when he aims to 'live and die' in Aristotle's works: 'Sweet Analytics, 'tis thou has ravished me!' Pretending to allude to Aristotle, he quotes instead from the French philosopher Ramus (who was said to oversimplify Aristotle) and then from the sceptical sophist Gorgias.

With this verbal sleight of hand, he gets rid of one discipline after the next. After philosophy swishes down the drain, he takes only a little longer to dismiss medicine, then law. 'When all is done', he seems to conclude, 'divinity is best.'

Here he is especially outrageous. He quotes twice from Scripture, but leaves out the crucial second parts of both biblical texts. 'The reward of sin is death. That's hard', Faustus reasons.

> If we say we have no sin,
> We deceive ourselves, and there's no truth in us.
> Why then belike we must sin,
> And so consequently die.
> Ay, we must die an everlasting death.
> What doctrine call you this, *Che serà, serà,*
> What will be, shall be? Divinity adieu![9]

In the Geneva Bible, the full text of Romans 6: 23 is:

For the wages of sin is death: *but the gift of God is eternal life through Jesus Christ our Lord,*

and that of 1 John 1: 8–9, is:

If we say we have no sin, we deceive ourselves, and the truth is not in us. *If we acknowledge our sins, he is faithful and just, to forgive us our sins, and to cleanse us from all unrighteousness.*

Why does Faustus leave out the Christian promise?

Whatever else he is, he is no careless fool. As a bright theologian and Protestant divine, he may be deliberately portrayed by Marlowe in a severe Calvinist light as a person who cannot obey God's Word, even though he is apprised of it. Possibly, according to P. R. Sellin, he has little freedom of choice. Calvin, in the *Institutes*, speaks of the Lord sending 'his Word to many whose blindness he intends to increase'—and who will

The Tragicall Hiſtory of the Life and Death

of *Doctor Fauſtus.*

With new Additions.

VVritten by *Ch. Mar.*

LONDON,
Printed for *Iohn Wright*, and are to be ſold at his ſhop without
Newgate, at the ſigne of the Bible. 1619.

22 Title page of the quarto of *Doctor Faustus* in 1619. This is the first
edition of the 'B-text' to mention 'With new Additions'

therefore be for ever lost. Moreover, the divine will is not to be questioned: 'God in His own nature and majesty is to be left alone', says Luther, and Calvin takes a step further in holding that the processes of God's will are closed to us and it is only blasphemous to try to lay them bare. So Faustus may be predestined to damnation before he speaks, and wicked to criticize or niggle over Scripture in any case.[10]

But then Marlowe is writing a play and not a theological treatise. He draws on modern Christian arguments, but without undercutting his hero by depriving him of free will. It is, I think, a mistake to assume that Luther's and Calvin's views were not openly and vigorously debated at Cambridge during Marlowe's six years at Corpus Christi. There was nothing especially hidden or 'crypto-Calvinist' in his formal training, nor does he satirize religion here. Like Shakespeare, he had begun to put a wide variety of details to use in the theatre. Still, he appears to draw specially and very interestingly on a university ambience he knows well.

For one thing, Faustus has the open, comradely manner of a Cambridge scholar in a small college—even his boredom, quickness, and lack of pedantry seem English. The Faust Book's German hero lives at an inn—half a mile from a university—where 'Students' regard him with awe and filial love. But Marlowe's hero is on equal terms with 'Scholars' who love him as fraternal colleagues, and he lives and dies in his 'study', near their adjoining rooms. He might even be at Corpus Christi College, where (at least in private) the scholars talked as they wished.

Marlowe may not have found a model for Faustus on the college's quadrangle steps, nor seen the devil near the Master's skeletal chapel, which nearly beggared Corpus—but, for six years, he had known the hopes, dreams, jokes, evasions, romantic crushes, and heresies of future clergymen. He knew Kett, later burned for what he said, and Greenwood, who was hanged by the government for what he wrote. In Cambridge's little intellectual furnace, no doubt there had been aberrations of every kind. One recalls, for example, Marlowe's wry, half-amused treatment of sexual impotence and of the lectured-to, disobedient, erect penis, under the sheets, in his smart college version of Ovid's *Amores*. But the energies and pent-up frustrations of young scholars had certainly poured into required 'disputes' on divinity. And it was this great topic, with its perils and rewards; this teasing, half-absurd, deadly serious

Queen of the Sciences; this master, divinity, which had sharpened many wits.

Faustus plans to fill the universities or 'public schools with silk, | Wherewith the students shall be bravely clad', and just as merrily quotes Ramus instead of Aristotle. But Ramus's logic—in Marlowe's time—was never put to a more moving or compelling purpose at Cambridge than in William Perkins's lectures at Great St Andrews in favour of Calvin's more severe doctrines. Perkins had raised the temper of debate, and his opponents countered in quick, simple, direct styles, of a sort Faustus uses in questioning Mephistophilis.

On the other hand, Marlowe's hero is more experienced, worldly, diverse, and hungry in his interests than the brightest college Fellow. He has 'attained the end' in philosophy, won every plaudit as a divine, cured bodies, and often defeated death. 'Are not thy bills [or prescriptions] hung up as monuments', Faustus assures himself,

> Whereby whole cities have escaped the plague
> And thousand desperate maladies been eased?[11]

What is most remarkable is that even in Act I such a meteoric man seems thoroughly human, sympathetic, far more concerned for his friends than his studies, and interested in worldly events, discussion, adventure, and living. With childish glee, he turns to magic at last, partly to see what it amounts to.

From time to time, Marlowe possibly draws on his own moods, and the hero's impatience might be that of an over-taught or over-confident young playwright at Corpus. But Faustus's casual, witty, seemingly reckless dismissal of the academic disciplines suggests a sense of having been cheated. He has seen the ends of study. What are the rewards of learning but more learning, a docile subservience, a bleak submission to the scheme of things? Magic gives power, delight, omnipotence, but above all can shatter divine mysteries since it

> Stretcheth as far as doth the mind of man,
> A sound magician is a mighty god.
> Here, Faustus, try thy brains to gain a deity.[12]

With this speech, he takes a step he never retraces: he implies that magic offers powers ascribed in the Bible (in Jeremiah 10, for example) to

God alone. A Good Angel, as if stepping in from a morality play,* warns him to desist, but an Evil Angel urges him on: 'Be thou on earth as Jove is in the sky'. Marlowe leaves us in no doubt that Faustus's pursuit of magic puts his soul in jeopardy.

But need he doom himself for ever? He summons his two preceptors in the arcane—Valdes and Cornelius—who claim to base their art on writers such as Roger Bacon, the thirteenth-century Franciscan philosopher who distinguished between legitimate magic and the evil invoking of demons. Faustus is urged to call up spirits who will appear in many guises—even as unwedded maids,

> Shadowing more beauty in their airy brows
> Than in the white breasts of the Queen of Love.

That is fairly innocent, and his instructors might be college Fellows dreaming idly of what they lack. Spirits are to bring them helpful 'Lapland giants', the world's adulation, or treasure taken from Venice, America, or sunken 'foreign wrecks'. In their random explicitness, Faustus's aims are just as weak and unfelt, as he thinks of attendants who will fetch him gold from India, dredge the sea for pearl, or enlighten him with odd facts—

> I'll have them read me strange philosophy
> And tell the secrets of all foreign kings.
> I'll have them wall all Germany with brass.[13]

One wonders if Marlowe's aims were any more focused when he became a secret agent. In *Faustus* he draws so astutely on his recent years that one feels he may not neglect his clandestine duties. Whether or not he betrayed Catholic students, he knew of other betrayers: it is indisputable that he was aware of the Walsinghams' methods. How many scholars had the Privy Council bought? There is an odd irony here, if Marlowe looks back on his crucial decision to work as an agent, and if he really pictures or parodies any of his own remembered, inchoate hopes. But even if that is valid, it would be an instance of drawing wryly on past experience—and, as a poet, he distances himself from any such wishfulness.

---

* One looks hard, I admit, to find warning or goading angels in medieval morality plays, but such emblematic devices are typical of the genre.

Left alone by fellow scholars, Faustus appears to conjure up an ugly devil, whom he bids return in the shape of a Franciscan friar, which 'suits a devil best'. That anti-Catholic joke is not surprising in a Protestant divine, but the act of summoning Mephistophilis implies a denial of God's power and very existence. Why risk Hell on the chance that the deity is a dream? Little else in the play supports atheism—what grounds does Faustus have for disbelieving in God?

'Put the case', writes Ernst Honigmann logically, 'that *one* of the super-natural beings of the Christo-Hebraic tradition incontrovertibly exists—good angel, bad angel, Lucifer—then there is an inherent likelihood that God "exists" as well.'[14] Mephistophilis himself—a hostile witness—refers to God, as well as to 'the saviour Christ', and incidentally adds that he, a devil, did not respond to Faustus's conjuring but came of his own accord when he heard the latter 'rack' God's name.

Yet again, the hero seems more than a vain fool. 'The play is irreducibly dramatic', writes C. L. Barber, who argues that Marlowe focuses upon 'blasphemy, but not with the single perspective of a religious point of view: he dramatizes blasphemy as heroic endeavour'.[15] At least that would imply Faustus is a heroic fool. Other critics have pointed to Marlowe's divinity studies and underlined what biographical evidence would sup-port—that he had an original, but also extremely rapid, well-informed mind, and had done well in Cambridge's MA course partly because he knew more than the required texts.

Faustus, moreover, shows that Marlowe has familiarized himself with occult literature. It is only a myth that John Dee (1527–1608), the ageing astrologer, magician, and royal astronomer, was a model for Doctor Faustus. Dee, at 61, had been abroad since 1583, and did not return until December 1589. He was an old St John's and Trinity College man, even a disciple of Cheke, a favourite of the queen, and often a bee in Lord Burghley's bonnet. His fame—if not his texts—could have whetted the poet's taste for Cornelius Agrippa's great *De Occulta Philosophia Libri Tres* (published in three volumes at Cologne in 1533), with its practical guides to conjuring. Faustus himself hopes to be 'as cunning as Agrippa was | Whose shadows made all Europe honour him'. That allusion recalls the phrase 'Agrippa his shadows' in Lyly's *Campaspe*. But Gareth Roberts has shown that Marlowe knew Agrippa's *De Occulta*, his *De Vanitate*, and almost certainly works such as the *Liber Quartus* (then attributed to

Agrippa) and Peter of Albano's *Magical First Principles*. As if to share his hero's experience, the poet is detailed and precise, and *Faustus* offers a technically more exact view of conjuring than any other sixteenth-century play.

It is worth pausing here over Marlowe's use of sources (other than the Faust Book), since he has looked into the bearing of occult ideas upon Christian belief. He has put himself into a seeker's mind, or pursued an intellectual voyage such as Faustus might have taken. Whether or not he had read far in Giordano Bruno, Marlowe knew something of the *Corpus Hermeticum* or writings by the supposed Egyptian seer, Hermes Trismegistus, which Bruno himself, as we have noticed, had brought to the attention of students and young poets in mid-1580s England. On the one hand, this occult tradition includes a Gnostic heresy, which denies the necessity or existence of a Supreme Being, and sees the individual as a potential demigod who is capable of embracing universal knowledge, and thus rising to divine status himself. On the other hand, writers such as Pico and Ficino, among the most influential Italian humanists, had tried to fit Hermetic viewpoints into a Christian framework. We need not imagine that Marlowe had read Pico or Ficino at the King's School (though works, in Latin, by both writers had been on Gresshop's shelves); their ideas were well known at Cambridge. Recent critics such J. S. Mebane and A. D. Nuttall interestingly suggest that Marlowe had turned from Christian interpretations to extreme Gnostic doctrines. In that case, Faustus's occult readings might explain his testy impatience with Scripture and offer a philosophical basis for his occasional denial of God. He can sound like a good Gnostic heretic when he boasts, 'A sound magician is a mighty god' ('a demigod', in the B-text).[16]

At any rate, it is clear that Hermetic ideas appealed to Marlowe, who uses many strands in the play. His hero's flexible, flitting mind is perhaps less stable (if even more bookish) than that of Shakespeare's Hamlet, who may have known less tedium at Wittenberg; but Faustus's mind is no more easily definable than that of Shakespeare's Prince. In Marlowe's tragedy, which helped to make the writing of *Hamlet* possible, there are no unmistakable 'value frames' to direct one's judgement, and no sign that one of the hero's moods or appearances is more deeply indicative than the next. Modern criticism itself suggests, above all, that *Faustus* is elusively complex and its interpretative problems inexhaustible.

The hero, for example, is less canny than the Faust Book's fairly simple protagonist, who endeavours to save his soul but trick the devil. In consequence, he is promised elegant clothes, free sex, or wonderful access to mines with 'the carbunckle, the diamond, sapphire, emerald, ruby, topaz, jacinth, garnet, jasper, amethyst'. The serving devil might be an agent for Barabas in *The Jew of Malta*.[17]

Faustus's devil, by contrast, is much less adroit in direct bribery, and frighteningly honest in admitting that he is miserable to be in Hell.

'How comes it then', asks Faustus, 'that thou art out of hell?'

'Why', replies Mephistophilis, with the strictest Calvinist orthodoxy in one of the play's most poignant speeches,

> this is hell, nor am I out of it.
> Think'st thou that I, who saw the face of God,
> And tasted the eternal joys of heaven,
> Am not tormented with ten thousand hells
> In being deprived of everlasting bliss?
> O Faustus, leave these frivolous demands,
> Which strike a terror to my fainting soul!

In his *Commentary on 1 John*, Calvin had said that if we neglect reconciliation, 'we shall always carry hell about within us', since 'hell reigns where there is no peace with God'.[18] If a devil can find that valid, why can't Faustus?

Critics frequently argue that Marlowe aims to mock belief. But there is no mockery of Calvinism here, and something other than theology or readings in the occult presses on the fabric of the play. As much as Marlowe cared for ideas, he cared even more for poetry, and it certainly appears that one of his efforts at Corpus had been to fashion a means to master tone, diction, flexibility and conciseness in English; that was one of the points of strenuous exercises in translating which led him at last to write *Dido* and *Tamburlaine*.

No problem in *Faustus* is more subtle, shifting, or difficult to assess in incremental effects than that of Marlowe's poetry. Faustus is not a poet, but he thinks as one, in the sense that he values what is sensuously apparent to his understanding, and it is this that makes him vulnerable. Beset by doubt, unsure of what he is, or of what he ought to desire most, he hungers for what is tangibly or imaginatively valid. 'Sweet Faustus', says the Good Angel in Act II, 'think of heaven and heavenly things'. But what is one to think of? Such vagueness leads the mind to so little; wickedness quickly seizes its chance:

EVIL ANGEL. No, Faustus, think of honour and wealth.
FAUSTUS. Of wealth?
   Why, the seignory of Emden shall be mine![19]

This, of course, is ironic. There is no other sign that he yearns for the lucrative governorship of Emden, a prosperous trading port on the North Sea, not that he despises power or wealth. His prize is in the image: the seignory of Emden—better than Heaven—supplies his imaginative intellect.

Since he is damned, he can be used with impunity to criticize God's order, and the play might be an extension of the author's divinity studies, except that Faustus is anything but an intrepid explorer of mysteries. He weakly ponders suicide: 'long ere this I should have slain myself', he laments even in Act II, 'Had not sweet pleasure conquered deep despair'. He mocks God foolishly by comparing himself with Christ, and makes absurd pledges for 'the love of Beelzebub':

> To him I'll build an altar and a church,
> And offer lukewarm blood of new-born babes.

The poet views him, it has been said, with 'a bemusement that ranges from exasperation to wry affection'. That may be so, or just as possibly the viewpoint is coolly neutral, but by keeping him at a distance, Marlowe is able to draw artfully on recent experience. The hero, for example, delights in walking with a comrade, in music and in Homer, and in hearing of 'Alexander's love and Oenone's death', as a Corpus poet might. Talks with Mephistophilis become 'disputes', as at Cambridge, and the tempter's world seems as agreeable as a university one, and, at one point, nearly defines Heaven. 'Now in hell?' Faustus tells the devil with amazement. 'Nay, an this be hell, I'll willingly be damned here. What, walking, disputing, etc.?'[20]

Modern critics nevertheless point to a problem here, since at times Marlowe may be too close to the hero, inextricably mixed up in the half-naive, half-alert musings of a Faustus, who, after all, believes and disbelieves in hell. But is the text the worse because its author may have felt what Faustus feels? What unifies the hero's moods is an implicit, terrible light, a sense that his intellect forces him to give up safety, and damn himself in order to exist. Hell inhabits his mind, and Marlowe may write to free himself from a dilemma. Yet to assume that Faustus is only a static, autobiographically drawn figure is to miss variations in his state of mind and the deeply convincing psychology of the work. There is nothing subjective, merely personal, lax, or untransmuted in this poet's art.

He uses the academic disciplines, and even shows the devil's confusions in an exchange on astronomy. Marlowe had little chance to hear of Copernicus's new idea that the earth revolves around the sun—no widely used textbook discussed it. A few up-to-date texts briefly denounced the heliocentric hypothesis. But—far from crediting Ptolemy's idea of an earth-centred universe—Marlowe expresses a sceptical cosmology, which he may take from Agostino Ricci, a converted Spanish Jew (whose brilliant work is *Augustini Ritii de motu octavae sphaerae*), though similar ideas were expressed by Oronce Finé, of the Collège de France. Faustus exposes Mephistophilis's naivety, and then, when he comes to astronomical facts which the Ptolemaic system cannot explain, drives him into vague nonsense. (Here the poet may be recalling an obfuscating lecture or two he has heard.)[21]

But why then, is the devil in control in sexual matters? Denied a wife three times, Faustus is made to feel disgusted by sex. Having bargained for twenty-four years of 'all voluptuousness', he is revolted by a 'hot whore' and then appeased by promises with a homosexual import. The devil will bring him anyone he likes, be she 'as beautiful | As was bright Lucifer before his fall'. If the male form once defined beauty in Heaven, men on earth are fairer still. 'Think'st thou heaven is such a glorious thing?' Mephistophilis remarks.

> I tell thee, 'tis not so fair as thou
> Or any man that breathes on earth.[22]

These overtures, though, do not quite explain why Faustus is chaste up to Act V. Marlowe's homosexual perspective is more serious and introverted here than in his earlier work, and I think that studies of gender have much to suggest about the play, if not indirectly about the author as well. 'Faustus thinks himself unworthy of making a sexual claim', according to Kay Stockholder, who adds that he 'fears parental reprisal for seeking sexual knowledge'.[23] In that case, he has to overcome the parental authority of demons, but, one might note, it is just as true that homo-social bonds protect him. Faustus—who yearns for a 'sweet chamber-fellow'—gives himself to diabolic powers who, as he supposes, may save him from divine wrath. Incapable of concealment, he is charmingly frank with Mephistophilis; and though waveringly defiant or terrified, he is bent on self-discovery up to Act III.

One feels, moreover, that he learns about his own nature, or that this is delicately implied. And yet the price of self-discovery would seem to be his own degradation, as if, in the modern world, there were no hope for any understanding of the self without a total abandonment of the propriety, pride, and self-respect which shield one from animality. The poet, as it were, reaches back to Canterbury's electioneering or moral plays for somewhat grotesque emblems which he now transforms. In this category is Lucifer's morbid display of the Seven Deadly Sins, which involves the topics of parentage and sexuality alike.

Starting with Pride, each sin, as it steps out to greet Doctor Faustus, refers to its begetting or to copulation. Pride and Wrath were born into a bleak, amoral wilderness without parents, but Envy was sexually created by a chimney-sweeper and an oyster wife. Covetousness was begotten by 'an old churl in an old leathern bag', and Sloth on a sunny bank from which he has never since moved.

After so much insemination, the minx Lechery pictures copulation itself: 'I am one that loves an inch of raw mutton better than an ell of fried stockfish.' At the time, 'raw mutton' was a term for lust or prostitutes, and 'stockfish' (or a dried-up piece of cod) was a slang word of abuse implying sexual deficiency. A modern, rather fastidious editor advises that Lechery says, in effect, that she 'prefers a small quantity of virility to a large extent of impotence'. There is, however, an explicit allusion to a small, active and sucking penis in Lechery's fondness for 'an inch of raw mutton', and to absolute sexual failure in 'an ell' (45 inches) of inadequate copulating. As in his version of Ovid's *Amores*, Marlowe comically heightens in this play not virility, but impotence, since this is what is most striking in Lechery's entire speech.[24]

Was Marlowe impotent? The truth of the matter is that he was extremely interested in desire, and also in what we might call the mythology of desire, or the boasts, the wishes, and hunger of the young in relation to the uncertainties of performance. Here, the poet counters the vague episodes of the Faust Book with sexual realism. And again, he draws on himself, as a writer must: he implicitly compares his own unsettled views of sexuality and faith with those of his hero. As Faustus explores himself, so the poet considers factors which affect self-possession and human volition. And one feels that Faustus gambles self-reflectingly and very well with devils; until he yields to their blandishments, he is not unwise.

In Marlowe's unusual art in this play, an explosion of the farcical incident, brutal, savage, or incoherent, gives a unique sense of the reality which he intends to represent. So it is with *Faustus*'s comic scenes, which at first alternate with the tense gravity of the hero's bartering with Hell. Comedy in this play has been ridiculed, especially by critics who once held that Marlowe wrote autobiographically, that his heroes were 'overreachers all', or that his structures were inept. To dismiss the work's comedy 'as textually extraneous or as unworthy of the play', as David Bevington noted some time ago, 'is a mistaken attempt'.[25]

One might note that *Faustus* appears to have been written outside London's walls, or near a suburb where Shakespeare 'wouldnt be debauched', and where procurers, maimed soldiers, unlicensed barber-surgeons, and others of no legal trade ordinarily mixed with the gentry. In their composition, the varying social ranks may have looked different early and late in the day. Yet failure and success rubbed shoulders at Shoreditch, and the common, the poorly employed, or destitute in their ways might have counterpointed the aplomb or fine airs in the wealthy. Marlowe reflects the mix of a crowded theatre suburb in *Faustus*. In getting his low-life folk to comment on his work's main action, to re-enact it, mock it, and now and then predict it, he opens up new possibilities for English tragedy. In broadening his art in this way, he at once makes the terrifying more intense but endurable for an audience.

Thus before the devil threatens to tear Faustus's limbs, we see pain as a joke. A boy named Robin is hired by the servant Wagner, who demands a seven-year contract in Act I, scene iv, 'or I'll turn all the lice about thee into familiars, and they shall tear thee to pieces'. Robin is paid in guilders, a word he hears as 'gridirons', or torture-instruments. Exasperated, Wagner calls for 'Balliol and Belcher' to fetch the lad, who now *runs up and down crying* according to the stage direction, as two devils appear. Even so, Robin is appeased to think that Wagner will turn him into a flea, to tickle the 'plackets'—slits in the petticoats, or the vaginas—of comely wenches. Faustus of course cannot be a flea, or anything but himself, and magic unfortunately can arrange for no transmigration of souls. No less predictive of Faustus's fate is Act II, scene ii, in which with a stolen conjuring book, Robin threatens the stable-boy Rafe: 'Keep out, keep out, or else you are blown up, you are dismembered.'

These scenes, although in some instances possibly revised by hack writers, prepare very well for later events. In Act III, Faustus has access to aerial viewpoints similar to those in the juvenile, anonymous play *Timon*, which exhibits so many of Marlowe's favoured devices. Lifted by dragons, Faustus rides in brightness up to Olympus's top, and then at lower levels over Trier and the river Main, as it plunges into the Rhine, then over Paris, Naples, and the golden tomb of Virgil, and so to Rome—where, invisible with the devil, he boxes the pope on the ear. His antics with the vicar of Christ are laughable, or grotesque, but lack the usual effect of Protestant propaganda. Marlowe perhaps undercuts all sovereignty, but he touches implicitly on Canterbury, the power of the sainthood, and the endurance of the papal power in England over the centuries. One might think sometimes, in reading More or Erasmus, that jokes and levity were nearly the life's blood of faith. At any rate, divinity, as a study, once gave meaning to all other knowing and experience. Faustus's conduct in the papal court leads him, as if shadowing a hierarchy in Cambridge's studies, downwards to the courts of Germany and mere statecraft, and then lower still, as G. K. Hunter has noted, to always more superficial areas of knowledge and experience, such as simple aristocratic pursuits, as when Faustus conjures up grapes for the Duke of Vanholt's wife, and down to the fairground trickery of a common horse-seller.

This view of his decline is valid, but taken alone, as Hunter is well aware, it is also too simple: it neglects Marlowe's paradoxical method and ability to depict contradictory themes.[26] As Faustus fades, so he succeeds. After all, he has hoped for mental access to politics and religion, to hidden reality, and to the specifics of power and control. Mephistophilis gives him intimate visions and other rewards, including a sense of commanding the past in its most exquisite greatness.

Simon Magus, or Simon of Samaria, is the magician in Act 8 who tries to buy from the apostles the gift of conferring with the Holy Spirit. Marlowe was possibly aware that Simon in legend had conjured up Helen of Troy, but he hardly needed to know that. In his main source, the *Damnable Life*, Wittenberg students ask to see Helen, who obligingly appears as a slender, tall beauty with a white neck, small mouth, and 'a sweet and pleasant round face'—so alluring that the goggling theologian gives her a child, Justus Faustus, who foretells the future. In Marlowe's version, the hero calls for 'that peerless dame of Greece' at the bidding of fellow scholars, and then gets the devil to summon her again as his paramour. When Helen appears for a second time, he exclaims in wonder, 'Was this the face that launched a thousand ships | And burnt the topless towers of Ilium?'[27] The scene underlines her appeal, but Faustus is as pleased by his own scenario. Yearning to resurrect Helen's milieu, or to re-enact it, he aims to discover and to feel rather than to possess:

> I will be Paris, and for love of thee
> Instead of Troy will Wittenberg be sacked.
> I will combat with weak Menelaus,
> And wear thy colours on my plumed crest.
> Yea, I will wound Achilles in the heel. . . .[28]

Thus Faustus would live as if the heroic, classical past were present. Marlowe's comic, many-edged *Hero and Leander* is the best evidence that he himself found such classical airs and hoodwinking of the self collegiate and jejune. Not the least of ironies is that Faustus cohabits with a devil in Helen's shape, and resorts to sensuality in panic: her 'sweet embracings may extinguish clean', he frets, 'these thoughts that do dissuade me from my vow'.

But since intercourse with demons—or the sin of demoniality—was not unpardonable in clerical eyes, why is it that, after indulging himself with Helen's image, the theologian cannot appeal to mercy and repent? An Old Man urges him in an evangelical vein, to no avail. Even so, Faustus would expand time, or stop it altogether, to bring himself to the deity:

> let this last hour be but
> A year, a month, a week, a natural day,
> That Faustus may repent and save his soul!
> *O lente, lente currite noctis equi!*[29]

The last line ('O run slowly, slowly, ye horses of the night!') is taken ironically from Ovid's *Amores*, at a point when the Student is begging for more time in Corinna's white arms. And yet Faustus's confused eroticism does not keep him from perceiving that one drop, or half a drop, of Christ's blood as it 'streams in the firmament' would save him, if he were not what he is: 'Curst be the parents that engendered me!'

His inability to repent, and his final 'Ah, Mephistophilis!', pose questions resolved, if at all, by teasing ambiguities. It may be unfair to say that God, or Christ, has no role in the play, if the Good Angel is Heaven's agent. The Chorus at the start is no more trustworthy than it is at last:

> Cut is the branch that might have grown full straight,
> And burned is Apollo's laurel bough.[30]

That is fine, but we are also told that Faustus's eternal damnation prompts us not 'to wonder at unlawful things'. His fate on the one hand is utterly cruel, harsh, and unjust, and on the other mysterious and inevitable. The subtle, complex consistency of his portrait, its representativeness of men and women in general, its lack of dependency on moral evaluation, as well as the poet's use of farce and comedy in aid of tragic effect were all to be gifts to Elizabethan and later dramatists.

T. S. Eliot approved the view that 'Marlowe follows Faustus further across the borderline between consciousness and dissolution than any of his contemporaries', and that he 'penetrates deeply into the experience of a mind isolated from the past'. Yet Faustus is at home in the Homeric past, and the implicit comparison with a sketch of 'dissolution' in, I suppose, Shakespeare's Jacobean *Macbeth*, is not convincing.[31]

'Tragedy is one of the rarest of flowers', says Albert Camus. 'Each time, in the history of ideas, the individual frees himself little by little from a corpus of sacred concepts and stands face to face with the ancient world of terror and devotion', as presumably Faustus does in Act V. 'We move from ritual tragedy and from almost religious festivals, to psychological tragedy'. With no fixed nexus, *Faustus* might be located all along the line of that movement. Its action reflects a paradoxical age of revolt, when, for example, divinity is conservatively redefined by Luther, Zwingli, Calvin, and Hooker, and claims of self-sufficiency are made by others.

The idea of human self-sufficiency appealed to Marlowe, but, says M. M. Mahood pertinently, 'he had a clearer understanding than any of his contemporaries of its disastrous effects'.[32]

Self-sufficiency is nonethless a timeless theme in human culture, and if Faustus defies God to obtain knowledge, his mistake is no worse than Adam and Eve's. Critics have seen the play as a prelapsarian 'tragedy of knowledge', or even as a conservative comedy of errors. What one is mainly left with in Faustus's defiance is his sense of the sacred, and his wish to participate in it even in a forbidden form.

The play's eerie, terrifying effects made it irresistibly appealing and legendary in the theatre. Edward Alleyn played Faustus in a white surplice with a cross stitched on his breast, and performances were full of roars, screaming, and fireworks. 'A man may behold shagge-hayr'd Devills runne roaring over the Stage with Squibs in their mouthes', wrote a witness who had seen the play at the Fortune theatre, 'while Drummers make Thunder in the Tyring-house, and twelve-penny Hirelings make artificiall Lightning in their Heavens'.

Marlowe's reputation as an atheist did not diminish, but among theatre men he was a celebrity. He could be trusted by colleagues to supply a good playbook, though a fee of £6 or £8 for *Faustus* was likely to be his only payment for the work. His insouciance was matched by Alleyn's actors since a certain 'T.M.' wrote later of 'a head of hayre' that reminded him of 'one of my Divells in Doctor *Faustus* when the olde Theater crackt and frighted the audience'.[33]

Anyway, Marlowe had become a maker of fashion in plays: his work stirred the theatrical community and evoked odd tales, such as that of 'the visible apparition of the Devill on the Stage', an extra devil to frighten actors. Marlowe was supplying an Industry which craved sensation and went to any ends to provide it. The star, such as Alleyn, had much help, since at the back of the stage there were 'diverse others', as John Gee noted somewhat later, 'that take a great deale of paines to project the plot, to instruct the Actor, and to furnish him with habit and ornament'.[34] This might be small consolation for a poet who found his text badly altered or degraded to suit public taste, but few playbooks survived unchanged, or, for that matter, at all. *Faustus*'s first performance on record was by the Lord Admiral's men at the Rose, on 30 September 1594, when it earned a handsome £3. 4s. 0d. for Henslowe, but it was not then a new play. Later,

23 The style of success. Joan Woodward married the actor Edward Alleyn in October 1592, after he had won fame as Tamburlaine and Doctor Faustus. She was a stepdaughter of Philip Henslowe, impresario of the Rose theatre

it had popular revivals, nine quarto editions between 1604 and 1631, and a curious fame abroad.

Versions of it were acted by roving English troupes at Graz, Austria, in January 1608, and at Dresden in July 1628, even as the drama suffered a sea-change. Its hero became a topic for pantomimes and fairground puppet-shows, as later at Frankfurt in the 1770s, where the Faust myth inspired Goethe. The first part of his *Faust* appeared long before Goethe exclaimed over Marlowe's *Faustus* to the patriotic Crabb Robinson in 1818, 'How greatly is it all planned!' In European music and fiction, versions of the Faust myth usually take their inspiration from Goethe. In music and text, Berlioz's *Damnation of Faust* in the 1840s profoundly explored a sense of alienation, a *mal de l'isolement*, and a century later Thomas Mann's novel *Doctor Faustus* used the myth to picture the artist in relation to Nazism. Yet no version of Faustus's tale is superior to Marlowe's brief one, in either human interest or dramatic intensity.

Today, significantly, *Faustus* on stage can be as powerfully moving for atheists and non-Christians as for othodox Protestants or Catholics, since it does not depend on our attitudes to a creed. A crass response to the sacred, or our robust individualism, presumptions of self-reliance, or moral experimentalism can be involved in Faustus's pride, as can the idea of a rightful struggle for access to experience and mental freedom. Marlowe's views of belief and evil were certainly not fixed, but he seems to accept that evil can come from within and result from human choice. Ben Jonson's amusing comedy *The Devil is an Ass* (1616), though it derives from *Doctor Faustus*, is in contrast literal and social. Jonson's hero is a devil named Pug, who tries to cause mischief in the city, but returns sadly to Hell because he finds Londoners more adept at wickedness than himself. In Marlowe's great symbolic tragedy, evil is darkly and strangely rooted in the psyche, and Hell is more than a fable.

Imprisonment

Living in the theatre suburbs, or to the west at Holborn and in the Inns of Court and Chancery, writers from the universities tested the market after *Faustus*. Marlowe became intimate with Thomas Nashe, lately down from St John's College; he was slight and active with porcupine hair, angled teeth, and a critic's disposition. His 'Epistle to the Gentlemen Students of Both Universities', prefixed to Greene's *Menaphon* (1589), struck at grammar-school writers who were then rivalling their betters from Oxford and Cambridge. The epistle refers to 'the trade of *Noverint*' (or scrivener) and to followers of 'the Kid in *Aesop*', so Nashe may perhaps be targeting

Thomas Kyd (a scrivener's son), or even a new actor-poet from Stratford in the Midlands, who, he says with ironic sparkle, will 'affoord you whole Hamlets, I should say handfuls of Tragicall speeches' to outdo the ancients. Neither Kyd nor Shakespeare, of course, had been to university. The allusions are obscure, but clouds move off across the sky, in Nashe's epistle, to reveal his own bright faith in 'George Peele' and a few others, who may revive the Muse of poetry.[35]

In fact, Peele, who had studied at Pembroke and Christ Church, Oxford before writing plays, was less offended than he seems by grammar-school men, and ready to make allowances for talent. He imitated *Tamburlaine* rather weakly in his *Battle of Alcazar*, but limited success hardly dampened his zeal for his model, and he was to recall Kit Marlowe as 'the Muses' darling'. John Lyly, at this time, was distant with most rivals, but still at work. As for Robert Greene, he in effect advertised Marlowe's genius by taunting him in print, though his final, brilliantly venemous attack on both Shakespeare and Marlowe in his *Greenes Groats-worth* was to have other consequences. Matthew Roydon, with an MA from Oxford, studied law at Thavies Inn; he closely befriended the poet, wrote verse himself, and became a secret courier with a penchant for Scottish intrigue.

The catalyst in this group of nervous, struggling University Wits was Thomas Watson. If Marlowe was kindly admired, 'witty Tom' was adored; he turned out Latin pastorals, mocked himself, and soothed mutual rivals. He did so on a scanty budget—whatever he inherited from his father—since he was forced to go in for tutoring. In 1585 he had wed Anne Swift, and had tried to support her in St Helen's parish; but four years later, he had taken cheap, affordable rooms in the liberty of Norton Folgate near Marlowe. (Despite what has been said, there is no sign that he left his wife or became Marlowe's roommate.)

The bowling alleys, cheap dens, and bohemian aspect of the theatre areas pleased Watson, and Marlowe's nearness to him, one suspects, did so even more. Watson thought of new projects, and became more productive than ever, after getting into the worst trouble of his life.

Though outwardly happy-go-lucky, he was always more than a prankster. His Latin version of *Raptus Helenae*, a Greek epic in 400 hexameters by Coluthus, the sixth-century poet of Lycopolis, had appeared back in 1586. It is said that Marlowe translated this into English as *The Rape of Helen* in 1587, but the *Rape* does not exist, and nobody claims to have seen the manuscript except for Thomas Coxeter, an eighteenth-century collector of dubious repute. Even so, Marlowe could have seen the *Raptus*—and dashed off a version in his last months at Cambridge.

He admired Watson, who took a high, serious view of poetry, and usually (but not always) kept his jokes out of his work. But in *Amintae Gaudia*, Watson calls Marlowe 'Faustulus', and briefly alludes to an incident which led the two poets to prison.[36]

Duelling in the city's outskirts had become fashionable. Not fond of corpses, the Guildhall had stationed officers at the city's gates, says John Stow, to 'cut the Ruffs and break the Rapier points' of all whose weapons exceeded a yard in length, or whose ruffs were more than 2¼ inches in depth. This law was carried out. The wide ruff—the starched frill worn around gentlemen's necks—was thought to induce fights.

Marlowe knew that if he killed an opponent he could be hanged or could die in prison. Neither fate in these years might have surprised Gabriel Harvey, who (at times) viewed Marlowe as an infidel, and likened him to 'Juno's gawdy Bird, that proudly stares | On glittering fan of his triumphant tail'.[37] It was, of course, a violent age—a playgoer was run through for disputing a theatre's gate-fee. Tempers quickly flared, and a scholar such as Sir William Sidney, aged 15, knifed his own schoolmaster. Ben Jonson killed Gabriel Spencer, and is said to have put out a boy's right eye. Moreover, prearranged duels were popular among well-heeled males, who sometimes died to prove how far they were from being ruffians. Fighting was a badge of gentility, a proof of courage, *virtu*, agility, and the passionate heart; and there were locales for duels. North of Bishopsgate, the highway had tenements on both sides, but at Norton Folgate one road branched due west. This was Hog Lane, and here Christopher Marlowe walked out near Finsbury's Fields on 18 September 1589.

Why was he ready to fight at this time? With success, Marlowe had become fonder than ever of personal display. He acted the gentleman with a few friends, and the cynical infidel with others, partly to show how far behind he had left Canterbury. Even so, his commitment to poetry had a far greater determining role in his behaviour than a care for his dress or society's esteem. The tensions in his work suggest that he had conflicting, unreconcilable promptings, elusive and hard to manage, as well as doubts about the validity of his art, and the fecundity his brain. Shakespeare, a company poet, recycled theatrical devices as a matter of habit, and repeated a few of his own phrases, image clusters, stage actions, scenic forms, and some of his own character-types from play to play, and to satisfy the hungry demands of repertory this had to be so. But with an abrasive, questioning intellect, Marlowe was likely to view his own repetition of words or phrases as a symptom of paralysis, blank ineptitude, or the dried-up well. One feels, too, that he tinkers almost to excess with his dramas, as brilliant as they are; he exerts himself in achieving a stylistic finish not for the actors, but for his own eyes, as if each play were a ticket entitling him to exist, and take up his pen again. Whereas Shakespeare is slightly strained in *Venus and Adonis* or *Lucrece*, and at ease as a play-wright, Marlowe is fully at ease only in *Hero and Leander*. It is not that self-doubt mitigates against his effectiveness, but he seems to worry over composing. His efforts involved a struggle for absolute artistic readiness, boldness, clarity, and pungency, or for a kind of procreative centre of his being. Not unlike his Faustus, he had little patience for pedants or dull-ness, and in Watson's easy, comic detachment, wit, and madness, he seems to have found an antidote to his own intellectualism. This friend had an underlying sense of purpose, evident in his Latin pastorals and minor epics; he was committed to classical forms, and to invigorating modern verse by exposing its roots in Ovid and Italy. Well before he roomed with Kyd, Marlowe had sought out writers, and he was not likely to fail Watson. Friendship, in this age, had imperative obligations, such as a disposition to supply funds, or to testify or to fight for one's soulmate. His friend was inclined to get into mix-ups, but this would not have kept Marlowe from risking himself for Tom Watson.

And what of the risk? There was a consoling factor in that duelling had become a matter of show, a figment of make-believe: the comic actor Tarlton had been a Master of Fence. Though weaponless in *Faustus*, Edward Alleyn had to play a role in Greene's *Orlando Furioso* which is scored *they fight a good while and then breathe*, and most fencing schools were in the theatre areas.[38] Rocco Bonetti had opened the premier one by buying from John Lyly a lease on rooms in the Blackfriars. Actors duelled expertly on stage, where the vogue of the *noblesse d'épée* spiritedly thrived, and the theatricality of a fight made its own apology. The long, thin Tudor rapier is difficult to manage, as one learns today at the Royal Armouries at Leeds. The weapon cannot be twiddled, or circled quickly round an opposing blade, and it is not easy to keep aligned. Marlowe's footwork with a good opponent suggests he had trained well with a rapier. There is no reason to think that he meant to kill or maim anyone, and surely not at a locale known for artful displays.

Not especially cautious, Watson had feuded with an innkeeper's son named William Bradley over an unpaid debt. On 8 March 1588 Bradley had borrowed £14 from one John Allen of London, innholder, and afterwards defaulted on the loan. A year later, Bradley requested sureties of the peace against Hugh Swift, John Allen, and Thomas Watson 'for fear of death'. Swift was Watson's brother-in-law, and John Allen was probably the actor Edward Alleyn's brother. The phrase 'for fear of death' (*ob metum mortis*) was a legal convention, used for example when William Wayte sued for sureties of the peace, seven years later, against 'Wilh*elm*um Shakspere' and four others. Bradley's father, the innkeeper, had premises well placed in High Holborn to receive visitors from Stratford, Oxford, and the west. He was fairly well off, and on the borderline of being genteel. His son was a touchy young man of 26, not sluggish, but vulnerable despite years of fencing with all the jingling, clattering accoutrements, and in one engagement he had been rather badly wounded.[39]

In Watson's case, friends were drawn into the quarrel over a debt: his relative Hugh Swift was sued by Bradley, and Swift, in turn, asked for sureties against a George Orrell. There was a chance that a brief, formal duel might reconcile all parties; but our chief guide to the affair is a coroner's report in Latin which opens *in medias res*. Bradley and one 'Christopher Morley, lately a gentleman of London', had begun fighting between 2 and 3 o'clock in the afternoon. Bradley used a sword and a dagger of iron and steel (*uno gladio et uno pugione de ferro et calibi*). Instead of tit-for-tat action—as in Hollywood films—there had probably been a slow, boxing-match exchange in which no one suffered any harm. After they had been at it for a while, says Finsbury's coroner,

a certain Thomas Watson, lately a gentleman of London, intervened upon the outcry of the bystanders, for the separation of the aforesaid William Bradley and Christopher Morley who were thus fighting.

'Art thou now come?' Bradley shouted at Watson. 'Then I will have a bout with thee.' Marlowe then withdrew, and Watson, taking out a rapier, was forced back and slashed. His time in Italy may not have included fencing lessons, and onlookers began to fear for him. The stuffed doublet protected the chest, but Watson seems to have been hurt. In a fight, the worst enemy can be a desperate, untrained amateur. At last with a ditch at his back, Watson lunged and killed Bradley with a thrust that penetrated six inches into the right breast; and then, amidst cries of the crowd, both Watson and Marlowe waited to be arrested *pro suspicione murdri.*[40]

They did not have long to wait, it seems, before Stephen Wyld, a tailor serving as a constable, took them to the nearest justice, Sir Owen Hopton, a lieutenant of the Tower who lived in Norton Folgate. He committed them to Newgate, though Wyld marched them there. On the next day, Ion Chalkhill, a Middlesex coroner, presided over an inquest at Finsbury, where twelve jurymen viewed Bradley's pale body. Watson was found to have killed in self-defence, and both poets went back to Newgate's dungeon to await trial. Marlowe was obliged to find £40 as bail, and also furnish two sureties of £20 each, as conditions precedent to his release.

Few of his friends could have put up £20 for him, or lend £40, so the two sureties he did get—Richard Kitchen and Humphrey Rowland—are interesting. With a large family, Rowland was a former constable who stood surety three times at least. In many years, he was too poor to be taxed (or to be on East Smithfield's subsidy roll), and he left an estate valued at just 35 shillings. It is unlikely that he had £20 of his own. Richard Kitchen, a lawyer of Clifford's Inn who came from Yorkshire, served for twenty years as a Queen's Bench attorney. Having married Agnes Redman in January 1580, he took on dangerous cases, and knew the usually placid vintners at the Mermaid tavern in Bread Street, including William Johnson who later helped Shakespeare as a co-signer in the Blackfriars gate-house purchase. Kitchen (whose name can appear as 'Kechin') may be the 'atorney Ceachen' used in the late 1590s by Henslowe of the Rose for legal work.

In the course of one investigation, Kitchen in 1594 was indicted at the Guildhall for a supposed assault on John Finch; but the case was removed to Queen's Bench and later discharged. He seems to have enjoyed trouble, and in the month of his recognizance for Marlowe (October 1589) he was chosen as an arbiter in a much-vexed dispute.

So far, we have little sign that either surety had met the poet before September. We know that Lord Burghley had helped one of them, Humphrey Rowland, a horn-cutter by trade, by getting him admitted to the Company of the Cutlers.[41] Rowland owed the Lord Treasurer favours, and obviously stood surety from time to time for small fees. In the light of new evidence, Rowland's relationship with a Privy Councillor is important, I think, in the history of Marlowe's life.

It is reasonably clear for the first time that the Privy Council appointed sureties for both Marlowe and Watson, and lessened their miseries at Newgate. Our chief evidence for this appears in Watson's Latin. As it happened, Sir Francis Walsingham died on 6 April 1590, and in dedicating his formal elegy upon him, *Meliboeus*, to the spymaster's cousin Thomas Walsingham, Watson states that the deceased had saved him in the past from dire storms:

> magnus enim (proh fata) diem Franciscus obivit,
>   Arcadiae nostrae qui Meliboeus erat,
> et mihi subtristes qui (te mediante) procellas
>   depulit, hyberno vela ferente Noto.

[For, alas the Fates, great Francis has died, he who was the Meliboeus of our Arcady, a man who warded off baleful storms from me when a winter tempest blowing from the south struck my sail, thanks to your intervention.]

The operative phrase is 'te mediante'. In pastoral guise, the words suggest that when Watson is in dire straits, he alerts a Seething Lane functionary, or case-officer, namely Thomas Walsingham, who 'mediates' for help from Sir Francis of the Council. In the elegy's concluding section, there is appropriately high praise for Lord Burghley himself, as well as for Sir Christopher Hatton, the Lord Chancellor, who 'tempers the wrath of the law'.[42]

Yet all of this is fairly discreet. Watson uses vague allusions, conventional imagery, and the plain see-through screen of Latin to express his thanks, but never explicitly discusses the 'baleful storms', or any recent 'tempest' which nearly sank him. He may allude to much earlier Privy Council help, but he refers to a *pattern* of aid which continued, and it is not surprising that Watson demonstrably thrived while in Newgate inasmuch as he had not carried official letters for Sir Francis in vain. The government came to his aid, and to Marlowe's as well, not out of loyalty, but because both were still potentially useful. Couriers were in short supply, especially well-educated ones familiar with both the Lowlands and France. As for Marlowe, after praising him in 1587, the government had

24 Newgate, where Marlowe and Thomas Watson were held after
the rapier fight with Bradley

not dropped him, and may well have used him in a damp prison even this September.

At any rate, he spent thirteen days in gloomy, dank Newgate. By luck or arrangement, he fell in with a prisoner then under Privy Council surveillance. This was John Poole of Cheshire, a counterfeiter and militant Catholic whose aim had been to mint coins for dissidents abroad. His wife was Mary Stanley, a sister of the traitor Sir William Stanley, who in Europe had been abetting a new and dangerous invasion scheme with considerable foreign support. Anything Poole said of his contacts was of use to Seething Lane. Marlowe later claimed (in Baines's words) that he 'was acquainted with one Poole a prisoner in Newgate who hath greate skill in mixture of mettals'.[43] Information that he picked up at Newgate later appears to have served, at least until things went wrong, when Marlowe used 'counterfeiting' as a cover on an odd, risky mission in the Dutch Zeeland.

Freed on 1 October, he saw Watson at the Old Bailey early in December. Their trial, on the 3rd, involved those in that month's 'Gaol Delivery of Newgate'. Sitting on the bench were the Lord Mayor of London, along with the chief justices Sir Christopher Wray of the Queen's Bench, and Sir Edmund Anderson of the Common Pleas. Also present were the Master of the Rolls, Sir Gilbert Gerrard, representing Chancery, and the fine old corrupt judge and helper of schools and scholars, Sir Roger Manwood, Chief Baron of the Exchequer.

Both poets were exonerated from guilt in the Hog Lane affair, although Bradley had sued for sureties of the peace only weeks before he died. Watson was remanded to custody to await the queen's pardon, and no doubt in order to avert violent reprisals by the deceased's friends.

However minor his role in the Hog Lane affair, an unreckoning Kit Marlowe had been involved in manslaughter: he was partly responsible for Bradley's death. At Norton Folgate, that may not have sat well on his conscience, and whatever his turmoil, pain, or misgivings on the day of the fight, his shock over seeing Bradley dead would have had a penetrating effect on his mind, as if he had ambled behind a trusty horse, which, with a kick of a hoof, had smashed his teeth down his throat. With his mouth full of blood, as it were, or in the presence of Bradley's lifeless, ruined body, he had a chance to consider. He had encouraged and abetted the mad, unworldly Watson, and but for his own self-indulgent inanity, the innkeeper's son might not have been killed. That much Marlowe may have recognized. Perhaps he took account of this episode for a few days, or made rigorous little adjustments with an idea of saving himself from future regrets, while feeling that he could use his own dilemmas advantageously, to flesh out a tragic personality in a stage drama. He may have reflected that he was not born to kill innkeepers' sons, and indeed— unlike Ben Jonson—he never hurt anyone badly, so far as we know. Probably Marlowe felt remorse, at least until he found more beguiling distractions; but, to salve his conscience or as a prudent gesture, he appears to have laid aside one of his beautiful, futile weapons. The effort cost him very little, and one cannot say that his troubles in managing his own impulsiveness and aggressiveness were over. This was not his last fight, but his only recorded one with a deadly rapier or sword.

Sir Walter Ralegh and the Wizard

The prestige of his dramas changed his life more than his brief stay in prison, and by 1590 he was seeing new acquaintances. He met scientists and mathematicians, hard-headed realists bent on innovation, discovery, and free thought. At the same time, Marlowe became more outspoken, and so took a path likely to complicate his reputation in the suburbs, if not in the city. These sociable days were abetted by the presence of Watson, who emerged from Newgate on 10 February, not at all ill, depressed, or half-starved, but apparently full of energy for composition and engagements: he printed three new volumes within a year, got involved in another wild prank, and for his splendid *First Set of Italian Madrigals Englished* inveigled some help from the composer William Byrd. Socially untarnished by the Hog Lane disaster, it seems, he courted influential men with somewhat varying results. In fact, he had dedicated two works to Henry Percy, ninth earl of Northumberland, the so-called 'Wizard Earl', whom Marlowe was able to meet at about this time.

Henry Percy, by 1590 or early 1591, was inviting some of the talented to Russell House in Charing Cross, which he rented because the two London houses he owned were unavailable: one was in poor repair, and his mother occupied the other. Born in the same year as Marlowe, he had a fragile, delicate charm, which was odd because he was a scion of the fierce, old rebellious northern family which included 'Hotspur'. His

25 Henry Percy, ninth earl of Northumberland, 'the Wizard Earl', from a
miniature portrait by Nicholas Hilliard, *c.*1595

grandfather had been executed for a role in the Catholic Pilgrimage of Grace, and his father, the eighth earl, died in the Tower. As a young man, Henry Percy had gone to Paris, where he fell in with Charles Paget, an agent of Mary Queen of Scots; but, tiring of intrigue, he developed a taste for art and science, without giving up other enthusiasms, which, as he later explained, were 'hawks, hounds, horses, dice, cards, apparel, mistresses'.[44]

A miniature portrait of him, by Nicholas Hilliard, shows a comely, languorous young man propped up on an elbow; he lies at full length on the grass, under a tree, oblivious to an open book nearby. At his estate of Petworth in Sussex Henry Percy did read at least a few dozen books (in which his spidery writing still appears), and amassed a library of between 1,500 and 2,000 volumes. He played at cards with Sir Walter Ralegh, but he also set up a scientific laboratory and conducted experiments. To keep track of expenses, he hired a fine mathematician named Walter Warner, whose left hand was missing: 'he had only a Stump with five warts upon it', according to Aubrey, and he 'wore a cuff on it, like a pocket'.[45] This aide kept Northumberland's accounts, and in his spare time devised a theory on the circulation of the blood which antedated the one of William Harvey. Valuing facts as much as creeds, Warner, with his restless, enquiring mind, was typical of a new breed of savants, who occasionally appeared at the Wizard Earl's soirées.

Marlowe conversed with him, and met others in a loosely knit Ralegh–Northumberland set. At first, he must have hovered at its edges, but at some point its star patron Sir Walter Ralegh wrote a reply to Marlowe's lyric, 'The Passionate Shepherd to his Love'. It is certainly doubtful that he had handed to Ralegh a copy of his own 'Passionate Shepherd', a poem which it is appropriate to consider here, in a few of its variants, since the work peculiarly illuminates its poet. A four-stanza version of Marlowe's work later appeared in *The Passionate Pilgrim*, an anthology of poems (by Shakespeare and others) printed by W. Jaggard in 1599. Evidently based on an early draft, the verses begin:

> Live with me and be my Love,
> And we will all the pleasures prove
> That hilles and vallies, dales and fields,
> And all the craggy mountaines yeeld.

A sharper version, included one year later in *England's Helicon* (1600), was to figure in anthologies of English verse down to our time. Marlowe reflects Watson's fondness for pastorals and the Italian madrigal in six well-polished stanzas, which begin:

> Come live with me and be my love,
> And we will all the pleasures prove,
> That valleys, groves, hills and fields,
> Woods, or steepie mountain yields.
>
> And we will sit upon the rocks,
> Seeing the shepherds feed their flocks,
> By shallow rivers, to whose falls,
> Melodious birds sing madrigals.

He even toyed with a seventh stanza, of which two versions survive from his own time. One of them occurs in a commonplace book kept by John Thornborough (1551–1641), dean of York and later bishop of Worcester,[46] and the other in the second edition of Izaac Walton's *The Complete Angler* of 1656. Here at last, the poor Shepherd comes into prosperity—

> Thy silver dishes for thy meat
> As precious as the gods do eat,
> Shall on an ivory table be
> Prepar'd each day for thee and me.

His revisions suggest that he cared for the lyric, although 'Passionate Shepherd' cannot be a literal statement of his views. Its passion is not necessarily homoerotic, nor does the poet aim to exalt a pastoral retreat, or argue for the bucolic. In its ideas, the work resembles other examples of Elizabethan 'pastoral suasoria', or those lyrics of the time which either praise or plead. Marlowe's image of the Shepherd obsessed him even so, and in his dramas he foreshadows or echoes this poem.

Although it is open to endless interpretation, there is an urgency in its deceptive serenity. Patrick Cheney, in an apt comment, finds a 'cultural energy' here, and in fact no other Tudor lyric was more popular, or found its way into so many song-books, or was more often satirized, burlesqued, alluded to, or refuted. The homoerotic poetry of Richard Barnfield, beginning with his 'The Affectionate Shepherd' (1594), for example, is deeply indebted to it. Marlowe's stanzas possibly evaporate a sense of time, but, then, time may allow the Shepherd to give his love only some of his well-chosen words. In one light, the poem is a manifesto about a difficult mission for the writer, and this, one feels, Marlowe had touched on in his version of Ovid's *Amores* (III. i), when the poet, or Ovid, is confronted by the Muse of tragedy, who bluntly calls him a time-waster and a laughing-stock 'to all the city', but offers him hope:

> Long hast thou loitered; greater works compile.
> The subject hides thy wit; men's acts resound,
> This thou wilt say to be a worthy ground.[47]

Habitually, Marlowe looked for remarks which upbraid the supposedly talented writer. In his mid-twenties, he could be confrontational, rash, or self-wasting, as the fatal duel at Hog Lane pretty well illustrates, but he was not always distractable. Needing to goad himself, he included hectoring lessons for the poet in his *Dido*, or translated them in *All Ovids Elegies*, or included goads to exertion in Faustus's monologues. Arguably, his interest in his failings was intermittent, or minimal and practical, but he responded to images of a poet's task. The 'Shepherd' might suggest a high, self-consciously defiant commitment to technical perfection in art. Perhaps that is why the lyric seems coolly distant, but also fragile and moving, and why it has usually appealed to writers. Marlowe views his task as heroic, possibly in order to continue in it at all. But comedy and wit belong to it, and Marlowe, in talk or with his pen, does not take himself too seriously. Anyway, as humour of one kind or another runs in his plays, so his poem sparks off comic replies. Donne echoes the lyric in 'The Bait', with no obvious satiric intent, and Shakespeare in *The Merry Wives* lets his Welsh parson recite a funny, mangled version of 'Passionate Shepherd' while awaiting a duel, though he also tries to calm himself with a psalm. 'Mercy on me!' exclaims Parson Evans,

> I have a great dispositions to cry.—
> (*Singing*)
> Melodious birds sing madrigals.—
> When as I sat in Pabylon—
> And a thousand vagram posies.
> To shallow rivers to whose falls . . .[48]

However, possibly the best response to Marlowe's work is the one by the queen's pearl-encrusted dragonfly and Captain of the Guard.

Amusingly, Sir Walter Ralegh becomes a disillusioned lady in 'The Nymph's Reply':

> If all the world and love were young
> And truth in every shepherd's tongue,
> These pretty pleasures might me move
> To live with thee and be thy love.

By 1589 Ralegh had enemies at court, where his glitter looked tarnished. Having lapped up favours with little care for public opinion, he had got his 'farm of wines', or the right to charge every vintner for the retail sale of wine, and then a patent for the export of broadcloths. He irked the Privy Council and maddened Lord Burghley, who hated favouritism. Dabbling in espionage, he tried to plant his captive Don Pedro Sarmiento de Gamboa as an agent in Madrid. When that failed, the queen consoled him with most of the traitor Babington's estates.

But if infatuated, she put a high premium on Ralegh's militant energy. As a gifted organizer, he seemed likely to outwit Catholic Europe and give her the most gigantic prize of America. Marlowe, though of gentlemanly rank thanks to Cambridge, was so far beneath him in status that he perhaps viewed him with half-awed amusement. Did he meet the great dragonfly? We only have a dubious report by the informer Cholmeley that Marlowe read to Ralegh an 'atheist lecture', possibly on biblical chronology (already questioned for decades) or on other topics likely to make a schoolboy tremble. What is certain is that he knew Ralegh's and Northumberland's intelligent aides: we have Kyd's remark that Marlowe conversed 'with Harriot, Warner, Royden, and some stationers in Paul's churchyard'.[49]

By 1590 or 1591 Marlowe had met Warner, most likely at Charing Cross, but he also had visited other lively houses. With colonies in view, Ralegh had begun offering seminars in navigation and astronomy to sea-captains. For that purpose, the colonial organizer invited graduates to Durham House, an old, rambling, draughty bishop's palace owned by the queen, who let Ralegh inhabit its upper floors, where the wind might have blown a scholar's papers off a desk.

Here, overlooking the river, he had fortuitously installed a lean Thomas Harriot. Born in Oxford in 1560, this disciple had taken a BA at St Mary's

Hall (later affiliated with Oriel College) and come to Durham House at about the age of 23. With a primitive telescope on the tiles at night, Harriot changed human history. He was the first being to view the moons of Jupiter. He mapped the earth's moon with an exactness which anticipated that of Galileo, and then began to revolutionize algebra. Marlowe appears to have met him at Durham House. Clad in divinity black, Harriot would have seemed unprepossessing, if the poet expected more shimmer and drama when pressing the hand of a living Doctor Faustus. Yet, even with his mathematics, Harriot was a good antidote to the timider beliefs of Cambridge, which *Faustus*'s author had wrung for what they were worth. Marlowe, sooner or later, found in him a prime thinker and scholar, one of his own ilk who was concerned with the demonstrable. Harriot, who smoked a pipe, lived in fumes of smoke. He would be the first on record to die of cancer from tobacco-induced causes. He disliked show, craved no fame, and wished for no high office. As a modest observer, he cared little for Hermeticism, mysticism, or the likes of Giordano Bruno, to whom he refers just twice in sixty volumes of his manuscripts now at Petworth and the British Library. But he cared for Ralegh's overseas enterprises.

Marlowe heard about those enterprises, and indeed some of his own chatter (though reports may be distorted) has an elated boastfulness, as if he had listened well at Durham House. He knows facts to support his quips. Also, Marlowe seems to allude to Harriot by name. It had happened that Ralegh's mathematician had, in the mid-1580s, taken charge of two American Indians, Manteo and Wanchese, who were brought to the capital from Roanoke Island off the Carolina banks. Lacking paint and dress, the voyagers from the New World arrived in brown taffeta smocks, which made them look like 'white Moors'. In London, they seemed pathetic and savage, ignorant and not engaging. They spoke unintelligibly, and a visitor noted that 'no one was able to understand them and they made a most childish and silly figure'.

But Harriot, after learning some Algonquian and teaching the two a little English, assessed their culture when he sailed to America with the first English settlers (all of whom were male) and spent a year studying the economy, habits, and religion of the tribes. The Algonquians are 'ingenious', he said in print, and 'although they have no such tools, nor any such crafts, sciences and arts as we; yet in those things they do, they show excellency of wit'. He had lost some notes at sea, but after returning home, he published, in 1588, *A Briefe and True Report of the New Found Land of Virginia*. Marlowe appears to have known Harriot's book, as well as John White's American engravings for it in an edition of the text printed two years later.[50]

This work had first appeared when the poet and his Stratford friend were 24. It helped to inspire, in time, more than Shakespeare's *The Tempest*, since the *True Report* had a strong, astonishing effect on the imagination of English writers. Yet since its author, in assessing a foreign, native religion, had not shown the Indians to be gross, vilely ignorant pagans, he was censured by those who began to find atheism in the Ralegh–Northumberland set. One of John White's engravings in the book, for example, is entitled 'The Conjurer'. It depicts a shaman or Algonquian medicine man, and Harriot explains that the Indians have 'conjurers or jugglers', who use odd gestures and enchantments to evoke devils, who, in turn, may tell a tribe 'what their enemies do'. His remarks are, of course, not impious, but his view of 'jugglers' was taken as an insult to religion, or anti-Christian mockery.

Marlowe himself was fascinated by 'jugglers', and in these details Baines seems to report at least his approximate words plausibly. According to that spy, Marlowe said that 'Moses was but a juggler, and that one Heriots [i.e. Thomas Harriot] being Sir W*alter* Raleigh's man can do more than he.' One often feels in judging the poet's reported talk that what he thinks is mainly, if not entirely, withheld, and that what surfaces is a distilled quip, which is meant to challenge or provoke. But he draws on Harriot more than once for his gullible or captious hearers. Apparently, Marlowe said in private, about the biblical view of the world's age, 'that the Indians and many Authors of antiquity have assuredly written of above [before] 16 thousand years agone, whereas Adam is proved to have lived within 6 thousand years'.

Harriot had written merely that the Indians were uncertain of the earth's age; they believed that woman was created before man, but just 'how many years or ages have passed since, they say they can make no relation'.[51] Presumably, the author of *True Report* did not mean to offend the sponsors of Ralegh's maritime exploits or colonies, but Harriot may have been less reserved in the Ralegh–Northumberland circle, so Marlowe possibly heard a little more about the Indians.

That topic was hardly a recondite one, and so far in his own dramas, his allusions to the Indians of Spanish America had run like a bright thread: he refers to them in both *Tamburlaine* and *Faustus*. He may have talked with Harriot before writing *The Massacre at Paris*, in which, in a fittingly violent image, the Guise vows to cause the 'Indians', under pressure, 'To rip the golden bowels of America'.[52]

In any case, the exploitation of America's land and Indians had begun to arouse concern and gossip, and Marlowe could have heard fresh details from his scientific friend at Durham House. Of the two 'white Moors' formerly tutored by Harriot, the Indian Wanchese, once back at Roanoke Island, had turned against his hosts, some of whom were attacked and mutilated. Only tactical bribery had kept the other captive Indian from defecting. Near Roanoke's fort, the obliging Manteo was christened and ceremoniously elevated as 'Lord of Roanoke and Dasemunkepeuc', and thereafter, as Walter Ralegh's feudal sub-tenant in the New World, he was expected to be helpful. And yet even that had not saved a second American colony, which soon had replaced the first. A small group of fourteen English families, including men, women, and children, as we know, had settled on Roanoke in 1587; they were unsupplied from home in the Armada year, and when, after some prolonged delays, ships finally reached the island in 1590, all the settlers had vanished without trace. Harriot and Marlowe never learned what happened to the colony, nor are we certain of the settlers' fate today. It appears that Ralegh, late in the 1580s, lost interest in his own venture; at any rate, no further attempt to set up an English colony in America was made in the sixteenth century.

Tales of greed, delays, or short-sightedness in these ventures could not have surprised Marlowe greatly. He was likely to hear as many reports of imaginary gold in Virginia as he did valid historical facts from Harriot; but what certainly braced him was that he had access to Warner and Harriot, and so could talk with aides who had special knowledge of discovery, politics, and modern science. Recently, Harriot had been occupying himself with optics, philosophical enquiry, and new chronological problems in Scripture with no evil intent, but the Ralegh–Northumberland set drew fire. Atheists, heretics, and men skilled in numbers, it appeared, were using mathematics and natives to undermine religion: 'I hear it say', Marlowe's friend Nashe wrote somewhat impishly in *Pierce Penilesse* in 1592, 'there be Mathematicians abroad that will prove men [lived] before Adam, and they are harboured in high places, who will maintain it to the death, that there are no devils.'

Marlowe, who enjoyed a fuss, was not necessarily offended by that allusion; but the fire directed at science and enquiry grew sharper. A well-written, rather facetious and witty Catholic pamphlet from Antwerp, called *The Advertisement*, was circulating in London by the autumn of 1592. This production assured the reader that green, gauche unbelievers were being tutored in London, and that 'Sir Walter Rawley's school of atheism', and the 'conjuror that is master thereof' (no doubt Harriot), were using sublime tactics and diligence

to get young gentlemen [into] this school, wherein both Moses and our Saviour, the Old and the New Testament, are jested at, and the scholars taught among other things to spell God backward.

Co-authored by several exiles, the polemic was a digest of *Responsio ad Edictum Elizabethae* by Father Robert Parsons who had expanded on foolish, heathenish things that might happen if the queen, as was then expected, made Walter Ralegh a member of her Privy Council. Some years later, Shakespeare in *Love's Labour's Lost* (iv. iii) supposedly joined the fray by having his King say to Biron in the play's quarto text:

> O paradox! Blacke is the badge of Hell
> The hue of dungions and the Schoole of night;
> And beauties crest becomes the heavens well.

Modern scholars have occasionally argued that 'the Schoole of night' must refer to Ralegh's School of Atheism, although the context of the King's speech, in the play, hardly supports the claim. The key word 'Schoole' in the comedy's quarto text looks, to recent editors, like a printer's misreading of 'Style'—not that the matter is quite settled. Navarre, Biron, and others, of course, join in a temporary academy, and Shakespeare, who may recall the public fuss, does make fun of a 'school'.

Marlowe, at any rate, joined no school, clique, or society of non-believers that we know of. He might have found Walter Ralegh's beliefs depressingly conventional, although, to his credit, that adventurer listened to sceptics. Harriot's religious views, at times, look fairly orthodox; he has been described as a Deist, though that may not suit him. In any case, Harriot refused to interpret biblical myths literally, or to confuse approximate or imaginary facts with recoverable, historical ones.[53] What most clearly emerges is that Marlowe was pleased to talk with a few thoughtful, brilliantly original mathematicians.

Warner and Harriot stretched his mind at about the time that he was planning or writing *The Jew of Malta*, a drama which seems to touch on a few topics which fuelled sentiment against Harriot and his Indians, such as a fear of alien beliefs, and alarm over the unorthodox 'stranger' in society's midst. To judge from what lay ahead, Marlowe courted about as much peril as he could wish for. He had a part-time career as a spy to consider, at a troubled time when even couriers abroad were in jeopardy. The enemy had good counter-agents, and the late Walsingham's 'system' had begun to falter.

In politics, there was a mood which is not fully explained by the reactions to Harriot. Anybody known as an 'atheist' began to look opposed to the Protestant state, or in league with the queen's enemies. The authorities were less resilient, and though so-called atheists had not been hanged, tale-tellers were eager to report on them. The government was nervous about its own intelligence operations. As a mood of fear and unease deepened, Marlowe was perhaps in danger from low-grade hirelings, or those most likely to be paid for stopping his breath.

8
A spy abroad

Danger's the chiefest way to happiness.
(Guise, *The Massacre at Paris*)

A room with Kyd

MARLOWE'S well-being, his career and living arrangements had been hinging on a need for funds. Apart from the spymaster's cousin, he had three known patrons after the Parker grant. One of them, Lord Strange, became wary of him, and neither the 'Wizard Earl' nor Sir Walter Ralegh, who had difficulties after an impolitic wedding, was likely to supply him regularly with cash. There was a shortfall in his expectations. Having bought weapons and smart attire he may not have lived above his means; but he had reason to worry. Near a brothel or a bowling alley, cheap rooms were available, and east of the Curtain were damp, underground dens in which one could live if funds ran short. If such arrangements did not appeal to him, he had to confront the fact, in 1590, that his best patron was in trouble.

After retiring to Kent, about a dozen miles from his office in the capital, Thomas Walsingham at first was prudent. But when sued for a large debt of 200 marks, by one Thomas Lund, he failed to turn up at the court's request and landed in the Fleet prison. 'Moved by pity', as the justices wrote on 27 May, 'we have pardoned the same Thomas Walsingham for the said outlawry.' Though freed, he had to find 200 marks, or £133. 6s. 8d., to pay off Lund (a sum equal to £67,000 or more today), and the debt suggests that his affairs were encumbered.[1]

With little aid from that patron, Marlowe looked to other sources. As for the intelligence services, they had suffered after Sir Francis died on 6 April 1590. The state's funding all but dried up, and payments to Marlowe, at least from Seething Lane, would have ended in April or May. He may have relied upon a miscellany of minor sources, as other theatre poets did, though evidence relating to his support after the Parker grant is fragmentary. He was not thrown into aching despair, to judge from his productivity or lively talk, but anyone who counted on the spy services had bad news. No Secretary was appointed to fill Walsingham's place, and Lord Burghley, at 70, had troubles. If Marlowe visited Seething Lane, he found little call for his help, and a depleted staff. Vital papers, after Sir Francis's demise, went missing; files were disturbed or emptied. It also appears that spies were defecting to serve the young earl of Essex, to whom Burghley lost key officers such as William Waad, Thomas Phelippes, and later Anthony Bacon, who was shocked by the government's cool reception after his ten years' work in France. Individual councillors paid out of pocket for intelligence-gathering operations while Burghley fretted over costs.

Lately, too, there had been timidities in policy which affected even Marlowe's friends. Lyly and Nashe for example were hired to reply to some Puritan 'Martin Marprelate' tracts, until the government turned sharply against its own helpers.[2] The deaths of Leicester, Walsingham, Mildmay, and Croft had left a power vacuum which the queen's much-favoured earl of Essex, though not in the Council, meant to fill, and yet the picture gradually changed. Burghley was not quite outdone: he had begun to groom as a future Secretary his own second son, Robert Cecil, who after an early tour of the Low Countries had become a specialist in the region. A humpbacked, deformed man, not an elf, but less than 5 feet tall, he soon proved himself and earned a knighthood. A trickle of funds could be drawn from the Privy Seal, but the two Cecils had to wait five years for a secret service budget. It appears that they did not quickly rescue the poet, or send him on a risky mission to Flushing, in Zeeland, before a good many months had elapsed.

With little to expect from Scadbury or the Cecils, Marlowe no doubt tightened his belt, but he meant to sell scripts. At least partly for reasons of economy, he entered into a modest though in some ways overly optimistic arrangement: near the end of 1590, or early in 1591, he agreed to share a writing room with Thomas Kyd, a London poet and author of

The Spanish Tragedy. They probably took a single chamber, either in Shoreditch or Norton Folgate, and vowed to make the best of it.

Unfortunately, our main knowledge of this arrangement comes two years later, at a tense, tragic time, when the Canterbury poet was dead and Kyd had been arrested, questioned, and probably tortured for libellous or even atheistical writing. Cleared of the charges, but still in shock and dismay, he needed to be reinstated in the good graces of a theatre patron. At the time, the blemish on his name was that he had lived with Marlowe, a reputed atheist, and shared his treasonous views. For help in clearing his name, he sent a letter and a note to the Lord Keeper of the Great Seal, Sir John Puckering, who presided at the Council. In the letter—written shortly after 30 May 1593—Kyd alludes rather mysteriously to a 'Lord', a patron who sponsored a troupe, which he and his former roommate had supplied with plays. 'My first acquaintance with this Marlowe', he bitterly tells Puckering,

rose upon his bearing name to serve my Lord although his Lordship never knew his service, but in writing for his players, for never could my Lord endure his name, or sight, when he had heard his conditions, nor would indeed the form of divine prayer used duly in his lordship's house, have quadred [squared] with such reprobates.[3]

In his two appeals, Kyd writes in a tone of candour and urgency, mixed with a deep affrontedness. He never mentions the name of his 'Lord', although the patron seems obviously to have been Ferdinando Lord Strange (the only nobleman who fits all the circumstances). We know that Strange's troupe when it included the actor Alleyn produced, in 1592 and 1593, both Kyd's *The Spanish Tragedy* and Marlowe's *The Jew of Malta*. 'That I should love or be familiar friend', Kyd comments retrospectively on his roommate, 'with one so irreligious, were very rare.' He shows that he had despised Marlowe's blasphemy, but implies that they had been close: 'An artist recognizes an artist by the slightest trace', he tells the Lord Keeper in Latin.[4]

In better times, the two writers may have lived in a half-pleasant oasis of quills, papers, and books, and possibly slept in the same room, or even for a while shared a bed. From Marlowe's viewpoint, any such arrangement would have had advantages. Baptized at St Mary Woolnoth's Church in London, on 6 November 1558, Kyd was five and a half years his senior, and by far the more experienced playwright. Francis Kyd, his father, was a respectable and moderately prosperous scrivener at Lombard Street. In that commercial area, the scrivener had befriended one of the most affluent of book-dealers, Francis Coldocke, Warden and Master of the Stationers' Company. At the time of the rooming arrangement in 1591, Coldocke was head of the guild which licensed all new books.[5] Such a man perhaps appealed to Marlowe, who chatted with booksellers, and Kyd's other connections were pleasant. It had done him no harm to grow up in an orthodox family, or to be sent along to Richard Mulcaster, master of Merchant Taylors' School when Edmund Spenser was a pupil there. From Mulcaster—another disciple of Cambridge's great John Cheke, the professor of Greek—he had received a training as good as anything given at Stratford or Canterbury. At 16 or 17, he had probably begun as a scrivener's apprentice; his clear, squarish handwriting and the calligraphic beauty of his signature are noted by the palaeographer A. G. Petti. This is the hand of a copyist—one of the 'paltry scriveners' as Nashe called them. Employed to indite letters and documents, the scriveners were indispensable in the city, but were often feared or disliked for knowing business secrets, or selling unauthorized manuscript copies of works.[6]

In his line of work Kyd had almost certainly picked up a few secrets about trade and finance. With an eye on the Mediterranean traffic in goods, Marlowe had been thinking of a colossal Jewish trader and entrepreneur, who takes risks for great profits. Also helpful was Kyd's art. With its five different avengers, his *Spanish Tragedy* became an enormously popular classic of revenge, and turned a good profit for Henslowe of the Rose. Interestingly, some traces of Watson's *Meliboeus*, written after 6 April 1590, appear in that play's speeches, so it may have been a fairly new work.[7]

Marlowe knew the *Spanish Tragedy* well, and its family values could not have struck him as utterly absurd. Kyd's supernatural framework (with a prologue in Hell), his portrait of a Machiavellian killer in Lorenzo, and above all his well-structured scenes, were impressive; the plot may have helped Marlowe with his design in *The Jew of Malta*. Often Kyd's best speeches are those of grief or complaint, as with his Turkish figures in *Soliman and Perseda*. He perhaps wrote a darker revenge play in *Hamlet*, the famously missing 'ur-Hamlet' which inspired Shakespeare, though the author of this work is still unknown.

What was Kyd like to live with? In our modern epoch, F. S. Boas has called him 'gloomy and rigid'. Arthur Freeman, on the other hand, finds him busy and 'at times humourless (though Jonson styles him "sporting"), professedly pious, meticulous in his handwriting as in his syntax, self-schooled, and a trifle pedantic'.[8] These are creditable attempts to judge him from his oeuvre and a few Elizabethan epithets, and perhaps from one or two of his pet theories.

Marlowe had survived among opinionated dons, but Kyd rode one hobbyhorse rather hard. He was obsessed with usurers, or those who lent money at high interest, and the vehemence of his prejudice is not untypical of the age. In print, he does not mention the Jews, but they were linked with 'usury' in the popular mind. Usury is 'a corrupter of a Commonwealth', Kyd announces late in the 1580s, 'a disobeyer of the Laws of God, a Rebel and resister of all humane orders, injurious to many, the spoil of those that most uphold it, only profitable to itself', and 'more infectious than the pestilence'. These remarks in Kyd's *Householder's Philosophy* are the more striking, because he claims to be translating from Tasso's *Il Padre di Famiglia*, whereas he adds his own diatribes to Tasso's work, in order to show that usury is 'never to be cured'.[9] Again in his prologue to *The Spanish Tragedy*, he sketches the deepest levels of Hell, 'Where usurers are choked with melting gold.'[10] He implies that moneylenders are the arch-enemies of society.

The evidence of his roommate's talk suggests that the Canterbury poet enjoyed such rant, and could outdo Kyd. In his table-talk, Marlowe was more nervy and specific, more outrageous, filthier, funnier, less restrained: he snipes at figures mentioned in the Bible, from Moses and the Jews to the Virgin Mary, Christ, or the Holy Ghost. There is a close similarity in Kyd's and Baines's accounts of his chatter, and in Cholmeley's allusion to it. None of these men is above suspicion, but their slightly varying impressions of what he said are convincing. It is wrong, I think, to predicate conspiracy theories in which Essex's or Ralegh's agents have somehow put blasphemous jokes in Kit Marlowe's mouth. While the *Spanish Tragedy*'s author was apparently in high dudgeon with vile talk, the shared room was obviously a happy place. On the other hand, Kyd's Christian pieties were mild, unobtrusive, and unremarkable, and these caused some trouble. His foul-mouthed roommate impugned the Protestant faith from the start: 'It was his custom when I knew him first',

Kyd explains about Marlowe, 'to jest at the divine scriptures, gibe at prayers, & strive in argument to frustrate and confute what hath been spoke or writ by prophets and such holy men.' There were bitter hours in the writing room, when Marlowe couldn't be repressed: 'he would so suddenly take slight occasion to slip out' a blasphemy. Upright souls, among their friends, took pains to 'reprehend him'.[11] But what could one do?

In his complaints, Kyd had some reason to exaggerate his irritation. He knew that Marlowe's blasphemies might be good evidence that he, Kyd the Christian, had suffered day by day, and in reading his letter one enters a kind of billowing cloud: he is acrid, pained, impassioned, but vague. Troubles surely came into the room, but the poets did not duel, go to law, or burn each other's scripts. Kyd insinuates, but specifies little in detail, as if his anguish were so deep that nothing might illustrate its causes.

He does, nevertheless, try to capture the horror of Marlowe's personality in a separate note. One reads it, of course, with some hope of finding base, obscene gutter talk, along with a truly depraved godlessness, of which a former reader of theology at Cambridge, perhaps, ought to be capable. Kyd recalls just four of his roommate's blasphemies. Marlowe had plagued him with a reference or two to Harriot's Indians and their 'jugglers'. One gathers that a little writing, now and then, occurred in the writing room. Hence when Kyd wished to compose a poem about St Paul's conversion, and felt keen to do it, Marlowe deflatingly replied that this 'would be as if I should go write a book of fast & loose, esteeming *Paul* a Juggler'. At another time, the younger poet began on biblical miracles, and, no doubt, Kyd tensed himself, or felt his ears were afire. Marlowe said that 'things esteemed to be done by divine power might have as well have been done by observation of men'. This did not remove God from the universe, but nearly removed him from literal-minded interpretations of Scripture. In alluding to what we can observe of nature's laws, Marlowe again seems to echo the view of an Elizabethan scientist such as Harriot or Warner.

Not stopping with these remarks, the poet also took up the parables of Jesus. Having searched for a damning example, Kyd recalls a comment on the Prodigal Son, in Luke (15: 11–32). Marlowe declared that 'the prodigal child's' patrimony consisted of a few coins, or only four nobles, worth about £2 in all, since the son gripped his purse so near its bottom in pictures of the biblical scene. That was Luke's joke, in Marlowe's view, 'or else four nobles then was thought a great patrimony'.[12] As biblical exegesis, the last remark is about as atheistic as off-hours talk in a divinity school, but the taunt for Kyd may be that the Jews, so-called usurers, were far from being wealthy among the ancients. It is hard to believe that these remarks, so far, had made the writing room shake. Kyd has trouble in reporting anything horrid enough to support his charges, but Marlowe had offered one prize: a blasphemous quip about the homoerotic Jesus.

On the topic of sex, Kyd was likely to feel somewhat off-guard. He could not afford to marry, whatever his hopes, and though he alluded to sex in his works (without an obvious qualm), he may have resented the poet's advances or insinuations, in close quarters, as much as a show of irreligion. He seems to complain of more than words, that is: of gestures, hands, seductive effects, as if his partner would not sit still at a writing table, or kept inching his table closer to Kyd's. Such inflictions, though 'monstrous' enough, may not have involved atheism. But, anyway, Marlowe claimed 'St John to be our saviour Christ's Alexis' (with reference to the gay Alexis in Virgil's second eclogue) 'that is, that Christ did love him with an extraordinary love'. Prizing that quip (it comes first in his list), Kyd offers it as an example of horrid atheistic perversity, although it sounds very typical of Renaissance wit, and might have been uttered quietly in a seminary at Paris or Rome. All in all, one is struck by the mildness and restraint of these exhibits: his friend was to be more snippety and vulgar in blaspheming with the literal-minded Baines.[13]

In some ways, Kyd was a *grand naif*. To his credit, he did not flatter, concede, or grovel to patrons as his roommate was capable of doing. He felt he had to cite 'Marlowe's monstrous opinions' to clear himself of 'being thought an Atheist', as he frankly told Puckering, for he hated atheism as 'a deadly thing which I was undeserved*ly* charg*e*d withal'. With regard to a break-up with Marlowe, he explained to the Lord Keeper that as 'God is my witness, as well by my lord's commandment, as in hatred of his life & thoughts, I left & did refrain his company'.[14] He does not say when he left Marlowe, or explain why he endured the latter's company at all, if it agonized him from the 'first'. As for the parting, he was possibly not being disingenuous, since it has emerged that Ferdinando Lord Strange had been under close surveillance for alleged links with a Catholic plot at least since 1591. Related on both sides to the royal family, and so in the line of succession, Ferdinando was being watched by the Crown and its ministers alike. The queen, in fact, had begun to fret over his religious loyalities when he was a boy of 12 or 13 in the Derby household in Lancashire. Though nothing else confirms it, Lord Strange—for the sake of his well-being or safety—could have advised Kyd to leave a deadly heretic.

Puzzles about the rooming arrangement remain. One wonders why, in the first place, Marlowe had bothered to irritate his friend with atheist jibes. Kyd was not of negligible talent, but he was 'middleclass' and mercantile to the soles of his boots, especially in sharing the capital's basest prejudices: he, at least, had the value of a creature, such as a wasp or a beetle, under investigation. It may have been of use to twitch or prod him with relation to his professed beliefs. The prodder, in this case, was a former student of divinity who was taking up religious hypocrisy and anti-semitism in his *Malta*; he possibly found Kyd's reactions to blasphemy of interest, though we may have to accept Kyd's hint that his friend goaded others as well.

Confrontation was one of Marlowe's vices; but it was a dramatic vice, not a sign of anti-social habits, or a psychotic tic. He defined his ideas in opposition to norms and popular myths, and did not share in any feeling against Catholics or Jews, either ancient or modern; nor did he torture his friends; it is clear that he was fond of Watson, Harriot, Roydon, Peele and Nashe, and probably of Kyd as well; he was not disposed to ruin or unnerve them, and, for the most part, he reined in his impulses, or behaved with restraint and an artist's self-discipline. If we doubt that, we have the evidence of his sane plays, which are as finely controlled as any other dramas up to 1593, and have fewer inconsistencies or minor con-fusions than most Elizabethan dramas (including Shakespeare's own). The government had already praised Marlowe for 'faithful dealing' and orderly behaviour. One concludes that his blasphemies were not always reckless: at times, they were a device for saying nothing, or for keeping his mind untrammelled. On the other hand, his behaviour with the crass Kyd, or with Baines, was not purely disinterested; so far as we can tell, Marlowe could be needling, insensitive, tactless, and presumptuous, if not down-right unendurable, though nobody on record ever found him tedious. Some of his reported quips are the tokens of atheist fashion, so unoriginal that one might imagine his brain was half-asleep; others are spontaneous, speculative, and refreshing in calling for logical argument or wit in return. In the best of his jokey and parodying taunts, he lifted theology and religion into the realm of the imagination, beyond pedantry or knee-jerk thoughtlessness alike, and, at the same time, he could use his taunts to reinforce a homosocial solidarity.

Kyd might have wondered if the Cambridge's Arts course normally bred atheists. Some years later, it appeared that Marlowe's crimes had begun with a seduction at Corpus Christi College: the evidence involves a species of pederasty. When at Cambridge, he supposedly damaged the faith of a boy of 13, one Thomas Fineaux, who matriculated in Easter term in 1587. We hear of Marlowe's crime from Henry Oxinden, a minor *littérateur* of Barham in Kent, who in turn heard of it from Simon Aldrich, a Canterbury man and a Fellow of Trinity College. Oxinden was intrigued enough to record versions of the matter in commonplace books, which still exist, as well as in the margins of his copies of Marlowe's *Hero and Leander* and Beard's *Theatre of Gods Judgments* in the 1640s.

The most neatly phrased of these entries about Marlowe's destruction of young Fineaux's faith is brief. First, we are allowed to hear of some later results in the moonlight. 'Mr Ald[rich]', Oxinden jotted around 1640,

> sayd that Mr Fin[eau]x of Dover was an Atheist & that hee would go out at midnight into a wood, & fall downe uppon his knees & pray heartily that the devil would come, that he might see him (for hee did not beleive that there was a devil) Mr Ald[rich] sayd that hee was a verie good scholler, but would never have above one booke at a time, & when hee was perfect in it, hee would sell it away & buy another.

The obsessed atheist in the moonlight, as it appears, had formerly 'learned all Marlowe by heart, & divers other bookes'. And so it was that 'Marlowe made him an Atheist'. This looks the more reprehensible since Thomas Fineaux had just left home when Marlowe worked on his mind. The boy survived to finish his studies, at any rate, and by chance he had to profess a Christian faith at the last minute. Oxinden's anecdote concludes: 'This Fineaux was faine to make a speech uppon *The foole hath said in his heart there is no God*, to get his degree.'[15]

The story looks substantial enough, the only trouble with it being that Marlowe was probably unable to meet the lad in question. It is fairly certain that 'Thomas Fineaux' never took a degree, so he may not be the boy who, as Simon Aldrich related, had to make a speech on 'The foole hath said in his heart' to get his BA. On the other hand, a *John* Fineaux, possibly of the same family, did leave the King's School in 1593 to enter Cambridge as an exact contemporary of Simon Aldrich; he went on to take two degrees just when Aldrich did in 1597 and 1600. Certainly, Aldrich had a good chance to hear about John Fineaux's habits (such as buying one book at a time, and selling it, before be bought another), whereas Thomas Fineaux had been at Cambridge six years before Aldrich arrived. The only atheist in the moonlight who fits Oxinden's report, in each detail, is John Fineaux, who matriculated too late to have seen Marlowe at Cambridge; he could easily have read his works or 'books' (which were mainly published between 1594 and 1603). Of course, it is possible that the poet, if new data comes to light, may yet be linked with the 13-year-old boy.

Not corrupting the innocent just lately, Marlowe had been sketching a mordant picture of life in a new drama. This work was probably finished months before he left on a difficult mission to Zeeland. As closely as evidence allows, we can follow him to a nest of vipers, but first it may be well to see what he had been saying about Christians and Jews.

The Jew of Malta

Even before Marlowe began to room with Kyd, a good deal had been happening at Burbage's propped-up Theatre at Shoreditch. The Admiral's company had been joined by an insolent, brilliant group of actors under Lord Strange's patronage. Some of those men and boys had been in prison after defying an edict and playing at the city's Cross Keys inn. The two troupes grudgingly co-operated until a quarrel between Alleyn and old James Burbage—at the back of the Theatre in May 1591— caused a bad rift.

In consequence, it appeared that Alleyn had taken the bulk of Strange's men down to the Rose at Bankside, where he threw in his lot with the impresario Henslowe. Just before that break-up, Marlowe may have completed *The Jew of Malta,* since he wrote this drama in 1590/91, and probably by the spring 1591 at the latest. Its leading role was meant for Alleyn, so the work perhaps had a debut at the Theatre, where all was done in haste. Seeking a licence from the Master of the Revels and casting roles, annotating the playbook, and transcribing each 'part', then getting costumes and properties ready and rehearsing the script would have taken about three weeks. The play could later have drawn crowds at the Rose, even before its first recorded performance on 26 February 1592, when Henslowe in his *Diary* does not mark it as 'ne' (presumably meaning either 'new' or 'newly licensed').

By then, a success was under way, and *The Famous Tragedy of the Rich Jew of Malta* (the title it had when first published in 1633) became one of the most popular dramas of the 1590s, and the most frequently cited in Henslowe's diary. Success may have surprised the author, whose methods were riskier than ever. His work opens as a tragedy, and veers towards wild farce after the second act. Full of 'asides', quips, and sentence fragments, it might have been written to mock the stage: typically, we first hear Jewish Barabas in mid-soliloquy. The action is clear, but the drama is bizarre and shifting in form, barbed and ironic in meaning, and troubling if not quite perverse.

Its success might be a sign that Marlowe has capitalized on his ability to shock, while appealing to racial prejudice. He focuses on an obsessive Elizabethan concern with Judaism and, in fact, counters anti-semitism, but keeps prejudice in the air to examine society. Barabas is what the alien is popularly taken to be; but, as a hero or anti-hero, he is also profoundly ambiguous, elusive, even sympathetic in his gaiety, wit, and role-playing, despite his violence and depravity. His portrait does not fit categeories; it will never be 'politically correct'. If we are offended by anti-semitism, Marlowe might ask that we be even more outraged, indignant, or mortified by the author and drama. Barabas is refreshingly candid: he conceals none of his ideas or feelings from an audience. He has been seen as a type of the diabolically entertaining 'Vice' figure, but even that will not do; he alters before our eyes, even as this play's genre changes, virtually from act to act.

One result is that *The Jew of Malta* remains the most thematically elusive of the classic Elizabethan plays, though it is exuberantly theatrical. Structurally, it is a masterpiece, strong in balance and symmetry, though it cannot be judged with principles derived from Shakespeare's plays. Marlowe opposes what he knows of Kyd's or Shakespeare's tidy genres, for it is only by mixing forms, traditions, and techniques, breaking up consistency, and allowing Barabas a dazzlingly Protean, witty intelligence,

The Famous

TRAGEDY

OF

THE RICH IEVV

OF *MALTA.*

AS IT WAS PLAYD

BEFORE THE KING AND
QVEENE, IN HIS MAJESTIES
Theatre at *White-Hall*, by her Majesties
Servants at the *Cock-pit.*

Written by CHRISTO: HER MARLO.

LONDON;
Printed by *I. B.* for *Nicholas Vavasour,* and are to be sold
at his Shop in the Inner-Temple, neere the
Church. 1633.

26 The title page of *The Jew of Malta*'s first known edition, 1633

along with a flexibility in being, that the age can be shown its social face. Comedy and tragedy mix here with farce and satire, and the play dances over precedents to mock fixities. There can be no tragedy for anyone, if society and politics are locked into the tragic and absurd. Kyd's fairly mindless Hieronimo in *The Spanish Tragedy* calls himself 'the hopeless father of a hapless son'. In Marlowe's apparent echo, Barabas's dim-minded daughter Abigail is 'the hopeless daughter of a hapless Jew'. Or again in Kyd's play, the hero bends over his son's corpse with the words: 'I am thy father, who has slain my son?' With snippety brevity, Marlowe has *two* anti-semitic parents lament their murdered sons in chorus:

FERNEZE. What sight is this? My Lodowick slain!

.   .   .   .

KATHERINE. Who is this? My son Mathias slain!

There are good signs that he has seen or read Kyd's play; it helps him to sharpen his methods, and *The Jew of Malta* gains from the energies of what it sends up.[16]

Marlowe exploits many other energies, including his city's myths about the alien. There had been Canterbury's 'prayer-books against the Turk', which remained in churches after the siege of Malta in 1565, and he could have read first-hand reports of the siege, as two contemporary English newsletter accounts of it have turned up in recent times. He also uses his family, or, perhaps, draws on intimate jokes or memories. He gives his Dover-born Christian mother's first name to the mother of one of Abigail's suitors, and conjures up Katherine Marlowe's favoured ring 'with the double posye' in writing of the other suitor.[17] He plays lightly on changing attitudes to the Ottoman empire, and treats Turks and Jews with a respect he denies to professing Christians. With the exception of Barabas, the only characters in the play who are not involved in a greedy scramble for land or wealth are the hero's Jewish daughter Abigail and the other Jews of Malta. Brought up near a former Jewish quarter, Marlowe clearly knew of insults relating to the Jews of Europe. His school had not neglected the Hebrew Bible or the authority of an ancient culture. God had spoken Hebrew at the creation of the world, and that language was taught in more than one English grammar school. The Psalms had become a bedrock of Christian faith, and indeed Oxford and Cambridge, for years, had had their professors of Hebrew. The dispersed exiles in the modern world, nonetheless, were said to crucify children, or threaten Christians with poison. The sagacity of the Israelites obviously did not remind people of contemporary Jews. Of course, there were mixed views. A lost play called *The Jew* is said to have illustrated greediness and 'the bloody minds of usurers', though Richard Wilson's *The Three Ladies of London* (1554) offered a favourable image of the Jew Gerontus to illustrate the hypocrisy of Christians.[18]

Few Londoners, though, had much contact with the city's tiny Jewish population. The Jew, for many, had become a scapegoat figure, a distant, shadowy foreigner who caused economic ills and plotted the downfall of Christians. London's anti-semitism thrived, and Marlowe, in embodying and satirically exaggerating it in a drama, risked contributing to it. By no means everyone who laughed, roared over, and applauded his Jewish villain would have found a satirical intent in the work. But his play brought mindless prejudice flamboyantly into the open; and by amplifying it with savage intelligence, *The Jew of Malta* encouraged people to think about the roots of prejudice in society. In effect, Marlowe began to lance a terrible boil, though art by itself cannot cure social insanity. Some of the best insights into his methods have come *after* the European Holocaust, in what has been shown about this play on stage, as in Clifford Williams's intelligent production of *The Jew of Malta* for the Royal Shakespeare Company at Stratford as well as at London's Aldwych theatre in 1964, or that at the Malvern and Almeida theatres in 1999 with Ian McDiarmid as Barabas.

Also, we learn something about the author's aims from his use of sources. Reaching back into old, popular myths about organized religion, his drama became more than a satire of Elizabethan attitudes, but Marlowe also looked into George Whetstone's smugly anti-semitic *The English Mirror* (1586), which he had used before. For Malta he found details in travel books, such as Nicholas Nicholay's *The Navigations, peregrinations, and voyages made into Turkie*, translated from the French by T. Washington (1585). Whether or not he hunted for remarks on Jews, he recalled what he had heard, and wrote the first great English play with a Jewish portrait. He relies, above all, on his nation's ferment over Judaism, a topic illuminated in a number of modern studies, such as James Shapiro's *Shakespeare and the Jews* or David Katz's *The Jews in the History of England,* though we need more research into local studies,

27 A purely romantic view of Malta, from a book which also gave Marlowe
useful details, *The Navigations, peregrinations and voyages made into
Turkie by Nicholas Nicholay*, translated by T. Washington in 1585

or the history of the Jews at Canterbury, Cambridge, and other communities.[19]

Gathering in a good deal, Marlowe planned something more complex than an ironic, half-farcical script. He enormously inflates anti-semitism, anti-Catholicism, and other misconceptions to hold them up to ridicule, but focuses on international trade, the cash nexus and power politics. Barabas's financial success and brief rise to be Governor of Malta contrast with the normal poverty, statelessness, and dispersal of the Jewish race. Rich Barabas cares nothing for others; he is self-centred, vicious, barely capable of love for his daughter Abigail, despising his fellow Jews (whom he misleads in Act I), and merciless in his treatment of Christians and Turks. Yet the satirical, evil, or diabolic features of his portrait do not overshadow certain humane features to which we respond.

This may be partly due to Marlowe's sympathy for a hell-raiser, but I think it has more to do with his familiarity with case histories. Any part-time agent, at some point, would have heard of officers, or others, at Seething Lane who made use of exiles from Spain and Portugal. The Privy Council had been relying on unpaid agents such as Dr Hector Nunez, or Nones, a Jewish physician with special contacts in Portugal and the Ottoman empire; Barabas, in the play, lists 'Nones in Portugal' among his wealthy peers. Nuñez, the one in London, helped in a plot sanctioned by Burghley to put Dom Antonio, the prior of Crato, on the Portuguese throne. Also there was Dr Roderigo Lopez, who reached London around 1559 and became the queen's chief physician, as well as being a secret agent in the pay of Spain. Lopez was to be hanged in 1594 for threatening the queen's life, and the fact that he was a Jew ensured his fate.[20]

There were luckier exiles in Marlowe's time, such as Joseph Mendez-Nassi (born João Miguez), who had led an exodus of 500 Jews from Venice to the friendlier Turkish capital of Constantinople, where he became an adviser to Selim, a son of the Turkish sultan. Then, in 1566, he was created duke of Naxo at an island in the Cyclades which Turks had wrested from Venetians. Here, then, was a Jewish grandee who came to rule a Mediterranean island with Turkish help, a situation very much like that of Barabas, although the poet could have drawn as well on the careers of David Passi, Alvaro Mendez, or others at Constantinople.

He opens the play, surprisingly, with the ghost of Machiavelli, the political philosopher who had been a topic of talk among up-to-date

Fellows at Cambridge. Copies of his most 'dangerous' works, *The Prince* and *Discourses*, in French or Latin, had excited the colleges. How painstakingly, if at all, had Corpus's poet read Machiavelli? Grammar-school training in the 1570s had made the best, most agile pupils into lambent readers: both Shakespeare and Marlowe sped through texts, to pounce like hawks. At Cambridge or in London, popular views, donnish talk, speculation, or jokes would have given a fertile complexity to Marlowe's attitude to *The Prince*'s author.[21] In *The Jew of Malta*'s Prologue, 'Machevill' embodies the popular, hostile English view of the malicious foreigner or 'stranger' who undermines Christian faith and ruins livelihoods: 'I count religion but a childish toy', he says, 'and hold there is no sin but ignorance'. Deeper, serious attitudes to Machiavelli intertwine in the play, and lend authority to its original ideas about social prejudice and government. Machevill merely asks the audience to view the distant Jew, at Malta, as they might be predisposed to do. Lately, he has been with the nation's enemy, the Duke of Guise in France; but now that the Guise is dead (Henri de Lorraine was assassinated two days before Christmas in 1588), he has journeyed to England to present

> the tragedy of a Jew,
> Who smiles to see how full his bags are crammed,
> Which money was not got without my means.

And sure enough, a grand Jewish trader and cross-cultural international trader appears in scene i, in the process of counting up his small cash or 'silverlings', a word used in one biblical translation for shekels. Oddly, he has little to do at first with the political ideas of Machiavelli, and more to do with Aristotle's *Nicomachean Ethics* and other, major streams of classical thinking about virtue. What unexpectedly happens in the play's opening, in the first of the Jew's permutations, is a kind of implicit examination of first principles in which he gains the authority to judge Malta's hypocrites. At the same time, Barabas becomes a spokesman for the estranged, independent critic of human society. For Marlowe, the dominant religion or moral system in any society becomes corrupt, since that is in the nature of things. The outsider, the Jew, even the poet, has a chance of showing up injustice or moral folly, at the risk of becoming as egocentric or corrupted as any of those he condemns. 'Who is honoured now but for his wealth?' Barabas deliciously asks himself, with an amused sense that he is, after all, the wealthiest soul on Malta. Still, he is franker, pluckier, and worthier than a brigade of Christian Maltese Knights:

> Rather had I a Jew be hated thus,
> Than pitied in a Christian poverty:
> For I can see no fruits in all their faith,
> But malice, falsehood, and excessive pride,
> Which methinks fits not their profession.[22]

His name suggests the murderer and thief spared instead of Jesus, or the biblical Barabbas. The poet, according to Baines, later said that 'Christ deserved better to die than Barrabas [*sic*] and that the Jews made a good choice, though Barrabas were both a thief and a murtherer'. But the play's figure is not much like his minimally characterized namesake. Critics have supposed that Henslowe's actors played him as a mock-Jew (mainly because William Rowley, in 1609, refers to 'the artificial Jew of Malta's nose'). But usurers and Jews were seldom depicted on stage in disguise, as James Shapiro notes, and there is no sign that Strange's Men regularly over-simplified him.[23]

At the outset he is comically awesome and enormously rich, as he greets ships from Cairo or Alexandria; we learn later that he keeps a 'factor' or agent even at remote Hormox on the Persian Gulf. He gives orders to lug up his vast loads from the port, and reassures a merchant captain who lacks credit at customs for such staggering imports:

> Go tell 'em the Jew of Malta sent thee, man:
> Tush, who amongst 'em knows not Barabas?[24]

The poet fixes him in the traditions of anti-semitic fantasy, as Harold Fisch notices, while also portraying him as an information-gatherer or bringer of light. The international trader transacts deals outside the limits of a nation-state, so he helps to preserve Malta, which is at the mercy of imperial Spain and the Ottoman empire. At the centre of a half-obscure network of exchanges, he is like an ideal agent for the Privy Council, or like a writer who brings exotic perspectives to the stage. Marlowe gives him characteristic phrases and tonal tricks, which Shakespeare later imitates in the generically different *Merchant of Venice*. Caring nothing for persons, Barabas repeats key facts: 'The ships are safe thou say'st, and richly fraught?' Men are significant to him in numbers: 'Why flock you thus to me in multitudes?', he tells three poor, worried Jews. Again, he is candid to a fault, as Shylock will be about his bond in *The Merchant*, I. iii. 'They say we are a scattered nation', he says of the modern Jewish predicament; 'I cannot tell.'[25]

In general, Barabas reflects the author's passion for ideas. The drama is nearly an essay-play, with a wider intellectual and geographical range of reference than is customary even for Marlowe. His Jew embodies a monstrosity of fears and resentments infecting every level of society, and although built up out of popular Tudor myths, he has an exotic, troubling, amusing pertinence for any audience: this is what good modern productions of the play show. We think we have one Barabas— perhaps we have ten of him. He registers an antipathy to foreign races and creeds, but also embodies the recognizable and respectable roots of suffering in both the Old and New Testaments—and Cambridge's former divinity student moves lightly in biblical history. Marlowe includes motifs which he takes seriously, without admitting their seriousness. Possibly because he cares for his themes, any indignation he feels is not allowed to show; he seems anxious to avoid any hint of know-all commentary, any suggestion that he has diagnosed England, or that he hopes for some ideal amelioration. His 'Machevill' in the Prologue will not lecture; he comes to present. So does Marlowe; he would present us as we are, in the sixteenth or any other century. He resorts to farce and irony to lift his art from pedantry, moralizing, or case-making, though he evokes the history of the Jews to expose what J. R. Siemon calls those 'attitudes, practices and associations' which always demonize the alien.[26]

The plot is brisk, clear, and lively, but what is most complex and nearly indefinable is the play's tone. This work anticipates the Jacobean dramas of Marston, Tourneur, and Jonson, as is often said, and these writers owe a great deal to it, but Marlowe here makes his most extreme demands upon an audience. He asks that we take his comic impossibilities and caricatures seriously, and his standard of 'reality' remains fluid in each scene. In contrast, there is a far more consistent standard of dramatic reality in *The Merchant of Venice*, with its romanticism and pathos, though Shakespeare's view of society is less ambiguous and questioning than Marlowe's.

The island's Christian governor Ferneze, we hear, has been lax in paying levies exacted by powerful Turks to the east. Selim-Calymath, a son of the Turkish emperor, arrives to flex his muscles and extract the overdue sums. Marlowe's Turks are not corrupt, but adamant: they are generous later on, and much too trusting of Barabas. Summoned by the local authorities, Malta's Jews are robbed of half of their assets to pay off the oppressors. Since Barabas protests at this, his house and entire wealth are claimed by the Christian state.

Lightly, this echoes a major crisis in English history. When the kingdom's Jews were expelled in the thirteenth century, their houses, their farms, their lands—down to the last half-acre—were forfeited to the state. Marlowe views that outright, gigantic robbery as a kind of unpublicized, silent theft, and implies that, as they were already demonized, the victims could not expect to find justice. In the play, Governor Ferneze and his knights are triumphant. The only protest we hear is that of Barabas, along with a faint murmur of his fellows. 'Alas, my Lord,' one of the Jews exclaims to Ferneze, 'the most of us are poor!'[27]

Thus Barabas's refusal to be cowed by Malta's knights is heroic. He has hidden away some of his assets, but his chances of prevailing against a hostile, venal government seem slight. His persecution in scene ii re-enacts the Passion of Christ. There is an echo of the biblical Caiaphas in Ferneze's claim, 'better one want for a common good | Than many perish for a private man'. Or we hear a reflection of Pilate's excuse (in Matthew 27: 24) when the Maltese governor, having confiscated the Jew's estate, alludes to hand-washing, 'Barabas, to stain our hands with blood | Is far from us and our profession.' Christian hypocrisy and villainy begin to look far worse than the Jew's plucky tactics. Barabas even merges with Job, not only in allusions to the man of Uz, but in the Malta trader's laments with their distinct Old Testament anguish—'For only I have toiled to inherit here | The months of vanity and loss of time | And painful nights have been appointed me.' These lines indicate a capacity for suffering, and it is characteristic of Marlowe's method not to exclude meanings from Barabas's portrait, but always to add to them and complicate effects.

If Job is a part of Barabas's mask, the poet lifts an audience's regard for him, and especially for his daughter Abigail, only to show later that the father is more lethal than we have thought, and that the daughter is a fool—as in her shallow laments: 'But I perceive there is no love on earth', she cries, 'Pity in Jews, nor piety in Turks.' Abigail is a convert to Christianity not once, but twice in the play. To gain access to wealth hidden in his rafters, Barabas persuades her to dissemble as a novice, so she can enter his house which has become a nunnery. Jewish dissembling is better than a Christian's perfidy, as he implies, or as he tells her, 'A counterfeit profession is better | Than unseen hypocrisy.'[28]

Marlowe had taken up a 'counterfeit profession' as an agent for the Privy Council, but far from justifying his dissembling or betrayals he offers no implicit self-apology. Nor does he in any sense exonerate his Jew, but instead depicts a nexus of trade, wealth, and power politics which begins to elude any moral evaluation.

Yet it is important that he treats his Jew and Catholic friars comically, whereas he reserves an acid pen for political grandees: he assumes that corruption and hypocrisy feed the state. Anti-semitism thrives because Ferneze requires that Jews be hated. Barabas needs to be ostracized by the community, despised for his race, religion, and gold, so that he can be cornered and squeezed.

Typically, the governor betrays the Turks as soon as he can. Offered Spanish support, Ferneze allows a victorious Admiral Del Bosco to sell his captives on Malta. The slave-market turns out to be profitable, and Barabas buys the slave Ithamore, to help with his revenge against the government.

In Acts II and III, the play's Apollonian lucidity gives way to a nightmarish, comic, and violent Dionysiac temper, of a sort which looks more bizarre than most of Nietzsche's Dionysiac examples in *The Birth of Tragedy*. The heartless hero is intoxicated by the idea of destroying Christians. We become aware of unleashed urges of the mind, as his revenge expands. To get back at the state, Barabas aims to kill Ferneze's genteel and pampered son Lodowick; but by Act IV he has caused the deaths of Abigail, both of her suitors, two friars, and a whole convent of nuns, as well as those of Ithamore, Pilia-Borza the pimp and thief, and Bellamira the courtesan.

He takes on lurid gleams and colours without losing his identity. Why, though, must he kill Abigail, his beloved daughter? It isn't easy to laugh at a father who eliminates his child and traps others, but he retains a hold on an audience's sympathy partly with the help of Marlowe's 'asides', such as when he meets Lodowick, who is a suitor for Abigail's hand. 'Thou know'st I am the governor's son', Lodowick tells him with smug gallantry in a crucial scene:

BARABAS. I would you were the father too, sir, that's all the harm I wish you.
[*Aside*] *The slave looks like a hog's cheek new-singed.* [*He turns away.*]

LODOWICK. Wither walk'st thou, Barabas?

BARABAS. No further. 'Tis a custom held with us
That when we speak with Gentiles like to you
We turn into the air to purge ourselves;
For unto us the promise doth belong.

LODOWICK. Well, Barabas, canst help me to a diamond?

BARABAS. Oh, sir, your father had my diamonds.
Yet I have one left that will serve your turn.
[*Aside*] *I mean my daughter—but e'er he shall have her, I shall sacrifice her on a pile of wood.*[29]

Do we wonder, in light of this, why Jonson found Marlowe's art useful when attacking social vices in *Volpone* or *The Alchemist*? The exchange has its sharp humour at the expense of the obtuse, self-enraptured Christian, and Marlowe opens a way for serious farce which can include believable feeling. Lodowick with pink, shaven cheeks ('*like a hog's cheek new-singed*'), disgusts Barabas, who is like a receptacle for the ferocity and disdain accorded to his race; and, for once, the Jew's prejudice is displayed at the expense of the pork-eating heretic. Abigail, his best 'diamond', is about to be lost, so his revenge involves a salvation of assets. Since Lodowick and Mathias both vie for her, he engineers a fatal duel for them, and they drop like puppets. Deaths in *The Jew of Malta* are meant to seem ludicrous, but the villain is always given realistic motives.

Implicit in Marlowe's treatment of his dramatis personae is a sense that vices flourish when the state is most manipulative. He writes from the viewpoint of an agent and dramatist who knows something of official duplicity and subterfuge, and of the Tudor policy of encouraging popular fears of Catholic Europe. Even his villain-Jew is partly formed by the state, and, psychologically, Barabas is more dependent on illusions of control over his fate than on wealth itself. He confuses girl and gold, since they equally sustain his narcissistic mind in his endless, politically enforced exile, which, at last, has driven him from humanity. His pride is damaged first by Abigail's love for a Christian and later by her choice to become a nun. Hence, he gladly and devilishly poisons her, along with the rest of her convent, with the help of Ithamore.

Born in Thrace and brought up in Arabia, this lean partner in evil appears to be a stateless former Christian. To gird him up for acts of mass murder, Barabas gladly portrays himself in the worst light. 'As for myself', he begins in a long tirade which neatly illuminates a dozen features of Elizabethan anti-semitism,

> I walk abroad o' nights,
> And kill sick people groaning under walls;
> Sometimes I go about and poison wells;
> And now and then to cherish Christian thieves,
> I am content to lose some of my crowns,
> That I may, walking in my gallery,
> See 'em go pinioned along by my door . . .[30]

This catalogue of popular Elizabethan complaints about Jews fittingly includes the loan-shark, or usurer, of Kyd's imagination. The splendid pointlessness of the Jew who risks his neck to 'kill sick people groaning under walls', or wastes his time in counting up suicides, exposes the speech as a compendium of anti-semitic nonsense. Yet it is in the light of these myths that the race of Isaiah is perceived.

Barabas's speech is as irreverent as Marlowe's reported talk, a difference being that jokes here are brought to serve the central irony that the theatre audience, in its prejudice, helps to create the alien whom they see on stage. As prejudice creates Barabas's roles, so Barabas creates Ithamore, who is useful until he falls in love with Bellamira the courtesan and tries to blackmail his employer. Disguised as a French lute-player, the villain finally kills off his slave and the slave's two friends with a poisoned nosegay.

In the denouement, the Turks make Barabas Governor of Malta, but he meekly hands that office back to Ferneze for fear of being killed for success he has achieved by the populace. He serves the state loyally by blowing up a Turkish army, and only errs in fatally trusting his old persecutor. Ferneze—a cynical, practical, rule-of-thumb version of Machiavelli's Prince—has no further use for him, and Barabas is left to boil in a cauldron he had prepared for Selim-Calymath.

Otherwise, little has changed in the island, except that its Jews are even worse off than before, and the Turks are held at bay. Ferneze, with Selim as a prisoner, remains imperturbably in control of Malta.

One of Marlowe's themes—in this great study of politics and prejudice—is that the prejudiced mind inhabits a small world cut off from the
real one. The play's most blinkered hypocrites (the friars Jachimo and
Bernardine) are trapped and killed easily, as are the anti-semitic romantics
(chiefly Mathias, Lodowick, and Abigail). Society itself in the play cannot
get rid of the evil it generates. The poet's views of entrenched power allow
for no political optimism, and the status quo in Malta appears to go
on for ever. However, at the outset the entrepreneur had thrived as an
independent trader before succumbing to pride. In contrast, Marlowe's
life entailed compromise in that he sought the good will of a state's
Council, working when he could—as an agent. Drawn into politics and
power, he lost the freedom of his own action. He generalizes this somewhat theoretical dilemma in his play, in which the only 'outsider' who
understands power is crushed by it. In Marlowe's view, the state reinforces
the myth of the dangerous alien, and the public ironically thrives in its
prejudices. T. S. Eliot once described this drama as 'farce of the old
English humour, the terribly serious, even savage comic humour'.[31] That
is valid, but hardly accounts for the work's uniqueness in form, its
openness to differing and playable versions in the modern theatre, or the
fact that it broadens and deepens one's sense of stage-tragedy. What
this drama can freshly tell us about the structures and combinations of
tragedy, social satire, and farce, and what it can inspire in new creative
developments, are matters for the theatrical future. Marlowe's intelligence
found one of its best vehicles and spurs in this play. He identifies with the
outcast, even as he develops an image of a psyche which, in effect, places
the artist outside society and also in its emotional depths. An image of
Jewish strength and intelligence appealed to him: Jews were victims of the
worst myths of the day, and hurt by them, but were not cowed or altered
by them. But he did not rest with tragic farce, or any other form, and this
work prompted him to look in new directions.

Henslowe may have bought the drama's playbook, since we know that
several companies staged *The Jew of Malta* at the Rose. It was performed
thirty-six times between February 1592 and June 1596, more often than
any other drama at the time. Productions of it were boosted, ironically, by
the trial of Dr Lopez, the queen's Jewish physician, who was executed on
7 June 1594. There were eight known showings in the first six months
of 1596.

Its popularity lasted for a while longer. In an inventory of stage properties, Henslowe lists a cauldron 'for the Jewe' in March 1598, and three years later he paid to buy 'divers things for the Jewe of malta'.[32] Shakespeare's *Merchant of Venice* increased the play's fame, and Jewish personae came to be modelled on the twin figures of Barabas and Shylock. Marlowe might have wondered if *The Jew of Malta*'s ideas were as well received as its protagonist's tragi-comic antics. The play was finally printed forty years after his death, and its 1633 quarto shows that it had been performed by Queen Henrietta's troupe at the court of Charles I, as well as at the Cockpit theatre, though by then its vogue was fading. In a prologue spoken at the Cockpit, Thomas Heywood briefly mentioned this drama's old Elizabethan origin: whether or not it suited the theatre, it was written 'by the best of poets in that age'.

Spying in Flushing and discovering in France

The *Malta* play did not make Marlowe rich, but it probably deeply satisfied the cognoscenti—the astute idlers at the lawyers' inns, for example— in its dark energy and bristling, timeless satire, its compressed verse and skill. It would have made him a folk hero again for the suburb's actors. Friends, such as George Peele and Tom Nashe, heroized him, if we judge from what they said of him later, or at least forgave his popular success. Nashe kept in touch with the grudging Robert Greene, whom he saw 'for a carouse or two'. Peele himself was in bad financial straits; in one year, he borrowed £30 from a mercer, then £2. 2s. od. from a goldsmith, and still ran through his first wife's inheritance, though he earned a little, now and then, by writing pageants for Lord Mayor's shows. For his part, Marlowe temporarily had the wherewithal to entertain a small gang for a 'carouse or two', and may have gone home to glitter under the tower of Canterbury Cathedral. In his play, he had touched on one of his city's events in having Barabas boil in a cauldron. That climax had a precedent in the hanging and parboiling of Canterbury's Friar Stone, who had refused to acknowledge Henry VIII's supremacy in the 1530s. People talked of such events long after they took place, and the fate of the Friar's body, bubbling in its 'kettle', remained in the city's accounts:

Item paid for half a tonne of tymber to make a paire of gallowes for to hang
    ffryer Stone ....ii^s vj^d
Item paid to ij men that fet*ched* the ketill & p*ar*boiled hym ....xij^d
Item paid to a woman that scowred the Ketyll...ij$^{d\,33}$

The 'kettle' practice did not quickly die out. The corpse of Robert
Southwell, the poet and Jesuit priest, was to be boiled in the 1590s. A
martyr's remains could be thought of as potent or infectious, and yet,
oddly, upsetting stage-dramas often thrived.

None of Marlowe's own plays appears to have been censored. He benefited from the Privy Council's discreet umbrella, but he had to be ready
for assignments. Lately, Robert Poley, after getting out of prison, had set
up an intelligence network while serving as a 'messenger of the court'.
Though living in Shoreditch, he went off for weeks to locales in Scotland,
the Lowlands, even Denmark. The zeal of one of his agents, Michael
Moody, embarrassed the government—but the Cecils had to use Poley's
men and others in an emergency.

Marlowe, in due course, heard of just that crisis. He may have seen
either Robert Cecil or Heneage before the autumn of 1591; and he agreed
to go on a mission himself. Either late in the year or early in January 1592
he left for Flushing or Vlissingen in the south Netherlands. This was a
'cautionary town', ceded to the English queen in return for her help
against Spanish armies in the Lowlands. Its governor Sir Robert Sidney,
a younger brother of the late poet, had charge of an ill-paid, restless
garrison. A good-looking, placid, mildly ambitious man, he led a hectic
life in the town's fortress, and would have had no advance warning about
spies sent from London. No doubt, the leakage of such information presented a great risk. Even so, we know of Marlowe's presence at Flushing
from a letter by the governor, which R. B. Wernham found in 1976 as he
was looking through uncatalogued data in the State Papers (Holland) in
the Public Record Office. The research of Millicent Hay and Charles
Nicholl has since filled in dark corners, and though I have not found
Marlowe's name at Vlissingen, its archivists and my Dutch-speaking son,
Matthew, have helped with the contexts of Sidney's letter.

In this episode, the poet took on a double risk, in that he had to avoid
being taken as a spy even by his countrymen. Early in 1591, Burghley had
interviewed a priest named John Cecil or Cycell—actually a double agent
who at Rheims used the alias of 'Juan de Campo'. Having been in Spain,

Cycell had headed back to England, only to be arrested at sea with a fellow priest, John Fixer, and brought before Burghley. Of keen interest to the Lord Treasurer was a letter on his person, dated 3 April 1591, and signed by Father Parsons, the Jesuit leader. This referred to *my cousin* and to a regicidal plot to put the poet's own theatre patron, Lord Strange, on the English throne. Cycell and Fixer were to apprise their leader of developments:

The form in the which you may advertise me may be this, and I pray you note it: '*Your cousin the baker* is well-inclined and glad to hear of you, and meaneth not to give over his pretence to *the old bakehouse* you know of, but rather to put the same in suit when his ability shall serve.

The code phrases were explained in a margin: 'by *baker* and *bakehouse* is understood my Lord Strange and the title they would have him pretend when her majesty dieth'.[34] This letter could be a forgery, since neither Father Parsons nor the poet's patron is known to have favoured the 'Stanley' claim; but the conspiracy itself was real. Lord Strange's cousin, Sir William Stanley, at Brussels, was getting support for an armed invasion of Scotland to be carried out by French Leaguers with help from Madrid. In the north, James VI was balancing his loyalty to Elizabeth by quietly encouraging the French; hence Scotland might be vulnerable.

Stanley moved regularly between Brussels and Spain, and the English Catholics had far-flung support. Burghley had already sent the poet's friend, Matthew Roydon, as a courier to Prague, where, amidst a group of English Catholic exiles, he met Sir Edward Kelley. 'I have cause to thank you, and do so very heartily', Burghley wrote to Kelley in May 1591, 'for your good, kind letter, sent to me by our countryman, Mr Roydon.' Kelley was an eccentric astrologer, but useful for what he knew of the Prague arm of the intrigue.

Marlowe was more reliable than many agents. As one of Strange's writers, he could be of interest to the group in Brussels, and he had met a Stanley relative, Poole the counterfeiter, at Newgate. The English Catholics were starved for cash, fake or real, and the poet's aim, so far as it can be deduced, involved bartering for intelligence in exchange for counterfeit cash. He may have hoped to go straight on to the Brussels Catholics, but he could expect difficulties enough at Flushing, which was under army rule. A spy caught by the garrison, whatever his nationality or

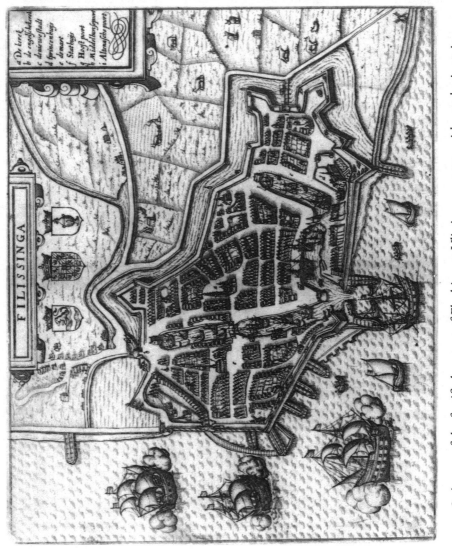

28 A map of the fortified seaport of Flushing or Vlissingen, *c.*1590, with emphasis on its harbour, defensive walls, and the estuary of the River Scheldt

allegiance, faced the hangman's rope or the loss of his ears. Probably with his eye on money and the government's help, Marlowe was disposed to take risks, and he may have known of Roydon's fairly tranquil success in Europe.[35]

In the dead of winter he reached Vlissingen, which was situated on an island in the Dutch Zeeland. Today it is a pleasant city, depending on the weather—and I myself have known its blustery January winds, cold streets, and white, frozen-looking seabirds. Late in 1591 some prosperity was evident in dwellings along the Palingstraat. New houses with step-gables clustered near St Jacob's Church, which had an 'English wing', but the town must have had a sullen, reproving air with its clots of soldiers. The garrison ran short of supplies, or went for days 'without a grain of powder'. Merchants fleeced the occupying army; this year, the English seemed less needed, and tables were turning. Sir Francis Vere's English field force, of 1,400 men, had become subordinate to a Dutch army under Count Maurice of Nassau, which had been driving Spanish forces out of the northen provinces. Zutphen was freed in May, Deventer in June, and Nijmegen in October. In his mild nepotism, Sir Robert Sidney peopled his underpaid staff with relatives, and felt he could trust his aides, but not his allies: 'If there were but one Englishman in the town', the governor remarked, 'they would wish him out.'[36]

At the port, consignments of salt were unloaded to preserve fish, and herring was sent out even to towns occupied by the Spanish; but plenty of goods came in, and a local 'Wijnhuis' had valuable, tempting supplies from Bordeaux. By mid-January, Marlowe, possibly in some comfort, had taken lodgings with two 'chamber-fellows'. One of them was a goldsmith named Gifford Gilbert (the name in reverse of an English spy), whose skills as a counterfeiter might interest the cash-starved enemy. The other chambermate, harder to account for, was the bluff, clumsy spy Richard Baines, who had meant to poison the seminary at Rheims. Exposed, tortured, and made to sign a long confession, he had become useless in France. Yet he definitely continued in espionage; either in the service of the earl of Essex, as Charles Nicholl supposes, or as an employee of one of the individual counsellors who were hiring agents in 1591, he had come to Flushing and fallen in with Marlowe and Gilbert.

At first, things may have gone well. But sooner or later Baines posed a distinct problem for his chambermates. He was a gross, shameless liar and a killer, with strength enough to have endured months of imprisonment, ratty food, and physical torture. If he looked ready to betray his fellows, he might be very dangerous. The throttling of Baines, however, did not seem a viable option; and how to get rid of a corpse may not have been included in the Cecils' instructions. The poet, at any rate, played a high-spirited game. The first duty of an agent, as Kim Philby put it in a later age of Cambridge-recruited spies, is 'to perfect his cover story as well as his cover-personality'.[37] Quite naturally, Marlowe posed as a footloose scholar with a right to mint money. He had 'as good a right to coin as the Queen of England', Baines heard him say. Having 'learned some things' in the dungeon at Newgate, he 'meant through the help of a cunning stamp maker to coin French crowns, pistolettes, and English shillings'.

Baines had blasphemed freely at Rheims, so he was not dumbfounded by the poet's talk. But he detested Marlowe, who treated him to a loose mishmash of 'atheist' gibes, only a bit cruder than those for Kyd. Treating that talk as damning evidence, and hoping to gain from it, Baines perhaps jotted down a few of Marlowe's words or phrases before 26 January 1592. Meanwhile, the chill of winter, nearby troops, and danger on the streets must often have kept the chambermates indoors. The wind howls at Vlissingen; so far as we know, the poet's spying came to a standstill. It may be that with his feet on a table, after glancing out of the window, Marlowe simply relaxed. He hardly excelled as a man of action, and his words were his gift to his fellows and the world. If mists settled over the North Sea and harbour, the room became a little more claustrophobic. Marlowe resolved on some mockery, and took up creeds, faith, and the Bible. 'All Protestants are hypocritical asses', he told Richard Baines, who was in holy orders. As for the Holy Trinity, 'the Angel Gabriel was baud to the Holy Ghost, because he brought the salutation to Mary'. Did Baines hope to destroy Catholic Rome? 'If there be any God', Marlowe said categorically, 'or any good religion, then it is the papists because the service of God is performed with more ceremonies, as elevation of the mass, organs, singing men, shaven crowns, & etc.'

All of this was a part of a facetious pose; but he was partial to Catholics with their ceremony, rituals and 'singing men', and may have felt that the papists, like the Jews and Turks, had been blamed enough of late. In his plays he often depicts representatives of each of these groups as caricatures of popular caricatures, but without the faintest disapproval. To entertain Baines, he declared that if Christ meant to institute 'the sacrament with more ceremonial reverence', it would have been 'much better being administered in a Tobacco pipe'. True to form, he referred to topics such as a homoerotic Christ, the whores of Samaria, or a 'filthily written' New Testament.

His remarks are unlike the dull, irreverent outbursts Baines had made at Rheims; one or two, such as that 'Christ was a bastard and his mother dishonest', were atheist commonplaces (not that Marlowe was ever likely to shun these). Later, in jotting what he supposedly heard, Baines possibly vulgarizes, forgets, mangles, or scratches his head, and invents—all of this may be true. His impression of Marlowe's character is hostile, but his account of the poet's talk is too consistent with Kyd's to be dismissed. When he had a fine, potentially lucrative chance to do so in England, Baines was to take revenge on his cocky friend: 'All men in Christianity', he finally wrote about Marlowe, 'ought to endeavour that the mouth of so dangerous a member may be stopped.' At Flushing, he could do little but wait for the heretic to do something damning enough to trip himself up.[38]

Marlowe faced some difficulties. If he meant to reach the Brussels group, he had to advertise Gilbert's skills discreetly. He could not stand on wet cobblestones at the harbour looking for papists, and, moreover, the Catholics were wary and alert. In the enemy's zone at Brussels, Sir William Stanley was little more than a figurehead; the Catholics' chief intelligence-gatherer was Hugh Owen, a sharp-eyed Welshman familiar with double agents, and a 'very active, diligent, faithful, and secret solicitor', in Father Parson's view. He took in intelligence from spies and priests in England, and passed it on to the duke of Parma, or directly to Spanish interrogators or Madrid. Could one fool Owen's men at Brussels or Flushing?[39]

It seems that Marlowe felt unrushed, and one wonders if his need for employment was his only reason for being in a Dutch seaport. A snugness indoors, the affordable wine, the drone of his mates, and a sojourn on foreign soil would have given him a chance to reflect. We know that Baines made no move before Gifford Gilbert was ready to mint a false coin to fish with in the sea of local agents. No such manufacturing occurred so long as Baines was hostile to his chambermates, and the poet had his own agenda. He was sensitive to locale, and inclined to think about history; his intellect and sense of atmosphere would not have failed him. He knew that there had been a deadly purity in the wars of rebellion in the Low Countries, when Dutch Protestants had attacked hundreds of Catholic churches, convents, and shrines. There had been hardly any looting at the time. Events such as the shattering of churches and burning of books were reminiscent of a far more horrific mood in France. Having referred to the duc de Guise in one play, Marlowe had him in mind as a symbol of modernity for a new tragedy, *The Massacre at Paris*. There is usually an element of *festina lente* in Marlowe's thinking and planning for a new work; he makes haste slowly in filling his mind with materials before he writes. In this case, the results that we have are fragmentary, but very interesting. His *Massacre* today exists in a garbled, skewed form reconstructed from actors' memories. Its text of about 1,250 lines, in an undated edition, suggests that about half of the original play is missing. He and Shakespeare are here together, since the actors borrowed a few lines from *2* and *3 Henry VI* in recalling his text.

It is likely that ideas for his play were in his mind at Flushing, when he was on Europe's soil. The St Batholomew Massacre had occurred twenty years earlier, but Marlowe had some reportorial connection with the events. In Paris at any time, he would have seen relevant locales, and met a few participants or survivors. In the French capital, the debacle had begun quickly. When Admiral Coligny, a Protestant figurehead, was shot and wounded on 22 August 1572, the duc d'Anjou, his mother, and advisers had decided to liquidate Huguenot leaders then in the capital. The next day, Coligny was thrown from a window, and this set off an orgy of killing, as mobs, Guisards, and royal guards hunted out victims. Two or three thousand Huguenots had died in less than a week. These events inspired blood-purges at Rouen, Orléans, Bordeaux, Toulouse, Lyon, and other towns, where ten or fifteen thousand more Protestants were slaughtered.

The French had not been at a loss for words, and the massacre had inspired a mountain of broadsheets, pamphlets, and books. Printers for the Catholic League alone, ground out over a thousand of these publications; in one year, 1587, as many as 362 appeared. Thus, some time before writing his play, Marlowe had much to beguile his imagination. Apart from representing 20,000 murders or so on a stage, he had to picture an immensely complicated panorama of incident and accident, political fissions and shifting alliances. He had to imagine the populace of France, characterize its leaders, and intuit meanings in the debacle.

For help, he was to draw amply on the vast publications mountain, especially on a study by the Huguenot lawyer François Hotman, translated into English in 1573 as *A true and plaine report of the Furious Outrages of Fraunce*. Among other works, he used Jean de Serres's bulky history, *Civill warres of Fraunce* (1574), and Simon Goulart's *Mémoires de l'Etat de France sous Charles Neuvième* (1576); and he drew on spoken accounts and a balance of pro-Catholic and Huguenot pamphlets.[40]

Marlowe, however, distances or stylizes the violence he takes from his sources, and by showing it as quick, routine and perfunctory, he heightens the mystery of its origins. Again, his stay at Flushing may have helped him, whether or not he saw hatred in the streets, in the burghers, or in Baines's eye. In the play, he struggles to come to terms with the roots of modern bestiality. He says nothing of the Parisian children who disembowelled the body of Admiral Coligny, or of copies of Huguenot bibles burned and stuffed in victims' mouths. 'Kill them all, the king commanded it', the duc de Guise had told the crowds, and ten years before the massacre, the *parlement* of Toulouse had legalized the slaughter of all Protestant heretics. The hangman at Carcassone had used his chance in a riot to kill five enemies, 'eating the liver of one of them'.

Having offered her atrocities, France in a flurry of inventiveness used the stage to begin to apologize for them. A *théâtre national ou historique* of political importance had focused on the religious wars. Marlowe possibly knew of Chantelouve's *La Tragédie de feu Gaspard de Colligny*, of the 1570s, with its ultra-Catholic party line, or of Matthieu's *La Guisiade*, not necessarily acted, but printed in three editions at Lyon in 1589. Such dramas were highly partisan, and in England, too, there was fierce partisanship with respect to France. Queen Elizabeth, at severe cost to herself, had sent her troops in support Henri IV, the Protestant king, against the Catholic League backed by Spain.[41]

At the risk of offending the English Revels Office, Marlowe was to bring his action virtually into the present. In less than half the *Massacre* he depicts the St Batholomew butchery of August 1572, and he then follows the reign of Henri III down to his recent murder in 1589. The English queen is flattered in the last scene, but the whole drama is a tissue of ironies.

A deft, very simple, mordant humour was to serve him in depicting Paris's murders, as when the Guisards search for Admiral Coligny:

ANJOU. In lucky time: come, let us keep this lane,
  And slay his servants that shall issue out.

GONZAGO. Where is the Admiral?

ADMIRAL. O, let me pray before I die!

GONZAGO. Then pray unto our Lady; kiss this cross.
  Stabs him.

ADMIRAL. O God, forgive my sins!

In the bloodiest sequence, he gives each killing a wry religious motif. 'Sirrah', the Guise demands of a Huguenot divine, 'Are you the preacher of these heresies?'

LOREINE. I am the preacher of the word of God;
  And thou a traitor to thy soul and him.

GUISE. 'Dearly beloved brother,'—thus 'tis written.
  Stabs LOREINE, who dies.[42]

Marlowe's stage manner is balletic and light, and yet he probes the underlying causes of events. He had no prophetic aims himself, although London had its own sorcerers, witches, 'wise women', and foretellers. In his French tragedy, he predicts nothing, but he is probably the first English writer to look into factors which, among other causes, contributed to the twentieth century's Holocaust.

In his vignettes, he shows that Parisians were led to forget that their victims were human beings, and that once a minority group is demonized, the persecutor has a sanction for massive crimes. Anjou, who in the play becomes Henry III, holds at the start that even 'Ladies of honour, knights, and gentlemen' must be eliminated lest they turn upon the state. He tells Charles I that the 'wisest' must

                    seek to scourge their enemies
        Than be themselves base subjects to the whip.

That in itself immobilizes a weak Charles: 'What you determine, I will ratify.'[43] Marlowe had learned enough to comment on political vacuums,

29 From the Collier or Folger leaf, with additional lines for *The Massacre at Paris*, scene 19. The leaf is probably a genuine playhouse document in the hand of a copyist

and into the French vacuum steps a svelte Duke of Guise, whom Henry III berates as a 'dictator' (scene xix, line 56). The play has been faulted for dwelling unpolitically on Guise's cuckoldry, but in his relations with his wife, her lover, and a ribald king, we see a political being in depth. Some light on that has come from a 'leaf' for the drama found by J. P. Collier, who transcribed it in 1831. Collier divided his time between antiquarianism and forgery, but the leaf exists at the Folger Library and scholars accept it as Marlowe's work, though it is not in his hand. A three-line monologue, in the play's octavo version, becomes in the leaf a fifteen-line speech, in which Guise is self-analytical. His scorn for faith and kingship is matched by his penchant for intrigue and subterfuge.[44]

Originally, the play may have had much more interior analysis, but as it is, Henry III is the work's key figure. Pamphlets had accused him of homosexual dalliance, weakness, and hypocrisy, all of which Marlowe accepts, though the king is given a secular 'born again' impetus once he kills the Duke of Guise and emerges from maternal clutches. Catherine de Médicis (queen mother to France's three kings from 1559 to 1589) is a malevolent but yearning, isolated figure, far more than a caricature drawn from Protestant sources. Marlowe unexpectedly arouses sympathy for her before she dies and shows that no one villain perpetrates the national tragedy. In a fine essay on the play (though it underrates theatrical details), Julia Briggs cites Natalie Zemon Davis's research into 'rites of violence'. Ms Davis, in *Society and Culture in Early Modern France*, does not refer to Marlowe, though it might appear that he understood how a modern society can create the psychological conditions of guilt-free violence, once murder is seen as a ritual purgation. His comic scene xi, for example, becomes deadly serious in suggesting that the killing of Admiral Coligny, the massacre's first atrocity, was undertaken to disinfect the state ritually and deprive the Huguenots of potency. In this case, no cauldron is at hand to boil an infectious martyr:

1ST MAN. Now, sirrah, what shall we do with [the body of] the Admiral?

2ND MAN. Why, let us burn him for an heretic.

1ST MAN. O, no! his body will infect the fire, and the fire the air, and so we shall be poisoned with him.

2ND MAN. What shall we do, then?

1ST MAN. Let's throw him into the river.

2ND MAN. O, 'twill corrupt the water, and the water the fish, and by the fish ourselves, when we eat them![45]

Marlowe avoids a sensational treatment to picture one of several root causes of the massacre.

Playing over the fractured text is his often wry humour. There is even a mild Cambridge joke in the murder of the philosopher Ramus, who had derided Aristotle. The Duke of Guise is full of Latin pedantry when he accosts the scholar, whereas the great logician is simple and plain. 'And this', Ramus states very simply before he dies,

> for Aristotle will I say
> That he that despiseth him, can ne'er
> Be good in Logic or Philosophy.

The drama ends with Navarre's or King Henry IV's anti-Catholicism, which reflects the very disease of stupidity and blight with which the debacle began. 'And then', says Navarre about Henry III,

> I vow for to revenge his death,
> As Rome, and all those popish prelates there,
> Shall curse the time that e'er Navarre was king.[46]

Marlowe might have enjoyed the fact that Henri IV, despite 'popish prelates', became a Catholic in 1594 to assume the crown of France.

One modern critic notes aptly that none of the play's characters manages to internalize an ideal. We might be able to confirm this if we had the whole work. What is more evident is that the author condemns political subterfuge, and thus the whole apparatus of state espionage.

But again, this play is only a fragment, and it is well to remember that other works by Marlowe may be wholly lost. In *Faustus*, there is a reference to what may be a missing drama, of his own, on Hannibal and the wars of Carthage; and in view of his need for money, he may have contributed to other scripts. Most Elizabethan playwrights collaborated, and his additions could well have been signed by other writers. Did Marlowe write lyrics which are now lost? Sukanta Chaudhuri has transcribed a series of manuscript English poems signed 'Ch. M.', once thought to be his, but these, including sonnets and the eclogue 'Amor constans', are the work of an unknown hand.[47] Nor can it be said that unattributed poems such as 'Ignoto' or 'Dialogue in Verse' are his, though he could have written one or two (unassigned) lyrics that were printed in John Bodenham's anthology *Belvedere* of 1600. There is still much to discover about the chronology of Marlowe's plays and their dates of performance. The *Massacre* itself was first staged at the Rose by Lord Strange's men on 30 January 1593, when Henslowe took an exceptionally high return of £3. 14s. 0d. Perhaps it was then new. It was acted ten times in a fairly brief period, and printed (almost certainly after the spring of

1593) in an undated octavo, as *The Massacre at Paris: With the Death of the Duke of Guise* and as *Written by Christopher Marlow*, as if to capitalize on his posthumous notoriety.

If being in Europe helped him with his ideas, Marlowe could not avoid a practical mission. One day in Flushing, Gifford Gilbert minted a Dutch shilling in pewter, so false in colour that it was clearly designed as a token of his skills. Marlowe perhaps felt resigned to fate; but it appears that by taking Richard Baines at face value he lost sight of his own danger. Baines, by then, had professed warm friendship, goodwill, or an approval of coining; tactically, he may have posed as a man hoping to profit from counterfeiting himself, and so wished the two chambermates all success. Whatever he said makes little difference. He misled Marlowe, who grossly misjudged the spy's character and underestimated him. Baines was not inclined to string along with his roommates' plans: he knew counterfeiting was treasonous. Having delayed overnight after seeing the false coin, he went straight to the governor of Flushing, who arrested both Marlowe and Gilbert.

Sir Robert Sidney appears to have interrogated the poet in prison. In his downfall, Marlowe acted the role of a gentlemanly graduate with high connections and keen curiosity. His questioner accepted that he was 'a scholar', without crediting his remarks about Baines. Some light on the governor's office itself has emerged in a note, dated 22 March 1593, which Sidney wrote about one Walter Marsh, a former Rheims seminarian who might 'discover' matters of interest to the queen.[48] Sidney's other letters confirm that he himself sent occasional intelligence to the Privy Council, and often appealed in vain for funds. He found Marlowe, on the whole, puzzling and interesting, and decided to send him with the coiner or 'goldsmith' back to England along with the following message to Lord Burghley, conveyed by the governor's 'ancient', who was David Lloyd.

The letter, interestingly, suggests the treachery of Baines, the meekness of the 'goldsmith' Gilbert, and the role Marlowe assumed in captivity as a polite, rather naive scholar with high-placed friends.

'Right honourable', Sidney tells Lord Burghley efficiently. 'Besides the prisoner Evan Flud, I have also given charge to this bearer, my ancient, two other prisoners, the one named Christofer Marly by his profession

INVENIAM VIAM
AVT FACIAM

30 Sir Robert Sidney, military governor of Flushing, from a painting of about 1588. Treated badly by the queen, he used a secret cipher to refer to his ally at court, Lady Walsingham, the wife of Marlowe's former patron

a scholar, and the other Gifford Gilbert, a goldsmith, taken here for coining, and their money I have sent over unto your Lo*rdship.*'

These arrests have come about as a result of suddenly acquired information:

The matter was revealed unto me the day after it was done, by one Ri*chard* Baines, whom also my ancient shall bring unto your Lo*rdship*. He was their chamber-fellow and, fearing the success, made me acquainted with all.

The men being examined apart never denied anything, only protesting that what was done was only to see the goldsmith's cunning, and truly I am of opinion that the poor man [Gilbert] was only brought in under that colour, whatever intent the other two had at that time. And indeed they do one accuse another to have been the inducers of him, and to have intended to practise it hereafter, and have as it were justified him unto me.

But however it happened, a Dutch shilling was uttered, and else not any piece. And indeed I do not think that they would have uttered many of them, for the metal is plain pewter and with half an eye to be discovered. Notwithstanding, I thought it fit to send them over unto your Lo*rdship*, to take their trial as you shall think best. For I will not stretch my commission to deal in such matters, and much less to put them at liberty and to deliver them into the town's hands. Being the Queen's subjects, and not required neither of this said town, I know not how it would have been liked, especially since part of that which they did counterfeit was Her Ma*jesty*'s coin.

The goldsmith is an excellent workman, and if I should speak my conscience, had no intent hereunto. The scholar [Marly] says himself to be very well known both to the Earl of Northumberland and my Lord Strange. Baines and he do also accuse one another of intent to go to the enemy, or to Rome, both as they say of malice one to another. Hereof I thought fit to advertise your Lo*rdship*, leaving the rest to their own confession, and my Ancient's report.

And so do humbly take my leave. At Flushing the 26 of January 1592.

Your Honour's very obedient
to do you service,

R. Sydney[49]

Marlowe may not have been as 'well known' to Lord Strange as this letter suggests. At any rate, by stressing his acquaintance with that patron (who was then being watched), he got back safely to England.

If conveyed home in irons, he was presently freed. We know that he was at liberty in England in March. Lord Burghley, who was often cold but seldom vindictive, may not have blamed his agents for coming to grief. Marlowe had talked his way out of a jam, but in Zeeland had achieved very little. He had charmed Sidney, which was a useless reprieve for his self-esteem, even if his charm helped to save his neck. But he was back in the suburbs, where nothing could have made up for the possibility that he had lost his chances as an agent. He had not exerted himself at Flushing, beyond, perhaps, his approval of minting a coin. Humiliated by Baines, he was probably in need of some good news, some nourishment for his ego, or sublime compensation, material or otherwise, if he lacked assurance just then that anybody would employ him again as a failed spy.

IV
Sexuality and Reckonings

9
The keen pleasures of sex

Ah, words that make me surfeit with delight:
What greater bliss can hap . . .
Than live and be the favourite of a king?
Sweet prince, I come! these, these, thy amorous lines,
Might have enforced me to have swum from France,
And, like Leander, gasp'd upon the sand,
So thou wouldst smile and take me in thy arms.

(Gaveston, *Edward II*)

Shakespeare and new fields

No spy or part-time agent who risks life and limb, and who then escapes from a dangerous, nerve-racking predicament is likely to be full of self-recrimination for long. And nothing suggests that Marlowe took pride in being a spy. His morale did not hinge on the technical failure of his stay on a Dutch island. After all, he had not really forfeited the Cecils' interest and protection. He had accustomed himself to duplicity, or the deception required in overseas work, or he could not have gone to Zeeland and survived. His nerve had not quite failed him, and after some weeks in London his optimism and self-esteem probably blotted out any sense of a lost chance. He was lucky to get back from Flushing without the loss of his ears: he had suffered no punishment after falling into the hands of the svelte, debonair, poetry-writing governor.

A dependency on secret work since his Cambridge days, though, had its drawback: he could not be sure of its continuance, or if he would ever be used again. No elegant, young, part-time spy had any such assurance; and there may have been difficulty in informing employers of his availability. Meanwhile, if he had a story to tell about Zeeland or Sir Robert, he is unlikely to have told it. He was probably as discreet as the Privy Council believed: whatever his shortcomings as an agent, he did not have a loose tongue. He knew the risk of compromising his employers, or of jeopardizing any frail hope he had for another assignment.

In London, he was capable of playing roles to cover up other roles: for his own safety, he tried not to resemble a pane of glass. Today, of course, he disappears from view if one takes him too literally, if one imagines that his plays or his personality are transparent, or that his works can be summed up as autobiography, and that everything Kyd or Baines report of him ought to stand as evidence of his convictions. His reported talk is not quite a guide to the man. His light atheistic quips and commonplaces, for instance, have no relation to the theological strands and ambiguities of his dramas. In the force and subtlety of their concern with religion, Marlowe's plays are unmatched in the Renaissance theatre. But he paraded as a blasphemer, rather than as an enquirer into beliefs, passions, or human behaviour. Fame assigned him the role of a jaunty wit, and in the taverns, with a few friends or Inns of Chancery idlers, he may have found it natural to sound as outrageous as his plays were said to be.

For a while that year a good deal ran in his favour, and the success of more than one work spoke for his popularity. *Tamburlaine* appears to have been read to pieces, and its second edition may date from 1592 (though the year is obscure in its only surviving copy). By coincidence, *The Jew of Malta* was staged on his baptismal day (26 February) by Lord Strange's troupe, which, in the same month, had been invited to perform for the fifth and sixth times in the season for the royal court. In contrast, Sussex's, Hertford's, and the Queen's men gave one play each for the court. With Alleyn as Barabas, *Malta* featured along with dramas by Shakespeare, Kyd, Greene, and others in a long season at the Rose which began on 19 February and lasted eighteen weeks.

Marlowe hardly needed encouragement, as a new script from him might have been snatched up by any troupe. There are too many imponderables for us to be exact about their dates, but he probably turned to English history and then French history, or finished his *Massacre* some time after *Edward II*.[1] There is some evidence that he revised his translation of Lucan's *Pharsalia* about the horrors of civil war, when he was immersed in the English and French historical projects. Finally, he was to write his fresh *Hero and Leander*, the most successful of all narrative poems of its kind, after planning it perhaps in 1592 or early in 1593. His mind and pen were not inactive in the eighteen months before he died.

The paradox of these efforts, I think, is that even as Marlowe continued to develop and find stimulus in his friends and, perhaps, Walsingham at Scadbury, he plunged into a kind of twilit zone of nerves and recklessness. He began to give in to pride, to take offence quickly, misjudge situations, and get into awkward trouble, and so he became a victim of himself. What had begun to beset him? His looks, his clothes, and his need to appear as a gentleman of taste, suavity, and leisure meant something to him, but fame did not come with gold in the fist. Instead, he struggled for money in order to seem what he pretended to be. He might have been a cobbler patching boots or supplying shoes, and indeed he was a supplier of actors, who profited from his works while paying nothing but a static, meagre fee.

Underlying his money troubles, and any fret over his dress, were tensions which may date from his early years in a cobbler's house. He had seen his path in life, but it is not certain, after all, that he had rebelled very bravely against his mother's wishes or any home comforts in his adolescence: we know that he lived well enough under his parents' roof until he went off to Cambridge. If he submitted outwardly to their wishes, then how much of his aggression, before leaving home, had he needed to disguise or repress? Marlowe, as an adult, sometimes gives the impression of needing to find enemies, and of taking refuge in savage wit, to save himself from challenging the hog-sellers. Still he did not riot night after night, or patrol the lanes with weapon in hand (or we would have heard of it). Biographers have slightly misreported his first scrape after the Zeeland episode, and perhaps made a little too much of the second. His failures in restraint are not many, though they look ominous in the months leading up to his murder.

It is probable that his need for cash increased, and that this annoyance worsened. The Cecils still looked for funds to pay agents, since there was not yet a budget for espionage; they did not necessarily line Marlowe's purse after the failure in Zeeland. His patron at Scadbury had been gaoled briefly for debt, and (though information about this matter is slight) there is no sign that Thomas Walsingham obliged poets with financial aid for some time after the spring of 1590. It is also clear that, since Sir Francis's death, Burghley's economies had a sharp, discouraging effect on the Council's agents, many of whom were seeking new employers. There are two signs that Marlowe was badly out of pocket, during a summer visit at Canterbury—quite apart from the fact that the whole entertainment industry suffered a setback in June.

Hence, by the spring, a need for cash may have rankled. Marlowe's self-esteem was easily punctured, and his dislike of petty, masculine authority was keen. In May he exchanged some words with a constable and a beadle in Shoreditch. The exact whereabouts of this row are unknown, but even Dogberry in a tavern knows a trouble-maker when he sees one. Some pushing, shoving, or insults were involved, but without grave result: the upshot was that Marlowe was bound over to keep the peace, a common penalty often meted out for wife-beating or simply threatening a neigh-bour. Brought before Owen Hopton—a justice of the peace for Middlesex, whom he had seen in the Bradley affair—he was quickly set at liberty. Though not obliged to pay a fine at once, he heard that he would have to appear at a session of the court in five months' time. Nobody other than the presiding justice and the two offended constables is mentioned in Marlowe's formal recognizance of 9 May 1592. 'There has appeared before me, Owen Hopton, knight', runs that document in Latin, 'Christopher Marle of London, gentleman, and he acknowledges that he owes our said lady the Queen twenty pounds of good and lawful English money, on the condition that he will personally appear at the next general session of the Peace.'

The accused is to keep the peace towards 'the whole people', and especially towards Allen Nicholls, constable, and Nicholas Elliott, sub-constable, of Holywell Street. 'And he agreed', Hopton concludes, 'that if he failed in the matters aforesaid, the said sum [of £20] should be levied by a form of recognizance from his goods and chattels, lands and tenements, for the use of our said lady the Queen.'[2]

The fact that he was apprehended by a constable of Holywell Street suggests that he was still living north of Bishopsgate in a theatre suburb. The old statute of 14 Henry VI, c. 4, had dispensed the magistrates from holding more than two General Sessions in a year, and Marlowe was supposed to present himself next in October 1592. By then, he was in Kent, where the magistrates would have found the forfeiture of £20 difficult to collect, though they may have rejoiced to be rid of him without more trouble.[3]

Rioting closed the theatres in June, and in the summer the plague ensured a prolonged closure. In the hot, clammy months when many of the well-to-do had left the city, the epidemic worsened; it reached a peak in August. In the following month, the poet was at home in Canterbury, and so at a remove from the infection, though with no chance of selling anything he wrote. London's theatre doors had shut. Groups of actors put on shows in the provinces without buying new material, and most of the cut-down troupes had to support a retinue of boys, carpenters, and others left behind. The entertainment industry was in a period of dispersal and chaos.

Marlowe would have had a few practical concerns in mind. Robert Poley was then in eastern Kent, as was the engineer and former Walsingham operative Paul Ive, ostensibly at work on a Canterbury canal scheme. Poley's organizing talent had impressed the government, and his movements often coincided with the poet's before their final rendezvous at Deptford. A chance of obtaining new employment in the Netherlands or Scotland—both Poley's bailiwicks—would have interested Marlowe. We do not know that a meeting occurred, but there are signs of his increasing sense of futility, of disappointment, even of wounded *amour propre* and an obscure crisis of nerves. It may be that, by September, he was ripe for a Kentish quarrel.

Anyway, he found one. Near the corner of Mercy Lane, below the city's main crossroads, a fairly well-accoutred Kit Marlowe reportedly attacked a local tailor, William Corkine, with a stick and dagger on 15 September. No one in the skirmish was badly hurt. The poet's first weapon, the stick, is vaguely described in Latin as 'baculo', so it is less likely to have been a deadly, metal pointed quarterstaff than a 'singlestick', which was a dummy or practice weapon.[4]

The law was treated to a charade. Corkine, through his attorney Giles Winston, on 26 September, sued the poet at Canterbury Civil Court for loss and damages to the extent of £5. John Marlowe, then serving as a constable, stepped into the scene handily as one familiar with the law courts. He paid a fee of 12*d.* as his son's surety, and Marlowe the next day submitted through his attorney, John Smith, a boldly ridiculous indictment to the effect that Corkine did 'beat, wound, and maltreat' him besides inflicting other atrocities (*enormia*). That fooled no one, but saved Marlowe from paying £5, which he may not have had.[5]

A grand jury quickly threw out the poet's indictment, which a clerk properly endorsed *Ignoramus* (legally, 'We take no notice'), and slashed three times with a penknife. After Corkine's charge was resubmitted, the case was adjourned for a week until 9 October, when it was dropped by mutual consent. Had Marlowe quarrelled with a tailor over the cost of a new, handsomely slit doublet (as it is tempting to think)? Corkine, we know, was an indigent married man in the run-down Northgate area; he had paid to be admitted to the freedom of the city, but waited six more years to join the Company of Woollen-Drapers and Tailors, probably because he couldn't afford the heavy entry fine of 40s. until then. Oddly, another William Corkine, perhaps his son, served as a choirboy and later published an air to Marlowe's 'Passionate Shepherd' in 1612.

'I have run up and down the world with this case of rapiers, wounding myself when I had nobody to fight withal', remarks Wrath demonically in *Doctor Faustus*—but one can underestimate the poet's self-awareness and commonsense.[6] Marlowe knew well enough, after the killing of Bradley by his friend Thomas Watson, that a serious duel is a foolish risk. His Canterbury skirmish was largely bluff: he had used no rapier, and only damaged his opponent's clothes or property. The tailor's attorney neither defines any grave injury nor bothers to explain why the scrap had begun. The poet's sister Margaret had wed the tailor John Jordan on 15 June 1590, so he might have turned to a tailor in his own family if he wanted a new doublet. It is nonetheless clear—whatever his grievance with Corkine— that his tensions, his excitable wit, his aggressive, confronting outspokenness had led again to violent results.

And yet so far, this is only a fragment of the extraordinary story of the last months of his life. His talent suffered no blight; his writing continued whether he was paid or not, and friends did not think of him as vicious. He was not 'Kind Kit Marlowe' (as one acquaintance remembered him) every day, and his pluck carried him through difficult times and through achievements which temporarily set him ahead of the most brilliant ones of Shakespeare.

Crucial to his late artistic development was his honesty with himself, and a painful understanding of sexual desire, sexual obsession, infatuation, and perhaps buggery. He willingly may have yielded to impulse, as in the fight with Corkine, in the process of coming to terms with himself. In any case, he had for months been alert to shifting, shadowy developments in the theatre world, to changes in allegiance and the migration of personnel.

Lately, most theatre men would have heard of the vigorous dispute between James Burbage and the actor Alleyn—at Shoreditch in May 1591—which had led Alleyn to perform with Lord Strange's troupe down at the Rose theatre on Bankside. Having thus suffered a setback in the north, James Burbage was not easily defeated. As impresario at Shoreditch, he benefited from certain warm, shrewd attachments and loyalties, and some actors and their suppliers remained with him. Among those who stayed north of the river were his son Richard Burbage, a skinny, small John Sincler, who was to act in *The Taming of the Shrew*, and other players such as John Holland and Humphrey Jeffes, along with several playwrights, who almost certainly included Kyd, Marlowe, and Shakespeare.

Before long, Burbage's new company seems to have attracted as their patron Henry Herbert, second earl of Pembroke, an elderly and distinguished Privy Councillor, then normally occupied in the Welsh Marches as lord president of the Council of Wales. In 1577 Pembroke, with good taste, had taken as his third wife Mary Sidney, a younger sister of the poet Sidney, and it is possible that the brilliant, literary countess of Pembroke soon took an interest in the new troupe. (We know that Simon Jewell, a former Pembroke actor, declared in his will of 19 August 1592 that: 'my share of such money as shal/be givenn by my ladie Pembroke . . . shal/be distributed and paide towardes my buriall'.[7]) But Pembroke himself had high standing at court and prestige enough to satisfy his actors.

It is reasonably clear that Shakespeare continued to act and write for the Burbages in this troupe. The playbook of his *Titus Andronicus* went from Strange's men to Pembroke's men, if we can believe in the succession of its owners as given on its quarto's title page. Moreover, in recent years, it has been shown that Shakespeare was probably on hand when the quarto and octavo texts of *2* and *3 Henry VI* (in versions known as *The Contention* and *Richard Duke of York*) were put on by Pembroke's company, which acted twice before the queen at the end of 1592. Altogether, this group performed in its short career at least four of the Stratford poet's plays; but, I admit, it is easier to see why Shakespeare, whose loyalty to the

Burbages was unvarying, might wish to write for James Burbage and Pembroke's men at the familiar northern Theatre, than to see why Marlowe suddenly chose to do so.

What of Marlowe's loyalties just then? The actor Alleyn had made the roles of Tamburlaine, Doctor Faustus, and Barabas famous, and yet he had left to play for the competing Strange group at the Rose south of the river. What kept Marlowe from following his star? We might imagine that he had quarrelled with Alleyn, although there is no other sign of such a break. It was perfectly evident at Shoreditch, at any rate, that Shakespeare's history plays were being staged by Burbage's new troupe. Whether moved by profit or other factors, Marlowe began to write a history play for the same company. He readied *Edward II* for Pembroke's men, the only group named on that play's title page in its sole sixteenth-century edition.

Thus, late in 1591 and in 1592, Marlowe and Shakespeare were not quite competitors, but, instead, were in a kind of business alliance to ensure the Burbages' financial success against Henslowe's strong drawing power at the Rose. Their relationship slightly changed, or at least they found themselves in conditions unlike those I tried to sketch in connection with Shakespeare's early, chancy meetings with poets in the suburbs. For Pembroke's men, there were signs of electric success in the air. A pushy, touchy, tough-minded impresario, Burbage broke the law repeatedly to supply nuts and drink to his gallery audiences without a catering licence, and, no doubt, he dined well. Needing many writers, he was likely to entertain them privately at a supper or luncheon; and Shakespeare and Marlowe, at convivial times, probably would have met with other poets whom they knew.

What was said when Burbage's wine flowed? 'There was no talk about literature or the arts, or friendship or nature or morality or personal relations or the ends of life', reports an observer who heard of a dinner attended by dramatic and other writers in London some years before the First World War. Possibly among male playwrights in the capital, a few things had hardly changed in 400 years. 'There was not a touch of anything faintly aesthetic', one hears of that gathering, in which the talk involved gossip, scandal, love affairs, or anecdotes about the famous, 'accompanied by gusts of laughter, puns, limericks' and a good deal to drink.[8]

It may be absurd (let alone unhistorical) to imagine Stratford's poet in such company, or making up 'puns and limericks', although in the only reports of his meetings with Ben Jonson, Shakespeare is full of such nonsense. At a tavern one day, Jonson begins his mock epitaph, 'Here lies Ben Jonson, | That was once one [?one's son]', and Shakespeare completes it for him,

> Who while he lived was a slow thing
> And now being dead is no thing.

Or the elder poet puns on some *latten* (brass-like spoons) which he plans to give as a chistening gift to Jonson's son, and says he will let Ben the Latinist 'translate them'.[9]

If these jokes are authentically his own, they may give us a hint as to how the writer of the *Henry VI* plays dealt with Marlowe, who was better known as a playwright in around 1591 or 1592 than Shakespeare himself. Whatever the blaze of his doublet, the groomed wave of his hair, the mock-insolence of his voice, or the intensity of his glance, Marlowe's fame was the most spectacular thing about him. Most probably, Shakespeare's light, witty, spontaneous banter put the proud achiever at ease. Marlowe's own talk, of course, was often non-literal, playful, or exaggerative: he sought out fellow writers and apparently expected them to tolerate his antics.

What else, one wonders, did he (or anyone else) see in his Stratford friend in these years? Shakespeare's character is pretty well attested to by Henry Chettle, in *Kind-Harts Dreame* of 1592, where he finds the playwright's 'demeanor no less civil than he [is] excellent in the quality [i.e play-acting] he professes', and adds that those of rank or 'divers of worship' have reported Shakespeare's 'uprightness of dealing, which argues his honesty'. In connection with the last word, we are told that Elizabethans who knew their Horace would think of '*honestus*', meaning 'decent, gentlemanly'. Jonson also calls Shakespeare 'honest'. And Heywood and Chettle agree in finding him capable of taking 'offence', or angry if badly provoked. Nobody calls him 'gentle' while he is alive.

A near-monotony of agreement about him, at least among theatre men, reinforces one's feeling that Marlowe found him bland, easy, likeable, and receptive, if also self-protective and not necessarily forthcoming, but these men also knew each other's playscripts. A script can proclaim its author, rather as the Duke of Somerset's severed, bloody head in *3 Henry VI* becomes eloquent, when hunchback Richard throws it down with the remark, 'Speak thou for me, and tell them what I did.'[10] What Shakespeare 'did' in his English history sequence was to achieve a new, authentic, convincing realism which won audiences, and opened Marlowe's eyes. No one was more famously admiring of the new realism than Nashe, who, in *Pierce Penilesse*, evoked the English general Talbot in *1 Henry VI*: 'How it would have joyed brave Talbot (the Terror of the French)', he wrote in 1592, 'to think that after he had lain two hundred years in his Tomb, he should triumph again on the Stage.' The new effects, moreover, allow for pathos, since Talbot's bones are new embalmed with 'the tears of ten thousand spectators at least (at several times)' who 'imagine they behold him fresh bleeding'.[11]

Shakespeare's Talbot is predictably heroic in speech and battle, one feels, but the *Henry VI* dramas go somewhat further than heroics, along the lines of *2 Tamburlaine*, in subjecting honour and integrity to fresh scrutiny. It is a mistake to think that Marlowe had dealt with these concepts merely in a romantic, abstract way in the *Tamburlaine* sequence, but Shakespeare's scrutiny powerfully involves kingship, political rivalry, and war in the landscape of fifteenth-century England and France. He uses rambling, recalcitrant chronicle material selectively, in order to show some causation and impose unity on a scattered array of persons, events, and locales, often at the expense of any sustained psychological analysis. Nevertheless, he was opening up English history to realistic and sceptically intelligent treatment.

Marlowe learned from *2* and *3 Henry VI*; in turn, in *Edward II*, he offered his colleague examples (especially for *Richard II*), though again, no simple formula accounts for this theatrical symbiosis. In recent times, Nicholas Brooke and Maurice Charney have been moderate and suggestive about its general development: 'Marlowe seems to have been for Shakespeare not only a great poet', writes Brooke, 'but the inescapable imaginative creator of something initially alien which he could only assimilate with difficulty, through a process of imitative re-creation merging into critical parody.' Charney adds logically that comparisons between the two writers depend on 'what criteria' we choose to invoke, and that 'dramaturgic criteria' will yield the sounder, more positive results.[12] It is no discredit to Shakespeare that he never matched the acid social satire of *The Jew of Malta*, or wrote speeches in the savage, farcical vein of Barabas's pure joy in mass murder:

> There is no music to a Christian's knell:
> How sweet the bells ring now the nuns are dead
> That sound at other times like tinkers' pans![13]

Barabas's exaggerated portrait is no less 'deep', varying, or functional in its rich, satirical context, than is that of the much more naturalistic Shylock in the different pattern of romantic and psychological comedy in *The Merchant of Venice*.

As unalike as the poets' interests were becoming, their methods nearly merged in the early 1590s—at the very end of Marlowe's stagewriting career. In *Edward II* he submitted himself to Shakespeare chiefly in the matter of style, although Marlowe's own verbal style, after the introduction of Gaveston in scene i, becomes even more astringent than that of his colleague. Marlowe is likely to have viewed *Titus* or *Two Gentlemen of Verona* as self-consciously poetic, but he did not find artificiality in his mentor's history plays. Rather, he found in *Henry VI* a full, fairly unadorned manner, astonishingly close to the human voice. The barons of Shakespeare can sound like one another, but without reminding one of the stage or make-believe. They emerge from history itself, or seem to do so, as if brought to life from chronicle, document, and memory, with no need for a writer's seemingly imposed strategies. As an artist, Marlowe had usually concealed his hand, but he found Shakespeare's cool disinterestedness undeniably fine and chastening. His manner in *Edward II*, on the whole, is starkly terse, economical, and restrained, though in separating himself from the eloquence of *Tamburlaine* and the sonorous despair of *Faustus*, he does not implicitly repudiate his earlier verbal styles, nor does it follow, necessarily, that *Edward II* is in any way more perfectly achieved than *Tamburlaine*, *Faustus*, or *The Jew of Malta*. Marlowe watched Shakespeare's history dramas sharply in order to follow a path of his own. He aimed to give his new play a special authenticity, or a convincingly developed inwardness in a sustained central portrait, and a more realistic sense of time, and of political milieu, than he had seen on the stage. Also, he interpreted the chronicle story of Edward II as that of a king undone by a genuine, natural, but blinding infatuation with a male lover.

To treat that theme well, he made expert use of the annalistic records of Edward's reign, but he also turned to a more intimate source than Holinshed's *Chronicles*. For his compelling, unprecedented effects, he drew on his own views and special understanding of a man's love for a man.

Sexual acts

Sexual desire fascinated Marlowe and had stimulated his pen at an early point, if we think of his randy Student with Corinna in *All Ovid's Elegies*. But his own sexuality was a tangled matter, a part of his nature which he did not resolve in easy definition. 'I prefer Spanish wine', would have been a vastly simpler affirmation than the provocative, 'All they that love not tobacco and boys are fools.' The remark about 'boys', which could include young men, if he said it, may not have affirmed his sense of himself, though the comedy, pathos, and tensions of sexual love had intrigued him for years. Sex, after all, had been a theme of his training.

In the Tudor schoolroom, however, one might expect to find a slight distancing of this topic, in order to save the pupil from too many thoughts of real-life complications, though treating him to pleasurable, masturbatory images. Pupils who read Ovid were bathed in the sexual exploits of the gods, or they laughed over the tricks of lovers in Plautus's or Terence's plays. Outside grammar school, sex was forbidding for many Tudor boys, and marriage could be a distant, unlikely prospect. Couples in any town were relatively few: they made up about a third of the populace, instead of about half the community as today. And Marlowe had grown up in a strongly male, homosocial culture—despite the influence of his sisters—and had experienced a fairly extreme separation of the sexes. Living in a shared bedroom at Corpus, he had formed close alliances—he let two friends benefit from his Parker allowance, or took holidays exactly when one of his roommates did. Homoerotic relationships thrived at Cambridge, and his extra-curricular translation of the *Amores* suggests an early determination to be realistic about passion and its failures. His need for male companionship mixed with his zest for poetry, and continued in London, if he was willing to fight on behalf of Watson, or eager to share a room with the bachelor poet Kyd.

In his dramas, he had sketched heterosexual love very well, as in Dido's passion for Aeneas, but his homoerotic scenes have an unusually elated quality. Jupiter's comic dalliance with Ganymede in *Dido*, or Tamburlaine's seductive words with Theridamas, or Dr Faustus's uneasy, half-fawning relationship with Mephistophilis can suggest a homosexual author.

The matter of his sexuality, though, is more elusive, if only because, in a strict sense, there were no 'homosexuals' in the realm; homosexuality is a modern concept, and few Elizabethans seem to have thought of homo-erotic desire in connection with a distinct personality type, or as giving an erotic identity. Marlowe is called a homosexual today, with some justice, if we think of his plays and his descriptions in *Hero and Leander*, but the anachronism may be false to his self-awareness. Today, psychologists often view homo- and heterosexuality as part of a 'spectrum', rather than as two incompatible tendencies, and claim that most of us experience both inclinations (as in adolescent crushes, or later on). In any social class, a small minority may be predominantly homosexual; but this view itself has been contested. In modern academic Queer Theory, which took a cheerful impetus from Michel Foucault's writings in the last century, sexual identity has been left in what is called 'definitional instability'. We may need to understand Marlowe's and Shakespeare's age to understand our own. Their society knew buggery, and linked the word 'sodomy' vaguely with debauchery, a wide range of sexual practices and even criminal activity against the state, as Valerie Traub, Jonathan Goldberg, and others have closely shown.

There was a difference between socially tolerated behaviour and the force of the law, but the law—as Marlowe understood it—was severe. The 'first buggery statute', passed by Henry VIII's Reformation parliament in 1533, had been aimed against clerical dissidents. Priests were associated with dark vices, and sodomy as a legal category had served as a device to trick Catholic heretics who faced death if convicted of 'the detestable and abhomynable vice of buggery'. The law was three times renewed under Henry VIII, repealed by Queen Mary, and reinstated with the original Henrician terms by Elizabeth to live a long after-life, inasmuch as sodomy was punishable by death as late as 1861.[14]

Nevertheless, something had happened to the law by Marlowe's time. Bruce Smith believes that the original idea of sodomy as 'religious heresy', under Henry VIII, changed with a new focus on its threat to the family. That might help to explain the fact that, of all crimes prosecuted in

Marlowe's day, the least noticed were sexual ones. Magistrates seldom imagined that sodomy undid families, or at least they believed that what males did, with minimal violence and no loss to others, was not actionable. Sodomy, when linked with atheism, popery, or an aristocrat's failure to uphold the ideals of rank, could be seen as a social threat. But in the assizes of Marlowe's Kent and the other five Home Counties, during the forty-five years of Elizabeth's reign, only one man was convicted of sodomy.[15]

Still, Marlowe obviously knew a chaos of attitudes to same-sex love. The sodomite might be thought of as a devil, a heretic, an Italian, or a Turk or an African, or even linked with Harriot's New World savages, to justify violence against Roanoke's Indians. However, orderly or quiet homoerotic acts were not often stigmatized, although sermons continued to attack the incitements of boys on stage in female dress. Marlowe was aware of a deep male fear of effeminacy, or of a 'womanish' sensuality which could lead a man into an excessive, depleting lust for either boys or women.

As for young poets and scholars, their intense friendships or crushes could not have surprised him. In overcrowded London, most people were obliged to share a bed; the rooms in tenements opened easily into one another; doors were left ajar, and one's 'bedfellow' was no mystery to anyone under one's roof. Male intimacy was publicly displayed in clinging relationships, and emotional language or embraces between men were among the commonplaces of friendship. But there were other conventions of friendship, too, and it does not follow that a young poet, jealous of his independence and wary of threats to his vigour, was often in someone else's arms. A good deal stood in the way of anyone's casual sexual affairs, and no value in Marlowe's early writing is more keenly stressed than that of homosocial solidarity. In reports about him, he rarely seems to have been alone: we hear of his relations with this group or that, or with patrons, stationers, fellow agents, scientists, or the aides of noblemen. He never came to anything like Robert Greene's solitary distress, or Tom Nashe's lonely turmoil at the time of *Christ's Tears over Jerusalem*, or Kyd's final, dispirited isolation. The bravado of Marlowe's talk bound him closely to male friends, partly because his jokes about the Holy Ghost or the Virgin Mary were treasonous: anyone could have seen lewd speakers in a London pillory, or wearing papers on their heads proclaiming their indiscretions. No matter how outlandish he might be, he implied that he trusted his auditors, and he even used blasphemy as a *passe-partout* for winning new allies. Little that Marlowe did was unrelated to his need for comradeship and the male gang; he made himself intriguing, inciting, a centre of stimulus, though without a hint of the provocative clown. 'Almost into every company he cometh he persuades men to Atheism', says the exaggerating Baines, who adds that Marlowe wills men 'not to be afeard of bugbears and hobgoblins' and is 'utterly scorning [of] both god and his ministers'.[16] If that had been strictly true, he might have bored sophisticated young graduates, booksellers, scientists, mathematicians, and patrons, let alone most of the wits and poets whom he knew. He seems to have reserved his silliest atheistic platitudes for wide-eyed dullards such as Baines or Cholmeley.

Implicitly, he had announced a homosocial ideal as early as *Tamburlaine*. After seducing Theridamas to his ranks, the play's hero alludes to two fabled lovers of his native Scythia:

> by the love of Pylades and Orestes,
> Whose statues we adore in Scythia.

The mutual love of Pylades and Orestes had figured in Lucian's Greek dialogue *Toxarus*, which Erasmus translated—though Marlowe could also have found the two warriors in the *Ex Ponto* of Ovid, who declares that 'The young men's love was astonishing' (*mirus amor juvenum*, III. 2. 95).[17] Only Lucian, though, mentions that statues of the two men had been worshipped; and just as Scythians 'adore' Pylades and Orestes, so Theridamas, in Marlowe's play, is urged to cling to his new confederates, who 'will never leave thee til the death'. At first, Theridamas responds somewhat contortedly to this lesson in male fellowship:

> Nor thee, nor them, thrice-noble Tamburlaine,
> Shall want my heart to be with gladness pierc'd . . .[18]

Whatever the sexual overtones may be in the image of a male organ 'pierc'd', there is no hint of sodomy in that drama. Nor is there in *Faustus*, though a pitying remark by the Third Scholar in Act V lights up the hero's need for comradeship: Faustus is 'not well with being over-solitary'.[19]

Marlowe might have said the same of himself, and his views of the homosocial gang evolved. His tragic analysis of same-sex love in *Edward II* has little in common with the lightness of Jupiter sporting with rakish Ganymede in *Dido*. Direct evidence of his own sexual life is lacking; but Marlowe understood desire, and there is no reason to think he was particularly chaste at Cambridge or later on. Obviously, he craved affection, and may have found it more easily among future clergymen in a bottled-up, monkish university than when trying to survive in the suburbs. Also, there is something intense and dedicated in Marlowe. He seems to have needed allies for their wit, thought, gutsiness and creative audacity much more urgently than for their love: men such as Watson, Nashe, Roydon, Peele, Shakespeare, and probably Chapman and Kyd in different ways sustained him. He could make himself amiable as he moved from group to group in London: he was 'our friend', the publisher Edward Blount recalled of Marlowe, 'the man that hath been dear unto us'.[20] Like Watson, he put writing above other concerns in his life, and tried to sketch desire impartially and in believable contexts. As an observer, he was obsessed with human passion in society. Vilifying and barely tolerating sodomy, the age, in denying same-sex love, raised the psychological cost for anyone indulging in it. In Marlowe's own writing, there is an underlying grievance linked with desire: he can suggest pain, hesitation, and defeat beneath his endorsement of Ovidian eroticism. It can be one thing to yearn for sexual fulfilment, and another to fear a loss of integrity, a diminishing of the self, or even a breaking off from other friends necessary to one's well-being.

In *Edward II* he legitimizes homoerotic desire by treating it more realistically than any English playwright had done before. To prepare for this, he must have undertaken a penetrating enquiry into experience, including his grievances, hopes, frustrations, or cowardice. He became clearer about himself, and ruthlessly analytical and detached. There is a savage economy in *Edward II*, in which those who oppose the self-indulgent hero are supported by the fabric of society; they may be evil and adulterous, but they do not have far to seek for social approval.

Marlowe had found ripe material in the second edition of Holinshed's *Chronicles* (1587), with its vague, tantalizing sketch of the erotic life of King James VI of Scotland. The young king had been subject to the 'craft and subtiltie of some lewd and wicked persons', the *Chronicles* announced, and these men kept 'his maiestie thrall to authorise by his roiall power their abhominable and execrable facts'. This is nearly the language of the sodomy law, and gossip in London had filled in some details. King James, at the age of 14, had begun an affair with his father's French cousin, Esmé Stewart, sixth Sieur d'Aubigny, who was then 37. As a result, Aubigny had gained royal favours—to the distress of the Scottish court. In 1580 he had become earl of Lennox, governor of Dumbarton Castle, and first gentleman of the bedchamber, as well as a Privy Councillor and Lord Chamberlain. Having helped to tarnish his rivals, he next emerged as duke of Lennox and began to favour a Franco-Spanish plot to overthrow Elizabeth with 20,000 troops, and install Mary and James as joint rulers of England and Scotland. That optimistic plan having come to light, he fled to France, where he died in 1583 after promising to send his royal lover his embalmed heart.

The elder Walsingham had gone to Scotland to remonstrate with the king when the affair was over. James, who in his maturity wrote of the crime of 'Sodomie' in his *Basilikon Doron*, soon found other favourites, such as George Gordon, earl of Huntly, and later Alexander Lindsay, Lord Spynie. These liaisons made it easier for those of anti-Scottish feeling to deride his maturing self-command and political astuteness even as reports amplified the importance of his private behaviour. At the end of the 1580s, it was still being said that 'this Kinge' was subject to 'yonge men that lyes in his chamber and is his mynions'. Lord Spynie was not forced to flee the Scottish court until December 1592. Queen Elizabeth had already written in alarm of a Catholic such as Lennox, who had insidiously been in 'possession' of James's person. Since the latter was a candidate for the English throne, Britain might one day be ruled by a sodomite enthralled by a papist.[21]

Some of these facts and fears were known to agents of the Cecils, and Marlowe must have had a good sense of the Scottish king's dilemma. His interests were turning to Scotland, and the *Chronicles* helped him in another way. In that same text, he had found an account of a monarch not wholly unlike James VI. The reign of Edward II (1307–27) was distantly medieval, but a play about him might be topical, and Marlowe—like Shakespeare—eyed the box office. On the other hand, there was a problem in that the medieval king's story was no story, but a large clutter of political details involving a struggle over Edward's favourite, Gaveston, who had died in 1312, a baronial revolt and late royal victory, as well as a new ascendancy of power-seekers culminating in Edward's deposition and horrendous murder. As usual, Marlowe plunged into a variety of parallel sources including the chronicles of Robert Fabyan and of John Stow, as well as Foxe's 'Book of Martyrs', and almost certainly Jean Boucher's pamphlet, *Histoire tragique et mémorable de Pierre de Gaverston* (1588), which draws parallels between Henri III's sexual liaison with his courtier Epernon, and Edward's dalliance with a reckless Gaveston.[22]

Also available, in several editions, was John Stow's stubby octavo, *Summarie of Englyshe Chronicles*, which offered no outline for a tragedy, but a digest of Edward's reign with a blurry, grainy verbal snapshot of the king: 'He was fayre of body, but unsteadfast of manners, and disposed to lightness: he refused the company of his lordes . . . and haunted the company of villeins and vile persons.' Stow does not describe the 'vile' companions or lovers, but from hints scarcely better than these the play-wright sketches a deeply ambiguous erotic affair.[23] Marlowe was drawn to tragedy partly because of his breadth of interest in society and history, but also, it seems to me, because of his acute, critical self-consciousness, his interest in his own sometimes wavering path in life, and his impulsive nature and behaviour. In a shadowy way, he can seem to be in each of his heroes, since he is not wholly unlike the beautifully articulate, boasting, self-deluding Tamburlaine, or the rashly intellectual, question-ing, upsetting, doubting Faustus, or the obsessive, jejune, easily entranced Edward II of England. But what is often overlooked is that Marlowe, in writing, comes to terms temporarily with himself, 'settles' his score, as it were, and by identifying his own traits frees his imagination and artistry. What he draws from the quarry of the self is combined with his observa-tions of others and vividly etched into something life-like, distinct, and essentially not autobiographical at all. The main movement of his art is away from heroism and romanticism of any kind, and towards a more complicating view of human society. It is true that Edward seeks pleasure and self-fulfilment with the zeal of a Cambridge poet gloating over the chance of outdoing Virgil or Plautus; but this hero is less important than his royal setting. Marlowe places him in a milieu of opportunism, egotism, greed, and wilfulness in which politics is nastier, grubbier, and more treacherous than Shakespeare had so far shown it. In using his sources, he eliminates time gaps, unhistorically heightens Mortimer as the king's antithesis and leader of a baronial clique, and develops Edward's relations with two male lovers, the barons, and his wife. The king's infatuation is treated as a human fact, not as a whim or as something to be got over, but as a need of the confused, immature, and headstrong Edward.

Edward II, no doubt, offers the first great depiction of same-sex love for the stage, but its dramatization of erotic behaviour is subordinated to its focus on power. The play makes no liberal case for sexual freedom, but takes up the cost of self-realization and the folly of the impulsive, unheeding will, while significantly doing justice to the temper of an English reign. 'Marlowe's play', says the modern historian Natalie Fryde, 'has captured the essential atmosphere of the regime perhaps better than any historian has since been able to do.'[24]

The regime was neither static nor colourless, and the drama brings energy and light to the theme of poor kingship. As green as Edward is, he takes the initiative when he accedes to the throne and invites his minion to share power. First banished by Edward's father, Piers Gaveston on returning to England aims to 'draw the pliant king which way I please'. Marlowe's key figures implicitly choose, proclaim, and 'act out' their sexuality, as, for example in Tamburlaine's or Faustus's acts of showily cutting an arm to shed manly blood, or in Barabas's lurid boasts or his slaughter of male rivals. Gaveston acts out his homoerotic desire, but also conveys a less selfish passion for art and fancy, and so takes on a strange and valid authority. The dramatist omits what historical sources had said of Piers de Gaveston's theft of royal treasures, or of his status as the son of a Gascon knight, and makes him reciprocate the king's love.

The French butterfly doubly offends as a commoner, and it is impossible not to sympathize with the barons' grievance as the kingdom goes to ruin. Homoerotic infatuation is shown in the worst light, except that the light is not especially lurid. In contrast, Michael Drayton's poem *Peirs Gaveston, Earl of Cornwall*, of 1593, moralizes on sensuality while also sentimentally exploiting it: 'His love-sick lips at every kissing qualm, | Cling to my lips, to cure their grief with balm.'[25] We are barely allowed to imagine a riot of senses in Marlowe's tragedy, for the interesting reason that sensuality is not seen as a dramatic, contentious issue, by either the barons or the playwright himself.

Here there is something strikingly different from the account of James VI in Holinshed's *Chronicles*, which Marlowe cannot have overlooked since it was a main source for his drama. (I waive for the moment anything he may have heard from Poley, who regularly visited Berwick-on-Tweed, which was a base for English spies in Scotland, or from Roydon or other informants concerning James VI.) Whereas the account in Holinshed implies that male lovers are nasty, perverted, slimy, insidious, and far worse than female vamps would have been in ruining Scotland's king, Marlowe will have none of this in his sketches of Gaveston or Spencer Junior with King Edward. If we think of *Edward II* as a 'homosexual' play, what is most striking is the normality it suggests in same-sex love. Nearly everything we hear of Gaveston suggests his fondness for dress, art, movement, lightness, and the sensual beauty of the classics—all appealing but doomed values; for what is at stake is Edward's conduct of the realm. In Marlowe's view, there is ultimately no privacy, retreat, or escape into romance for anyone, and every bedroom door is open. Whatever is done or experienced affects the fabric of a surrounding world. In fact, the presence of Gaveston figures in an epic conflict between the king and his opposing noblemen, who are goaded by Young Mortimer. That confrontation involves virtually everyone else in the play; Kent, the king's brother, wavers between the two camps, but only the author remains neutral. 'Was ever king thus overruled as I?' Edward weakly complains, as he shrugs off duties of state. At any cost, he will have Gaveston, and there is no special emphasis on the latter's selfishness or exulting in royal favours.

Typically, Marlowe defeats expectations to show balanced values, which generate a dialectic, so that an audience is called upon to interpret and evaluate rather than to rest in sympathizing with either camp. We do not observe Gaveston flattering or manipulating the king or mocking the peers, and at first the barons are no more effectual than the flaccid, weak-minded Edward himself. Not for the first time, Marlowe draws on an amusing relationship between power and dress, which in light of his own habits might be half-responsible for his penury in London. Gaveston 'jets it', Mortimer Junior remarks. 'I have not seen a dapper jack so brisk; | He wears a short Italian hooded cloak | Larded with pearl.' The upstart lover even animates his enemies, who speak colourfully or accept his mode even as they denounce him.[26]

Gaveston's own beautiful, sensual lines early in the play, and later his naive Italianate aspects, suggest the imagination, poetry, and sexual fantasies of youth. From a biographical viewpoint, no other figure in Marlowe's works is more nearly a product of his own schooldays, or more indicative of his sense that hard political reality will destroy anyone incapable of changing imaginatively in order to cope with it. Oddly isolated by art and shows, Gaveston and Edward are threatened by the barons' images of maiming, beheading, and symbolic castration, which itself underlines the king's horror of a feminine role in same-sex love. Despairing over Gaveston's banishment, Edward most freely expresses his desire when his lover is absent.

His French-born wife Queen Isabella, who later sanctions his murder, is seen in fleeting glimpses as the king might have perceived her, and the tragedy treats no figure as independent of time, process, and deep self-contradiction. Time had been nearly palpable in Marlowe's version of Lucan's account of the civil war horrors of Caesar's day in the *Pharsalia*. His version of Book I of the *Pharsalia*—probably drafted at Cambridge, but revised later in London—catches the cold, imperious height and rush of a poem which suggests that historical forces are beyond control and indifferent to human suffering or awareness. Nearly the central experience of Marlowe's life was his own quick, half-illusory success as a theatre poet. If he draws on Lucan and on valid personal experience in writing *Edward II*, he demands a special alertness of theatre-goers, for in some scenes he more nearly gives us the bones of a history play instead of its flesh, and there is hardly any relief from the forward surge of the stage action. Unstable identities give us little chance to form fixed judgements of the king's enemies, and yet the effect is realistic. Marlowe learns from Shakespeare's examples of lean, expository style, but he avoids the comforting expansions of feeling, emotive redundancies, and fixed delineations of knowable 'personality' in the *Henry VI* dramas. Queen Isabella is in some ways more life-like than other females depicted on the English stage up to her time, since she is varying, fitfully glimpsed, and plausibly untheatrical. Far from believing in unified psyches, Marlowe allows for the coexistence of incompatible traits, such as loyalty and egoistic self-regard. Refusing to separate love from politics, Isabella does not reveal the *process* of her corruption, but she is unpredictably horrendous, persuasive as a liar, half-sympathetic before her treachery, and always a riveting index of her unsparing milieu.

Gaveston is trapped and killed by Warwick. Dreadful news of beaten garrisons in France, or of the aggressive Irish, of the Scots at the walls of York, or haughty Danes at sea, and unrigged English ships in port, comes in to King Edward from all sides, but the reports do not come in, as it were, to a bleak cell. So far, there is nothing claustrophobic in the action. Music, lavish costume, space, and resurgence fill the court scenes, even after most of the peers defect. Marlowe's sense of the interconnection between the personal and political allows for no salvation for his king, two of whose late companions, Spencer Junior and Baldock, express just such bitterness over lack of preferment as might have been heard at the author's Cambridge. Edward not only takes Spencer Junior as a new lover, but begins to attend unselfishly to his companions in adversity. The later scenes were to be one template for Shakespeare's construction of Acts III–V in *Richard II*, and may not have been forgotten by the author of *King Lear*. Disguised as clergy and hounded by enemies, Edward with his two exiles takes refuge in the countryside with a Welsh abbot, who presides over a belated seminar on governance. 'Come Spencer, come Baldock, come sit down by me', the hero orders, as he makes trial of the pomp and empery of kingship. 'For God's sake let us sit upon the ground', Shakespeare begins in his finely expansive, but not more life-like variation on this episode in *Richard II* (III. ii). Edward is histrionic almost to the end, but not at the cost of failing to identify his solipsistic illusions. In captivity, he removes his crown, pretends to surrender it to Leicester, and snatches it back in a rage. More sharply than in the imitative scene in *Richard II* (IV. i), his antics suggest his earlier, irresponsible play-acting in his sacred royal role.

That consistency typifies Marlowe's unromantic and sceptical attitude to the possibility of redemptive changes in human nature. He allows for discovery, recognition, and a play of the mind over personal failings, but not for the leopard's changing of his spots. It is a mistake to simplify his attitudes as if they responded only negatively to religion, or to suppose that he shuts himself off to any possibility of illumination. But the here and now, for him, exists in the order in which social reality conditions the psyche and exacts penalties for barbarity, or even for a lack of awareness of the duty one human being owes another. Edward's own torture befits a tragedy which involves broken trust, political depravity, and outright treachery. Since Kent aims to restore Edward to the throne, Mortimer

Junior orders that the deposed king be made to droop and fret. He is hurried from Berkeley to Kenilworth's dungeons, and left ten days in sewage, with drumming to keep him awake in the stench. His beard is shaved in puddle-water—an echo of Edward's order for Coventry's bishop to be plunged in it. His death scene is the most terrible of any episode that survives from the Elizabethan theatre. Marlowe does not originate it, but takes most of its details from Holinshed, who is more luridly specific, although Marlowe invents the perpetrator Lightborne (the name is an Anglicizing of 'Lucifer'), who increases the tension and horror of the scene through his pretended kindness. Edward must be dispatched cunningly, with no trace of harm to be seen on his corpse. Accordingly, as he lies forcibly on a bed, a red hot spit is shoved up into his fundament, and rolled about, to and fro, to burn his entrails.

'I fear me', says Maltravers of the victim's excruciating scream, 'that this cry will raise the town.'[27]

In its ghastly way, Edward's death mimics a male sexual act. What are we to make of this? Does Marlowe punish the hero for buggery, or punish the excoriating vileness of his own desires, or show the Elizabethan age an image of its own frightful inhumanity? If he pictures sex in the light of brutal political reality, that is not surprising for a poet who has worked as a government agent, but there is a tragic vision here which is as terrifying and inexplicable as that of his rival's perceptions in works to come.

Love is corrupted in this play not only by politics but by a resiliently evil, existential self-regard. Isabella has sent a jewel to Edward in prison as a token of 'my love', after subscribing to his death. When at last Mortimer and Isabella are caught, exposed, and condemned, she is shown to plead very well as a blameless mother to her stern, just son, King Edward III. 'Away with her!' cries Edward, who sends her to prison in the Tower, 'her words enforce these tears.' The queen may yet save her own head.[28]

In 1592 no more powerfully unified history play had been written for the London stage. Though borrowing from Shakespeare, Marlowe for the moment eclipses him in a fresh, astute development of psychology and in fresh techniques in dramaturgy, including sharply contrasting styles of speech. It is likely that *Richard III* was performed some months after Marlowe's opus, and it is in his later ritualistic *Richard II* that Shakespeare makes the most considerable use of Marlowe's historical tragedy. Staged in around 1595, *Richard II* has a richly worked, ceremonial effect in its demystification of monarchy. Marlowe's tragedy, in contrast, exhibits the haunting sacredness of kingship, and, as actors and critics have noticed, this is one reason why Edward's final scream can seem to echo long after it is heard.

That pitiable scream, and the story of the king's deposition, may not have pleased Queen Elizabeth, who presumably saw this drama acted at court. Registered on 6 July 1593, it appeared as a well-printed quarto, of 1594, in a title which exalts its villain, as *The troublesome raigne and lamentable death of Edward the second, King of England: with the tragicall fall of proud Mortimer.*

In modern times, it has had a high reputation, usually for the wrong reasons, since it has been taken to be the most 'Shakespearean' and so the most correct of Marlowe's works. But unless one credits the uniqueness of his own dramaturgy, one's understanding even of his rival's developments will be the poorer. The two writers innovated very differently with regard to time, history, causation, and tragic effect. If Marlowe's play is satisfying, that is largely because it eludes all rules but its own.

There were further quartos of *Edward II* in 1598, 1612, and 1622. Unlike his other dramas, this one did not devolve into Philip Henslowe's hands at the Rose, but was acquired by Queen Anne's men, a troupe which secured a new theatre in the Red Bull to the north of the city in Clerken-well, in about 1603. Actors performed there in that year, and must have staged Marlowe's drama at that playhouse. His originality in *Edward II* is impressive, and if the play lacks the full imaginative brilliance of *Tamburlaine*, or the depth and exuberance of *The Jew of Malta*, or the intensity and pathos of *Doctor Faustus*, it is like those works in extending our ideas of what stage tragedy may be, especially in its intelligently sensitive portrayal of homoerotic passion. Plays were only a trifling segment of the Jacobean book trade; but it is not hard to believe that *Edward II*'s contemporary editions sold well, or that the fourth edition sold out. Its quarto of 1622, itself, may reflect a late stage revival, in assigning the play to the 'Queenes Majesties Servants at the Red Bull'.

Love in a cold climate

Unfortunately, a long, dreary interval elapsed between the selling of *Edward II* and the date of its first known staging. The theatres had been closed since 23 June 1592. 'The plague still encreaseth in London', wrote the Catholic spy Richard Verstegan in October.[29] At that time, only some of the wealthy had returned to the capital; apprentices were being discharged from service, and rituals of life and trade were already breaking down. Less grain was being imported into the city and 'dead carts' rolled in the streets. By 10 November, after a stay in Kent, Marlowe had a sight of the area north of Houndsditch, but may not have rushed into the theatre suburbs to face an entanglement with constables and an unpaid fine of £20, which, by then, he owed to a law court. He often behaved as if he were immune to danger, or happy to trust in fate, but he was slow to risk his physical freedom. For him, there was probably a sense of endings and new beginnings; plague ticked away more quickly than time, divesting him of his worst enemy in Robert Greene, and of one of his close friends in Thomas Watson. Greene had died on 3 September, after eating a meal of pickled herring which made him ill. In a final fling at the actors, he had left a clever work, which Henry Chettle copied out and saw through the press as *Greenes Groats-worth of Witte*.

Licensed on 20 September and printed in about 500 copies, the pamphlet had the vogue of a small, irritating *cause célèbre*. Greene mainly attacks a crass, tigerish 'Shake-scene', a grammar-school upstart and protégé of the Burbages (the 'burrs') who take the bread out of poets' mouths. But he also attacks Marlowe for a lack of faith, and implies that he has been beguiled by Italian sophistry, or Machiavelli's godlessness. 'Wonder not', warns Greene, who calls Marlowe a 'famous gracer of Tragedians' and admits his own earlier fall from grace. 'Why should thy excellent wit, *His* gift, be so blinded, that thou shouldst give no glory to the giver? Is it pestilent Machiavellian policy that thou hast studied? O peevish folly!'[30]

This was fairly mild, and since Greene had played the 'atheist' card earlier, Marlowe cannot have been greatly surprised; but there was a twist late in the year. Either Shakespeare or his friends complained of insults to 'Shake-scene' in *Groats-worth*, and noticed that Henry Chettle had sent the work to the press. Chettle, with an air of innocence, finally apologized in his *Kind-Harts Dreame* (licensed on 8 December). He notes that Greene has offended several 'playmakers'. With two of the aggrieved souls, Chettle is not acquainted, 'and with one of them [Marlowe] I care not if I never be'. Yet in all his years in the printing trade, he has spared scholars from grief. Indeed, he had deleted a passage aimed at Marlowe, 'whose learning I reverence', since he felt that poor Greene had written it in displeasure, 'or had it been true', he adds, 'yet to publish it, were intolerable'. He hopes that Marlowe 'will use me no worse than I deserve'.[31]

This oily, self-righteous, and side-stepping apology made up for nothing, and reinforced the hoary atheistic charge, but if Marlowe protested to Chettle, he soon let the matter drop. He was unlikely to fret over what was said of him, and might have been glad to be damned, but for the fact that what was said could damage his chances with a sponsor; he needed material help, so it was useful to brighten his name if he could. The theatres in closing down, after all, freed him from catering to the public. He had a chance to pick up half-abandoned threads, weave anew, cater to patrons, or put himself on a fresh footing with the moneyed gentry. He had not sold his brains to the Shoreditch impresarios, but, in turning away from playwriting, he gave up a crucial outlet for his energies.

No doubt, there was an abiding, inner restlessness in Marlowe's nature, as well as a craving for risk and confrontation. Restlessness appears varyingly in his works, as in Tamburlaine's need for endless campaigns, or in Faustus's penchant for a 'desperate enterprise'. Stephen Greenblatt, in a brilliant and influential essay, relates the poet's temperament to an instinctive sympathy for the remote and alien, a fondness for repetition, and to an admiration for the 'playful courage' of his own stage heroes. If Marlowe feared satiety or personal fulfilment, he may have had an obsessive 'will to absolute play'. However, he had to spin out new dramas in order to live; he continually explored new themes, locales, situations, or personality types (as Greenblatt recognizes), and could not afford to keep his pen idle.[32] For the time being, he wrote two brief pieces in Latin, a dedication to the countess of Pembroke and elegiac lines on Sir Roger Manwood, both of which seem to have preceded his writing of *Hero and Leander.*

Even in the plague, booksellers outside St Paul's did a fair business, and Marlowe chatted with them now and then, under the high, garish shop signs. Some of these shops were three or four storeys tall, as good as anything a bibliomaniac could find outside a Frankfurt fair. Probably in the autumn, he was glimpsed in the area by Gabriel Harvey. The living hero of *Pedantius* had come up to the capital to work for his printer (John

Wolfe) in St Paul's churchyard, after failing at Cambridge to get a Public Oratorship or the Mastership of Trinity Hall. After the poet's death, he published in *A New Letter of Notable Contents* a poem called 'Gorgon, or the Wonderful Year', which has often been taken to be wholly about Marlowe.

'Weep Paul's', he writes with irony, 'thy Tamburlaine vouchsafes to die.' Harvey appears to imply that *Tamburlaine*'s poet had insulted the sick and dying in London before being killed by the plague. 'The haughty man extolls his hideous thoughts', he bitterly complains,

> And gloriously insults upon poor souls,
> That plague themselves: *for faint hearts plague themselves.*

The poem is, in fact, chiefly about a dim-witted eccentric named Peter Shakerley, who had paraded in a bizarre fashion at St Paul's, and also about Harvey's enemy Tom Nashe ('the second Shakerley'). But in *A New Letter* itself, Harvey goes out of the way to attack not only Nashe but Nashe's friends: he calls Marlowe a 'Lucian', or scoffer at religion, and links him with 'extreme *Vanity*' and implicitly, I think, in the poem, with peacock pride and ostentation.[33]

Marlowe would have had little time for Harvey, but he had some feeling for Thomas Watson, who was buried at St Bartholomew's churchyard on 26 September, and may have died at St Bartholomew's Hospital. Watson had nearly finished a Latin *magnum opus*, written in the vein of Roman erotic pastorals, called *Amintae Gaudia* ('The Joys of Amyntas'), and, for once, his jokes had assisted his genius. This large poem celebrates young lovers who know almost nothing of love: Amyntas at 15 is a naive or bogus shepherd, who adores little Phyllis, whom he congratulates for having no dandruff in her hair. Watson includes some gorgeous mythology in ten separate eclogues, one of which amounts to a minor epic, and the poem has other effects which remind one of Ovid's *Metamorphoses*. The *Amintae* has been called 'the most successful Ovidian performance by any Englishman writing in Latin',[34] and its naive lovers especially have a relation to Marlowe's *Hero*.

Watson had meant to inscribe the work to Philip Sidney's sister, the countess of Pembroke. As a duty to his friend, Marlowe wrote a Latin dedication to her some time before 10 November, when the *Amintae* was licensed. Having looked into other dedications to the countess, he borrowed lightly from one by Samuel Daniel, who had been among the crush of Walsingham's couriers at Paris. Not staying long at the rue St Jacques, Daniel had travelled in the 1580s with a spy named Julio Marino, alias Renat, who is said to have killed the queen of Navarre. (Complete with poisoned gloves, Renat makes a brief debut as the apothecary in scene iii of *The Massacre at Paris*.) In his dedicatory letter, Marlowe is florid and graceful, with the excuse that hyperbole looks better in Latin than in English: 'Descendant of the gods who impartest now to my rude pen breathings of a lofty rage', he writes, 'deign to be patron to this posthumous Amyntas.'[35] Mary Sidney, of course, put up with more absurd encomia than that.

Probably, in helping along Watson's poem he was angling for the countess's attention. He was ready to try for new patronage, and baited his hook as he could, and yet he did credit to Watson's work. In the past, that friend had been ill used by the poet Abraham Fraunce, and this interested Marlowe. After translating Watson's earlier Latin *Amyntas* of 1585 into English, Fraunce had passed off the result as his own *Lamentations of Amintas* without acknowledgement. Also in an effort to appeal to Mary Sidney, he had lately collected a book of verse tales about the pagan gods, and issued it as *The Third part of the Countesse of Pembroke's Ivychurch, entituled Amintas' Dale.*

One of the stories, as Marlowe noticed, was about Venus and Adonis. The Queen of Love mentions 'how Leander died, as he swam to the beautiful Hero'. The narrator goes on to say that '*Leander* and *Hero*'s love is in every man's mouth', inasmuch as Ovid had exalted the two lovers in the *Heroides*, and their story even has filled a book in Spanish called *Historia de Leandro y Hero.*[36]

Marlowe must have read *Amintas' Dale* since its phrases echo in his dedication of Watson's volume, but he felt Fraunce had underestimated the lovers, Hero and Leander. He himself saw their beginnings in a short Greek poem by Musaeus, of which there were handy Latin versions. Musaeus had treated the tale as a mythic tragedy, but Marlowe, with a cool sense of rivalry, meant to stand it on its head and make it partly comic, exuberant, and modern.

It is difficult to date his own poem *Hero and Leander* exactly, but with its mature grace of style, it probably responds to Watson's *Amintae* and Fraunce's *Amintas' Dale*. Far from being like his college exercises, it has the merit of making one forget that it is a poem. It is one of the most original works ever written about love, though it has affinities with Shakespeare's *Venus and Adonis*, which appears to have been written at nearly the same time.

Late in the autumn, the weather began to help both Marlowe and Shakespeare, and mercifully diminished the weekly death-tolls. In December, freezing winds swept the British Isles, with the result that Londoners were more likely to die of hypothermia than the epidemic. On Christmas day, the cold was so intense (says *The Book of Days*) that starved wolves were said to have entered Vienna to prey on people and cattle. Four days later in England, the authorities lifted the ban on play-acting for about a month.

Actors and their suppliers then rushed back to the suburbs in a busy, flurried round of activity. At the Theatre and the Curtain, people weary of plague flocked to entertainments, and the taverns and alehouses did good business. Modern editors are right, I think, in believing that Shakespeare did not begin *Venus and Adonis* before the autumn, but the autumn itself had left playwrights free, so *Venus* may have existed in some form by January. In his works, Shakespeare was not averse to using topical puns, or disguised allusions relating to the theatres, himself, or his fellows. In *Venus* there is an alehouse joke of some topicality about 'shrill-tongued tapsters, answering every call' and 'Soothing the humour of fantastic wits' (ll. 849–50). The joke is odd, since it has little to do with *Venus*'s setting. We lack proof that it refers to Marlowe, but whether or not the two met at an alehouse before stepping into the sub-zero dusk, Marlowe and his colleague became aware of each other's Ovidian projects. Shakespeare's fragile, lovely, shrinking-violet boy Adonis evokes the same kind of male beauty that Marlowe praises in Leander, and gods and mortals mingle in both erotic poems. *Venus*'s narrator is barely characterized, but in remarks such as 'Being proud, as females are, to see him woo her' (l. 309), he can sound like Marlowe's deliberately crass tale-teller.

Neither poet was very proprietary about his non-dramatic works, and both were turning to a fashionable genre. Thomas Lodge, in *Scillaes Metamorphosis* (1589), had produced the first Ovidian epyllion. That term itself, meaning little epic, was not used by Tudor poets (though 'epyllion' does occur in an index to Callimachus in 1543). Drayton, Daniel, and others were beginning to follow a new vogue, at any rate. In the epyllia fashion of the 1590s, the writer typically offers a tale of two lovers or would-be lovers, usually either as a pitiful complaint or as a third-person history which ends tragically. Emphasis falls on the effects of passion, hence on lyric beauty, pathos, and tragic irony. Benefiting from a group identity, epyllia poets borrowed each other's phrases, or even finished each other's works, as both Henry Petowe and George Chapman were to write completions for Marlowe's *Hero and Leander*.

Shakespeare's *Venus* opens with originality and decorum. Marlowe makes his own work as outrageous as possible, but he begins rather timidly, as Gordon Braden (a good student of his Greek bearings) has shown. We might be back in a Cambridge bedroom with a translator of the classics who has some Latin versions of 'Hero and Leander' as well as a copy of Musaeus's Greek poem at his elbow, though Marlowe at least *gazed* at the old Greek version.

Musaeus had written, for example,

Σηστὸς ἔην καὶ Ἄβυδος ἐναντίον ἐγγύθι πόντου· γείτονές εἰσι πόληες.

[There was Sestos, and Abydos opposite near the sea. They are
neighbouring cities.][37]

Marlowe—apparently—imitates that balanced simplicity as he evokes the cities of two lovers at either side of the Hellespont, the ancient name for the Dardanelles:

> On Hellespont, guilty of true love's blood,
> In view and opposite two cities stood,
> Sea-borderers, disjoined by Neptune's might:
> The one Abydos, the other Sestos hight.[38]

And yet *Hero and Leander* soon takes leave of literary models. Its narrator might be a college Fellow given to crass remarks on women, or else a drinking mate who cracks off-colour jokes with Ovid in a Roman bistro. In a brisk narrative, one witty absurdity leads to the next. Hero is so sexually alluring that her very fragrance turns heads, and yet she is virginal and demure in a blue kirtle 'whereon was many a stain, | Made with the blood of wretched lovers slain'. Did she stab her lovers day by day without changing the kirtle?

Many of these details are comic, and yet as hyberbole runs nearly wild we become aware of a stunning tension. No other short narrative in

English is so filled with the bustle and turmoil of erotic power, or has such an overwhelming mood of amorousness. Because nature is bent on desire, practically everything flatters Leander and urges him to success in love. The cities on either side of the Hellespont are divided by 'Neptune's might'—as if this deity were holding them apart. All nature is personified—and the sea is throbbingly sexualized by Neptune, who nearly drowns Leander while making love. Here a sense of the amorality of the classics, and of the relief the poet knew in finding a sounder, saner world in his early reading, lie behind Marlowe's best writing. Yet all of this looks as if it were tossed off in an instant—the sea-god plays with the boy's tresses,

> watched his arms, and as they opened wide
> At every stroke, betwixt them would he slide
> And steal a kiss, and then run out and dance,
> And as he turned, cast many a lustful glance,
> And threw him gaudy toys to please his eye,
> And dive into the water, and there pry
> Upon his breast, his thighs, and every limb,
> And up again, and close beside him swim,
> And talk of love. Leander made reply,
> 'You are deceived, I am no woman, I.'[39]

The colour and amusing homoerotic effects of *Hero* are, at least in part, Marlowe's response to deprivation. The poem appears to have been written during a plague which lifted for a few winter weeks, only to return. With little or no income, he had to depend on the resources of a patron who had been in debt, but whom he needed to please. Walsingham knew him well enough, and could be expected to approve his art. But Marlowe's reputation as a daring, outlandish heretic or 'atheist' stood in the way of finding new sponsorship, and he may have suspected that not everyone at Walsingham's Scadbury approved of him. No doubt, there were obstacles and uncertainties in his temperament, his habits, his jokes and exaggerations, his eagerness to irk and incite comment. In the gloom of the suburbs, he may have felt that his part-time government work could tell against him, or that he already had some obscure enemies.

In *Hero*, his wit and gorgeous lyric effects belong to a fabric of deception, and the work's power arises from a realistic, underlying concern with the human psyche. Leander's words are hardly needed to persuade Hero to make love, as she is won by a glance at the outset. Leander speaks with the naivity of an adolescent who has rehearsed arguments against virginity, and still the poem is subtle and disturbing. In Musaeus's version, Hero's parents have kept her nearly as a prisoner, and she devotes herself to the goddess Aphrodite with a firm belief in chastity. Eliminating the parents, Marlowe develops the irony of her being a chaste and sacred advocate of love, and calls her 'Venus' nun'. He apparently lifts the phrase from Stephen Gosson's *School of Abuse* (1579), in which prostitutes just outside London are 'like Venus nuns in a cloister' in the bordellos of Newington and Islington.[40] In Elizabethan slang—as in Hamlet's insults to Ophelia—'nun' and 'nunnery' signify prostitute and bordello, and Marlowe finds a 'nun' in the psyche of every young woman who makes love. Yet his concern is to highlight both lovers, who seem innocent of sexual experience and at first even of gender identity.

Leander is gorgeous enough to delight any male whom he meets—

> His body was as straight as Circe's wand;
> Jove might have supped out nectar from his hand.
> Even as delicious meat is to the taste,
> So was his neck in touching, and surpassed
> The white of Pelops' shoulder. I could tell ye
> How smooth his breast was, and how white his belly
>
> .   .   .   .
>
> Had wild Hippolytus Leander seen,
> Enamoured of his beauty had he been;
> His presence made the rudest peasant melt,
> That in the vast uplandish country dwelt.
> The barbarous Thracian soldier, moved with nought,
> Was moved with him, and for his favour sought.
> Some swore he was a maid in man's attire,
> For in his looks were all that men desire,
> A pleasant smiling cheek, a speaking eye,
> A brow for Love to banquet royally;
> And such as knew he was a man would say,
> 'Leander, thou art made for amorous play:
> Why art thou not in love, and loved of all?
> Though thou be fair, yet be not thine own thrall.'[41]

Yet Marlowe does not indulge in homoerotic fantasies for their own sake. The poem has been called a 'bisexual fantasy', but it is also a study of adolescent love, of experience in general and the human dilemma. Biographically viewed, it offers through its snippety narrator a sense of violence barely under control, and of the author's frail hope and recent pessimism. Hero's own shock and dismay after love-making become magnified as if they are preludes to tragedy, and the groping of the lovers begins to look as important as anything that can happen to them. Far from denying pleasure, Marlowe enormously heightens it and locates its essence in sexuality, with the instincts of a theatre man, since Leander's appeal is similar to that of Elizabethan boy actors in silks, wigs, and cosmetics. The cross-dressing tradition was never legally forced upon English acting companies, and when a foreign troupe acted in England, women took the female roles. The poet grants a temporary freedom to sexual desire, not for the sake of indulging himself but to create the utmost intensity in an amorous design.

Also, he discovers an advanced method. His narrator is abrupt, devil-may-care, often unreliable, but brilliant enough to be worth listening to, even though he might be asking us to buy him another drink. One thinks of Chaucer's Canterbury-bound raconteurs, but a much closer parallel exists in works such as T. S. Eliot's 'The Love Song of J. Alfred Prufrock', or again in monologues by Frost, Lowell, or Tony Harrison. In other words, Marlowe foreshadows the method of the dramatic and psychological monologue. What the narrator says is slanted, but one is encouraged to see through the aberrant report to the real state of psyches, and beyond that to symbols of the human condition. The poem takes a giant step ahead in form, and the form itself partly arises from Marlowe's need to conceal his feelings; he never permits himself, here or elsewhere, a direct viewpoint of his own. He uses hyperbolic images to distance sexual love, but then explores what might be his, or anyone's, initial experience of it. If the action is cruel, its shame and pain are offset by fumbling tenderness. Nor can we blame the tale-teller for being perverse or inconsistent. Typically, the narrator digresses in an anecdote about Mercury, loses the story's thread or its relation to the love-story, and so becomes irrelevant, only to enthral in all that he says. His voice has so strong a movement that nothing impedes it, and the poem's beauty begins to look inevitable, though no more consciously planned than nature's forms may be. Nothing is overtly patterned in *Hero* except for the stepping stones of its couplet rhymes. One result is that it becomes a laboratory of the imagination, even a discourse *about* writing, and a work so free of correctness that it exhibits at every turn the primacy of creativity itself.

Marlowe's major poem has been admired for centuries, though never more avidly than by the Victorians. Its 'riot of passion and of delight in the beauty of colour and form', wrote George Saintsbury, 'has never been approached by any writer'. For Havelock Ellis, the poem was 'the brightest flower of the English Renaissance', and Swinburne, with *Hero and Leander* doubtless in mind, called its poet 'alone the true Apollo of our dawn'.[42] Such praise had been foreshadowed in lines which Sir Francis Verney sent to Robert Cecil, then earl of Salisbury, only a few years after *Hero* was published. Verney hails Marlowe as 'the splendour of our worthless time', as if no other Renaissance poet could touch him.[43]

There are one or two mysteries in relation to the poem's fate. After Marlowe died, Gabriel Harvey's printer, John Wolfe, licensed the work on 28 September 1593, but if he printed an edition, no copy survives. Later, he sold his rights to Edward Blount, who brought out a quarto in 1598, printed by Adam Islip. Blount inscribed this edition to Sir Thomas Walsingham in a dedicatory letter which summons up Marlowe's corpse, or at least evokes his burial: 'when we have brought the breathless body to the earth', Blount solemnly tells Walsingham, 'for albeit the eye there taketh his ever farewell of that beloved object, yet the impression of the man that hath been dear unto us, living an after life in our memory, [puts] us in mind of farther obsequies'. In his afterlife, it seems, Marlowe has no reason to complain, since Walsingham of Scadbury had attended to him discriminatingly, 'entertaining the parts of reckoning and worth which you found in him, with good countenance', as Blount tells that patron.[44] This suggests that some 'parts' or abilities of Marlowe had not come up to scratch. Blount's remarks are curiously ambiguous, but his dedicatory letter was later omitted or suppressed, and never appeared again in any editon of the poem until modern times.

A second edition, which featured George Chapman's additions to the poem, was somewhat odder. Chapman dedicated this to Walsingham's wife (the former espionage officer, by then, was well married), and explained, none too clearly, why he had troubled to finish the work. He was 'drawn by strange instigation to employ some of my serious time in so trifling a subject' as this poem.[45] Whose instigation might this refer to? Chapman divided Marlowe's 818 lines into two sestiads (taking that name from 'Sestos'), and added four fresh sestiads, or nearly 1,600 fresh lines of his own with arguments to go at the head of each section. In consequence, about two-thirds of the poem in this edition is written by Chapman, in a manner unlike Marlowe's handling of the story. Blount sold a part of his interest to Paul Linley, who then brought out the second edition in 1598 as 'HERO AND LEANDER: Begun by Christopher Marlow; and finished by George Chapman'.

Though he had broken off his writing at a natural point, Marlowe, of course, may have meant to finish the poem himself. He alludes to the story's climax, or to Leander's drowning in the Hellespont, as if he had meant to describe it. Admittedly, if he felt that his life was in danger in May 1593, it is possible, though not very likely, that he asked Chapman to complete the production. A man of abstemious habits and rare talent, Chapman was well admired among Marlowe's friends. He dedicated two volumes of obscure verse, *The Shadow of Night* (1594) and *Ovid's Banquet of Sense* (1595) to Matthew Roydon, and also felt it his duty to translate Homer. And he issued a first instalment of that famous project as his *Seven Books of the Iliad* in the same year as *Hero*.

More than one critic has argued, however, that he damaged Marlowe's work by adding to it. Chapman's splitting of the opening section into two parts is probably defensible, but his long, linked-up sestiads are ingenious, rather than life-like or illuminating of the lovers. At least, Chapman's moralizing, philosophical sestiads suit one side of the Elizabethan Ovidian tradition, and by way of contrast heighten what is unique in Marlowe's writing. There was a romantic side of the tradition, too, which Henry Petowe supports in a weaker completion of the poem in 1598.[46] Yet, finally, it is odd that Marlowe never finished *Hero and Leander*. What mainly emerges from the work's aftermath is the troubled, but no doubt sincere, interest of Marlowe's patron Sir Thomas Walsingham in its achievement.

In the early weeks of 1593, Marlowe's patron had been busy in Kent. Not yet knighted, Thomas Walsingham occupied himself behind a drawbridge not far from Chislehurst, and also took advantage of the fact that Scadbury was barely more than a dozen miles from royal Westminster. It is fairly clear that Marlowe, by the spring of that year, knew his way to

Thomas's domain. Indeed, the poet may gladly have accepted hospitality there. But there were, no doubt, considerations in the spring which would have made Scadbury especially attractive. For one thing, Marlowe appears to have taken delight in writing poetry acceptable to his patron. Also the plague raged in London's suburbs, and his own funds may have run low.

Whether or not he requested leave to visit, he found Thomas ready to receive him, perhaps at some point well after the re-closing of the theatres. One feels that Marlowe, finally, would have been glad to be out on the road. He did not have far to travel, since Scadbury was six or seven miles south of the Thames. No doubt, he looked forward to talk and Latin poetry with Thomas Walsingham in Kent, even if his stay were to be short. Not later than the middle of May, he would have had a sight of woods and of his great patron's white, handsomely moated house, well set on a hillside which offered a view of the poet's own county.

10

A little matter of murder

O Envy for his virtues spare one man.

('Sir Roger Manwood')

We are in fact convinced that no human experience is without
meaning or unworthy of analysis, and that fundamental values,
even if they are not positive, can be deduced from this particular
experience which we are describing.

(P. Levi, *Se questo è un uomo*)

A great house in Kent

THOUGH the queen was entertained at Scadbury manor, and
business agents, spies, poets, and officers of the Crown dined
there, little of this remarkable house remains today. It was pulled
down in about 1734, but its moat-surrounded island still exists. The locale
is eerie and beautiful for a visitor who comes upon dark water near
Kentish woods; a black, water-filled moat protects the ruins of brick
cellars, undercrofts, and brewery areas of Thomas Walsingham's former
edifice. Thanks to the Orpington and District Archaeological Society, its
compact size has become clear, but formerly it was an attractive retreat
with many chambers.

In an underground, silted-up drain near the old kitchen, debris has
come to light—including a newborn baby's skull. This skull (lately
inspected by the Kent police) might be a cruel symbol of Thomas's problems. At 31, Marlowe's patron was a bland, cultivated former espionage
officer who meant to excel at the royal court. To succeed as a courtier, he
needed to detach himself from spies or 'projectors' to a degree; and yet if

31 Sir Roger Manwood, Chief Baron of the Exchequer

he had a past to bury, he found that he still required a few practices of London's Seething Lane, a few old, safe, sure lines to power. He had been worried by debt, but his finances began to right themselves when he undertook little, sharp, wise economies. Even so, his retrenchments do not account for his rising fortune.

On his moated island, Thomas might appear unfairly as a Prospero with magical spirits, an ape on his shoulder, or strings in his hand leading to the collars of beasts with men's faces, tricksters, thugs, lackeys, and killers. Yet there is no need to romanticize Thomas of Scadbury, and the facts of the poet's life outclass any fiction about himself or his patron.

By the time of Marlowe's visit in the spring, his host was making use of men such as Peter Manwood, MP for Sandwich. He was a son of the corrupt judge Sir Roger Manwood, who had died in disgrace on 14 December 1592. Marlowe had seen Sir Roger at the Old Bailey, and in all likelihood had received the judge's practical help earlier. It came to light, however, that, as Chief Baron of the Exchequer, Sir Roger had used his office for personal profit. He had stolen a house in Sandwich by bullying and terrifying its legal owner in court, before turning over its deed to his son Peter (who sent the owner a receipt). Taking bribes, Sir Roger had let at least two murderers off scot-free; he tampered with juries; he behaved so outrageously that Lord Burghley and the Privy Council denounced him. An absurd but venal incident involving a 'golden chain'—in which Sir Roger had retrieved the item without paying the £30 due for it—became a minor *cause célèbre* in London, by which time many of the Chief Baron's iniquities had been exposed.[1]

Even before reaching his host, Marlowe seems to have written a brief Latin elegy on Sir Roger. Its witty exuberance suggests that he had been amused by the judge's predatory look, his hatchet-like features, and receding forehead. Though calling him a 'vulture', the poem implies that Sir Roger had preyed on hardened criminals:

Noctivagi terror, ganeonis triste flagellum, | *Et Jovis Alcides, rigido vulturque . . .*
Within this urn lies the terror of night thieves, the harsh scourge of the profligate, a vulture to the resolute criminal, Jove's Alcides. Rejoice, sons of the wicked![2]

The Chief Baron may have gone to his alabaster tomb with a fairly good conscience—he was as paradoxical as the age. He had aided the highways and churches in Kent, and founded an excellent free school which thrives today as Sir Roger Manwood's School at Sandwich.

The judge's ruin was no earthquake at Scadbury—a few of his misdeeds had been known for years—and Marlowe's poem looks like an acknowledgement of help received, though its whitewashing effect was not needed at Scadbury. Thomas's son was to marry Elizabeth Manwood, a granddaughter of the fallen judge, but that could not have been fore- seen. The poem was not printed in its day, and only survives by a happy chance. Its key feature was probably that it was composed in Latin, for Latin was the music of the spheres for Walsingham. At Scadbury, the poet's remarks in Latin to his host may have lifted discourse above the level of servants or, perhaps, business agents, and reinforced Marlowe's bond with his patron.

New light on Thomas's situation might almost be found in his moat, or its history. Chislehurst, a mile away, was once a tiny hamlet. Vulnerable to predatory gangs along the main route from Dover, the hamlet had enjoyed the De Scathebury family's aid until the advent of the Walsing- hams in 1475. Thomas's ancestors came from Norfolk, but a branch settled in the capital, and a succession of Thomas Walsinghams occupied the wattle-and-daub manor. Thomas I, a successful vintner, practically rebuilt the parish church with the help of his son, Thomas II. After Sir Edmund Walsingham served for some years, not necessarily with blood on his conscience, as Henry VIII's Lieutenant of the Tower of London, public service became a family tradition, except that cash ran low. Thomas III, a son of Sir Edmund, left the bulk of his property in the hands of executors to pay off debts and legacies when he died in 1584, but the executors did not release the legacies while his namesake was alive.

Hence, when Thomas IV (our Thomas) inherited Scadbury in 1589, he was embarassed for funds. But a few days in the Fleet prison did him little harm. He found out that he could easily borrow cash, but had to repay creditors. Emerging from a debtor's cell he played trump cards, or I should say that he played some, and held back a few. One was his grand old name, and his family's gloomy Scadbury Chapel at St Nicholas Church, not far away over the fields. Marlowe, in all probability, knew the church, where the rector was Richard Harvey, a younger brother of Gabriel of Cambridge. Once Richard had predicted a disaster with two planets in conjunction, and heard tart remarks when the heavenly blast failed to occur. Cambridge, of course, laughed again at a Harvey, and 'Little Dick' retreated to a safe pulpit. The poet heard him, I suppose, since Nashe tells us—'Kit Marloe was wont to say that he was an ass, good for nothing but to preach of the Iron Age.'[3]

That allusion to Ovid's distaste for the Iron Age might not have upset the Latin-loving Thomas, who had other cards to play. Related ancestrally to Mary Boleyn, the sister of Queen Elizabeth's mother, he was not too poor to entertain people at Chislehurst who had duties at the royal court. Thomas did not give New Year's gifts to the queen before 1599, and until then he found it cheaper to be affable at home. In our time, Patricia Fumerton and Jennifer Stead have noted a niceness of ritual in dinners given by the aspiring Tudor gentry. Imported from France was the *voidée*, or void, in which guests stood in an inner chamber, to take the final wine, comfits, or spices of an evening.[4] On a lesser occasion, most probably, the poet had a chance to see his patron's business agent Mr Ingram Frizer.

A discreet man, Frizer lived in the capital, but evidently had retreated from the plague. In two documents from this spring, he is said to be 'lately of London' (*nuper de Londonia*). As Thomas's servant, he had to call upon his master, and so may have had a bedchamber at Scadbury. Formerly, he had been occupied in Hampshire, where there were two (doubtless related) Ingram Frizers. This Frizer had entered the legal record on 9 October 1589, when he bought the Angel inn at Basingstoke for £120. Two months later, he sold it for a 'competent sum' to James Deane, a wealthy draper who later left him £20, with black cloth for a mourning gown and forgiveness for a debt of £5. Clearly, the draper had been satisfied with the Angel.

When he bought it, Frizer had managed to offer a cash loan to one of its vendors, a Thomas Bostock. Having signed a bond for £240, Bostock failed to discharge the debt, whereupon Frizer sued, won his case in the Exchequer in 1592, and received back the sum owed plus £4 in costs. That was a paltry return, but in these years he was testing the waters between crime and legitimacy, and learning details of finance and semi-legal man-oeuvre which led him to become the business agent of Thomas's wife, Lady Audrey Walsingham, and profit at last from England's Scottish king.

Marlowe, with time on his hands, did not merely listen to the song-thrush or nightingales: we know that he met the business agent at some point before 30 May. There was in Frizer's bulk, as one gathers, little sign of the rugged persuader, or the hand quick to reach a knife. In Thomas's former calling, murder had nearly gone out of fashion. In espionage, it told nothing; it silenced a voice, whereas a living spy could be turned and used. Frizer had avoided any indictment for violence, though he had a raw accomplice in Nicholas Skeres. A minor tool of the earl of Essex, Skeres had helped as an informer but he did not work for Marlowe's patron; he was a half-educated thug, often in and out of gaol, a tough, shadowy veteran of Francis Walsingham's bleak network.

Looking at his childish signature, one wonders why Frizer used him at all as a con man, or 'coney-catcher' (the 'coney' being the rabbit or victim who is fleeced). One known example, I think, testifies to the smooth hand-in-glove performance of two con artists, with a touch of Scadbury for the finale. Early this year, young Drew Woodleff and his widowed mother Anne had urgently needed money. Feeling an 'affection' for Skeres, Drew applied to him for help. Skeres led him on to Frizer, who promised him a loan of £60, and extracted an IOU for that sum, but, later on, explained that he lacked cash. Instead, the young man was offered a 'commodity'.

It says much for Frizer's air of reliability that his victim agreed, for the scam was notorious. It involved offering in lieu of cash a 'commodity', worth far less than the stated sum and often wholly imaginary. Marlowe's Barabas refers to such 'tricks of brokery', which lead victims to bankruptcy or suicide, and later Shakespeare, in *Measure for Measure*, alludes to 'young Master Rash' who is 'in for a commodity of brown paper and old ginger, nine score and seventeen pounds' (IV. iii. 4–6). There were expert variations abroad, as Molière's Harpagon in *The Miser* shows in his behaviour with his own son.

Frizer persuaded his victim to accept 'a certain number of guns or great iron pieces', stored on Tower Hill. With that settled, he pretended to sell the guns, and gave Drew Woodleff just £30, which he said was all he could get, and so charged 100 per cent interest on a loan of £60.

Next, Skeres came back into the picture. Claiming that he owed Frizer twenty marks (£4), he made Woodleff sign a bond for that sum to Frizer. By then Woodleff, already in debt for £64, needed money at any price, and Frizer induced him to sign a 'statute staple', on 29 June 1593, for all of £200. In the twentieth century, Leslie Hotson was surprised to find that the bond was made out to 'a gent. of good worship', who turned out to be 'Thomas Walsingham of Chislehurst, Kent, esquire'.[5]

Marlowe's patron had underwritten the climactic swindle, whether or not he knew of its details. No word about the amazingly gullible Drew, or his mother, would have been spoken openly at the patron's table.

As for Marlowe, the water-voles in a moat, one suspects, might have weighed more with him than any concern for his patron's virtues; he plainly admired Thomas, and not only for the latter's charm. As a poet, he had interested himself in clandestine power, tricks, abasement, and immoral force, but he found in Thomas something more than the amoral manipulator, for his patron was a generous man of taste. Also, with the return of plague, theatre doors had shut, and Marlowe had no hope of immediate cash from his calling, though even that is less important, I think, than an abiding fact of Elizabethan life: almost any writer, unattached to a troupe or university, looked to patronage in order to live. Thomas offered a respite from want, a pledge of future help, immediate comfort, a sophisticated ear. Nor was any of that illusory; and in the light of George Chapman's future sonnet and play dedications to (Sir) Thomas Walsingham, it is certain that this patron's aid, when he could give it, was unstinting and real. Thomas gained a social veneer by sponsoring writers of classical excellence, and the grateful few sang his praise.

Furthermore, he was habitually alert. He was politically attuned at a time when England was at war—and questions about an ageing queen, the maddeningly unsettled succession problem, and the conundrum of King James VI of Scotland were in the air. This spring, or on former occasions, Marlowe may have noticed his patron's interest in Scotland. Years earlier, Thomas, as an officer, had interviewed Robert Poley, and the two had worked together in the Babington case. Lately, Poley had endured bad roads and a Scottish winter for weeks. His movements were kept on record (on vellum at the Pipe Office) just because they were of the utmost importance; for Poley was no ordinary court messenger, but a messenger extraordinary. In December, for example, he had been paid for carrying letters 'of great importance' into Scotland, and riding 'in sondrye places within that province by the space of twoe whole monethes'. He had recently gone back and forth, too, from Scotland to the Netherlands.

Poley was at least partly involved with the government's interest in King James's overtures to Catholic France and Spain. There had been a need to ferret data from listening-posts in the Netherlands, where spies, informers, and a Scottish regiment were at hand. Married to a young Danish wife, James had become politically mature, subtle, and intuitive; he was 'one of the most secret princes', as Henry Wotton said, and he had begun to get on craftily and well with his nobles. As Jenny Wormald has noted in our time, he aimed to keep Queen Elizabeth guessing about his foreign policy, partly because she had refused to grant any open recognition of his claim to be her successor.

Thomas knew that if James VI acceded, those who had supported him would be rewarded. He not only favoured James's claim, but formed alliances with a few who suffered from Queen Elizabeth's neglect or dislike. One of these was Sir Robert Sidney, who was wounded shortly after his arrest of Marlowe at Flushing, and was still affected by the petulant wrath of his queen. New evidence shows how disaffected Sidney had become in the early 1590s. Thomas's wife, Lady Audrey Walsingham, was to be given a secret cipher to correspond with Sidney after she became a Lady of the Bedchamber in Elizabeth's court. (We hear of the cipher in a letter by Sidney's agent, Rowland Whyte, of 20 September 1599.) In that fashion, Lady Audrey became a spy; even if she only reported gossip of the court she played two sides of the street, as did Thomas. By appearing to be utterly devoted to Elizabeth, the Walsinghams gained her trust and favours, while doing all they could for James of Scotland. Such duplicity was to bring manors and new wealth to the Walsinghams, rewards to Ingram Frizer, and high office to Sidney as soon as James came to England's throne.[6]

One or two men of the Privy Council—notably Sir Robert Cecil—also played the hazardous game. In the 1590s they flattered or pleased the two proud, often mutually offended rulers of England and of Scotland, without apprising the queen of their loyalty to James. Few played the game more delicately than Thomas, who knew its danger. He had the advantage of his contacts in the secret service, and of having been a go-between for field agents such as Poley and his own cousin the Secretary of State. One returns to Watson's Latin writings, and to his remark *te mediante* about Thomas as a mediating figure—part-time couriers had had his help before. Indeed, men of strategic importance were in his debt, and Poley was clearly among them. Whether or not Thomas heard often from Sir Robert Cecil is more difficult to say; both men were secretive, and they were almost equally concerned with Scottish intelligence.

Thomas lacked a government office, but as an appendage of the court he was strangely effective in this decade. That may be, in part, because the queen doted on a handsome face. Marlowe's patron, however, had another appeal at a time when reticence and self-deprecation were valued by the nobility. A politic diffidence, not unlike that '*sprezzatura* of non-chalance' recommended in Castiglione's *Book of the Courtier*, had come more fully into vogue. The trick was to display an indifference, even a seeming carelessness which disguises or hides insouciant mastery. In art, this effect appears rather gorgeously in Marlowe's *Hero and Leander*, and in politics it begins to appear in Walsingham's very blandness. Espionage had given a gritty substance to his mildness—and he was helped by his sense that the queen knew that intelligencing was required for the nation's survival. In any case, Thomas was favoured. When he worked on defence problems in Kent, Queen Elizabeth granted him the manor of Dartford for a prolonged period. A year or two later in 1597, she herself came to Scadbury and knighted Thomas, and in the next year, granted him a valuable house at the lower end of Whitehall's tiltyard—and this is not to list the grand benefits that were to flow to the two Walsinghams from King James I.

Marlowe couldn't have foreseen his patron's success, but he could enjoy his hospitality. One can forget how much the scenic, plastic side of life meant to the poet. In his works, it is true, he had undertaken a grave, doubting enquiry into accepted notions of human society and behaviour; but he had aimed to make his enquiry colourful, sensuous, tactically naive, and emotionally powerful, in an art which does not judge life but evokes, challenges, disturbs, and delights. One of his resources (and compensations) had been his love of landscape, and in this month he had the loveliness of Scadbury as a reward.

For a while, he had a chance to know his patron's grounds, which are approximately described in a later inventory as including 'Gardens and Orchards enclosed with Brick walls and planted with excellent fruit, 3 Barnes, 3 large Stables, a Granary, Pigeon house and fish ponds, a Parke well impaled about, 400 acres stored with Deere and Conies [rabbits] and other Stocke of Cattle, and Timber, Trees . . .'[7]

All that this omits is an old moat which has survived. The corbels for its drawbridge are still in place, with the socket holes 'in near perfect condition', according to a modern survey. Scadbury's patron was as adequate, as unyielding as the corbels of his bridge—whereas the poet, at the best of times, was vulnerable, inconsistent, excitable. There was, as ever, a gap between Marlowe's well-disciplined life of art and thought and the loose and easy exuberance of his talk. But his patron was affable, or at least attuned to his nonsense and laughter, and Marlowe can hardly have worried among the fishponds, let alone in a meadow with long views. So he must have thrived at Scadbury, until an odd event occurred. Just after the middle of May, a messenger from the government arrived to put him, in effect, under arrest. The apprehension was fairly grave, or potentially grave enough to change his relations with the Council and his patron at a stroke.

Mercury in the form of Mʳ Maunder

On 18 May, the poet was sought for; but his dilemma was more worrisome and uncertain—in the next few days—than dangerous. He was wanted not by a sheriff of Kent, or a justice of the peace, but by an authority which controlled life and death: the Queen's Council. He was not a fugitive; he was not in hiding, but available at his patron's estate a few miles south-east of the capital. That locale is the only one explicitly cited in the order to apprehend him. There is a good tradition that he worked on his *Hero* when at Scadbury, and the fact that he was there, with his patron, was to offer him an alibi, removing him from suspicion of having committed a treasonous offence in London.

The pursuer knew where his victim was; and the estate's pigeon house or quiet ponds, its mansion, even the ample green park with its palings, might have put an apprehending officer at ease. Mʳ Henry Maunder, who arrived to escort the poet, served as a 'messenger' of the Council for more than twenty years; he had little in common with a courier such as Poley; and as a delegate from their lordships, this particular Mercury did not arrive and depart on winged feet. He was well armed but the armament consisted largely, if not wholly, of a piece of paper.

Mʳ Maunder's warrant, in fact, directed him

to repair to the house of Mʳ Tho: Walsingham in Kent, or to anie other place where he shall understand xtofer Marlow to be remayning, and by vertue hereof to apprehend and bring him to the court in his companie. And in case of need to require ayd.[8]

The truth is (as Tucker Brooke noted, in his 1930 *Life* of Marlowe) that individuals who were ordered to answer charges or to serve as witnesses in often trivial cases were known to ignore a Council summons, or simply to evade the attending officer. The result, for failing to comply, was usually no more than a reprimand and a strongly phrased repetition of the order to submit to arrest. The warrant for Marlowe does not indicate that he was called in to answer charges, since it does not include a variant of the phrase 'to answer matters as should be objected against him before their Lordships'.

The fact that Marlowe did not flee, and that forty-eight hours passed before he was brought in, suggests that Mr Maunder paused for breath. It would not have been untoward if the officer had stayed overnight at the moated manor before leaving with his charge the next day. Any such delay would not necessarily have soothed Marlowe's nerves, particularly if he did not know why the Council wanted him. In general, his own quickness, imagination, and impatience did him little good in the latter part of that May.

But if we imagine that his apprehender stayed for supper at Scadbury's small 'island', a pause in the crucial rush of events of this time can give us a chance to look widely into events that bore on Marlowe's fate. He had an eye for politics and geography, and would have been aware of current events. Even during the plague, Queen Elizabeth had attended the opening of her eighth parliament in February, or rather, she had arrived by barge from Somerset Place one afternoon to hear her Lord Keeper's remarks on the Spanish war and to try to raise more funds. England was nearly in the grip of Spain this year, it appeared: King Philip had gone far towards establishing himself on Elizabeth's southern threshold in Normandy, while intriguing in Scotland to secure a potent base in the north. The earl of Essex had failed with his army at Rouen in Normandy; this was tactfully not alluded to. But the diplomatic manoeuvres of James VI of Scotland were implicit in the bleak picture, and by the spring Marlowe himself may have heard fresh news of the Scottish king from Walsingham at Scadbury. The Lord Keeper—Sir John Puckering—at any rate referred to Philip's aim of making 'a party there' in Scotland 'ready to receive an army', and then to invade England by land from the north and assail her by sea from the south.[9]

All of this, dire as it was, introduced a theme close to Puckering's heart. 'Secret intelligencers', he claimed, were reporting to the enemy about incidents of religious heresy and discontent, as well as informing them about the separatism of extreme Puritans in England, thus convincing the king of Spain that he was about to take over a weak, divided nation. Harsh measures were therefore urgently required for England's internal security. Parliament, along with John Whitgift, the obdurate archbishop who had been enthroned ten years earlier at Canterbury, was in general agreement.

Then, on 6 April, a few days before the session ended, Marlowe's Cambridge friend John Greenwood (who once had used the poet's bursary allowance) was hanged at Tyburn along with Henry Barrow. Both young men were devout Christian separatists who had written tracts against the Anglican Church, but, interestingly, they were found guilty of endangering the state, and subsequently hanged for sedition rather than for nonconformity—a sign of the times. A better-known Puritan propagandist, John Penry, was to be hanged late in the next month.

It may be that Marlowe's occasionally savage political and religious satire has some bearing on these dangerous times in which dozens of Cambridge men, before Greenwood, were hanged by the state, not for any harm they ever did but for their beliefs. In any case, if word of Greenwood's fate reached Kent, Marlowe perhaps wondered how anyone linked with outright 'atheism' might soon fare.

Other news likely to have trickled through at Scadbury concerned the new power of the young earl of Essex. Even Mr Maunder knew what all of London knew and, as a Westminster courtier, Marlowe's patron also had cause to follow Essex's career. The great shimmering aristocratic darling of the queen was no longer a mere 'court pet'. Since 25 February, Essex had emerged as a new Privy Councillor and major force in the nation's life. Thirteen MPs owed their seat to his backing; all the chief captains in the Low Countries, including Robert Sidney at Flushing, were already reporting to him; and for months, Essex had wooed King James VI of Scotland.

Even Thomas Walsingham, with his feet on the ground, may not have known all that is still coming to light about Essex's tactics. For six years, he had pressed to get his friends appointed as justices of the peace—as we learned in 2004; and he had begun to keep secretaries busy in organizing his espionage service, and finding replacements for unlucky agents (such as Marchant and LeBlanc, who were later hanged in Spain).[10] He was becoming a shrewd, powerful 'patronage broker' or intermediary between the queen and aspiring suitors for office. Little wonder that Skeres,

Ingram Frizer's creature, could boast of being Essex's servant. Disturbingly for some, the earl was barely 20 when he became colonel-general of the horse in the Netherlands, and only 26 when elevated to the Privy Council. Fiercely ambitious and eager to pursue the Spanish war, he was at the moment on cordial, if not sparkling, terms with that potent little dynamo, Sir Robert Cecil, who was also ambitious but far more amenable towards Spain. Though the average age of the Privy Councillors was about 60, the nation was now in the hands of largely untried, newly elected parliamentarians and two canny young manipulators, Essex and Cecil. In the background were the ageing queen and her often incapacitated, elderly adviser Lord Burghley, as well as figures such as the Lord Keeper, who expressed alarm over religious dissidents of every kind.

At least when under the eye of Mr Maunder at Scadbury, Marlowe knew nothing more potent or hazardous than his host's wine cellars and brewing facilities. Archaeological evidence tells us about the latter—and, standing on Scadbury's island today, I find its brewery area impressive. What lasts in the world? In May 1593 Marlowe had begun *Hero and Leander*, one of the most psychologically intense love poems in any language, still as fresh as it ever was; and for one afternoon or evening Thomas Walsingham's hospitality, the decanted liquids at a table and the charms of a bakery and kitchen, gave him a welcome respite. Probably, too, Marlowe's morale was affected for the better. When he rode off to court, presumably on a May morning, he was protected by something more than his pluck, well-being, defiance, and indispensable arrogance.

Six years earlier, Lord Burghley—as Chancellor of Cambridge and leading spirit of the Council—had sat at the meeting which approved Marlowe's secret work and saved him from forfeiting his MA degree. Even earlier, the government had taken an interest in writers, and in due course poets such as Watson, Roydon, and Marlowe came to be well respected as couriers or agents for their lordships. The state looked after its dependable hirelings, and after the duel with Bradley, Marlowe and Watson had received some official aid. Or again, their lordships could be lenient. Marlowe's episode with a counterfeiter at Flushing may have had a poor result, but since counterfeiting was a capital offence any fieldwork involving it was likely to be hazardous; the Privy Council had credited his persistence at Flushing, and might in future be expected to offer further tolerance and protection.

Even so, complications did not favour the outspoken, and integrity did not fare very well. The guarding shield of the Cecils was not made of steel or cast iron. The Lord Treasurer, despite efforts, had failed to save Greenwood and Barrow from the gallows. Sir Walter Ralegh, exiled to Devon after a rash marriage, had fluttered back to parliament to speak—uselessly, as it turned out—in favour of liberty of conscience, and had not prevented a bill for the further harsh enforcement of religious conformity in March.

Ralegh, as it happened, had also opposed a bill that offered an extension of privileges to Dutch merchants and other foreign traders in the capital. It is easy to believe that Ralegh hated the Dutch. But with inflation, plague, then falling demand and an exodus of well-to-do buyers from the city, xenophobia was likely to smoulder. The measure that gave new privileges to Dutch and other immigrant merchants in London had the effect of dry, resin-soaked timbers tossed on smoky embers. About a month after the session ended, the Privy Council met to consider an inferno of angry complaints from shopkeepers that aliens, mostly from the Lowlands, were illegally buying and selling foreign goods. Placards appeared, and inciting tracts had begun to circulate.

Next, the Council authorized the torture of writers. At midnight on 5 May, an especially insolent rhymed ultimatum had been found on the wall of the Dutch churchyard, Broadsteet Ward. Vicious and anti-semitic, it gave notice that the throats of alien traders would be cut, characterizing in fifty-three lines the 'Machiavellian merchant' who spoils the state:

> Your usury doth leave us all for dead,
> Your artifex & craftsman works our fate,
> And like the Jews, you eat us up for bread.

Signed '*per* Tamberlaine', as if to conjure up that avenger, the verses even alluded to Marlowe's recent play, *The Massacre at Paris*:

> Not paris massacre so much blood did spill
> As we will do just vengeance on you all.[11]

Possibly tipped off by an informer, a commission set up by the Council seized on Marlowe's former roommate Kyd as the most likely author of this libel. Kyd had railed at 'usury' in two works, and his clear penmanship as a former scrivener may in itself have pointed to him as the perpetrator. To fix his guilt or extract information he was perhaps tortured or hung up on manacles. If suspected persons 'refuze to confesse the truth', as the Star Chamber order of 11 May put it, 'you shal by authoritie hereof put them to the Torture in Bridewel' and 'as often as you shal think fit'.

When the authorities entered his room, it appears that Kyd had tried to co-operate, or at least had handed over some 'waste and idle papers'—a few of which were subsequently extracted and labelled:

> 12 May 1593
> vile hereticall Conceiptes
> denyinge the deity of Jhesus
> Christe our Savio^r fownd
> emongest the pap^{r}s of Thos
> Kydd prisoner

to which someone later added, in a different-coloured ink,

> wch he affirmeth that he
> had from Marlowe[12]

These few pages, which he thought were Marlowe's, had been accidentally 'shufled' with his manuscripts when the two men shared a room, as Kyd later told Puckering. In a neat hand, the incriminating pages included extracts from an old theological book which had been on Gresshop's shelves at the King's School. This work was John Proctor's *Fall of the Late Arian*, published in 1549—a refutation of Arianist ideas which questioned Christ's divinity. Unfortunately, the book included large portions of the same heterodox views that it was meant to confute. Hence the search of Kyd's room took a new turn, in that the authorities concerned themselves not just with a Dutch Church libel but with the papers and propagandists of atheism.

In all likelihood, Mr Maunder was unaware of the reason for apprehending the person he was asked to bring in, and Marlowe, in riding over the countryside among the young green leaves and fresh breezes of the season, was possibly none the wiser either. In the event, he was simply taken to court, where a clerk noted that, on 20 May, one 'xtofer Marley of London' had appeared in accordance with their lordships' warrant, 'for his indemnity herein; and is commanded to give his daily attendance on their lordships, untill he shalbe lycensed to the contrary'.[13]

What emerges, on the face of things, is how little the Council—or its clerk—cared about his behaviour or alleged views. He was possibly asked about Kyd or the Arianist tract, but not thought guilty of writing the Dutch Church libel. An 'indemnity'—a fairly minor routine sum—was required as bail, along with his daily attendance upon their lordships; but neither on this day or later was any charge against him indicated.

In court, he rose slightly in status from the 'Marlow' named in the warrant to 'Marley of London gent'—and indeed he may have favoured the spelling 'Marley' which his father had used with excellent results in courts of law.

At liberty—or nearly so—he probably rode back to Scadbury within a day or two, certainly arriving before the month's end. Flutters of the government affected his patron, and it may be that Walsingham was particularly anxious about the concern with religious dissidents. By this time, 'atheism', as a political issue, was more showily in the air than ever. Because of Walsingham's ties to the court, it is possible that he talked to Marlowe at this point about 'atheism' as it concerned Sir Robert Cecil.

Only recently put in charge of intelligence operations, Cecil lacked the well-attuned espionage system formerly in place at Seething Lane. Lord Burghley had let the old arrangement almost fall to pieces, yet with the help of a little more funding it was now being threaded together, patched up, and tailored anew by Burghley's deft son. Indeed, Cecil kept his eyes open, his mind primed and alert. In two years on the Council, he had found his colleagues and agents often as adversarial or detrimental to his interest as the state's enemies. His own youth helped him: he was a new broom; he found fresh corners to sweep. As the Catholic menace shrank, so did legitimate targets for his spies. As always, many of these men belonged to a competing underworld of liars and inventive informers, including those who manufactured threats and incriminating data in order to be paid for reporting on what they brought to light. Cecil was healthily sceptical and quietly pragmatic. He saw the value of keeping his counsel, though his discretion had been tried lately by a wild, irregular operative named Richard Cholmeley.

As a son of Sir Hugh Cholmeley who reported on heresy in Cheshire, this agent must have begun with good credentials. Employed by the Council 'for the apprehension of papists and other dangerous enemies',

Richard worked with his brother Hugh and other, shadier informers to gain access to Catholic households; he took bribes from those he betrayed; he brought about the arrest of one fellow agent; and he mocked and denounced members of the Council. In a letter to Cecil in 1592, his brother refers to Richard's 'conceit of hatred' and 'ambitious infirmity'. Finally, in March 1593, a warrant was issued for his arrest, and by mid-May an informer had sent in a report entitled 'Remembrances of Words & Matter against Ric: Chomeley'.

The allegations may not have been altogether new to Cecil, but they were many and detailed. One was that Cholmeley had said he regretted not having 'killed my Lord Treasurer'. Another was that 'he speaketh in general all evil of the Council, saying that they are all atheists & Machiavellians, especially my Lord Admiral . . .'.

One of the most specific was this:

hc saith & verily believeth that one Marlowe is able to show more sound reasons for atheism than any divine in England is able to give to prove divinity, & that Marlowe told him he hath read the atheist lecture to Sr Walter Ralegh & others.

This is the only passage in the 'Remembrances' which mentions Marlowe. Later on, the same informer sent in a letter (perhaps to Justice Young) which specially targets Cholmeley's atheism. In this, almost exactly the same quips and scoffs which the spy Richard Baines reports that Marlowe had said are repeated—only now it is Cholmeley who is supposed to have uttered that 'the Angel Gabriel is bawd to the Holy Ghost' or that 'Moses was a juggler', for example.

Lest this virulent chatter be thought just a matter of atheist quips and clichés, the informer outdoes himself. He claims that Cholmeley has a political gang of sixty followers—all men of 'resolute murdering minds'—whose aim, after Queen Elizabeth's death, will be to crown one of themselves as king and live by their own laws. Furthermore, Cholmeley and his crew believe that there will soon be 'as many of their opinion as of any other religion'.

Pretty clearly, the informer caters to what the government most fears: the possibility that atheists have seditious aims and murderous means at hand. Cholmeley himself, in due course, rather unwisely sent a petition along to Archbishop Whitgift, of all people, with the result that the archbishop's own agent for rooting out heresy, Dr Richard Bancroft, took an interest in this case. When Cholmeley, a month after Marlowe's death, finally turned himself in on 28 June, Bancroft ordered him to be imprisoned with 'the rest that should be found of his sect'. But the sect, or 'terrible crew' of sixty, turned out to be just four men, all of whom at one time or another had been government spies or turncoat Catholics.[14]

In our time, much has been made of Marlowe's relations with Cholmeley (who has also been mistaken for another Cholmeley who happened to know the earl of Essex)). It has been supposed that the author of the 'Remembrances' was Cholmeley's fellow agent and enemy Thomas Drury. But that is impossible, as C. B. Kuriyama has shown. For one thing, Drury's nearly illiterate prose is very different from the lucid, cogent style of the 'Remembrances', whose author seems to have been in touch with the spy Baines. It is clear that there was a feeding frenzy over the rewards of exposing atheism after the eighth parliament. Feverish, self-serving accusations were traded between underpaid spies, but there was no 'smear campaign' against Marlowe or Ralegh. Nor, despite an ingenious theory, is there any evidence that an excerpt from the anti-Arianist tract found in Kyd's room was a 'plant' to trap Marlowe. Anyone wishing to accuse the poet of atheism would not have needed to suborn the searchers of Kyd's papers; and if the authorities meant to be rid of him, they only needed to throw him in prison where anything could happen to a man.

The furore over heresy, stoked by creative reports of seditious talk or incidents, at least fired up the intelligence services. There is no doubt that Sir John Puckering and Lord Buckhurst, of the Council, wanted to be given evidence of an atheist threat. It is not difficult to see how Marlowe came to be fingered. His works had a seditious taint, or at least his notoriety made it profitable to cite his name; hence he became a card, a golden chip, an icon to be used by informers. The very strongest evidence of his heresies, or Baines's 'Note', with quoted phrases of Marlowe's talk, reached the Council by Saturday evening, 26 May. This paper (or a copy) was endorsed 'Bayns Marlow of his blasphemyes', and a hand with an index finger pointing to 'Marlow' was drawn on the document.[15]

Marlowe's alleged quips, many apparently recalled from Baines's stay at Flushing, are listed in a seemingly haphazard order. Several (such as 'all they that love not Tobacco & Boies were fools', or the remarks on coining) have nothing to do with blasphemy, and two lines near the end are so cramped that they may have been inserted some time later:

That one Ric Cholmley hath confesst that he was perswaded by Marloes reasons to become an Atheist.[16]

The reference to 'Ric Cholmley' in itself might have assured Cecil that Baines's Note contained a little fancy footwork by avid, hungry agents. And one doubts that Cecil would have been alarmed by Marlowe's blasphemies if they looked authentic: of course, any government 'projector', in the line of duty, would have been at liberty to say nearly whatever he liked as a cover. What is slightly more remarkable is that nobody on the Council, not even Puckering or Buckhurst, seems to have taken any immediate action over the poet's 'atheist' talk.

Shortly after Marlowe's death, however, someone did make a hastily edited copy of Baines's Note for the queen. I think Charles Nicholl rightly detects Sir John Puckering's hand in this. Items with no direct bearing on Marlowe's religious views were deleted, and, whereas the Note claims he had said that 'Moyses [Moses] was but a Jugler, & that one Heriots being Sir W Raleighs man can do more than he', the revised version omits any mention of Ralegh's name. The omission looks intentional, and it would be hard to reconcile this absence with the theory that the Council meant to smear Ralegh, or 'that Ralegh was the target of the attacks on Marlowe'.

The rough draft of Baines's Note is endorsed:

> Copye of Marloes blasphemes
> As sent to her H.[ighness]

An edited copy reached her majesty in June, when the poet was already dead. There is no historical evidence of any kind that Queen Elizabeth personally had anything to do with Marlowe's fate. The draft for the version of Baines's Note prepared for her began with a heading that referred to 'one Christofer Marlye' who 'since Whitsundy dyed a soden & vyolent deathe', though this was slightly reworded to read in full:

> A note delived on Whitsun eve last of the most horrible
> blasphemes and damnable opinions uttered by xtofer
> Marly who within iij dyes after came to a soden & fearfull
> end of his life.

Obviously, she could not prosecute the blasphemer 'Marly', who in June was already buried. Since every remark in the edited Note for her perusal concerned religion, there was a natural emphasis on the final item, which concerned the still living, active, and officially wanted Richard Cholmeley, who had been 'perswaded by Marloes reasons to become an Atheist'. Opposite Cholmeley's name was the notation, 'he is layd for', that is, being sought for.[17]

If one can trust a somewhat vague letter which the agent Thomas Drury sent to Anthony Bacon several months later on 1 August 1593, the queen, in noting the report of Cholmeley's atheism, gave an order 'to prosecute it [i.e. this matter] to the full'. In the same letter, Drury hints at much more data that he can reveal to Bacon, who had become the earl of Essex's director of intelligence.[18]

Though Drury does not refer explicitly to Marlowe, he gives a certain retrospective light on the events of May. As an informer, he was a man whom the Cecils thought worth listening to. A younger son of Robert Drury of Hawstead, Suffolk, he was related through his mother, Audrey, née Rich, to his first cousin Robert, Lord Rich, who in 1581 had married the earl of Essex's sister Penelope Devereux—the Stella of Sir Philip Sidney's sonnet sequence *Astrophil and Stella*. Born on 8 May 1551, Thomas Drury at first had given some promise of not becoming his family's black sheep. However, after an aborted career as a young scholar at Caius College, Cambridge, he had drifted into money-lending, dodgy schemes, outright swindles and in and out of the Fleet and Marlshalsea prisons. His nephew later referred to 'that degenerate rogue Tom Drury' and to his 'plots that he deviseth to beg and get money with', but Tom Drury found out a good deal, while keeping up a litany of his woes.

In his letter of August 1593 to Essex's chief agent, for example, Drury hints that he had discovered the identity of the Dutch Church libeller. He had pried out 'the desired secret' of this from Baines, only to be cheated of the City of London's reward for naming the miscreant author. He also claims that he had received not a penny for prompting someone to 'set down' some flagrant 'articles of atheism' for the Council. In this, he may possibly allude to Baines's Note, as has been supposed, except that it is hard to see why Baines would have needed prompting to send in a full, explicit list of Marlowe's 'atheistical' remarks to Pickering and Lord Buckhurst. A few days after writing to Bacon, Drury was suddenly imprisoned on orders from the Lord Chancellor (Henry Carey, the first Lord Hunsdon). 'I am committed', he then wrote familiarly to Sir Robert Cecil that August, 'for abusing him unto you, as also for wicked speeches that I could say I was able to make any Councillor a traitor.' His miseries in prison, this time, were not prolonged, since Cecil arranged his release and sent him money. Drury's gratitude was immediate and unusually eloquent: 'In all duty and lowliness of heart', he wrote to Cecil, 'I most humbly thank your Honour for your liberality, as also for my liberty.'[19] Significantly, the agents whom the Cecils took care to foster and protect they also frequently used; and Drury, within a few months, found himself working as a well-paid government courier for Lord Burghley.

That was a happy result, though courier duties were hardly his speciality; but he was thus kept on leading-strings and out of trouble by Cecil, who valued Drury's close family connection with Anthony Bacon. As the earl of Essex's intelligence director, Bacon had been seeking on behalf of his aristocratic master a cordial understanding with James VI of Scotland, and this particularly interested Cecil.

Four years earlier, Essex—with the help of his sister Penelope Rich— had made overtures to the Scottish king, but these had come to little. Nevertheless, Bacon's moves on behalf of his master were having more effect in Scotland by 1593. In wooing James VI, Essex meant to be in the king's good graces for the next reign in England.[20] As Sir Robert Cecil was one of the queen's chief ministers, his own support of James could not be overt, but he had been relying on operatives such as Poley for northern intelligence, and clearly holding others in reserve. There is reasonable evidence, as I shall try to adduce, that men such as Roydon and Marlowe were thought available for courier duties or similar work in Scotland.

Cecil could not guarantee the safety of his agents, and Essex could be ruthless, harsh, and unreckoning even in the days before he challenged the queen and instigated a rebellion that sent him to the scaffold. But as a new councillor, ambitious but temporarily docile, he must have seemed unlikely to oppose the government's northern plans. There had been tension between Essex and Ralegh, but even that was in abeyance to the extent that Essex, lately, had temporized by nominating his rival for membership of the Order of the Garter, and by standing godfather to a child of Ralegh's illicit marriage. Ralegh, at least, would not be a competitor in the Scottish arena where Cecil meant to prevail.

At Scadbury, Thomas Walsingham had interests not dissimilar to Robert Cecil's in the north, and a concern for political developments. There is good evidence that he had fresh news of Scotland at the end of May. The Council's lasting, mad fuss over libels and atheism, as well as the news of the persecution of Kyd, affected patrons of poetry such as Strange or Walsingham; the latter could hardly ignore topics which could affect his repute or estate. From Marlowe's agitated viewpoint, Scadbury's owner might have looked rock-like in composure late in the month. Hollow, empty days, it seems, had passed for the poet since his apprehension. With heresy in the air, he might yet have to answer charges; but if examined by Buckhurst or Pickering, Marlowe could have said that he had not written atheist tracts, and that his plays neither supported nor subverted the state. He inflated misconceptions to expose them to his wit, and had gone beyond satire. Did the state wish to kill him? Well then, do it with nerve and Lucan's style! Far from countering vices, he was bent on probing into the human situation, and not even a well-wishing Cecil or Burghley could accuse him of being a tame moralist. He stylized experience to get a pressing immediacy into his imaginings, the fictive world being an intensification for him of the real one.

But the Cecils had more on their minds than the art of drama, and Marlowe's fame could not guarantee his future or safety—after all, the authorities had not spared Kyd. Marlowe's patron had influential friends and indirect power, without being affluent or prominent at court. The memory of a debtors' cell may not have haunted Thomas, though he skirted the law to keep his estate on a sound footing. He was ready to aid the Canterbury poet however he could, if not to the detriment of his balance sheets; his own needs at least heightened the value to him of Frizer, his business agent, who lately had been active in an obscure affair with his accomplice Skeres. At some point, Marlowe had a chance to see these two operatives together.

The tumult over heresy might test any patron's tolerance of the heretic. Ralegh himself—though Marlowe never knew it, and there had been no secret, concerted plan to undo Ralegh—was to be targeted for atheism in the next year. An ecclesiastical commission under Viscount Bindon was to meet at Cerne Abbas in Dorset, in March 1594, to pry into the 'atheism or apostasy' of Ralegh and his adherents. Thomas Harriot was then cited for having 'brought the Godhead in question, and the whole course of the scriptures', although Ralegh, Harriot, and their circle at last escaped charges.

This spring, Marlowe was much more at risk; his patron could not be expected to vouch for an 'atheist' at the royal court, and even a servant such as Frizer had an interest in the prosperity of Scadbury, which depended on its owner's impeccably good taste and devotion to the monarch. Marlowe was too quick to be disaffected, too outspoken and impish to be any sponsor's tame beast: and yet Walsingham had invited him into Kent, and shared a passion which nearly put other concerns in the shade. Their mutual love for Latin and classical decorum might have guaranteed their friendship; and then, too, it may have been clear to Scadbury's master that the poet was still of value to the Cecils.

While staying in Kent, Marlowe possibly had not endeared himself to Frizer, or to Essex's minor helper Nick Skeres. But before the month ended, it appeared that Robert Cecil's interest in Scotland was undiminished, and that agents, perhaps, might have more work. There was new intelligence from Scotland and the Lowlands. That would have pleased Walsingham, whose longstanding friendship with Robert Poley cannot have faded away, and Poley's service for the Council, especially in the north, certainly interested Marlowe's patron. The news at hand was that Poley was back in the country. That special 'messenger' for Scotland had just returned hurriedly from abroad, with a desire to see persons at Scadbury or elsewhere on government business, no doubt in accordance with stated instructions. Before delivering foreign letters to the court, Poley was to spend a whole day in conference with Marlowe and two of Walsingham's associates in a house beside the Thames.

The river at Deptford

Some ten days after Mr Maunder apprehended the poet and took him to court, four individuals met at Mrs Bull's house in Deptford, along the river three miles east of London, on Wednesday, 30 May 1593. At this point, the Thames in the winter and spring was rapid; its rushing water swirled in from the north-west, and moving past Deptford Strand and the royal docks bent off in a north-eastern curve. For a voyager, the scene was map-like and promising. A strong current might impede navigation, but the wharves here were usually busy the year round. Those intending to sail for Berwick-on-Tweed, an organizing point for Scottish espionage, often embarked at the Strand.

The four guests who reached Mrs Bull's at about 10 a.m were Marlowe, Ingram Frizer, Nicholas Skeres, and the 'special messenger' Robert Poley, who had just returned from the Hague. In need of privacy, they stayed all day at Mrs Bull's, which was not a tavern but a rooming-house in which meals were served. Her normal clientele would have included supervisors or inspectors at the dockyards, exporters of quality goods, and merchants involved in imports from Russia and the Baltic ports. Deptford was more nearly a country village than a grimy dockside town. Mrs Bull's house and garden lay in the Strand, which bordered on the river between Sayes Court and Deptford Creek, but even here there was a large Common Green. One looked downriver to the pennons of Greenwich Palace, and opposite to the Isle of Dogs, a scrubby wasteland almost screened off by the waterfront. Drake's *Golden Hind* still lay in sight, to tempt souvenir-hunters who pried wood from its timbers. Naval vessels, awaiting refitting, stood with their high masts and welter of spars and ropes at the royal docks.

Mrs Bull was a widow of good family lineage, whose likely discretion would have suited secret agents. Born as Eleanor Whitney, she was related to a family at Whitney-on-Wye which had produced men who rose to be MPs, sheriffs, and minor officers at court. Her 'cousin' Blanche Parry, Chief Gentlewoman of the Privy Chamber, had been a favourite of the queen. When Blanche Parry died in 1589, she left Eleanor a legacy of £100, to be paid out of a debt recoverable from a third party. The legacy, though generous, thus had an awkward string attached, and it does not follow that Eleanor, whether or not she received £100, was prominent enough to have known all of the 'cousins' and legatees of the former Chief Gentlewoman, who included Lord Burghley and even the alchemist Dr John Dee.[21]

As a well-bred woman, she had married Richard Bull, probably the son of a local 'master shipwright' of that name who was still living in 1571, the year of her wedding. Richard Bull the younger held the post of sub-bailiff at Sayes Court and worked for the Clerk of the Green Cloth, until his own death in the spring of 1590. Unless her offspring predeceased her, Mrs Bull was childless since the beneficiary of her estate in the mid-1590s was George Bull, yeoman of Harlow, Essex, who was cited as her next of kin, but was too old to have been her son.

A family named Bull had been at St George's parish, Canterbury, but there is no sign that Marlowe had an early acquaintance with his hostess. A certain Anthony Marlowe, who is described as chief agent of the Muscovy Company, supervised imports of timber and cordage at Deptford in this decade, but his relatives were from Yorkshire, not Kent; he was not a blood relative of the poet. Nor does Edmund Marlowe, a sea-captain, appear to have any relation to the poet or to the rendezvous this spring. One must look elsewhere for facts about the meeting at Mrs Bull's.

Just back from the Continent, Robert Poley was a spy of varied experience, subtlety, and craft. Ten years older than Marlowe, he was the senior person at this meeting. If he had a rugged or weather-worn look, he also had a delicacy, a finesse, a psychological gift which set him apart from other operatives. In Poley's assignments, nothing was allowed to go 'wrong', or, as in the Babington case, he quickly made up for a setback. He was not a man to let events, in intimate company, occur to his disadvantage. Utterly ruthless, he acquired a small fortune even when inside the Marlshalsea, where he entertained a cutler's wife to 'fine bankets'. Lately, for work in Scotland and the Low Countries, he was being well paid: in eight months, he received fees of £116 from the Vice-Chamberlain Sir Thomas Heneage. Poley used several letter-drops, as his cipher-keys show. He had two safe houses in Antwerp, two in London, and a convenient drop at the broker Robert Rutkin's house in Shoreditch. An enquiry into Rutkin's loyalty had stimulated Cecil's interest in Poley's ability: 'I have spoken with Poley, and found him no fool', Cecil told Heneage on 25 May 1592.[22]

Since then, Poley's missions in Scotland had been more frequent, and a year later he found messages which kept him busy for more than a week. On 30 May, the letters he was carrying from the Hague must have been on his person; he did not take these to the court until 8 June. His employers noted of his movements, between early May and up to that June day, that he had been 'in her majesties service all the aforesaid time'. Nowhere else, among the entries of payments to messengers, does that statement occur. The Cecils had evidently requested something special, in all likelihood that he prepare Marlowe for work.[23] A plan to send the poet into Scotland had been mooted; Kyd suggests as much in his final allegation to the Lord Keeper:

He [Marlowe] would persuade with men of quality to go unto the K*ing* of Scots, wither I hear Roydon is gone, and where if he had lived, he told me when I saw him last, he meant to be.[24]

Marlowe's loyalty to James VI has a certain plausibility in the light of his patron's and Cecil's concerns, as does a touch of braggadocio in what he is supposed to have said.

The Council knew where to find him, and Poley may have called at Scadbury. So far as we know, Ingram Frizer saved his master from any trouble in entertaining secret agents and invited Marlowe (and possibly Poley and Skeres as well) to a 'feast' at Deptford. The invitation is mentioned by William Vaughan, in the most credible of the relevant accounts which followed the inquest into the poet's death.

Poley thus reached M[rs] Bull's, seven miles from Scadbury's moat. There was a queerness in this 'feast', in that Frizer and Skeres had little to gain from talk about Scotland or the Dutch Lowlands, but Poley had an insider's view of the crises. The queen's relations with James VI had reached boiling point with the discovery of 'the Spanish blanks', sheets in which the Scottish earls of Angus, Huntly, and Errol pledged to give support to an invading Spanish army of up to 30,000 men. James VI's failure to suppress the earls, and his delays, had begun to lead the English queen to coerce him by supporting the earl of Bothwell, a thorn in the king's flesh. Poley had gone straight back to James's court in December when the 'blanks' came to light, and later to Brussels, again to Edinburgh and back to the Low Countries where he may have trawled for data at the Hague. Plums could be had by quick, secret couriers, rich opportunities: there could be more in the game than carrying the post.[25]

After M[rs] Bull's luncheon, the four men 'were in quiet sort together & walked in the garden of the said house until the sixth hour after noon'. In the infected suburbs, Poley had been too rushed to change his lodgings; but he kept up with events, and no doubt viewed the poet with interest. If heretic-hunters such as Whitgift, Bancroft, Puckering, and Buckhurst set the tone of the day, Marlowe could be seen as a liability to his sponsors.

As a finance clerk, Poley had once served the poet Sir Philip Sidney, and stayed behind with the poet's wife, Frances Walsingham, when Sidney went to his death in the Lowlands. Another friend to poets in M[rs] Bull's garden was Nick Skeres, who had helped to bilk the poet Matthew Roydon, then studying law at Thavies inn in 1582. After Roydon signed a bond for £40 to a London goldsmith, with Skeres and his brother as co-signatories, Skeres drew Roydon into a money-lending trap set up by John Wolfall of Silver Street. At the time of the Deptford meeting, Roydon, with two others, was bound to Wolfall for the large sum of £150. Yet the scams had not gone altogether well; just a month earlier, in April 1593, a law-suit had led the Star Chamber to question Skeres, who confessed that for ten years or more he had been an 'instrument' used by Wolfall to 'draw young gents into bonds'. For drawing in the 'gents', he was paid a small commission of 'xl shillings, or some suchlike petty sum'. A month later, Wolfall's man, no doubt, had a similar set-up with Ingram Frizer.

All the same, Skeres had to scrape for work. He had been a courier for the earl of Essex and soldiered for him at Rouen, but we lack any sign that he ever had a close connection with the earl. Paul Hammer has found a letter Skeres sent to Gelly Metrick, Essex's man of business in around 1596, in which, after having 'forsaken the waies of my good', as he says, Skeres tries hard to get into that agent's favour.[26]

It is a paradox that Marlowe's three friends at Mrs Bull's were not free-spirited rogues, but wary, dependent manipulators skilled in dodgy business transactions or espionage; each had to please an employer. Even Skeres was subject to Frizer. If Marlowe eyed them with interest, they in turn, saw him, perhaps, as a theatre man in mortal trouble over atheism, but not unlike a certain type of Londoner.

'The English', wrote Van Meteren the Dutch consul, who eyed young gentlemen at the great law Inns, 'are not vindictive, but very inconstant, rash, vain, glorious, light, and deceiving', and also 'full of courtly and affected manners and words, which they take for gentility, civility and wisdom', and they 'dress in elegant, light and costly garments'. Marlowe could be 'deceiving' in a way which annoyed Kyd, though at Mrs Bull's, his outspokenness may have been a fatal defect in Poley's eyes. At any rate, at 6 o'clock the four men went indoors for supper. By then, they had been talking for eight hours.[27]

When dining, they cannot have been alone; one or two servants entered and left. The room Mrs Bull allowed them had a long, typical wooden bench next to a table, as well as a bed. After supper, Marlowe lay on the bed, and Poley and Frizer, with their backs to him, sat at the bench to play at 'tables' or backgammon. Skeres may have waited a moment before sitting next to his master, so that Frizer was wedged between two companions. As the coroner's report says, an argument then began: Frizer and Marlowe 'were in speech & offered one to another divers malicious words . . .'.

The dispute flared up—but, I think, it will allow us a pause. Mr Frizer—to give him again a gentlemanly rank, as the royal coroner did— was normally a sedentary man, of some gravity, who wore a dagger for the purpose of cutting meat. The dagger was carried in a sheath transversely across the small of the back, and might be used for defence. Frizer pre- ferred to fight in law-courts, and, as we know, he engaged in litigation and some extra-legal trickery. He took an illegal profit of £30 early in the Woodleff scam, and later blocked his victim's suit of complaint. A year after that gulling, he was expelled from a domicile in St Saviour's parish, Southwark, after which he sued his opponent for recovery of the house plus £40 damages. The court awarded him the house, but cut the damages down to £5, with sixpence costs. The fact that he got only an eighth of the sum requested, with a pittance for costs, suggests that he may have used the house to milk a tenant or a former owner for damages.

In financially gouging a victim, Frizer took risks. But if he walked on eggs, he stepped with care. He befriended respectable tradesmen—often present or future aldermen such as James Deane or Andrew Chamberlain. His acquaintance Paul Banning, or Bayning, was about to become one of the two sheriffs of London in 1593, and this, in itself, could have emboldened Frizer.[28]

He meant to thrive as a business agent, but his chances—as well as Scadbury's solvency, and Walsingham's life as a courtier—were affected by Christopher Marlowe. At Mrs Bull's, Frizer provoked and killed the poet (later in the presence of the royal coroner, he confessed to the homicide). On 30 May he had bided his time until he had a chance to maim or kill with impunity.

Certainly, he had a strong motive. Early in the year, parliament had ensured that heresy was akin to treason; dissidents were being hanged. The royal court, thereafter, was unlikely to reward any sponsor of heretics. How could the law tolerate atheism, or the queen herself continue to favour Walsingham as the patron of a heretic, if, in law, all heresy was treasonous? Marlowe, the famous 'atheist' had become an intolerable, ruinous, and deadly burden for anyone who hoped to profit at Scadbury. As patron of a well-known, flagrant 'atheist', Walsingham risked damaging his own reputation, and so depriving his agent of profits and security. Had the earl of Essex wished to be rid of Marlowe, he could have been dispatched and thrown in the Thames any night.[29] But Walsingham's business agent faced a trying, appalling task. Indeed what emerges is the hard eye that Frizer had for money, and his desire to foster a cash source, and do anything to keep it.

He stood to gain from a rich and varied flow of benefits which could accrue to Thomas, if no albatross hung on the master's neck. The flow involved land grants, tangible honours and reversions while the queen was alive, and much more, if Scottish James acceded. Benefits could devolve down to an agent, if his master unfailingly pleased the feeding hand. Jealousy, too, can move a knife. The opposing Latin and English portraits of Thomas Walsingham in Watson's curious *Meliboeus*, in its two versions, suggest that the master of Scadbury imparted to elegant friends far more than he admitted to others and made nice distinctions between those he honoured, and those who served him. His habits were typical of the age, but they were likely to exalt Marlowe, with his ruinous 'atheism', at Frizer's cost. Taking risks for practical ends, Frizer may have felt that Marlowe was provocable. That was pretty apparent to anyone who knew the poet. A terrible wish can forbid itself action, until hours pass, and good luck, uncannily, allows for the deed.

After the fight, the killer was to languish briefly. Having received a royal pardon in the astonishing space of a month, Frizer, only a day later, was doing business for his master. With contacts in the Council, Thomas Walsingham may have accelerated the pardon, whoever else approved it. There was an advantage in the '*sprezzatura* of nonchalance', and especially in Thomas's mild, knowing yet unknowing habit of not looking far into Frizer's financial trickery, while profiting from it. Neither vicious nor evil, Thomas might express a worry to a faithful subordinate, in an off-hand, implicit way, and then, later, notice that affairs resolved themselves. No doubt, life brings poignant loss. On tragic days, one grieved, one stood in wise, reflective sorrow at a graveside, and then rode back to one's fishponds and profitable pigs, or shot at vile, squealing water rats in black water.

*

In later years, Sir Thomas Walsingham married a knight's daughter and descendant of a sister of the royal Boleyns, the vivacious, clever Audrey Shelton. She was born in June 1568. Not long before Lady Audrey employed Frizer as her own agent, the queen granted to the master of Scadbury in reversion the keepership of the Royal Park at Eltham, nearby in Kent. In due course, Frizer settled at Eltham for the rest of his life, and attended to her ladyship. James I, once enthroned, recalled the handsome Walsinghams, and beginning in the year of his accession granted a series of valuable leases of Crown lands to Lady Audrey Walsingham, or to Ingram Frizer for the lady's use.

One relevant indenture, now at the Yorkshire Archaeological Society, begins to indicate the handiness of these gifts. Frizer's name, at last, appears with the best of names in 1605:

James by the grace of God King of England Scotland Fraunce and Ireland defendour of the faithe etc. on the one parte[,] And Ingram Frizar then servant to the right honorable the Lady Audrey Walsingham (by the name of Ingram Frizar) on th*e* other parte, sealled with the sealle of the Dutchy of Lancaster[,] dated the seaventh day of January in the second yeare of his Ma*jes*ties raigne . . . to farme did let to the aforesaide Ingram Frizar amongest other things the aforesaid one messuage in Scotton and a half acre of land late in the tenure of Walter Pulleyne . . . **To have and to holde** . . . for the term of forty yeres[30]

With the king's lease, Frizer could sublet applicable grazing rights and the like. In this case, he paid Lady Audrey for the lease, so that the messuage and half-acre became his 'to have and to hold' for the stated forty-year term. Formerly owned by the Catholic Church, the property in this instance belonged to the chantry of Scotton in Yorkshire, and as Crown land existed as a part of the Duchy of Lancaster. Having acquired his rights, Frizer sold the lease just two months later, no doubt for a quick profit.

With his income and respectability assured, he had little need for bold scams—and Scadbury's owner did far better. The queen granted to Sir Thomas the manor of Dartford, together with Cobham, Combe, and Chislehurst for twenty-one years in 1597. At that time, he became MP for Rochester, and later in the new reign he represented Kent with Sir Peter Manwood. The offices and honours which the two Walsinghams received from King James may have enabled Sir Thomas to buy four manors outright, along with the county tracts or hundreds of Washlingstone and Littlefield, in 1611. Two years later, he sold three manors, but retained Chislehurst, the hundreds, and other lands.

So Marlowe's patron made no debilitating error in his arrangements, and lived to a ripe old age. Nor did Frizer go seriously astray after the spring of 1593, and in the months after the murder at Mrs Bull's house he devoted himself to tasks which helped his master to flourish.

At Deptford, the river changes in its character week by week. It has picked up streams from the Chilterns, and from others which arise to the south on the hills of the Weald in Kent and Sussex. Three billion gallons a day flow past the Chiltern scarp. In the spring, the great river is less agitated, but by no means lacking in its power. When Marlowe saw the Thames, he was nearly saved—if we credit the remark that he planned to be in Scotland. His streams are more exotic ones, such as the Nile and the Euphrates and the Tyros and Araris, but every foreign locale in his plays has a relation to England.

When he came indoors at 6 o'clock, the room was still suffused with daylight. After the evening meal, he lay down because he was disconcerted by events and perhaps hazy with drink. Few men handled situations better than Robert Poley, but judging from the coroner's report, neither he nor Skeres spoke or intervened when the argument began.

Malicious words, between Frizer and Marlowe, arose because of a dispute over the bill, or *le recknynge*, says the coroner. But the inquisition sketches an odd, almost hallucinatory scene. The three men, Skeres, Frizer, and Poley, sit with their backs to the poet, and they remain squeezed together and glued to a bench. Frizer speaks to a wall, and Marlowe on a bed replies to the ceiling. Possibly, the room begins to contract; one might think that the furniture is on the move, for twice, in Latin and in English, Mrs Bull's long table comes *nere the bed*. Poley and Skeres hear nothing. When violence begins, nobody can move, stand up, shout for help, or even turn his head. The most spectacular, bloody events occur next to Poley's elbow, but he has no idea that a man is being killed.

'Is it not odd', John Bakeless once asked, 'that there is nothing to explain why three men could not overpower Marlowe without killing him?' And yet the coroner addresses just this point: 'Ingram Frysar could in no way flee' from a mortal attack by Marlowe. Again: Frizer 'was not able to withdraw in any way', or again, 'the same Ingram could not withdraw further from the aforesaid Christopher'. In Elizabethan fights the safest way to draw blood without inflicting serious harm was to reverse the dagger, and pummel an opponent's scalp with the hilt. 'If thou dost lay thy hands on me I will lay my dagger on thy pate', says an earl's agent at Stratford in 1582.[31] The scalp wound, like the threat of it, is meant to confuse or intimidate, but not to kill.

Leaping from his bed, the poet grabbed at Frizer's dagger, and with the hilt gave him two wounds on the scalp, each two inches long and a quarter of an inch deep. The poet's 'rashness in attempting sudden privy injuries to men' was later noted by Kyd, possibly only with reference to verbal injuries; but Marlowe could be violent, and his attack left his enemy free to respond. Poley and Skeres may have pinioned his arms, or simply let Walsingham's business agent do as he wished. Frizer recovered his weapon and drove it hard at Marlowe's face.

According to the original report, this blade struck 'above his right eye' (*super dexterum oculum suum*), or just under the thin, bony ocular plate which roofs the eyeball. The dagger apparently penetrated two inches to the internal carotid where it divides into its terminal branches, the middle and anterior cerebral arteries. Modern medical opinion is sceptical of the view that Marlowe died of an air embolus, since the normal pressure in the sinus approximates to atmospheric pressure, as J. Thompson Rowling, a surgeon at Sheffield, has noted. It is hard to see how an embolism would result from a long, thin wound. The likeliest cause of death would be intracranial bleeding from a major vessel, such as the carotid, just punctured by the weapon. This would have left Marlowe conscious for five or six minutes; he is unlikely to have died at once.[32]

Such a detail may catch Poley, Skeres, and Frizer in a lie, since they told the coroner that Marlowe had died instantly—*et ibidem instanter obiit*. With access to details not in the official report, both Vaughan and Beard indicate that the poet remained conscious for a while: 'he shortly after dyed' or 'hee even cursed and blasphemed to the last gaspe'.[33] If the coroner's report is false in one detail, it may be false or distorted in others.

In theory, we are left with a question as to what Marlowe said in his last moments. If he simply ranted, there would have been no need to fabricate a story of instant death. But once he was silenced, his killer did not flee

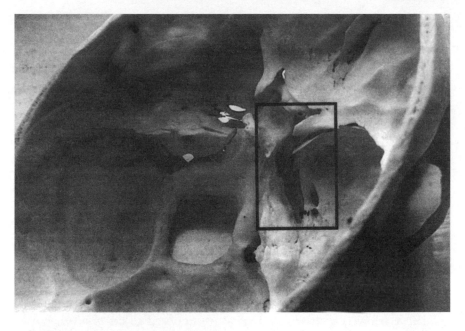

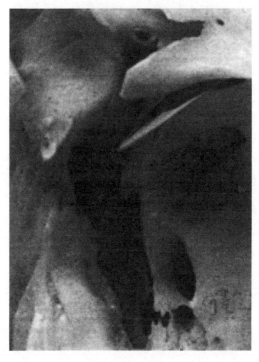

32 Marlowe's wound. Here, in a modern skull, the point of a dagger barely impinges on the internal carotid artery. Research suggests that Marlowe lost consciousness only after a few minutes, and probably died from haemorrhaging into the brain (not from an unlikely air embolus), in which case the witnesses lied about his 'instant death'. The coroner gives the wound's depth as two inches, which is almost exactly the distance from the skin of the eyelid to the internal carotid, as measured with a skull and callipers by the Sheffield surgeon J. T. Rowling from Mrs Bull's house, and Frizer and his friends had time to agree on a story before the coroner's inquest began two days later, on Friday, 1 June.

William Danby, Coroner for the Queen's Household, acted illegally, since the county coroner was required to be on hand, according to statutory law. The death occurred 'within the verge' (*infra virgam*), or within twelve miles of the physical presence of the sovereign. The queen was then at Nonsuch Palace, near Cheam, or about sixteen statute miles by road from Deptford Strand, but our statute 'mile' is shorter than the Tudor one.[34]

Danby ought to have arrived with a county coroner, but similar irregularities were common. Peter Farey, in looking into Middlesex records for 1589–92, finds six cases of death 'within the verge', in which not even the Coroner of the Verge was involved

In practice, Danby was fairly correct and meticulous. He was about 70 years of age, if he is the same William Danby who entered Lincoln's Inn on 1 August 1542. He had to lead sixteen jurors into Mrs Bull's room to gaze at Marlowe's body. The jurors were supposed to be 'good men and true', though picked more or less at random from a local poll. The initials of the surnames of most of Marlowe's jurors come from the first part of the alphabet (A, seven Bs, C, two Ds, ff, G, H, R, and W).[35]

Henry Dabyns and George Halfepenny were bakers with tenements in Deptford, and William Curry had a house near the Strand. Giles Feld was a local grocer, and Henry Awger was a tenant at Sayes Court manor. Robert Baldwin came from Greenwich, across the Ravensbourne Creek, and James Batt, a husbandman, rode in from Lewisham about a mile away. Wolstan Randall, gentleman, held a house and stable on lease from the Lord Admiral at Deptford. Of the others so far traced, the head of the jury, Mr Nicholas Draper, was perhaps the gentleman of that name who lived at Leigh, not far from Tonbridge in West Kent. The others were John Baldwyn, Thomas Batt senior, John Barber, Henry Bendyn, Alexander Burrage, Edmund Goodcheape and Adrian Walker.

It would have been difficult to suborn such a large, miscellaneous group from the middle ranks to get a false verdict. The coroner had to proceed *super visum corporis* (in view of the body), probe the corpse and take measurements, or evaluate Frizer's dagger (a cheap one worth 12*d.*).[36]

One suspects that the two witnesses told their tale with restraint, and very well. If Frizer mentioned that he was in the service of Walsingham, the allusion did him no harm. A writ of certiorari was issued on 15 June, for the purpose of requesting the result of the coroner's inquest, in order to determine whether 'Christopher Marley's' killer had acted in self-defence. Matters thereafter ran quickly, and the Crown's pardon exonerated Ingram Frizer on 28 June.

One may infer that Lord Burghley and Sir Robert Cecil were inconvenienced by Marlowe's death. Spies swarmed at Berwick-on-Tweed, where Roydon and Marlowe perhaps were meant to go. And still, the Council's exact plans are veiled. We know something about the poet's last weeks, but much remains unknown and troubling. If Cecil meant to get him safely out of the way and indeed use him, why had Marlowe been asked to call daily at the court—or had he perhaps been freed from the obligation? With Cholmeley still at large, the authorities may have wished to keep Marlowe on a loose rein to serve, at some point, as the state's witness, but might they not have dealt with Cholmeley, without impeding the poet's movements?

Neither Essex, Ralegh, the Cecils, nor any of the state's heretic-pursuers stood to gain by killing the poet. None would have bothered with Mrs Bull's house and servants, nor perhaps implicated Poley, whose work in Scotland and the Netherlands was urgent. We do not know if others backed Frizer, who killed to remove an obstacle which imperilled his profits. Further enquiry can tell us more. Useful research has been stimulated by the infinitesimally thin possibility that Marlowe did not die when we think he did, just as it has been by improbable theories about Shakespeare's 'Dark Lady'. History holds its doors open.

At some hour on 1 June, Marlowe's body was carried to St Nicholas Church in Deptford. Today, the church is surrounded by blocks of flats and thronged streets, but it is not far from greenery and the river. St Nicholas's had its origins in the twelfth century, and later acquired a tower and then a great bell in 1500. After Marlowe's time, most of the edifice was rebuilt, though the lower part of the tower is about the same as it was on 1 June 1593.

On that day, a group of mourners at the church may have included Scadbury's master, along with Edward Blount the publisher. In his edition of the poet's version of Lucan's *Pharsalia*, Thomas Thorpe

33 St Nicholas Church, Deptford, at the end of the nineteenth century.
Today, the tower's lower part is about the same as it was when
Marlowe was buried in the churchyard, 1 June 1593

imagines Marlowe arising as a ghost to stalk the grounds in St Paul's churchyard. 'Blount', begins Thorpe, who later baffled the world by dedicating Shakespeare's sonnets to 'Mr W.H.',

I purpose to be blunt with you, & out of my dullness to encounter you with a **Dedication** in the memory of that pure Elemental wit **Chr*istopher* Marlow**: whose ghost or **Genius** is to be seen walk the **Churchyard** in (at the least) three or four sheets.[37]

As it happened, in the sheets of St Nicholas's register, a mistake was made in the burial entry. The name of Marlowe's killer was incorrectly given by the vicar:

Christopher Marlow slaine by ffrancis ffrezer; the · I of · June.

There were at the time two Francis Frisers, one at Kingsclere in Hampshire, and the other in Essex or West Kent, though it is obvious and provable that neither had a connection with the Deptford murder.

Somewhat wryly, John Bakeless records the dilemmas of investigators, starting in the nineteenth century, who aimed to figure out who really killed Marlowe (a question which has helped to fuel Nicholl's *The Reckoning* and many a biography, play, and novel). James Broughton, the literary antiquary, heard in 1820 from the vicar of St Nicholas that the register gave the information: '—1st. June, 1593. Christopher Marlowe, slain by Francis Archer.' A misreading of what was already an error led searchers further from the quarry. John H. Ingram, in *Christopher Marlowe and his Associates*—in 1904, the first full-length biography of its subject— copied the vicar's errors and even added one or two. He read the entry:

> Christopher Marlowe, slain by ffrancis Archer, sepultus I. of June.

Halliwell-Phillipps, the Victorian scholar, had settled on 'Frezer', and a later Deptford clergyman opted for 'Frazer'. Among the Elizabethans, William Vaughan had given the killer's name as 'Ingram'. Vaughan, in 1600, had been plausible with other details, and thus Leslie Hotson in the twentieth century suspected the truth when, in the Public Record Office, he stumbled on the name 'Ingram Frizer' in the Calendar of Close Rolls. In the list of pardons in the Patent Rolls of Chancery, of 35 Elizabeth (1593), he found the entry:

> *Regina* xxviij° die Junij con*cessit* Ingramo ffrisar perdon*am* de se defend*endo*

This was dated just four weeks and a day after Marlowe's murder on 30 May. Hotson came upon this gem as the Public Record Office was closing. He spent a long night, almost too excited to sleep, before returning in the morning to find two documents—the coroner's formal investigation and the pardon—'which', says Mr Bakeless, 'told the whole story in minute legal detail'.[38]

Arguably, the trouble is that the legal details tell the 'whole story' about as well as a sieve holds molasses. The Latin pardon for Frizer repeats the wording of the coroner, and Danby's report seems incredible—if we are to assume that Poley and Skeres were paralysed, and that Frizer was unable to move away from Marlowe, but able to shove a dagger into his brain. Was this, after all, an unplanned brawl, a bar-fight, an accident, of a sort that can happen in a city any week? It can seem so, except that 'accidents' with Poley, Skeres, and Frizer were not normally allowed to happen, unless they wanted them to.

Marlowe was not forgotten by those who cared for him, and the balance of comment for the rest of Queen Elizabeth's reign was in his favour. Praise began on 26 June, a month after he was killed, with George Peele's tribute in *The Honour of the Garter* to 'Marley, the Muses darling'. Thinking of the spring of the Muses, George Chapman later asks a 'strangely intellectual-fire' to seek out Marlowe,

> free soul, whose living subject stood
> Up to the chin in the Pierian flood.

Henry Petowe's tribute is more banal, but no less interesting as an example of the enthusiasm in 1598 for 'Marlowe admired',

> whose honey-flowing vein,
> No English writer can as yet attain;
> Whose name in Fame's immortal treasury
> Truth shall record to endless memory.

Similarly, the conventional Francis Meres links him in that year, in *Palladis Tamia*, with 'Aeschylus, Euripides, Sophocles', and calls Marlowe along with Shakespeare one of 'our best for Tragedie'.

Some of the finest lines are in Michael Drayton's elegy on 'Henry Reynolds' (1627), though they say the least about the dramatist:

> Marlow, bathed in Thespian springs
> Had in him those brave translunary things,
> That the first Poets had, his raptures were
> All air, and fire, which made his verses clear
> For that fine madness still he did retain,
> Which rightly should possess a poet's brain.[39]

There had been a 'fine madness' in Marlowe's quips, provocative exaggerations, and wry humour. In London, he could be like an amused, solemn Doctor Faustus among those who mouthed truisms or the prejudices of the suburbs, though exhilarating spirits saved him from the boredom of literalness or complacency. In moving from group to group, he sought out those of audacity, independent views, or creative enterprise: John Greenwood, the Christian who was hanged; or Watson and Roydon, who wrote poetry and served as secret couriers; or Kyd, who innovated in tragedy; or Nashe, who criticized society as a pamphleteer. Marlowe had a committed habit of studying politics and power. His work as an agent focused his attention on the state, but also helped him as he enquired into overseas rivalry and the long-tenacled trade routes into the Middle East.

For all his apparent self-consciousness, he displayed a tough-minded, objective attitude to society. His morality as a playwright exists in his clarity, and in his trust in our ability to think for ourselves. He is enormously refreshing, and lightens our lives because he tests any 'truth' that belittles us. No dramatist ever affirmed human strengths more thoughtfully, or with a more exuberant gaiety. He finds the human psyche too complex for the requirements of a neat plot, in which the protagonist suddenly awakes in Act V to luminous wisdom, so that a play can end tidily. Our lives do not fit into the conventional genres of the stage, as he knew. This is partly why, in his experiments with 'tragedy', he lifts that form to levels of credibility which no other English writer had reached up to the year of his death. He was not a romantic, but a questing realist. His plays have become 'myths of modern existence', as Philip Edwards has said, because they show conflicting urges and impulses which still prevail in Western life. In dramatizing faith, desire, and our other attributes in their ambiguity, Marlowe belongs to us.

He never isolated himself from others. His quips, jokes, laughter, and enquiring wit are balanced by his sympathy for men and women, and by his indignation over social unfairness and hypocrisy. Certainly, the same Kit Marlowe who with gaiety, wit, and force examined follies could be foolishly violent. In his behaviour, he suffered from a blight of the age. Genetically and in other ways, he was a true son of a popular but enrageable John Marlowe, who did battle in punch-ups with shoemaker apprentices. But the son, as seems likely, may have given up fighting with a rapier after one duel in which he himself had not hurt the opponent. If he never fully checked his sillier impulses, Marlowe committed no deadly offence; he pictured some of his lapses and errors, and enquired intelligently into human behaviour wherever he found it. He began by studying his mother and sisters, and drew on his Canterbury days for the rest of his life. For him, too, there were old and not so old companions to turn to: the satirical Nashe or the classical Watson, the poetry-writing Roydon, the dramatist Peele. Needing the friends whom he twitted and tried, Marlowe might have been especially amused by a sketch in Thomas Dekker's *A Knight's Conjuring*, in which he is pictured with a group of fellow Elizabethan poets transposed to another world:

These were likewise carousing to one another at the holy well, some of them singing Paeans to Apollo, some of them hymns to the rest of the gods, whil'st Marlowe, Greene, and Peele had got under the shades of a large vine, laughing to see Nashe (that was but newly come to their college), still haunted with the sharp and satirical spirit that followed him here upon earth.

Epilogue

You see my lord, what working words he hath.

EWS and rumours of Christopher Marlowe's violent fate in a brawl—and casual legends about him as a heretic or rake-hell—increased the popularity of his plays in London. Even in their 1594–5 season, the Admiral's men staged the first part of his *Tamburlaine* fourteen times, and the second part six, *Faustus* twelve times, *The Massacre at Paris* ten, and *The Jew of Malta* nine.

At Canterbury, his parents John and Katherine had to come to terms with their shock and to learn to live with their recollections; but they gained no tangible benefit from his posthumous fame. In 1593 they were left with their daughters: Margaret, who was married to the tailor John Jordan, and her sisters Anne, then 21, and Dorothy, who was 19. (It is not known if their younger son, Thomas, was still alive.) Shortly after the playwright's death, Anne Marlowe married the shoemaker John Cranford on 10 June 1593. Since the old cobbler was a freeman of Canterbury, that status was automatically conferred upon his sons-in-law. Literate and skilful, Cranford paid 11½*d.* to be made free of the city, and rose to become one of the four serjeants-at-mace of Canterbury, with duties of making arrests and serving writs. Pregnant when she married, Anne in time gave birth to about twelve children, and lived to be 81. She was buried on 7 December 1652 (see the family tree in the appendices).

Dorothy Marlowe, in turn, was married to Thomas Graddell, on 30 June 1594. A glover, innkeeper, and hackneyman, Graddell was irregular in mood and behaviour. As landlord of the George inn, he did illicit deals in grain, received stolen goods, and tried to dodge payment of his debts. More than once, he and his wife were denounced for not attending church, or for not receiving Holy Communion. Having fathered two boys—both named John—he finally left his 'loving wife' an annuity of £3 when he died in 1625, after which Dorothy may have wed again.

In the year of Marlowe's own death, the plague nearly eliminated his uncle Thomas Arthur's family. In a merciless summer, Thomas Arthur died along with his wife Ursula, their two sons and two of their daughters. The family's only survivor—Dorothy Arthur, then aged 11—came to live with the old cobbler, who set about trying to take over the administration of her father's property. But John Marlowe had other concerns, too, and he and Katherine cannot have been indifferent to news about tributes to their lost, murdered son.

Christopher Marlowe's talented friends, in stressing his art, began to counter the slanders on his name. An informal campaign had begun when George Peele took the occasion of the investiture of the 'Wizard Earl' of Northumberland as a knight of the Garter, in June, to offer praise in *The Honour of the Garter*. Though this work alludes to other poets, Marlowe is the only playwright it singles out; he is said to be 'Fit to write passions for the souls below | If any wretched souls in passion speak.' In that Dantean capacity, Marlowe, in effect, has the courage and dark talent to render articulate even the terrible pangs of Pluto's wretched souls.[1]

Thomas Nashe, with great vigour, also subscribed to the genius of 'Kit Marlowe'. For one thing, he readied a quarto edition of the poet's *Dido* and wrote elegiac lines on Marlowe to go with it. Nashe's elegy is, sadly, missing today, or at least it is not in our four extant copies of *Dido*. But in the eighteenth century Bishop Tanner evidently saw a copy, and later described Nashe's verses as *Carmine Elegiaco tragediae Didonis praefixio in obitum Christoph. Marlovii* ('an elegiac song on the death of Christopher Marlowe, prefixed to the tragedy of Dido'). Thomas Warton, who became poet laureate, also found Nashe's elegy included in a copy of *Dido* in Osborne's bookshop in 1754. Warton told Edmond Malone that it was 'inserted immediately after the title page',[2] which suggests that the poem was on a printed single leaf, inserted in some copies but not in others.

Nashe had to be indirect in his praise, as it was risky—especially in 1593—to argue in favour of an 'atheist'. He took one clue from his enemy Gabriel Harvey, who in *Four Letters* (1592) had called Nashe 'the Devil's Orator', and Marlowe 'Aretine'. The latter name referred to the great Italian dramatist Pietro Aretino, a shoemaker's son who had died six years before Marlowe's birth. Witty, impudent, and falsely known for atheism, Aretino had been a critic of moral corruption in Roman life. In Nashe's novel *The Unfortunate Traveller*, which he finished on 27 June 1593, he breaks into the story at one point to praise Marlowe explicitly as 'Aretine'. The tribute applies partly to the Italian writer, but it is meant chiefly to illuminate the passion and integrity of Marlowe's art. First, there had been the impact of his plays, with their agility and imaginative intelligence. He was 'one of the wittiest knaves that God ever made' and 'his style was the spirituality of arts', writes Nashe.

No leaf he wrote on but was like a burning-glass to set on fire all his readers. With more than musket shot did he charge his quill, where he meant to inveigh.

In showing up hypocrisy, prejudice, and the lies of governments, Marlowe wrote with an eye on the faults of power:

He was no timorous servile flatterer of the commonwealth wherein he lived. His tongue and his invention were foreborn; what they thought, they would confidently utter. Princes he spared not, that in the least point transgressed.

Nashe adds a remark about Marlowe's outspokenness, which inadvertently suggests the poet's relations with Walsingham and Ingram Frizer: 'His life he contemned in comparison of the liberty of speech'.[3]

Publication of *The Unfortunate Traveller* was delayed until the spring of 1594. The previous summer, Nashe—in a bleak, guilt-ridden nervous crisis—had written *Christ's Tears over Jerusalem*, a product of 'days of dolour and heaviness', as he said; it landed him briefly in prison. In the second edition he refers to 'poor deceased Kit Marlow' who has been 'most notoriously & viley dealt with'. After that, Nashe fell silent for about two years, but in response to the charge that he had 'shamefully and odiously' mistreated others, he finally replied in *Have with You to Saffron Walden* (1596): 'I never abused Marloe' who had 'used me like a friend'.

That statement must be taken as truthful. His pamphlet-warfare with Harvey, though it exhausted Nashe, had given him good opportunities to praise Marlowe and respond to detractors who labelled the poet as a scoffer or 'Lucian', an atheist, or (implicitly) a social liability or mere peacock. When recovered from his battles, Nashe wrote a hilarious parody of the Hero and Leander tale in *Lenten Stuff* (1599). Without satirizing

Marlowe's poem, he refers to the Greek love-story as one that 'divine *Musaeus* sung, and a diviner Muse than him, *Kit Marlow*'.[4]

However, despite the hopes of well-wishers, the tables were turning. New, explicit reports suggested that Marlowe, a heretic, had been killed by God's wrath. Two accounts by Puritans are especially revealing, since despite their confusions they offer details about the murder at Deptford. In 1597 Dr Thomas Beard, a Cambridge graduate, soon to be rector of Hengreave in Suffolk, collected some histories of 'transgressors' for his first, mightily instructive work, *The Theatre of God's Judgements*. For him, Marlowe had been guilty of 'Atheism and impiety' as well as having been 'a playmaker, and a Poet of scurrility'. Beard confuses a 'London Street' with the capital itself, though he begins to paint the final skirmish at M[rs] Bull's:

But see what a hook the Lord put in the nostrils of this barking dog. It so fell out, that in London streets as he purposed to stab one whom he owed a grudge unto with his dagger, the other party perceiving so avoided the stroke, that withal catching hold of his wrist, he stabbed his own dagger into his own head, in such sort, that notwithstanding all the means of surgery that could be wrought, he shortly after died thereof. The manner of his death being so terrible (for he even cursed and blasphemed to his last gasp, and together with his breath an oath flew out of his mouth) that it was not only a manifest sign of God's judgement, but also an horrible and fearful terror to all that beheld him. But herein did the justice of God most notably appear, in that he compelled his own hand which had written those blasphemies to be the instrument to punish him, and that in his brain, which had devised the same.

In the cruel hook put into 'nostrils of this barking dog', one begins to see the outlines of Beard's later career. He became headmaster at Huntington grammar school, where he taught—and, as tradition has it, vigorously flogged Oliver Cromwell. At any rate, Beard offers the first independent account of Marlowe's death.

In 1598 Francis Meres, in *Palladis Tamia*, cited Beard's story and added vividly that Marlowe was 'stabbed to death by a bawdy Servingman, a rival of his in his lewd love'. This was new; but in the next century there were less incisive reports of the poet's death. With a few variations, Edmund Rudierde's *The Thunderbolt of God's Wrath* (1618), despite its title, repeated Beard's story without adding much smoke or fire to it; and Anthony à Wood used both Beard and Meres in *Athenae Oxonienses*

(1691), but made Marlowe 'deeply in love with a certain woman', and humiliated because his rival in love was a base serving-man. The poet's story, by then, was far advanced in a rosy world of fiction.

After Beard, just one other report of Marlowe's death is particularly important. Born in 1577, and a graduate of Jesus College, Oxford, William Vaughan was a Welshman with religious and medical interests. His family owned a vast estate called Golden Grove, of about 50,000 acres in Carmarthenshire. In 1600 he wrote a medical guide, *Natural and Artificial Directions for Health*, which went into seven editions in a brief period. In the same year, more remarkably, he included a paragraph on Marlowe's death in a book called *The Golden Grove*, which comes closer to the facts than any previous report. After dilating on the ultimate fates of Diogenes and Pliny, he takes up Marlowe as a topical example:

Not inferior to these was one Christopher Marlow by profession a playmaker, who, as it is reported, about 7 years ago wrote a book against the Trinity: but see the effects of God's justice; it so happened, that at Detford, a little village about three miles distant from London, as he meant to stab with his poniard one named Ingram, that had invited him thither to a feast, and was then playing at tables, he quickly perceiving it, so avoided the thrust, that withal drawing out his dagger for his defence, he stabbed this Marlow into the eye, in such sort, that his brains coming out at the dagger's point, he shortly after died. Thus did God, the true executioner of divine justice, work the end of impious Atheists.

In their accounts, both Beard and Vaughan reflect popular rumours in London about the circumstances of Marlowe's death. But, clearly, Vaughan had had access to special facts. His stepmother, Lettice Vaughan, was a sister-in-law to Dorothy née Devereux, the younger sister of the earl of Essex. A few years before *Golden Grove* was composed, Dorothy Devereux had taken as her second husband Henry Percy, the earl of Northumberland or the 'Wizard Earl'.

Marlowe had been admired by the Wizard Earl, and had boasted of that connection to Sir Robert Sidney. It is possible, then, that the earl himself spoke to one of the Deptford jurors, and passed along what he heard to Vaughan. In any case, Vaughan correctly identifies the scene of the fatal fight as 'Detford'; he specifies the game in progress at Mrs Bull's ('tables' or backgammon), and knows of the wound to the eye; he also names the killer, as 'Ingram', and mentions the latter's 'invitation to a feast'. Since all of this is consistent with the inquisition, it is reasonable to credit Vaughan's details.

The Puritans' harsh view of Marlowe was slightly offset by praise for *Hero and Leander* when it appeared in 1598. A year or two later, in *As You Like It*, Shakespeare has his shepherdess Phoebe remark in an aside:

> Dead Shepherd, now I find thy saw of might,
> Whoever loved that loved not at first sight?

The Dead Shepherd is probably Marlowe, and the 'saw' or maxim is a well-known line from *Hero and Leander*. In Shakespeare's play, Touchstone, the wise clown, may be referring to the quarrel over the *recknynge* at Mrs Bull's, when he says, 'it strikes a man more dead than a great reckoning in a little room'. Yet the clown's scene is richly comic; and Touchstone compares himself with Ovid in exile, so the famous line may instead be playing on Chapman's phrases, 'riches in a little Roome' and 'strooke dead', in a description in *Ovid's Banquet of Sense* (1595).[5]

Both of Marlowe's parents died in the early months of 1605. By then, those who had helped the cause of James I had been rewarded. Sir Robert Cecil was made Viscount Cranbourne in 1604, and a year later he became earl of Salisbury. Sir Robert Sidney, who had arrested Marlowe at Flushing, was created Baron Sidney of Penshurst on 13 May 1603, only a few weeks after the king's accession.

Not many of the spies of Marlowe's day thrived for long. Nicholas Skeres perhaps returned to the earl of Essex's service. A few weeks after the Essex rising in 1601, one Nicholas 'Skiers' was taken to the political prison of Bridewell, a locale with a fearful reputation for torture and no return. In that same year, Robert Poley received his last payment as a messenger and informer. Earlier, in 1597, when Ben Jonson was imprisoned in the Marlshalsea (with Nashe) for writing the seditious play *The Isle of Dogs*, Poley had been one of the 'two damn'd villains' sent to pry data from him. Jonson took revenge on Poley (or 'Pooley') in the poem 'Inviting a Friend to Supper', about the bliss of dining and drinking without spies on hand:

> And we will have no Poley or Parrot by;
> Nor shall our cups make any guilty men,
> But at our parting we will be as when
> We innocently met.[6]

Richard Cholmeley, the reckless informer, disappeared from record after his arrest on 28 June 1593. Thomas Drury, after courier work, returned to a life of hoaxes and swindling, and died of the plague at the Swan inn, Southwark, in 1603.

Matthew Roydon, the courier, apparently fared well in Scotland, and later settled in the house of William Haddington, earl of Hamilton, a favourite of King James. Among Marlowe's other acquaintances, George Peele is said to have died of the 'pox' around 1596. Archbishop Whitgift's orders against 'Satyres & Epigrams' and his command to confiscate 'all Nashe's books', in 1599, struck against one of Marlowe's best defenders. Partly as a result, Thomas Nashe gave up writing and sequestered himself; he died in about 1601. Gabriel Harvey also suffered from Whitgift's censorship, but retired to Saffron Walden and lived on in fussy bachelorhood into his eighties.

The murderer Ingram Frizer—and even the elegant Walsinghams—were of fairly minor interest to James, but Frizer settled into yeomanly respectability at Eltham. After the parish's vicar let him dig a well at a corner of the vicar's close, Frizer typically failed to pay for the privilege, but used the water to brew his ale. In 1604 he became churchwarden, and in 1611 the parish's tax-assessor. Frizer kept a servant, 'Margret', and had two daughters—one lived in the capital, as Alice Dixon, and the other married a man named Banks. A 'Mrs Ingeram', buried at Eltham in 1616, was possibly Frizer's wife. An odd payment he made, 'for putten forth of Sheeres child', may indicate that he dealt with a dependent child, or orphan, of his old fellow con man Nicholas Skeres. Having outlived his employer Lady Audrey, Ingram Frizer was buried in Eltham churchyard on 14 August 1627.[7]

By then, changing tastes in London had made Marlowe's plays look antiquated, if not boorish and crude, to many of the gentry. His works deeply appealed to Ben Jonson—whom T. S. Eliot later described as the 'legitimate heir of Marlowe'.[8] But Jonson's plays, too, went out of fashion in the seventeenth century, and even Shakespeare's works suffered from deletions and bland rewriting. And yet, even when Marlowe's reputation was at its lowest, the beauty of his verse drew attention—a sign that he would keep his power.

Appendices

1 Family trees

Marlowe, Arthur, and Moore Family Relationships

Born at Ospringe in Kent, John Marlowe the shoemaker married Katherine Arthur at Canterbury in May 1561. They both died early in 1605. Of their nine offspring, Christopher Marlowe (the poet), Thomas (a choirboy) and Margaret, Jane, Anne, and Dorothy all survived childhood. Raised at Dover, the poet's uncle Thomas Arthur married Ursula Moore, a daughter of Thomasina and Richard Moore, a blacksmith who died in 1582. Ursula's brother Thomas was wed to Mary Aunsell, a fact which led the Aunsells to sue Ursula and her mother in wrangles over the blacksmith's goods. The entire Arthur family, except for 11-year-old Dorothy, died in the plague of 1593. The poet's sister Jane Marlowe at 12 had married the shoemaker John Moore (her Aunt Ursula's brother) and died in childbirth. Later the widower took as a second wife his probable relative, Jane Moore.

The Families of Jordan, Cranford, and Graddell

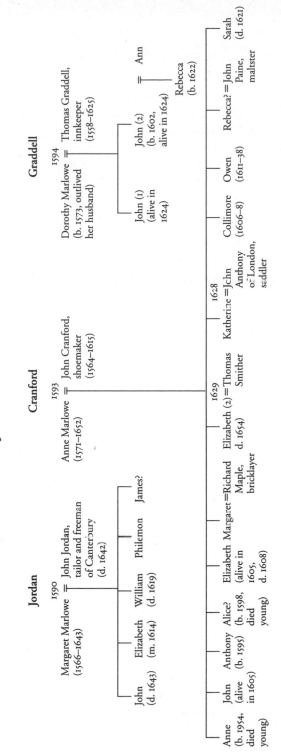

Three of Christopher Marlowe's sisters had offspring. In June 1590 Margaret Marlowe was wed to the local tailor John Jordan. They possibly had five or more children, but only four can be definitely traced; the name 'Jordan' occurs often at Canterbury. Anne Marlowe, who was pregnant when the poet died, married the shoemaker John Cranford in June 1593; the names of ten and perhaps of twelve of their children are recorded. In the following June, Dorothy Marlowe married the glover and innkeeper Thomas Graddell, and later gave birth to two sons named John (both were alive at the same time). The most enduring of the poet's sisters was Anne, who despite her alleged blasphemies, fighting with knives and other weapons, and defiance of her parish's churchwardens, died not far from Canterbury Cathedral at the age of 81.

2 Richard Baines on Marlowe

Baines's Note survives in the papers of Sir John Puckering, but may be a copy rather than the original document. The author is clearly the same Richard Baines who caused the arrest of Marlowe at Flushing in January 1592. The original Note is likely to have reached Puckering or Sir Robert Cecil, at Nonsuch Palace, not later than 26 May 1593. The signature here is in a plain, bold hand, differing a little from the slightly varying styles of handwriting in the text. (MSS BL Harleian 6848, fos. 185–6. By permission of the British Library.)

A note containing the opinion of one Christopher Marly concerning his damnable ⟨opini⟩ Judgment of Religion, and scorn of Godes word.

That the Indians and many Authors of antiquity have assuredly written of above 16 thousand yeares agone whereas ⟨Moyses⟩ Adam is ⟨said⟩ proved to have lived within 6 thowsand yeares.

He affirmeth that Moyses was but a Jugler, & that one Heriots being Sir W Raleighs man can do more than he.

That Moyses made the Jewes to travell xl yeares in the wildernes (which journey might have bin done in lesse than one yeare) ere they came to the promised land to the intent that those who were privy to most of his subtilties might perish and so an everlasting superstition remain in the hartes of the people.

That Christ was a bastard and his mother dishonest.

That he was the sonne of a carpenter, and that if the Jewes among whome he was borne did crucify him they best knew him and whence he came.

That Christ deserved better to dy than Barrabas and that the Jewes made a good choise, though Barrabas were both a theif and a murtherer.

That if there be any god or any good Religion, then it is the papistes because the service of god is performed with more ceremonies, as Elevation of the mass, organs, singing men, Shaven Crownes, &cta. That all protestants are Hypocriticall asses.

That if he were put to write a new religion, he would undertake both a more Exellent and Admirable methode and that all the new testament is filthily written.

That the woman of Samaria and her sister were whores & that Christ knew them dishonestly.

That St John the Evangelist was bedfellow to Christ and leaned alwaies in his bosome, that he used him as the sinners of Sodoma.

That all they that love not Tobacco & Boies were fooles.

That all the apostles were fishermen and base fellowes neyther of wit nor worth, that Paull only had wit but he was a timerous fellow in bidding men to be subject to magistrates against his conscience.

That he had as good right to coine as the Queen of England and that he was aquainted with one Poole a prisoner in Newgate who hath greate skill in mixture of mettals and having learned some thinges of him he ment through help of a cuning stamp maker to coin French crownes, pistoletes and English shillinges.

That if Christ would have instituted the sacrament with more cermoniall reverence it would have bin had in more admiration, that it would have bin much better being administred in a Tobacco pipe.

That the Angell Gabriell was baud to the holy ghost, because he brought the salutation to Mary.

That one Ric Cholmley ⟨hath Cholmley⟩ hath confesst that he was perswaded by Marloes reasons to become an Atheist.

These thinges with many other shall by good & honest witnes be aproved to be his opinions and comen speeches and that this Marlow doth not only hould them himself but almost into every company he cometh he perswades men to Atheism willing them not to be afeard of bugbeares and hobgoblins and utterly scorning both god and his ministers as I Richard Baines will Justify & approve both by mine oath and the testimony of many honest men, and almost all men with whome he hath conversed any time will testify the same, and as I think all men in Christianity ought to indevor that the mouth of so dangerous a member may be stopped, he saieth likewise that he hath quoted a number of contraieties oute of the Scripture which he hath given to some great men who in convenient time shall be named. When these thinges shalbe called in question the witnes shalbe produced.

Richard Baines

3 The coroner's inquest of 1 June 1593

The inquest on Marlowe's death was slightly irregular, since the county coroner failed to attend the proceedings at Deptford. However, the authority of William Danby, the Royal Coroner, or Coroner of the Verge, is stressed here in the repeated phrase 'within the verge' (*infra virgam*), which signals that the homicide had occurred within twelve miles of the queen. The inquisition is in Latin, except for several phrases, *nere the bed* and *le recknynge*. Paragraphing and punctuation are added in this translation, from MS C260/174, no. 127, by permission of The National Archives (PRO).

Kent. Inquisition made in two copies at Detford Strand in the aforesaid county of Kent, within the verge, on the first day of June in the thirty-fifth year of the reign of Elizabeth, by the grace of God Queen of England, France & Ireland, defender of the faith, etc., in the presence of William Danby, gentleman, coroner of the household of our said lady the queen, in view of the body of Christopher Morley, there lying dead & slain, upon the oath of Nicholas Draper, gentleman, Wolstan Randall, gentleman, William Curry, Adrian Walker, John Barber, Robert Baldwin, Giles Feld, George Halfepenny, Henry Awger, James Batt, Henry Bendyn, Thomas Batt senior, John Baldwyn, Alexander Burrage, Edmund Goodcheape & Henry Dabyns.

These [jurors] say upon their oath that when one Ingram Frysar, late of London, gentleman, and the aforesaid Christopher Morley and one Nicholas Skeres, late of London, gentleman, and Robert Poley of London aforesaid, gentleman, on the thirtieth day of May in the thirty-fifth year above mentioned, at Detford Strand aforesaid in the aforesaid County of Kent, within the verge, around the tenth hour before noon of the same day, met together at the house of one Eleanor Bull, widow, and there passed the time together and ate lunch, and after lunch were in quiet sort together & walked in the garden of the said house until the sixth hour after noon of the same day, and then returned from the said garden to the room mentioned, and there and in company dined, it befell that after dinner the aforesaid Ingram and the said Christopher Morley were in speech & offered one to another divers malicious words, because they could not concur nor agree on the payment of the sum of pence, which is to say, *le recknynge*.

And the said Christopher then lying on a bed in the room where they dined, and moved by anger towards the aforesaid Ingram Frysar because of the aforesaid words that had passed between them, and the aforesaid Ingram then and there siting in the aforesaid room with his back towards the bed where the aforesaid Christopher Morley then lay, near the bed, that is sitting [at table] *nere the bed* and with the front part of his body towards the table, and the aforesaid Nicholas Skeres and Robert Poley sitting on either side of the same Ingram, so that the same Ingram Frysar could in no way flee, it happened that the aforesaid Christopher Morley suddenly and of malice aforethought towards the aforesaid Ingram, then and there maliciously unsheathed the dagger of the aforesaid Ingram, which was visible at his back, and with the same dagger then and there maliciously gave the aforesaid Ingram two wounds on his head of the length of two inches and in depth a quarter of an inch.

Whereupon the aforesaid Ingram, in fear of being killed and sitting on the aforesaid bench between the aforesaid Nicholas Skeres and Robert Poley, so that he was not able to withdraw in any way, in his own defence and to save his life then and there struggled with the aforesaid Christopher Marley to take back from him his aforesaid dagger, in which same affray the same Ingram could not withdraw further from the aforesaid Christopher Morley.

And so it occurred in that affray that the said Ingram, in defence of his life, and with the aforesaid dagger of the value of 12 pence, gave the aforesaid Christopher then and there a mortal wound above his right eye to the depth of two inches and in breadth one inch, of which same mortal wound the aforesaid Christopher Morley then and there instantly died. And thus the aforesaid jurors say upon their oath that the aforesaid Ingram killed the aforesaid Christopher Morley the same thirtieth day of May in the thirty-fifth year cited above, in the aforesaid Detford Strand in the aforesaid county of Kent within the verge, in the room aforesaid within the verge, in the manner and form aforesaid in defence and for the saving of his life, against the peace of the said lady the queen, her present crown and dignity.

And further the said jurors say upon their oath that the said Ingram, after the killing aforesaid perpetrated & done by him in the manner & form aforesaid, neither fled nor withdrew himself. But as for what goods or chattels, lands or tenements the said Ingram had at the time of the aforesaid slaying done & perpetrated by him in the manner and form shown, the said jurors are totally uninformed. In witness to which, the aforesaid Coroner, as well as the jurors aforesaid to this inquisition, have in turn set their seals.

Dated the day and year mentioned above, etc.

by William Danby
Coroner

4 Kyd's letter to Puckering concerning Marlowe, *circa* June 1593

Kyd was arrested for libel, but 'vile hereticall' papers turned up in his room. When released from prison, he sought Sir John Puckering's help in recovering favour with his patron Lord Strange, and tried to dissociate himself from any taint of Marlowe's 'atheism'. Kyd's letter and note (see item 5 below) are of major interest for what they say of his rooming arrangement with Marlowe. The Lord Keeper took a special interest in heresy. Undated, the letter has Kyd's artful signature. (Harleian MS 6848, fo. 154; by permission of the British Library.)

[Addressed] To the R[ight] honorable Sir John Puckering Knight Lord Keeper of the great seale of England.
[Annotated] Kidde

At my last being with your L[ordshi]p to entreate some speaches from you in my favor to my Lorde, whoe (though I think he rest not doubtfull of myne inocence) hath yet in his discreeter judgm[en]t feared to offende in his reteyning me, without your honors former pryvitie; So is it nowe R[ight] ho[nourable] that the denyall of that favor (to my thought resonable) hath mov'de me to conjecture some suspicion, that your L[ordshi]p holds me in, concerning *Atheisme*, a deadlie thing which I was undeserved chargd withall, & therfore have I thought it requisite, aswell in duetie to your L[ordshi]p, & the Lawes, as also in the feare of god, & freedom of my conscience, therein to satisfie the world and you:

The first and most (thoughe insufficient surmize) that ever as [MS defective] therein might be raisde of me, grewe thus. When I was first suspected for that Libell that concern'd the state, amongst those waste and idle papers (which I carde not for) & which unaskt I did deliver up, were founde some fragmentes of a disputation toching that opinion, affirmed by Marlowe to be his, and shufled with some of myne (unknown to me) by some occasion of our wrytinge in one chamber twoe yeares synce.

My first acquaintance with this Marlowe, rose upon his bearing name to serve my Lo[rd] although his L[ordshi]p never knewe his service, but in writing for his plaiers, for never cold my L[ord] endure his name, or sight, when he had heard of his conditions, nor would in deed the form of devyne praier used duelie in his l[ordship]s house have quadred with such reprobates.

That I should love or be familier frend, with one so irreligious, were verie rare. When *Tullie* saith *Digni sunt amicitia quibus in ipsis inest causa cur diligantur*

378

[Those whom there is reason to esteem are worthy of friendship] which neither was in him, for person, quallities, nor honestie, besides he was intemperate & of a cruel hart, the verie contraries to which, my greatest enemies will saie by me.

It is not to be nombred amongst the best conditions of men, to taxe or to opbraide the dead *Quia mortui non mordent* [because the dead do not bite]. But thus muche have I (with your L[ordshi]ps favor) dared in the greatest cause, which is to cleere my self of being thought an Atheist, which some will swear he was.

For more assurance that I was not of that vile opinion, Lett it but please your L[ordshi]p to enquire of such as he conversed withall, that is (as I am geven to understand) with *Harriot, Warner, Royden,* and some stationers in Paules church-yard, whom I in no sort can accuse nor will excuse by reson of his companie, of whose consent if I had been, no quetion but I also shold have been of their consort, for *ex minimo vestigio artifex agnoscit artificem* [an artist recognizes an artist by the slightest trace].

Of my religion and life I have alreadie geven some instance to the late comis-sioners & of my reverend meaning to the state, although perhaps my paines and undeserved tortures felt by some, wold have ingendred more impatience when lesse by farre hath dryven so manye *imo extra caulas* [nay, outside the sheepfold] which it shall never do with me.

But whatsoever I have felt R[ight] ho[nourable] this is my request not for reward but in regard of my trewe inocence that it wold please your l[ordshi]ps so to [use] the same & me, as I maie still reteyne the favors of my Lord, whom I have servd almost theis vi yeres nowe, in credit untill nowe, & nowe am utterlie undon without herein be somewhat donn for my recoverie. For I do know his L[ordshi]p holdes your honors & the state in that dewe reverence, as he wold no waie move the leste suspicion of his loves and cares both towards hir sacred Majestic your L[ordshi]ps and the lawes whereof when tyme shall serve I shall geve greater instance which I have observd.

As for the libel laide unto my chardg I am resolved with receyving of the sacrament to satisfie your l[ordshi]ps & the world that I was neither agent nor consenting therunto. Howbeit if some outcast *Ismael* for want or of his own dispose to lewdnes, have with pretext of duetie or religion, or to reduce himself to that he was not borne unto by enie waie incensd your l[ordshi]ps to suspect me, I shall besech in all humillitie & in the feare of god that it will please your l[ordshi]ps but to censure me as I shall prove my self, and to repute them as they ar in deed. *Cum totius iniustitia nulla capitalior sit quam eorum, qui tum cum maxime fallunt id agunt ut viri boni esse videantur.* [There is no more capital injustice than that of those men who strive to seem good at the time they are being particularly deceitful.] For doubtles even then your l[ordshi]ps shalbe sure to breake [?open] their lewde designes and see into the truthe, when but their lyves that herein have accused me shalbe examined & rypped up effectually, soe maie I chaunce with Paul to live & shake the vyper *off* my hand into the fier for which the ignorant suspect me guiltie of the former shipwrack. And thus (for nowe I feare me I growe teadious) assuring your good L[ordshi]p that if I knewe eny whom I cold justlie accuse of that damnable offence to the awefull majestie of god or of that other mutinous sedition towrd the state I wold as willinglie reveale them as I wold request your L[ordshi]ps better thoughtes of me that never have offended you.

Yor L[ordshi]ps most humble in all duties
Th Kydde

5 Kyd's unsigned note to Puckering, *circa* June 1593

Evidently Puckering wanted to hear more about Marlowe's associates and views. In his note, Kyd is careful not to finger anyone but Roydon (the courier and poet, mentioned in Kyd's letter). Memory may be conveniently failing him, but he recalls a few of Marlowe's 'monstruous opinions' and refers interestingly to Scotland. The numbers in the margins, not exactly aligned with the religious comments, may have been added by a later hand (BL Harleian MS 6849, fo. 218, by permission of the British Library).

> Pleaseth it your honorable L[ordshi]p touching Marlowes monstruous opinions as I cannot but with an agreved conscience think on him or them so can I but particulariz fewe in the respect of them that kept him greater company, howbeit in discharg of dutie both towrdes god your L[ordship]s & the world thus much have I thought good brieflie to discover in all humblenes.
>
> First it was his custom when I knew him first & as I heare say he contynewd it in table talk or otherwise to jest at the devine scriptures gybe at praiers, & stryve in argument to frustrate & confute what hath byn spoke or wrytt by prophets & such holie men/
>
> 1 He wold report St John to be our Savior Christes *Alexis* I cover it with reverence and trembling that is that Christ did love him with an extraordinary love/
>
> 2 That for me to wryte a poem of St *Paules* conversion as I was determined he said wold be as if I shold go wryte a book of fast & loose, esteming *Paul* a Jugler.
>
> 3 That the prodigall childes portion was but fower nobles, he held his purse so neere the bottom in all pictures and that it either was a jest or els fower nobles then was thought a great patrimony not thinking it a parable.
>
> 4 That things esteemed to be donn by devine power might aswell been don by observation of men all which he wold so sodenlie take slight occasion to slyp out as I & many others in regard of his other rashnes in attempting soden pryvie injuries to men did overslypp though often reprehend him for it & for which god is my witnes aswell by my lords comaundment as in hatred of his life & thoughts I left & did refraine his companie/
>
> He wold perswade with men of quallitie to goe unto the K[ing] of *Scotts* whether I heare *Royden* is gone and where if he had livd he told me when I sawe him last he meant to be.

Notes

Unless otherwise stated, a book's place of publication is London. I have used short titles for Marlowe's works, and occasionally his initials, 'CM'.

Citations from Marlowe are normally to the texts and line numbers in *The Complete Works*, 5 vols. (Oxford, 1987–2000): vol. i, ed. Roma Gill, *All Ovids Elegies, Lucans First Booke, Dido Queene of Carthage, Hero and Leander* (1987; we cite the corrected reprint of 1997); this volume also includes 'The Passionate Shepherd' and Marlowe's Latin works; vol. ii, ed. Roma Gill, *Dr Faustus* (1990; repr. 2000); vol. iii, ed. Richard Rowland, *Edward II* (1994); vol. iv, ed. Roma Gill, *The Jew of Malta* (1995; repr. 2000); vol. v, *Tamburlaine the Great*, Parts 1 and 2, ed. David Fuller; *The Massacre at Paris with the Death of the Duke of Guise*, ed. Edward J. Esche (1998). The spelling in poems and plays has been modernized. References to *Faustus* give both the scene divisions from Gill's edition and, in square brackets, act and scene divisions from the Revels edition: *Doctor Faustus A- and B-Texts (1604, 1616)*, ed. David Bevington and Eric Rasmussen (Manchester, 1993; repr. 1995).

The following abbreviations have also been used in the notes:

Bakeless	John Bakeless, *The Tragicall History of Christopher Marlowe*, 2 vols. (Cambridge, Mass., 1942)
Boas	F. S. Boas, *Christopher Marlowe: A Biographical and Critical Study* (Oxford, 1940)
Concordance	Louis Ule, *A Concordance to the Works of Christopher Marlowe* (Hildesheim, 1979)
MS BL	Manuscripts at the British Library, London
MS Bodleian	Manuscripts at the Bodleian Library, Oxford
MS Cant. Cath.	Manuscripts in the Canterbury Cathedral Archives
MS Corpus Christi	Manuscripts in the Parker Library, at Corpus Christi College, Cambridge
MS Folger	Manuscripts in the Folger Shakespeare Library, Washington, DC
MS Kent	Manuscripts in the Centre for Kentish Studies, Maidstone
Nicholl	Charles Nicholl, *The Reckoning: The Murder of Christopher Marlowe*, 2nd edn. (2002)

REED   *Records of Early English Drama: Cambridge*, ed. Alan H. Nelson, 2 vols. (Toronto, Buffalo, and London, 1989)

Thomas and Tydeman   *Christopher Marlowe: The Plays and their Sources*, ed. Vivien Thomas and Walter Tydeman (London and New York, 1994)

TNA(PRO)   Manuscripts in the National Archives (formerly the Public Record Office), London

Urry   William Urry, *Christopher Marlowe and Canterbury*, ed. with an introduction by Andrew Butcher (1988)

1 Birth

1. For Canterbury before the poet's birth and in his early years, I have drawn upon MS Chamberlains' accounts and MS court records in the Canterbury Cathedral Archives, and churchwardens' reports and other material in *Archæologia Cantiana*. The study by Urry was a welcome guide, and the following were especially helpful: P. Collinson, N. Ramsay, and M. Sparks (eds.), *A History of Canterbury Cathedral* (Oxford, 1995); Frank Barlow, *Thomas Becket* (1986); John Brent, *Canterbury in the Olden Time* (1879); William Somner, *The Antiquities of Canterbury*, introd. William Urry (East Ardsley, Wakefield, W. Yorks., 1977); and Peter Clark, *English Provincial Society from the Reformation to the Revolution: Religion, Politics and Society in Kent 1500–1640* (Hassocks, Sussex, 1977).

2. *Jew of Malta*, I. i. 6.

3. Barrie Dobson, 'The Monks of Canterbury in the Later Middle Ages, 1220–1540', in Collinson *et al.* (eds.), *A History*, 142, 144.

4. See J. F. Davis, 'Lollards, Reformers and St. Thomas of Canterbury', *University of Birmingham Historical Journal*, 9 (1963), 1–15. The smith was William Ayleward.

5. *Archæologia Cantiana: Testamenta Cantiana* (1907), p. 122.

6. MSS Cant. Cath. BAC B/C/S/II/2 and BAC J/B/353.

7. Urry, 14.

8. The Chamberlains' accounts (in MS Cant. Cath. BAC FA/19, fos. 184–5) mention about a dozen 'little gardens' evidently within the city's walls: e.g. 'one other little garden in the hands of John Edwards' or 'in the hands of Alexander Thorneley'. For descriptions of the goblins and other building ornaments, see Brent, *Canterbury in the Olden Time*, 188–9.

9. *Victoria History of the County of Kent*, ed. William Page, 3 vols. (1926), ii. 83.

10. No. 27 of the Thirty-Nine Articles (1563), on baptism as a 'sign of Regeneration' in which one is 'grafted into the Church'. See also David Cressy, *Birth*,

Marriage, and Death: Ritual, Religion, and the Life-Cycle in Tudor and Stuart England (Oxford, 1997), 109; and Brent, *Canterbury in the Olden Time*, 252.

2 Petty school and the parish

1. MS Kent, PRC 16/36. Boas, i, lists thirteen variants of 'Marlowe', and Cambridge citations of the poet's surname give four more.
2. MS Cant. Cath., accounts, 1558–68; Bakeless, i. 21.
3. William Urry, *Saint George's Church Canterbury*, Canterbury Local History Pamphlet no. 3 (n.d.).
4. MS Cant. Cath., PRC 39/5, fos. 55 ff. Involved in the defamation case of *Hurte v. Applegate* was a deposition concerning Laurence Applegate given by 'Johannes Marley . . . shomaker' on 19 Feb. 1565. (Bakeless, i. 24–5, offers a useful transcript; later biographies summarize.) The cobbler's walk to Barham had occurred early in 1564.
5. John Marlowe's words were so reported on 12 Oct. 1570. MS Cant Cath., BAC, J/B/370, iv, fo. 4.
6. See Bakeless, i. 5–11, Urry, 12–19, and Michael Frohnsdorff, *Christopher Marlowe: The Local Connection and New Research*, Faversham Society (Faversham, Kent, 2003), pp. i–xii.
7. In 1605 (a year of three Marlowe family documents), no cash on hand is indicated in the cobbler's will of 23 January, or in the inventory of 21 February. But in her will of 17 March, Katherine Marlowe leaves the sum of £5 (which she appears to have saved), or 40s. to her son-in-law John Moore, and 40s. and 20s. respectively to her daughters Margaret and Dorothy.
8. MS Kent, PRC 3/26, fo. 105.
9. MSS Cant. Cath., DAC X.4.4, BAC J/Q/425, 426. Urry, 34.
10. MS Kent, PRC 16/127.
11. Accounts of the churchwardens of St Dunstan's and St Andrew's parishes, edited, respectively, by J. M. Cooper and Charles Cotton, in *Archæologia Cantiana*, 17 (1887), 119, and 35 (1921), 68.
12. Accounts, ed. Cooper, *Archæologia Cantiana*, 17 (1887), 121, for 1566 Malta's siege occasioned prayer-books 'against the Turk' in some urban churches, as did a concern for English trade in the Mediterranean.
13. Francis Clement, *The Petie Schole* (1587), 4.
14. In the *Concordance*, see the following lines: *First Book of Lucan*, 243; *1 Tamb.*, 692; *Faustus* (1604), 956, (1616), 714–15; and *Jew of Malta*, 1747–8.
15. On these events and English reactions, I have found of particular interest G. K. Hunter's 'Elizabethans and Foreigners', in *Dramatic Identities and Cultural Tradition* (Liverpool, 1978), 1–30; Jonathan Israel's *The Dutch Republic* (Oxford, 1995), and N. M. Sutherland's *The Massacre of St Bartholomew and the European Conflict 1559–1572* (1973).
16. N. W. Bawcutt, 'Marlowe's "Jew of Malta" and Foxes's "Acts and Monuments" ', *Notes and Queries*, 213 (1968), 250. Despite its large size and costliness,

Foxe's 'Book of Martyrs' was kept in some parish churches; two copies were set up, in the choir and north aisle, of Canterbury Cathedral.

17. *Certain Sermons or Homelies* (1547) and *A Homily against Disobedience and Wilful Rebellion* (1570), ed. R. B. Bond (Toronto, 1987), 180.

18. Ibid. 210, 214.

19. Lisa Hopkins, 'Fissured Families: A Motif in Marlowe's Plays', *Papers on Language and Literature*, 33 (1997), 198–212, esp. 209.

20. F. B. Tromly, *Playing with Desire: Christopher Marlowe and the Art of Tantalization* (Toronto, 1998), 38–9. In *All Ovids Elegies*, II. xix. 36, CM translated Ovid's line, 'quod sequitur, fugio; quod fugit, ipse sequor' (from *Amores*), as 'What flies I follow, what follows me I shun'. For the version given to the Duke of Guise: *Massacre at Paris*, sc. ii, 42.

21. See S. M. Deats, *Sex, Gender, and Desire in the Plays of Christopher Marlowe* (1997), 101, 117–18.

3 The King's School

1. William Urry, *Chief Citizens of Canterbury* (Canterbury, 1979), 54; Somner, *The Antiquities of Canterbury*, 183.

2. W. D. Rubenstein's *A History of the Jews in the English Speaking World: Great Britain* (Basingstoke, 1966), and Cecil Roth's *A History of the Jews in England*, 3rd edn. (Oxford, 1964) are standard histories. Data about Canterbury's medieval Jewish quarter is not plentiful, but for a beginning, with names and dwellings, see Audrey Bateman, *One Small Part of Canterbury* (Canterbury: St Mildred's and St Margaret's Conservation Society, n.d.), and Daniel Cohn-Sherbok, *The Jews of Canterbury, 1760–1931* (Canterbury: Yorick, 1984); see also S. Williamson, in *Bygone Kent*, 4 (1983), 174–6, and M. E. Simkins, in *Victoria History*, ed. Page, ii. 47–8. On the problems in recovering data, see Patricia Skinner (ed.), *The Jews in Medieval Britain* (Woodbridge, 2003), and the remarks in *English Historical Review*, 119 (2004), 495–6.

3. *Victoria History*, ed. Page, ii. 48.

4. *The Antiquities of Canterbury*, 66. Somner's comments first appeared in about 1640.

5. Urry, *Chief Citizens*, p. viii.

6. *Matthew Parker . . . Letters*, ed. John Bruce and T. T. Perowne (Cambridge, 1853), 475.

7. *1 Tamb.*, II. v. 53–4.

8. Matthew Parker to Lord Burghley, 19 May 1572.

9. Patrick Collinson, *The Elizabethan Puritan Movement* (1967), 175; Peter Clark, 'The Prophesying Movement in Kentish Towns during the 1570s', *Archæologia Cantiana*, 93 (1978), 81–90.

10. C. L. Barber, *Creating Elizabethan Tragedy* (1988), 82–3.

11. 'Churchwardens' Accounts of the Parish of St Andrew', *Archæologia Cantiana*, 35 (1921), 72.

12. Ethel Seaton, 'Marlowe's Light Reading', in Herbert Davis and Helen Gardner (eds.), *Elizabethan Studies Presented to Frank Percy Wilson* (Oxford, 1959), 17–35, esp. 23.

13. *1 Tamb.*, II. iii. 22–4.

14. *Dido*, III. i. 116–25.

15. A. F. Leach, *Educational Charters and Documents 598 to 1909* (Cambridge, 1911), 456–7.

16. On the King's School, see Urry, 42–54, 108–22, as well as D. L. Edwards, *A History of the King's School Canterbury* (1957), 13–90, and Bakeless, i. 31–6. Though worth consulting, C. E. Woodruff and H. J. Cape's *Schola Regia Cantuariensis: A History of Canterbury School commonly called the King's School* (1908) is at times plainly inaccurate.

17. See Judith Weil, *Christopher Marlowe: Merlin's Prophet* (Cambridge, 1977), 20, 29.

18. Ibid. 44.

19. Eric Jacobsen, *Translation, a Traditional Craft. An Introductory Sketch with a Study of Marlowe's Elegies* (Copenhagen, 1958), 116–17.

20. MS Kent, PRC 21/4.

21. Loeb edn. Lucian's early modern reception is treated well in Duncan Douglas, *Ben Jonson and the Lucianic Tradition* (Cambridge, 1979), esp. 30–115.

22. *Faustus* (1604), sc. xii, 81–2 [V. i. 91–2].

23. Rosemond Tuve, *Elizabethan and Metaphysical Imagery* (Chicago, 1947), esp. 27–105. This classic study bears partly on Elizabethan criteria for poetry, and the teaching of rhetoric, logic, and composition. Tuve's studies of allegorical imagery are related; see Margaret C. Evans's interesting *Rosemond Tuve: A Life of the Mind* (Portsmouth, NH, 2004).

24. *All Ovids Elegies*, II. xv. 1–6.

25. Urry, 43–5; Leach, *Educational Charters*, 468.

26. G. K. Hunter, *John Lyly* (Cambridge, Mass., 1962), 37–47; Mark Eccles, 'Brief Lives', *Studies in Philology*, 79 (1982), 86–8; Urry, 46–7; J. R. Henderson, 'Euphues and his Erasmus', *English Literary Renaissance*, 12 (1982), 135–61.

27. Urry, 51, 99, 102–7.

28. Anthony Gash illuminates the Erasman synthesis and 'holy fools', in 'Shakespeare, Carnival, and the Sacred', in Ronald Knowles (ed.), *Shakespeare and Carnival After Bakhtin* (1998), 177–210. For CM's use of the Geneva and Bishops' bibles, see e.g. *Faustus*, sc. v, 57–8, as well as J. H. Sims, *Dramatic Uses of Biblical Allusions in Marlowe and Shakespeare* (Gainesville, Fla., 1966), 1–28; R. M. Cornelius, *Christopher Marlowe's Use of the Bible* (New York, 1984); and Naheeb Shaheen, in *Notes and Queries*, NS 47 (2000), 94–7.

29. *A Catechisme, or first Instruction and Learning of Christian Religion*, trans. T. Norton (1571), sig. C4ʳ.

30. G. K. Hunter, 'The Beginnings of Elizabethan Drama: Revolution and Continuity', *Renaissance Drama*, NS 17 (1986), 29–51.

31. [Matthew Parker], *The whole Psalter translated into English Metre* [*c.* 1567], STC 2729. Cf. Roland Greene on the Psalter, in *Studies in English Literature*, 30 (1990), 19–40.

32. *Kent: Diocese of Canterbury*, ed. J. M. Gibson (2000), i. 191; iii. 1287–8.

33. *King Johan*, ed. B. B. Adams (San Marino, Calif., 1969), 1, 803–4.

34. *Jew of Malta*, II. iii. 209, III. iv. 81, V. i. 90–1 and iii. 36–7.

35. *Timon*, ed. J. C. Bulman, J. M. Nosworthy, and G. R. Proudfoot (Oxford, 1980), ll. 771–4.

36. Ibid., ll. 1656–69.

37. Dyce MS 52 ('Timon MS'), at the Victoria and Albert Museum, copied out in haste by two hands, has been dated variously between 1580 and 1611; but portions of the play appear to have been composed at different times. In summary, the pro-Marlowe case might be this. Some scenes may allude to 'showy', Kent-related events of 1580. A few of CM's favoured rare words, place-names, phrases, dramatic devices, and jokes (such as that of an 80-year-old lover, as in *Dido*) are reflected. But several explanations are possible, and whether a school play, of *c.* 1580, here leaves its traces in a much later revision, by another author, is very questionable. See esp. James C. Bulman Jr., 'The Date and Production of "Timon" Reconsidered', *Shakespeare Survey*, 27 (1974), 111–27, and John C. Baker, 'Towards a New Date and Suggested Authorship Attribution for the Timon, MS', *Notes and Queries*, NS 45 (1998), 300–2.

4 Corpus Christi College, Cambridge

1. See esp. John Lamb, *Masters' History of the College of Corpus Christi and the Blessed Virgin Mary*, 2 vols. (1831), and D. R. Leader, *A History of the University of Cambridge . . . to 1546* (Cambridge, 1988). Older guidebooks help with the Tudor college's layout, as does R. Willis, *The Architectural History of the University of Cambridge*, ed. J. W. Clark, 4 vols. (Cambridge, 1886).

2. *REED*, ii. 747–78.

3. Archbishop Parker's will (5 Apr. 1575) mentions the room which his scholars, elected from the schools at 'Cantuar.', 'Aylesham', and 'Wymondham', were to have in the court: 'in eo collegio [Corporis Christi], jam vocatum *a Storehouse*'. A copy of the will is at the college; his chained books were for the use of his Norwich scholars, but CM may have had access to them. Cf. G. C. Moore Smith, 'Marlowe at Cambridge', *Modern Language Review*, 4 (1909), 167–77.

4. Harvey, *Works*, ed. A. B. Grosart, 3 vols. (1884), i. 137–8 (italics have been added to book titles in this excerpt).

5. E. R. Sandeen, 'The Building of the 16th-Century Corpus Christi College Chapel', *Proceedings of the Cambridge Antiquarian Society*, 55 (1962), 23–35.

6. C. H. Cooper, *Annals of Cambridge*, 2 vols. (Cambridge, 1843), ii. 410–15.

7. *The Repentance of Robert Greene* (1592), sig. C1.

8. MS Corpus Christi, 'Buttery Book 1579–1581', fos. 67^r, 68^r.

9. *REED*, ii. 714–22; A. H. Nelson, *Early Cambridge Theatres* (Cambridge, 1994), 71, 86–7, 102–17.

10. MS Corpus Christi, 'Statuta', fos. 56–7.

11. Oxford *DNB*.

12. W. M. Palmer, 'John Hatcher, M.D.', *Proceedings of the Cambridge Antiquarian Society*, 9 (1910–11), 238–45.

13. There is no need to imagine that CM received aid from 'outside' sources before he took the BA in 1584; before then, his known expenditures did not appreciably exceed his grant. Entries bearing on the Pashley trouble were first printed by Moore Smith in 'Marlowe at Cambridge', 170–1. Cf. Bakeless, i. 68.

14. Moore Smith, 'Marlowe at Cambridge', 168.

15. MSS Corpus Christi, Buttery Books. John Bakeless locates and transcribes the relevant entries, in *Christopher Marlowe* (New York, 1937), app. A.

16. MS Corpus Christi, '1579–1581'.

17. Urry, 59–60, 81.

18. Bakeless, i. 72–5.

19. See R. F. Hardin, 'Marlowe and the Fruits of Scholarism', *Philological Quarterly*, 63 (1984), 387–8 (italics for titles added). Especially useful, too, are Lisa Jardine's 'Humanism and the Sixteenth Century Cambridge Arts Course' and C. Webster's 'Review', in *History of Education*, 4 (1975), 16–31, 51–68.

20. MS BL Lansdowne 43, fo. 85.

21. The syllogism is from a late Elizabethan dispute in Latin: see W. T. Costello, *The Scholastic Curriculum at Early 17th Century Cambridge* (Cambridge, Mass., 1958), 19–21.

22. Christopher Haigh, 'The Taming of the Reformation', *History*, 85 (2000), 572–88.

23. MS Corpus Christi, 'Supplicats', 1583–4, no. 199.

24. *All Ovids Elegies*, I. ii. 1–2, 8.

25. Ibid. III. vi. 67–70, 73–8.

26. Ibid. I. v. 20–6.

27. Ibid. I. iv. 33–4.

28. Ibid. III. ii. 3, 9–14.

29. Ibid. II. i. 25, I. viii. 56.

30. R. J. Dingley on 'Dominicus Niger', *Notes and Queries*, NS 27 (1980), 315–18. Also pertinent are M. L. Stapleton, *Harmful Eloquence: Ovid's Amores from Antiquity to Shakespeare* (Ann Arbor, Mich., 1966), Jacobsen, *Translation, a Traditional Craft*, and I. F. Moulton, ' "Printed Abroad" ', in P. W. White (ed.), *Marlowe, History, and Sexuality* (New York, 1998).

31. Nelson, *Early Cambridge Theatres*, 66. Sandra Billington, 'Sixteenth-Century Drama in St John's College, Cambridge', *Review of English Studies*, 29 (1978), 1–10.

32. *Sermons of M. John Calvin upon the Fifth Booke of Moses Called Deuteronomie*, trans. Arthur Golding (1585), 773–4.

33. Watson, *Complete Works*, ed. and trans. Dana F. Sutton, 2 vols. (Lampeter, Wales, 1997), ii. 191 n.
34. Hunter, *John Lyly*, 71.
35. *Dido*, I. i. 28–35.
36. Ibid. I. i. 56–61.
37. Ibid. II. i. 195–6, 247–8.
38. Ibid. IV. v. 22–34.
39. Ibid. V. i. 27–9.
40. Ibid. IV. iv. 48–51, 94–5.
41. See the analysis of Shakespeare's uses of Marlowe's work (and of the latter's precedents in emotional intensity) in Brian Gibbons, *Shakespeare and Multiplicity* (Cambridge, 1993), 182–202.
42. *Dido*, IV. iv. 99–102.

5 Into espionage

1. MS Kent, PRC 16/36. Boas and Urry mistake the date; the will was signed on 19 Aug. 1585, as C. B. Kuriyama established in *Marlowe* (2002), 194.
2. G. Dyer, *The Privileges of the University of Cambridge*, 2 vols. (1824), i. 189–92. Peter Roberts, 'The "Studious Artizan" ', in D. Grantley and P. Roberts (eds.), *Christopher Marlowe and English Renaissance Culture* (Aldershot, 1996), 25.
3. *1 Tamb.* I. i. 75 and ii. 36, 95–8.
4. Ibid. I. ii. 139–40, II. i. 7–30.
5. In legend, the portrait was first seen in 1953 in the Master's Lodge; in fact, enquiries about it began in November 1952, after it turned up at a south-eastern corner room of Corpus's Old Court.
6. B. D. [Bruce Dickins], 'The Emergence of a College Portrait', *Letter of the Corpus Association*, 45 (Michaelmas 1966), 24.
7. MS Corpus Christi, 26 May 2000.
8. Ibid.
9. B.D., 'Emergence of a College Portrait', 24.
10. MS Corpus Christi, Hall to Cannell, 26 May 2000.
11. MSS Corpus Christi, Adams to Bury, 17 Nov. 1952; Boas to Bury, 27 Nov. 1952; Bakeless to Bury, 27 Dec. 1952.
12. MS Corpus Christi, Freeman to Bury, 9 Dec. 1952.
13. MS Corpus Christi, Holder to Bury, 24 Aug. 1953.
14. *Cambridge Review*, 4 Mar. 1967; *Letter of the Corpus Association*, 46 (1967), 30–3.
15. Roy Strong, *The English Renaissance Miniature* (1984), 10.
16. *Autobiography of Thomas Whythorne*, ed. J. M. Osborn (Oxford, 1961), app. V.
17. L. C. Knights, *Further Explorations* (1965), 86.
18. Marlowe, *Complete Works*, i. 220: 'Insons luctifica sparsis cervice capillis | Plange'.
19. T. Birch, *Memoirs of the Reign of Queen Elizabeth*, 2 vols. (1754), i. 26, 39.

20. W. S. Hudson, *The Cambridge Connection* (Durham, NC, 1980), 81.

21. John Bossy, *Under the Molehill: An Elizabethan Spy Story* (2001), 152.

22. Ian Arthurson, 'Espionage and Intelligence from the Wars of the Roses to the Reformation', *Nottingham Medieval Studies*, 35 (1991), 134–54. A small library of sources now pertains to Elizabethan espionage; see esp. Bossy, *Under the Molehill*; Nicholl *The Reckoning*; Alan Haynes, *The Elizabethan Secret Services* (Reading, UK, 2000); and Roy Kendall, *Christopher Marlowe and Richard Baines* (1993) and 'Richard Baines and Christopher Marlowe's Milieu', *English Language Review*, 24 (1994), 507–52. Much is to be found in the State Papers. Especially useful on the changes after April 1590, which indirectly affected CM, is P. E. J. Hammer, *The Polarisation of Elizabethan Politics: The Political Career of Robert Devereux, 2nd Earl of Essex, 1585–1597* (Cambridge, 1999).

23. Nicholl, 132–3.

24. Conyers Read, *Mr Secretary Walsingham and the Policy of Queen Elizabeth*, 3 vols. (Oxford, 1925), i. 24 5. Alan Haynes explores this career in *Walsingham: Elizabethan Spymaster and Statesman* (Stroud, 2004).

25. Scott McMillin and Sally-Beth MacLean, *The Queen's Men and their Plays* (Cambridge, 1998), 24–32.

26. P. Neville-Singleton on Hakluyt, in C. C. Brown and A. F. Marotti (eds.), *Texts and Cultural Change in Early Modern England* (1997), 66–79.

27. Nicholl, 139.

28. Ethel Seaton, 'Marlowe, Robert Poley, and the Tippings', *Review of English Studies*, 5 (1929), 280–1.

29. Prefatory verses, *Sophoclis Antigone* (1581), ll. 27–32.

30. See Watson, *Complete Works*, ed. Sutton, and A. Chatterley, 'Thomas Watson's Works, Contemporary References and Reprints', *Notes and Queries*, 246 (2001), 239–49. On the late Tudor manuscript culture see H. R. Woudhuysen, *Sir Philip Sidney and the Circulation of Manuscripts* (Oxford, 1996).

31. By means of spies, informers, or part-time observers (not co-ordinated dragnets) the names of Catholics were collected whether or not they were suspected of being agents. Before the anonymous informer at Paris reported on Thomas Watson on 27 Apr. 1580 (*Calendar of State Papers, Foreign Series, 1579–80*, 250), the spy Davie Jones in October 1578 had listed a 'Papist' named Watson, living at London's 'Great St Helen's', but the latter may not be Watson the poet. Thomas Watson had been at the Jesuit English College at Douay before Walsingham used him, and the profile of the 'double agent', reporting to a Jesuit such as Father Parsons and serving as a courier, is not unusual; but there is no hard evidence that CM's friend was a spy.

32. See *Works*, ed. Sutton (1997), i. vii–xi.

33. *Hecatompathia* (1582), no. IV.

34. MS BL Add. 48029, fos. 121–30, has a transcript of Charles Sledd's diary. Martin Haile, *An Elizabethan Cardinal, William Allen* (1914), esp. 145.

35. M. L. Carrafiello, 'English Catholicism and the Jesuit Mission of 1580–1581', *Historical Journal*, 37 (1994), 761–74, esp. 765.

36. *The First and Second Diaries of the English College, Douay*, introd. T. F. Knox (1878), 124, 127; Mark Eccles, *Christopher Marlowe in London* (Cambridge, Mass., 1934), 140–4.

37. *Works*, ed. Sutton (1997), i. xvii–xviii; Nicholl, 220–2.

38. *An Eclogue upon the death of the Right Honourable Sir Francis Walsingham* (1590), ll. 117–20.

39. *Meliboeus sive Ecloga Inobitum*, ll. 132–4, trans. in *Works*, ed. Sutton, ii. 117.

40. *Jew of Malta*, III. i. 5–9.

41. Nicholl, 216.

42. Urry, 113, 117.

43. Frances A. Yates, *Giordano Bruno and the Hermetic Tradition* (Chicago, 1964), 235–56, esp. 251.

44. Ibid. 211.

45. MS Corpus Christi, Grace Book, fo. 152^r.

46. *Jew of Malta*, III. iv. 113–15. Baines is not to be confused with a 'Wanes' noted 'At Paris', in the spy Sledd's diary, in April 1580; see *Miscellanea: Recusant Records*, ed. Clare Talbot, Catholic Record Society, vol. 53 (1961), 202–3.

47. Kendall, 'Richard Baines and Christopher Marlowe's Milieu'; Nicholl, 149.

48. *Calendar of State Papers, Scotland (1585–1586)*, viii. 595, 601.

49. Babington's note became famous in its time: at least three copies exist (MS BL Lansdowne 49; MS BL Add. 33938; MS Bodleian, Rawlinson D264).

50. On hearsay and CM's *Massacre*, see Thomas and Tydeman, 252; on the shortage of couriers or messengers in 1585–6 see R. C. Bald, *Donne and the Drurys* (Cambridge, 1959), 74–8.

51. Eccles, 'Brief Lives', 73–7; Thomas and Tydeman, 79–80. *Faustus*, sc. i, 92–7 [I. i. 94–9].

52. See Bossy, *Under the Molehill*, 16–28.

53. Bald, *Donne and the Drurys*, 72.

54. *Massacre at Paris*, sc. ii, 80–5.

55. *La Vicissitude ou Variété des Choses en l'Univers* (Paris, 1575; repr. 1576, 1577), sig. Aiij.

56. J. S. Nolan, *Sir John Norreys and the Elizabethan Military World* (Exeter, 1997), 92–3.

57. *Massacre at Paris*, sc. xxi, 100–2.

58. A. K. Gray, on 'Rheims and Cambridge', *PMLA* 43 (1928), 687–90; Urry, 49. Some who went to Rheims from Cambridge were undergraduates whose fates elude the *Alumni Cantabrigienses*.

59. Lamb, *Masters' History of the College of Corpus Christi*, i. 129–39.

60. *Acts of the Privy Council*, VI, 29 June 1587.

6 The Tamburlaine phenomenon

1. John Stow, *A Survey of London*, ed. C. L. Kingsford, 2 vols. (Oxford, 1971), ii. 367–9 nn. P. Honan, *Shakespeare: A Life* (Oxford, 1998), 102.

2. MSS Folger Z.c.39(7) and Z.c.(144, 150) suggest that views of time were expansive and not always strict, but many shows began at 2 or 3 p.m. For the shored-up Theatre or Theater see J. P. Lusardi, 'The Pictured Playhouse', *Shakespeare Quarterly*, 44 (1993), 202–27. On 'void' seats or pews, the letter of 25 Jan. 1587 to Walsingham, transcribed in E. K. Chambers, *Elizabethan Stage*, 4 vols. (Oxford, 1923), iv. 303–4.

3. On overseas trading consortia in relation to Marlowe, see Jonathan Burton, 'Anglo-Ottoman Relations', *Journal of Medieval and Early Modern Studies*, 30 (2000), 125–56; Nabil Matar, *Turks, Moors, and Englishmen in the Age of Discovery* (New York, 1999); and Emily C. Bartels's arguments with their critical implications for CM's works, in *Spectacles of Strangeness: Imperialism, Alienation, and Marlowe* (Philadelphia, 1993).

4. Edwin Nungezer, *A Dictionary of Actors* (New York, 1968), 4–11; see also W. A. Armstrong, 'Shakespeare and the Acting of Edward Alleyn', *Shakespeare Survey*, 7 (1954), 82–9, and A. J. Gurr, 'Who Strutted and Bellowed?', *Shakespeare Survey*, 16 (1963), 95–102.

5. C. P. Cerasano, 'Tamburlaine and Edward Alleyn's Ring', *Shakespeare Survey*, 47 (1994), 171–9; useful modern accounts of Timur (1336–1405) include Hilda Hookham, *Tamburlaine the Conqueror* (1962), and Justin Marozzi, *Tamerlane: Sword of Islam, Conqueror of the World* (2004).

6. Thomas and Tydeman, 69–168.

7. See Ruth Lunney, *Marlowe and the Popular Tradition* (Manchester, 2002), 3–7.

8. *1 Tamb.*, I. i. 23–4, 97–8.

9. Ibid. II. iv. 1–6.

10. M. C. Bradbrook, *The School of Night* (New York, 1965), 133; Brian Gibbons, 'Romance and the Heroic Play', in A. R. Braunmuller and M. Hattaway (eds.), *Cambridge Companion to English Renaissance Drama* (Cambridge, 1990), 207–36.

11. *1 Tamb.*, I. ii. 167–77.

12. T. Norton and T. Sackville, *Gorboduc*, ed. W. Tydeman (1992), ll. 764–5 and 1648. *1 Tamb.*, II. vii. 18–29.

13. *2 Tamb.*, I. iii. 194–7. Ethel Seaton, 'Marlowe's Map', *Essays and Studies*, 10 (1924), 13–35.

14. Burton, 'Anglo-Ottoman Relations'; Halil Inalcik, *From Empire to Republic* (Istanbul, 1995), esp. 117.

15. *1 Tamb.*, III. i. 48–55.

16. Ibid. V. i. 108–18.

17. Richard Levin, 'The Contemporary Perception of Marlowe's Tamburlaine', in J. L. Barroll and P. Werstine (eds.), *Medieval and Renaissance Drama* (New York, 1984), 51–70.

18. Vladimir Propp, *Theory and History of Folklore*, trans. A. Y. and R. P. Martin (Manchester, 1984), 133–4.

19. R. W. Battenhouse, 'Protestant Apologetics and the Subplot of *2 Tamburlaine*', *English Literary Renaissance*, 3 (1973), 30–43. Andrew Gurr, 'The Great Divide of 1594' in *Words That Count*, ed. B. Boyd (Newark, Del., 2004), 24–50.

20. *2 Tamb.*, Prologue, 1–4.

21. Ibid. I. i. 62.

22. Ibid. II. ii. 36–8.

23. Ibid. I. i. 36; iii. 101, and V. i. 170–1 ('Techelles, drown them all, man, woman, and child, | Leave not a Babylonian in the town').

24. Ibid. I. iii. 85–7.

25. Ibid. II. ii. 47–54.

26. P. H. Kocher, *Christopher Marlowe* (Chapel Hill, NC, 1946), 100; John Proctor, *Fal of the Late Arrian* (1549), sig. F8ᵛ.

27. *2 Tamb.*, IV. iii. 1–2. E. M. Waith, 'Marlowe and the Jades of Asia', *Studies in English Literature 1550–1900*, 5 (1965), 229–45.

28. Rick Bowers, 'Tamburlaine in Ludlow', *Notes and Queries*, 243 (1998), 361–3; the hero also later inspired student plays, e.g. Charles Saunders' 'Tamberlaine', written at Trinity College, Cambridge in 1681, and staged before royalty.

29. *Letters of Philip Gawdy*, ed. I. H. Jeayes (1906), 23.

30. Robert Greene, *Perimedes the Blacke-Smith* (1588), sig. A3.

31. Greene, *Works*, ed. A. B. Grosart, 15 vols. (1881–6), vi. 86, viii. 132, ix. 230.

32. Marlowe, *Complete Works*, v. 2: 'To the Gentleman Readers: and others that take pleasure in reading Histories'.

33. Middlesex Sessions Roll 282, nos. 12 and 22. On Tudor taverns, see esp. Peter Clark, *The English Alehouse: A Social History* (1983), 11–13.

34. *Henslowe's Diary*, ed. R. A. Foakes and R. T. Rickert (Cambridge, 1961), 88, 201; Clark, *The English Alehouse*, 12; Honan, *Shakespeare: A Life*, 123–6, 202, 251–3.

35. Eccles, *Marlowe in London*, 123.

36. Mary Edmond, 'The Burbages and their Connections', in R. B. Parker and S. P. Zitner (eds.), *Elizabethan Theater* (Newark, Del., 1996), 30–49.

37. MS Bodleian, Aubrey, 8, fo. 45ᵛ.

38. See Adam Fox, *Oral and Literate Culture in England 1500–1700* (Oxford, 2002), 68.

39. See John Southworth, *Shakespeare the Player* (Stroud, Glos., 2000), app. A. This list of verbal echoes is helpful, but Shakespeare's use of *1* and *2 Tamb.* extended well beyond such borrowings.

40. A. H. Nelson, 'George Buc, William Shakespeare, and the Folger *George a Greene*', *Shakespeare Quarterly*, 49 (1998), 74–83.

41. See Honan, *Shakespeare: A Life*, 326–8, 387.

42. *2 Henry IV*, II. iv. 160–4. See James Shapiro, *Rival Playwrights: Marlowe, Jonson, Shakespeare* (New York, 1991).

43. Nashe, *Works*, ed. R. B. McKerrow, 5 vols. (Oxford, 1966), i. 215; Hunter, 'The Beginnings of Elizabethan Drama', esp. 45.

44. *Lear*, I. i. 113–20, and *2 Tamb.*, III. iv. 19. Michael Holahan comments on the *Tamburlaine* allusion, in ' "Look, her lips": Softness of Voice, Construction of Character in *King Lear*', *Shakespeare Quarterly*, 48 (1997), 406–31.

45. *Greenes Groats-worth of Witte* (1592), F2ᵛ. See Ernst Honigmann, 'Shakespeare's Life', in Margreta de Grazia and Stanley Wells (eds.), *Companion to Shakespeare* (Cambridge, 2001), 1–12, esp. 4 and 12 n. 2.

7 *Doctor Faustus*

1. The National Archives (PRO), C 3/229/121. Eccles, *Marlowe in London*, 125.

2. J. R. Williams, *Goethe's Faust* (1987), 3–12. Very useful on the antecedents are *The English Faust Book*, ed. J. H. Jones (Cambridge, 1994), and Thomas and Tydeman, 171–248.

3. William Prynne, *Histrio-Mastix* (1663), pt. 1, fo. 556.

4. *Doctor Faustus, A- and B-Texts (1604, 1616)*, ed. David Bevington and Eric Rasmussen (Manchester, 1995), 1–2.

5. Ibid. 63.

6. See Huston Diehl, *Staging Reform, Reforming the Stage: Protestantism and Popular Theater in Early Modern England* (1997), 97, and M. H. Keefer, 'Verbal Magic', *Journal of English and Germanic Philology*, 82 (1983), 324–46.

7. Cf. e.g. the rather unconvincing, contradictory results of function-word analysis in Rasmussen's *A Textual Companion to 'Doctor Faustus'* (Manchester, 1993), 62–75; Shapiro's comment is in *Studies in English Literature*, 36 (1996), 502–3.

8. *Faustus*, Prologue, ll. 1–6 (A-text; the last line adopts B-text's 'vaunt' instead of A-text's 'daunt').

9. *Faustus*, sc. i, 6, 37, 40–8 [I. i. 6, 37, 41–50].

10. See P. R. Sellin, 'The Hidden God', in R. S. Kinsman (ed.), *The Darker Vision of the Renaissance* (1974), 147–96, and Pauline Honderich, 'John Calvin and Doctor Faustus', *Modern Language Notes*, 68 (1973), 1–13.

11. *Faustus*, sc. i, 20–2 [I. i. 20–2]. G. M. Pinciss, 'Marlowe's Cambridge Years and the Writing of *Doctor Faustus*', *Studies in English Literature*, 33 (1993), 249–64.

12. *Faustus*, sc. i, 61–3 [I. i. 63–5].

13. Ibid., sc. i, 76–145 [I. i. 78–147].

14. Ernst Honigmann, 'Ten Problems in *Doctor Faustus*', in Murray Biggs *et al.* (eds.), *Arts of Performance* (Edinburgh, 1991), 173–91, esp. 188.

15. C. L. Barber, ' "The form of Faustus' fortunes good or bad" ', *Tulane Drama Review*, 8 (1964), 92–119.

16. J. S. Mebane, *Renaissance Magic and the Return of the Golden Age* (1989), 113–36; A. D. Nuttall, *The Alternative Trinity* (Oxford, 1998), 41–76.

17. *The Historie of the Damnable Life*, trans. P. F. Gent (1592), ch. 18.

18. *Faustus*, sc. iii, 75–82 [I. iii. 77–84]. John Calvin, *Commentary on 1 John*, trans. T. H. L. Parker (1994), 240; Adrian Streete, 'Calvinist Conceptions of Hell in Marlowe's *Doctor Faustus*', *Notes and Queries*, 245 (2000), 430–2.

19. *Faustus*, sc. v, 19–23 [II. i. 20–3].

20. Ibid., sc. v, 12–209 [II. i. 12–II. iii. 27].

21. F. R. Johnson, 'Marlowe's Astronomy and Renaissance Skepticism', *ELH* 13 (1946), 241–54.

22. *Faustus*, sc. v, 160–1, 186–8 [II. ii. 160–1, II. iii. 5–7].

23. Kay Stockholder, 'Faustus's Relation to Women', in K. Friedenreich *et al.* (eds.), '*A Poet and a Filthy Playmaker*' (New York, 1988), 208.

24. *Works*, ed. Gill, ii. 77 n. See *Faustus*, sc. v, 291–345 [II. iii. 110–63].

25. David Bevington, *From 'Mankind' to Marlowe* (Cambridge, Mass., 1962), 252.

26. G. K. Hunter's 'Five-Act Structure in *Doctor Faustus*', in *Dramatic Identities and Cultural Tradition* (Liverpool, 1978), 335–49, allows for parody, multiple themes, and a paradoxical struggle against carnal opportunism in the tightly written play.

27. *Faustus*, sc. xii, 81–2 [V. i. 91–2].

28. Ibid., sc. xii, 88, 90–2 (A-text), and l. 89 (B-text's 'Wittenberg' instead of A-text's 'Wertenberge') [V. i. 101–5].

29. Ibid., sc. xii, 76–7, sc. xiii, 67–70 [V. i. 86–7, V. ii. 71–4].

30. Ibid. sc. xii, 107, Chorus, 1–2 [V. ii. 113, Chorus, 1–2].

31. T. S. Eliot, 'Shakespeare and the Stoicism of Seneca', in *Selected Essays* (1951), 133.

32. Albert Camus, 'The Future of Tragedy' (1955), in *Selected Essays and Notebooks by Albert Camus*, ed. and trans. Philip Thody (Harmondsworth, 1955), 190–203; M. M. Mahood, *Poetry and Humanism* (1950), 86–7.

33. See Andrew Gurr, *Playgoing in Shakespeare's London* (1988), 140; T. Y. Grande, *Marlovian Tragedy* (1999), 97; and Suzan Last on a 'Comedy of Error', in *Renaissance et Réforme*, 24 (2000), 23–44.

34. John Gee, *New Shreds of the Old Snare* (1624), sig. D4.

35. Nashe, *Works*, ed. McKerrow, iii. 315.

36. Watson, *Complete Works*, ed. Sutton, ii. 204–7. John Stow and E. Howes, *Annales* (1631), 869.

37. Harvey, *Works*, ed. Grosart, i. 292, 297.

38. Gurr, *Playgoing in Shakespeare's London*, 132.

39. See Eccles, *Marlowe in London*, 43–68.

40. Middlesex Sessions Roll 284, no. 12. See Watson, *Complete Works*, ed. Sutton, i. xxv–xxix, and, on late Tudor duels, Craig Turner and T. Super, *Methods and Practice of Elizabethan Swordplay* (Carbondale, Ill., 1990), and Sydney Angelo, 'Dueling Ethic', in his *Chivalry in the Renaissance* (Woodbridge, Suffolk, 1990), 1–12.

41. Eccles, *Marlowe in London*, 70–99.

42. 'Generosissimo viro Thomae Walsinghamo armigero', in Watson, *Complete Works*, ii. 108–9; see also ii. 130–3 and 140 nn.

43. MS BL Harleian 6848, fos. 185–6.
44. *Advice to his Son*, ed. G. B. Harrison (1930), 81.
45. G. L. Batho, on the ninth earl's books, in *The Library*, 15 (1960), 246–61; *Aubrey's Brief Lives*, ed. O. L. Dick (Harmondsworth, 1978), 475–6.
46. MS Folger, 2973, fo. 100.
47. Patrick Cheney, *Marlowe's Counterfeit Profession* (1997), 68–87. *All Ovids Elegies*, III. i. 24–6.
48. *Merry Wives*, III. i. 21–5.
49. MS BL Harleian 6849, fo. 218.
50. See *The Roanoke Voyages, 1584–1590*, ed. D. B. Quinn, 2 vols. (1955), i. 116 n. and 371.
51. MS BL Harleian 6848, fos. 185–6. *The Roanoke Voyages*, ed. Quinn, i. 373, 442.
52. *Massacre at Paris*, sc. xix, 50.
53. See E. A. Strathmann, *Sir Walter Ralegh: A Study in Elizabethan Skepticism* (New York, 1951), ch. 2, and Scott Mandelbrote, 'The Religion of Thomas Harriot', in Robert Fox (ed.), *Thomas Harriot: An Elizabethan Man of Science* (Aldershot, Hampshire, 2000), 246–79.

8 A spy abroad

1. TNA(PRO), C66/356, M.35 (27 May 1590).
2. Hammer, *The Polarisation of Elizabethan Politics*, ch. 5, esp. 153–7. Bossy, *Under the Molehill*, 146–8. The anonymous and illegal 'Martin Marprelate' tracts, issued by Puritans from a secret press in 1588–9, had devastatingly attacked Anglican Church practices. Both Nashe and CM may have learned from the rollicking satirical methods of 'Martin', who infuriated the government.
3. MS BL Harleian 6848, fo. 154.
4. Idem ('ex minimo vestigio artifex agnoscit artificem').
5. Arthur Freeman, *Thomas Kyd: Facts and Problems* (Oxford, 1967) 1–5.
6. A. G. Petti, *English Literary Hands from Chaucer to Dryden* (Cambridge, Mass., 1977), 82–3.
7. *The Spanish Tragedy*, ed. Philip Edwards (Manchester, 1977), app. D.
8. Thomas Kyd, *Works*, ed. F. S. Boas (Oxford, 1901), p. lxvi; Freeman, *Thomas Kyd*, 39.
9. See Lukas Erne, *Beyond 'The Spanish Tragedy'* (Manchester, 2001), 217–19.
10. *The Spanish Tragedy*, I. i. 67.
11. MS BL Harleian 6849, fo. 218.
12. Ibid.
13. MS BL Cotton, Titus C6, fos. 17–18; Nicholl, 389–90.
14. MSS BL Harleian 6848, fo. 154, and 6849, fo. 218.
15. MS Folger, V.b.110; Mark Eccles, 'Marlowe and Kentish Tradition', *Notes and Queries*, 169 (1935), 20–61. Kuriyama, in *Marlowe*, 158–60, was the first to suggest that CM's rapt disciple was not Thomas, but John Fineaux.

16. *The Spanish Tragedy*, II. v. 18, IV. iv. 84; *Jew of Malta*, I. ii. 313, III. ii. 10–12.

17. MS Kent, PRC 16/127; *Jew of Malta*, II. iii. 297–8; and M. G. Brennan, 'Two Newsletter Accounts of the Siege of Malta (1565)', *Notes and Queries*, 238 (1993), 157–60.

18. A. C. Dessen, 'The Elizabethan Stage Jew and Christian Example', *Modern Language Quarterly*, 35 (1974), 231–45, and L. E. Kermode, 'The Jew as Critic at the Rose in 1592', *Studies in English Literature*, 35 (1995), 215–29.

19. I found these particularly helpful on themes relating to Barabas: Harold Fisch, *The Dual Image: The Figure of the Jew in English and American Literature* (1971); David S. Katz, *The Jews in the History of England, 1485–1850* (Oxford, 1994), esp. ch. 2; James Shapiro, *Shakespeare and the Jews* (New York, 1996); and Peter Berek's 'The Jew as Renaissance Man', *Renaissance Quarterly*, 51 (1998), 128–62.

20. Katz, *The Jews in the History of England*, ch. 2.

21. Marlowe mixes serious attitudes to Machiavelli with various shades of popular myths or misconceptions about him. The Prologue 'establishes that "machiavellism" is widespread, even among those who openly repudiate it': *The Jew of Malta*, ed. T. W. Craik (1988), p. xi. See esp. *The Jew of Malta*, ed. N. W. Bawcutt (Manchester, 1978), 11–16, and Bawcutt's 'The "Myth of Gentillet" Reconsidered', *Modern Language Review*, 99 (2004), 863–74.

22. *Jew of Malta*, Prologue and I. i.

23. MS BL Harleian, 6848, fos. 185–6. Shapiro, *Shakespeare and the Jews*, 240 n. 96.

24. *Jew of Malta*, I. i. 65–6.

25. Ibid. I. i. 54–141.

26. *The Jew of Malta*, ed. J. R. Siemon (Manchester 1997), pp. xix–xxxviii.

27. *Jew of Malta*, I. ii. 57. See the discussion of 'reality' in H. S. Babb, 'Policy in Marlowe's *The Jew of Malta*', *ELH* 24 (1957), 85–94.

28. *Jew of Malta*, I. ii. 196–291, III. iii. 51–2.

29. *The Jew of Malta*, ed. David Bevington (Manchester, 1997), II. iii. 40–51.

30. See *Jew of Malta*, II. iii. 175–201.

31. Eliot, *Selected Essays*, 123.

32. *Henslowe's Diary*, ed. Foakes and Rickert, 170, 321.

33. MS Cant. Cath., accounts, 1539–40; Bakeless, i. 38. David Horne, *The Life and Minor Works of George Peele* (New Haven, Conn., 1952), 82–8, 128.

34. Cf. Nicholl, 271–3. The agent who had been in Madrid was John Cecil, but the spelling 'Cycell' also occurs.

35. The myth that Marlowe risked the loss of good credit with the Privy Council, as well as maiming or death, by setting up as a counterfeiter, in a town under military rule, for personal profit, is sufficiently negated in Nicholl, 278–98 (see also pp. 310–11). From time to time, the Council employed the poets Watson, Roydon, and Marlowe (the latter two in the same crisis of 1590–1); in England, Marlowe escaped any known charge for counterfeiting (punishable anywhere by death), just as he did, later, from any known charge for heresy; he benefited intermittently from the Council's favourable treatment,

starting in June 1587, when he was praised unreservedly for his secret government work.

36. Millicent V. Hay, *The Life of Robert Sidney, Earl of Leicester (1563–1626)* (1984), ch. 4; P. E. J. Hammer, *Elizabeth's Wars* (Basingstoke, 2003), 172–3; R. J. W. den Broeder *et al., Wonen in Vlissingen* (Vlissingen, 1983).
37. Kim Philby, *My Silent War*, introd. Graham Greene (1968), 154.
38. MS BL Harleian, 6848, fos. 185–6.
39. See Albert J. Loomie, *The Spanish Elizabethans* (New York, 1963), 52–93.
40. P. H. Kocher, 'Contemporary Pamphlet Backgrounds for Marlowe's *The Massacre at Paris'*, *Modern Language Quarterly*, 8 (1947), 157–73, 309–18; Thomas and Tydeman, 251–60; *The Massacre at Paris*, in *Complete Works*, v. 307–9.
41. Richard Hillman, *Shakespeare, Marlowe and the Politics of France* (New York, 2002), ch. 4.
42. *Massacre at Paris*, sc. vi, 25–30, sc. vii, 5–8.
43. Ibid., sc. iv, 14–16, 25,
44. MS Folger, J.b.8.
45. *Massacre at Paris*, sc. xi, 1–8. Natalie Zemon Davis, *Society and Culture in Early Modern France* (Oxford, 1998), ch. 6; Julia Briggs, 'Marlowe's *Massacre at Paris*: A Reconsideration', *Review of English Studies*, 34 (1983), 257–78; and David Potter, 'Henri III', in Grantley and Roberts (eds.), *Christopher Marlowe and English Renaissance Culture*, 70–95.
46. *Massacre at Paris*, sc. ix and xxiv.
47. Sukanta Chaudhuri, 'Marlowe, Madrigals, and a New Elizabethan Poet', *Review of English Sudies*, 39 (1988), 199–216.
48. PRO SP 84/44, fo. 145.
49. See R. B. Wernham, 'Christopher Marlowe at Flushing in 1592', *English Historical Review*, 91 (1976), 344–5; paragraphing added.

9 The keen pleasures of sex

1. *Henslowe's Diary*, ed. Foakes and Rickert, 16; *Edward the Second*, ed. C. R. Forker (Manchester, 1995), 14–17.
2. Middlesex Sessions Roll 309, no. 13.
3. Eccles, *Marlowe in London*, 107.
4. MS Cant. Cath., BAC J/B/S/392.
5. Ibid.
6. Urry, 65–6; *Faustus*, sc. v. [II. iii].
7. For the will, see Mary Edmond's transcript in *Review of English Studies*, NS 25 (1974), 130. On the fate of Pembroke's troupe see Lawrence Manley, 'From Strange's Men to Pembroke's Men', *Shakespeare Quarterly*, 54 (2003), 253–87.
8. Isaiah Berlin, 'Edmund Wilson at Oxford', in *Personal Impressions* (1998), 176.
9. Honan, *Shakespeare: A Life*, 253–4.
10. *3 Henry VI*, I. i. 16.

11. Nashe, *Works*, ed. McKerrow, i. 212.

12. Nicholas Brooke, 'Marlowe as Provocative Agent in Shakespeare's Early Plays', *Shakespeare Survey*, 14 (1961), 34–44; Maurice Charney, in *Renaissance Drama*, NS 10 (1979), 33–44; Shapiro, *Rival Playwrights*, ch. 3.

13. *Jew of Malta*, IV. i. 1–3.

14. On Renaissance sexuality and Marlowe, I have learned from Mario DiGangi, *The Homoerotics of Early Modern Drama* (Cambridge, 1997); Jonathan Goldberg, *Sodometries* (Stanford, Calif., 1992); Stephen Orgel, *Impersonations* (Cambridge, 1996); Ian McAdam, *The Irony of Identity* (1999); and several classic studies: Alan Bray, *Homosexuality in Renaissance England* (1982) and 'Homosexuality and the Signs of Male Friendship in Elizabethan England', in J. Goldberg (ed.), *Queering the Renaissance* (1994), 40–61; and Bruce R. Smith, *Homosexual Desire in Shakespeare's England* (1991). I am also indebted to G. W. Bredbeck, *Sodomy and Interpretation* (1991), and to works by Valerie Traub, including her survey (of post-Foucault ferment), 'Studies in Homoeroticism', *English Literary Renaissance*, 30 (2000), 284–329.

15. Bruce Smith, *Homosexual Desire*, 41–53; DiGangi, *The Homoerotics of Early Modern Drama*, 19–20. See also David Stymeist, 'Status, Sodomy, and the Theater in Marlowe's *Edward II*', *Studies in English Literature*, 44 (2004), 233–53, esp. 233–5.

16. MS BL Harleian, 6848, fos. 185–6.

17. B. P. Fisher, 'Pylades and Orestes', *Notes and Queries*, 232 (1987), 190–1.

18. *1 Tamb.*, I. ii. 248–50.

19. *Faustus* (1616), V. ii. 34–5.

20. Edward Blount, dedication in *Hero and Leander* (1598).

21. See Holinshed's *Historie of Scotland* in *The First and Second Volumes of Chronicles* (1587), 446–7; *Edward II*, ed. Richard Rowland (Oxford, 1994); and Lawrence Normand, '*Edward II* and James VI', in Grantley and Roberts (eds.), *Christopher Marlowe and English Renaissance Culture*, 172–97.

22. Thomas and Tydeman, 341–81.

23. Cf. M. Godman, in *Notes and Queries*, 238 (1993), 160–3.

24. Natalie Fryde, *The Tyranny and Fall of Edward II, 1321–1326* (Cambridge, 1979), 7.

25. Lines 233–4.

26. *Edward II*, sc. iv, 38, 408–14.

27. Ibid., sc. xxii, 113.

28. Ibid., sc. xxiii, 85.

29. *Letters and Despatches of Richard Verstegan*, ed. Anthony G. Petti (1959), 92: Antwerp, 30 Oct. 1592.

30. *Greenes Groats-worth of Witte* (1592), E4ᵛ.

31. 'To the Gentlemen Readers', in *Kind-Harts Dreame. Conteining five Apparitions, with their Invectives against abuses raigning* (1592).

32. Stephen Greenblatt, *Renaissance Self-Fashioning: From More to Shakespeare* (Chicago, 1980), 193–221; this unusually insightful essay was later published

under the title 'Marlowe and the Will to Absolute Play', as in Richard Wilson and Richard Dutton (eds.), *New Historicism and Renaissance Drama* (1992), 57–82.

33. Harvey, *Works*, ed. Grosart, i. 258–97. Harvey's 'Gorgon', in *A New Letter*, alludes to Peter Shakerley, Nashe, and Marlowe. The poem's main topic is Shakerley, but Marlowe is in view often in the *Letter*, as well as in the lyric: see Nicholl, 70–6, and, for related biographical details, Virginia F. Stern, *Gabriel Harvey* (Oxford, 1979).

34. D. F. Sutton, introduction to *Amintae Gaudia*, in Watson, *Complete Works*, ii. 190.

35. Ibid., dedication by 'CM', trans. Sutton, 210.

36. *The Third part of the Countesse of Pembroke's Yvychurch, entituled, Amintas' Dale* (1592), sigs. M2, M4; Eccles, *Marlowe in London*, 167–8.

37. Gordon Braden, *The Classics and English Renaissance Poetry: Three Case Studies* (1978), ch. 2, esp. 125–6. *Venus and Adonis* was licensed 18 Apr. 1593.

38. *Hero and Leander*, 1–4.

39. Lines 15–16, 667–76.

40. William Keach, 'Marlowe's Hero as "Venus' Nun"', *English Literary Renaissance*, 2 (1972), 307–20; Georgia E. Brown, 'Breaking the Canon', in White (ed.), *Marlowe, History, and Sexuality*, 59–75.

41. Lines 61–90.

42. See Millar Maclure, *Marlowe: The Critical Heritage* (1979), 163–75.

43. Cecil Papers 233/9, at Hatfield House: see Eccles, 'Brief Lives', 91.

44. Edward Blount, dedication in *Hero and Leander* (1598).

45. Chapman, dedication to Lady Walsingham (1598).

46. Stephen Orgel, in editing CM's poem, has found no sign that Chapman's continuation was felt inappropriate; Petowe's own taste is less likely to have troubled readers than his humdrum skill.

10 A little matter of murder

1. See John Cavell and Brian Kennett's closely detailed account of the judge, in *A History of Sir Roger Manwood's School, Sandwich, 1563–1963, with a Life of the Founder* (1963), 191–220. The Latin elegy on Sir Roger was written soon after Marlowe's Latin epistle for Watson's *Amintae*, though later than 14 Dec. 1592.

2. Marlowe, *Complete Poems*, ed. Stephen Orgel (Harmondsworth, 1987), 217.

3. Nashe, *Have with You to Saffron-Walden* (1596), sig. N3ᵛ. On the manor and its owners, see F. A. Hart and S. M. Archer, *Scadbury Manor* (Orpington and District Archaeological Society, 2003), and also E. A. Webb, G. W. Miller, and J. Beckwith, *The History of Chislehurst, its Church, Manors, and Parish* (1899; repr. 1999). Archaeology has continued at Scadbury's 'island'.

4. Jennifer Stead, 'Bowers of Bliss: the Banquet Setting', in C. Anne Wilson (ed.),

'*Banquetting stuffe*' (Edinburgh, 1991), 115–57, and Patricia Fumerton, *Cultural Aesthetics* (1991), ch. 4.

5. Leslie Hotson, 'Marlowe among the Churchwardens', *Atlantic Monthly*, 138 (July 1926), 37–44.

6. On James VI's foreign policy, see Jenny Wormald's 'James VI and I', *History*, 68 (1983), 187–209. For Lady Audrey's cipher: Arthur Collins, *Letters and Memorials of State* (1746), ii. 126. On Poley's travels: Eugénie de Kalb, 'Robert Poley's Movements as a Messenger of the Court, 1588 to 1601', *Review of English Studies*, 9 (1933), 13–18, and Ethel Seaton, 'Marlowe, Robert Poley, and the Tippings'. On Sidney's disaffection: M. G. Brennan, N. J. Kinnamon, and M. P. Hannay, 'Robert Sidney, the Dudleys and Queen Elizabeth', in Carole Levin *et al.* (eds.), *Elizabeth I* (Aldershot, Hants., 2003), 20–42.

7. Hart and Archer, *Scadbury Manor*, 7–8. On 'sprezzatura', see Harry Berger, Jr., *The Absence of Grace* (Stanford, Calif., 2000), and Frank Whigham, *Ambition and Privilege: The Social Tropes of Elizabethan Courtesy Theory* (1984), esp. chs. 1 and 2.

8. TNA(PRO), Acts of the Privy Council, 18 May 1593.

9. J. E. Neale, *Elizabeth I and her Parliaments 1584–1601* (1957), 241–50.

10. Alison Wall, ' "The Greatest Disgrace": The Making and Unmaking of JPs in Elizabethan and Jacobean England', *English Historical Review*, 119 (2004), 313–32, and Hammer, *The Polarisation of Elizabethan Politics*, ch. 5.

11. Arthur Freeman, 'Marlowe, Kyd, and the Dutch Court Libel', *English Literary Renaissance*, 3 (1973), 44–52.

12. MS BL Harleian 6848, fo. 189.

13. TNA(PRO), Acts of the Privy Council, 20 May 1593.

14. MSS BL Harleian 6848, fos. 190–1, and 7002, fo. 10. The notion that Marlowe was killed as an impediment to a 'shoddy enterprise against Sir Walter Ralegh' may be usefully speculative, but it is not evidenced. Nor was Cholmeley (the informer) in the employ of the earl of Essex, as P. E. J. Hammer firmly establishes in 'A Reckoning Reframed', *English Literary Renaissance*, 26 (1996), 225–42.

15. MS BL Harleian 6848, fos. 185–6.

16. Ibid.

17. MS BL Harleian 6853, fos. 307–8. D. Riggs, in *The World of Christopher Marlowe* (2004), is in error in assuming that 'infra virgam' ('within the verge') had anything to do with Greenwich, late in May 1593, when the queen was at Nonsuch Palace, and again wrong in implying that it is known that 'Baines's Note arrived at Greenwich' (p. 334). There are a few other mistakes here: Poley and Frizer are not known to have 'worked with one another before' (p. 331). It is not true that Lord Burghley, who tried in vain to save Barrow and Greenwood from charges of heresy, supervised a 'heresy hunt'. Further, the spy Drury's letter, of August 1593 (which does not mention Marlowe), is not proof that 'articles of atheism', concerning Marlowe, were sent to the queen in advance of Sir John Puckering's edited copy of Baines's 'Note', which was prepared for

delivery to her in June. Nor is there support for the notion that Puckering 'extricated' Elizabeth I (p. 336) from 'machinations', guilt, subterfuge or any particular circumstance bearing on the poet's death.

18. See S. E. Sprott, 'Drury and Marlowe', *TLS*, 2 Aug. 1974.

19. See Nicholl, 378–80.

20. On Bacon's helping to improve the earl of Essex's relations with James VI, see Hammer, *The Polarisation of Elizabethan Politics*, 164–5.

21. H. A. Shield, 'The Death of Marlowe', *Notes and Queries*, 202 (1957), 101–3.

22. See de Kalb, 'Robert Poley's Movements', 16–17; Ethel Seaton, 'Robert Poley's Ciphers', *Review of English Studies*, 7 (1931), 137–50; Nicholl, 300–5.

23. De Kalb, 'Robert Poley's Movements', 13–14, 17.

24. MS BL Harleian 6849, fo. 218.

25. See Jenny Wormald's 'James VI and I', and 'Tangles and Tongues', *TLS*, 14 Mar. 2003. On the 'Spanish blanks' and Bothwell crises, there are many sources; W. T. MacCaffery offers an overview of Anglo-Scottish relations in this decade in his *Elizabeth I* (1992). De Kalb accurately lists Poley's movements from the Declared Accounts.

26. Paul Hammer, 'A Reckoning Reframed', *English Literary Renaissance*, 26 (1996), 225–42; Nicholl, 29–30.

27. E. Van Meteren, the Dutch consul in London (1583–1612), arguably offers a generic frame for some of CM's more overt traits and behaviour, e.g. as they are reported (in a malicious vein) by informers in May 1593: see *Pictures of the English in Queen Elizabeth's Reign*, translated from the Dutch (1865).

28. Arthur Freeman, 'The Deptford Killer', *TLS*, 28 May 1993.

29. John Carey makes the logical remark about Essex and murder: *Sunday Times*, 7 June 1992.

30. See Yorkshire Archaeological Society, MS DD56.DI (13 Oct. 1612).

31. John Goodman so threatens Mr Francis Smyth, at Bull Lane, Stratford, in 1582, in one of many Tudor examples of the threat of rapping with a dagger's hilt. If the skull is not fractured, scalp wounds can look colourfully worse than they are.

32. J. Thompson Rowling, 'The Death of Christopher Marlowe', *Journal of the Royal Society of Medicine*, 92 (1999), 44–6.

33. William Vaughan, *The Golden-grove, moralized in three Books* (1600), sig. C4^v; Thomas Beard, *The Theatre of Gods Judgements* (1597), 147–8.

34. See Peter Farey's appendix 1, on distances and on 'within the verge', in 'Marlowe's Sudden and Fearful End', at <http://www2.prestel.co.uk/rey/index.htm>.

35. Gavin Thurston, 'Christopher Marlowe's Death', *Contemporary Review* (Mar./Apr. 1964), 1–12.

36. TNA(PRO), C260/174, No. 127.

37. *Lucans First Book Translated Line for Line, by Chr. Marlow* (1600), dedicatory letter.

38. Bakeless, i. 151–3.

39. George Peele's *The Honour of the Garter* (1593), sig. A2ᵛ; George Chapman's *Hero and Leander* (1598), sestiad III; Henry Petowe's *Hero and Leander* (1598), ll. 59–62; Francis Meres's *Palladis Tamia* (1598), sig. 003ʳ; Michael Drayton's 'Elegy to my most nearly-loved friend Henry Reynolds' (1627); and Thomas Dekker's *A Knight's Conjuring* (1607), sig. L.

Epilogue

1. See Horne, *Life and Minor Works of George Peele*, 246.
2. Nashe, *Works*, ed. McKerrow, ii. 335–6.
3. Ibid. ii. 264–5; Nicholl, 63–5. Nashe's use of 'Aretine' (for Marlowe) was first explored in Lynette and Evelyn Feasey's still useful 'The Validity of the Baines Note', *Notes and Queries*, 194 (1949), 514–17.
4. Nashe, *Works*, ii. 180–1; iii. 131, 195.
5. See the remarks in *A New Variorum Edition of Shakespeare: As You Like It*, ed. Richard Knowles and E. J. Mattern (New York, 1977), 188–90, and *As You Like It*, ed. Alan Brissenden (Oxford, 1994), III. iii. 11–12, III. v. 82, and IV. i. 86–98.
6. *Ben Jonson*, ed. Ian Donaldson (Oxford, 1985), 259–60.
7. Eugénie de Kalb, 'An Elucidation of the Death of Christopher Marlowe' (Ph.D. diss., University of Cambridge, 1929). Bakeless, i. 166–71, offers a summary of the murderer's last years.
8. T. S. Eliot, 'Ben Jonson', in *Selected Essays* (1951), 154.

Index